PENGUIN BOOKS

ABRAHAM LINCOLN AND THE
ROAD TO EMANCIPATION, 1861–1865

William K. Klingaman's books include *1919: The Year Our World Began*; *1929: The Year of the Great Crash*; and *1941: Our Lives in a World on the Edge*. He lives in Columbia, Maryland.

ABRAHAM LINCOLN AND THE ROAD TO EMANCIPATION, 1861–1865

WILLIAM K. KLINGAMAN

PENGUIN BOOKS

PENGUIN BOOKS

Published by the Penguin Group
Penguin Putnam Inc., 375 Hudson Street,
New York, New York 10014, U.S.A.
Penguin Books Ltd, 80 Strand, London WC2R 0RL, England
Penguin Books Australia Ltd, 250 Camberwell Road,
Camberwell, Victoria 3124, Australia
Penguin Books Canada Ltd, 10 Alcorn Avenue,
Toronto, Ontario, Canada M4V 3B2
Penguin Books India (P) Ltd, 11 Community Centre,
Panchsheel Park, New Delhi - 110 017, India
Penguin Books (N.Z.) Ltd, Cnr Rosedale and Airborne Roads,
Albany, Auckland, New Zealand
Penguin Books (South Africa) (Pty) Ltd, 24 Sturdee Avenue,
Rosebank, Johannesburg 2196, South Africa

Penguin Books Ltd, Registered Offices:
Harmondsworth, Middlesex, England

First published in the United States of America by Viking Penguin,
a member of Penguin Putnam Inc. 2001
Published in Penguin Books 2002

1   3   5   7   9   10   8   6   4   2

THE LIBRARY OF CONGRESS HAS CATALOGED THE HARDCOVER EDITION AS FOLLOWS:
Klingaman, William K.
Abraham Lincoln and the road to emancipation, 1861–1865 / William K. Klingaman.
p.   cm.
Includes index.
ISBN 0-670-86754-3 (hc.)
ISBN 0 14 20.0043 4 (pbk.)
1. Lincoln, Abraham, 1809–1865—Views on slavery.   2. Lincoln, Abraham,
1809–1865—Relations with African Americans.   3. United States. President (1861–1865:
Lincoln). Emancipation Proclamation.   4. Slaves—Emancipation—United States.
5. African Americans—Legal status, laws, etc.—History—19th century.   6. United
States—Politics and government—1861–1865.   7. United States—Race relations.
8. Whites—United States—Attitudes—History—19th century.   I. Title.
E457.2 .K57 2001
973.7'092—dc21   00–043993

Printed in the United States of America
Set in Fairfield LH Light
Designed by Jennifer Daddio

For Joan and Jim McCrumb

CONTENTS

PREFACE

When the Civil War began in April 1861, President Abraham Lincoln had no intention of issuing an emancipation proclamation. Lincoln believed he lacked the constitutional authority to interfere with slavery in any state, even when the government of that state insisted it was no longer a part of the Union. The president feared that emancipation would shatter the northern consensus in favor of a war to preserve the nation, and might alienate the border slave states that remained in the Union—possibly leading them to secede and join the Confederacy.

Lincoln also shrank from emancipation because he did not know if four million free African-Americans could find a place in American society. Slavery—and the racism that sustained it—had deep roots in the nation's psyche. Viewing the effects of more than two centuries of slavery, white Americans doubted whether blacks could sustain themselves in a competitive economy, or fulfill the responsibilities of citizenship in a democracy. Lincoln understood that every part of the nation shared this prejudice; his only solution was to colonize free blacks outside the United States.

This book recounts Lincoln's gradual conversion to the cause of emancipation. I have written it as a narrative to re-create the pressures and events that led Lincoln to adopt the role of emancipator, a role he accepted with great reluctance. In a recent biography, David Donald has emphasized Lincoln's essentially passive nature, his willingness to allow circumstances to narrow his options or even determine his policy. Nowhere was this tendency more evident than in dealing with slavery.

Lincoln's decision in the summer of 1862 to issue an emancipation proclamation represented one of the boldest gambles of his presidency, but it was a gamble born of desperation and frustration from repeated military failures. "Things had gone on from bad to worse," Lincoln later recalled, "until I felt that we had reached the end of our rope on the plan of operations we had been pursuing; that we had about played our last card, and must change our tactics, or lose the game." The Emancipation Proclamation was a weapon to help the Union win the war. When Lincoln finally issued the proclamation on January 1, 1863, he hedged his bet by couching emancipation in conservative, legalistic language. There were no inspiring words about racial justice, no commitment by the government to help the freed slaves obtain equality.

What began as a study of the Emancipation Proclamation soon led me into a broader examination of racial attitudes in the United States. Throughout the narrative, I have attempted to convey the pervasive nature of certain assumptions held by most white Americans about blacks in the mid-nineteenth century. Many whites believed that the behavior of slaves reflected the inherent nature of blacks, rather than the deadening effects of chattel slavery. Even those whites who were willing to grant blacks a measure of humanity felt that it would take several generations to eradicate the deleterious consequences of slavery and bring blacks close to the level of whites. To help re-create this mind-set, I have used the most common contemporary term of "Negroes" to refer to African-Americans. For the same reason, I have retained the word "nigger" wherever it appeared in quotes—as jarring as it may be—as well as the black dialect quoted by whites in contemporary sources. Interestingly, most writers transformed Lincoln's western speech into grammatically correct English; they did not afford the same privilege to African-Americans.

Like anyone who writes about the Civil War era, I owe a great deal to a multitude of historians who have studied the period from nearly every angle. The continued publication of diaries, memoirs, letters, and other contemporary sources provides writers with an abundant harvest that kept me eager to add newly discovered material throughout the publication process. My deepest thanks go to my agent, Donald Cutler, who first encouraged my interest in this topic and guided me with an expert hand through several early drafts. My editors, Sarah Baker and Michael Millman, have smoothed the publication process and improved the manuscript substantially with their insightful observations. M. H. Lankin and Joan McCrumb also provided support and excellent suggestions. Any flaws that remain are entirely my responsibility. Finally, I would like to thank my wife, Janet, and my children, Nicholas and Marianne, for their patience and love while I completed this study.

1

INAUGURATION DAY: MARCH 4, 1861

Shortly after dawn, Abraham Lincoln awoke in his second-floor suite at Willard's Hotel, two blocks from the White House. Outside, the city was stirring earlier than usual. Through his window above Pennsylvania Avenue, Lincoln could hear delivery wagons driven by Negro laborers rattling over the rutted, unpaved streets, bringing fresh oysters, shad, and eggs to the hotel's kitchens for breakfast. Young boys were already circulating through the gathering crowds, hawking American flags, sheets with the lyrics of patriotic songs, and newspapers featuring lithograph portraits of the incoming president. On the street corners, the long cast-iron handles of wooden water pumps creaked as visitors unable to find hotel rooms washed their faces after spending a chilly evening in the city's parks. From a distance came the less familiar sound of troops marching through the streets to take up their stations along the inaugural parade route.

Lincoln was not yet aware of what was happening on Capitol Hill, at the other end of Pennsylvania Avenue. Thirty-six weary senators were wrapping up an all-night session with a vote on a final compromise to save the Union by allowing slavery into the New Mexico territory. With every senator of Lincoln's Republican Party voting against it, the measure failed by a narrow margin. Visitors leaving the galleries wondered aloud if the nation would survive until April.

There were men in Washington who hoped this would be the last day of Lincoln's life, and Lincoln knew it. Threats had been made against him even before he arrived in the capital nine days earlier. After several reliable sources reported evidence of a conspiracy to assassinate Lincoln as his train passed through Baltimore, the president-elect had altered his original itinerary and entered Washington secretly, ahead of schedule, disguised in an overcoat, muffler, and plaid cap—almost, noted one observer, like a fugitive slave, "seeking concealment . . . arriving not during the sunlight, but crawling and dodging under the sable wing of night."

Although many of the most outspoken advocates of slavery and states' rights had left the city in disgust following Lincoln's victory the previous November, Washington was still predominantly southern in its culture and sympathies. When Lincoln checked into Parlor Number 6, an elegant suite at Willard's, he found an anonymous letter calling him "nothing but a god-damn Black nigger" and warning that his enemies would "play the Devil" with him if he did not resign at once. A local secessionist paper, the *Constitution*, was urging its readers to employ whatever force might be necessary to prevent Lincoln's inauguration. Government officials heard rumors that a band of southern sympathizers planned to ride into the city from neighboring Virginia, kill or kidnap Lincoln before he could be sworn in, replace him with the outgoing vice president—the Kentuckian John C. Breckenridge—and make Washington the capital of a Confederate nation.

To protect Lincoln during the inaugural parade and ceremony, General Winfield Scott, the seventy-five-year-old general in chief of the United States Army, had mobilized the scanty forces at his command in the District of Columbia: 653 regular army troops, a squadron of cavalry, a handful of marines from the Navy Yard, an assortment of state militiamen, and three artillery batteries. Scott was deploying sharpshooters on rooftops along Pennsylvania Avenue, cannons outside the Treasury building and the north entrance to the Capitol, cavalry on all the side streets, and fifty riflemen to stand guard beneath the temporary platform at the east portico of the Capitol, where Lincoln would take the oath of office. Then Scott called for reinforcements to handle unforeseen dangers.

A Nation Falling Apart

Washington seemed a city under siege. The capital had never witnessed anything like this grim military display on such a festive occasion, but then the nation was closer to dissolution than ever before. Special conventions in seven states of the Deep South, from South Carolina to Texas, had already voted for secession. Less than a month before Lincoln reached Washington, delegates from those states met in Montgomery, Alabama, to establish the Confederate States of America. Southerners were leaving the Union because they knew that Lincoln, as the candidate of the Republican Party, adamantly opposed the spread of slavery past its present boundaries; after all, that was the fundamental principle upon which the party had been founded in 1854. They suspected that a Republican administration would also threaten slavery where it already existed, despite Lincoln's repeated assurances to the contrary.

Most of all, southerners saw that the political balance of power in the United States had shifted, depriving the South of the self-protective dominance it had enjoyed in Washington for three-quarters of a century. At times their anxiety verged on sectional paranoia, as when southerners accused Lincoln and the Republicans of seeking to turn the racial structure of society upside down—"to free the negroes and force amalgamation between them and the children of the poor men of the South." "If you are tame enough to submit," warned the prominent Baptist preacher James Furman, "Abolition preachers will be at hand to consummate the marriage of your daughters to black husbands."

To justify secession, Confederate officials argued that the Union was merely a compact between states that could be broken whenever a state felt its vital interests threatened by an oppressive majority. Now that "the evil days, so dreaded by our forefathers and the early defenders of the Constitution, are upon us," as the *Dallas Morning Herald* put it, leaders of the seven Confederate states wished to depart in peace.

No one really knew how Lincoln would respond to secession. For that matter, most Americans knew little at all about the man, even after they elected him president. At age fifty-two, Lincoln was the third-youngest man ever to win the presidency. To official Washington, he seemed the quintessential outsider, an undistinguished western politician with only two years of experience in Congress in the late 1840s, who had never moved among the political or business elite of the East either in or out of office.

Only a small minority of northerners, and virtually no southerners (except Washingtonians who remembered him from his days as a congressman), had ever seen or heard Lincoln in person. His campaign literature extolled his log-cabin origins in Kentucky, although Lincoln was always embarrassed by his lack of education and his family's poverty. He had grown up near Pigeon Creek, Indiana, and had learned enough law to make a living as an attorney in Illinois, riding circuit to drum up cases. Lincoln began his political career in his midtwenties as a member of the Whig Party; at the time, he was more concerned with economic issues than slavery, which he considered a "minor question."

Although Lincoln's family never owned slaves, he was less eager than most northern politicians to condemn slaveholders. He described slavery as "the disease of the entire nation," and insisted that "the people of the North were as responsible for slavery as the people of the South." Lincoln pitied southerners because they had become so dependent upon the institution—and so corrupted by it—that they could not uproot slavery without wrenching consequences.

At the same time, Lincoln condemned slavery on humanitarian grounds as "a great crying injustice" and "an enormous national crime." He sought to contain it within its existing boundaries, trusting that it would atrophy and eventually die, although he never developed a plan to eradicate it without violating slaveowners' property rights and tearing the Union apart. Nor did Lincoln know how free Negroes could be assimilated into American society. "If all earthly power were given to me," he once admitted, "I should not know what to do, as to the existing institution."

Congressional approval of the Kansas-Nebraska Act of 1854, which threatened to introduce slavery into free western territories, finally persuaded Lincoln to join the antislavery crusade. He cast his lot with the fledgling Republican Party, but he remained a moderate by Republican standards. In 1858, in his race for the Senate seat held by Stephen Douglas, Lincoln never strayed from the mainstream of Republican ideology, denouncing slavery as a threat to American ideals of liberty, and calling on the national government to reserve the western territories for white settlers.

Lincoln's debates with Douglas and his subsequent speaking tours through the North brought him to the attention of Republican Party leaders, but he remained far down on the list of choices for the 1860 presidential nomination. Lincoln won the nomination as a dark horse because the four leading candidates were each burdened with critical weaknesses, while Lincoln—who had made few enemies in his brief political career—could unite Republicans and attract northern Democrats who opposed the spread of slavery. Still, his antislavery credentials were sufficiently suspect that the abolitionist Wendell Phillips referred publicly to Lincoln as the "Slave-Hound of Illinois."

During the fall 1860 campaign, Lincoln followed the accepted practice of his day (and the unanimous recommendation of his advisers) and made no speeches of his own, relying instead on the party's printed pamphlets and on local orators to drum up enthusiasm for the Republican ticket. The strategy worked; Lincoln managed to win all but one state north of the Mason-Dixon line, though none below it. Between his election and inauguration, Lincoln remained silent, anxious to avoid alienating either residents of the upper South—Virginia, North Carolina, Kentucky, Tennessee, Arkansas, Missouri, and Maryland—who had not yet decided to join the Confederacy, or his own supporters in the North, who would view any substantive concession to the South as a betrayal of Republican principles. No one knew whether Lincoln intended to coerce the Confederate states back into the Union, or to employ a patient, conciliatory policy, hoping that the seceding states would return of their own free will.

Nor had the sphinxlike Lincoln provided any clues about his intentions during the triumphal train ride from his home in Springfield, Illinois, to Washington in February. He had left Springfield on February 11—"not knowing," he said, "when, or whether ever, I may return"—in a richly appointed railroad car, accompanied by an entourage of family, friends, and political cronies from Illinois. Self-appointed bodyguard Ward Hill Lamon, Lincoln's former law partner, armed himself with pistols and knives and came along for protection. To attend to the presidential party, Lincoln hired a young Negro servant named William Johnson.

For nearly two weeks the three-car private train wound eastward, zigzagging through Ohio, Pennsylvania, and New York State to allow as many people as possible to see Lincoln. Then it headed southward through New Jersey and Pennsylvania again, crossing the Mason-Dixon line into the more dangerous border slave state of Maryland, before finally arriving at Washington's Union Station, two blocks from the Capitol. The long journey exhausted everyone. Not even the luxurious fittings of the presidential coach could compensate for overheated cars filled with stale air, jouncing over rough roadbeds and crooked track, and switching onto eighteen different railroad lines. At most stops along the route, Lincoln appeared briefly to wave to the waiting crowds and tell a few stories, but nothing more. "He keeps all people, his friends included, in the dark," complained one reporter. "Mr. Lincoln promises nothing, but only listens."

Whenever he had to deliver a formal speech, Lincoln limited himself to optimistic generalities, depreciating the seriousness of the secession crisis and claiming that it had been "gotten up . . . by designing politicians." "Why all this excitement?" he asked his audience in Cleveland. "Why all these complaints? . . . The crisis is artificial."

Lincoln did insist that he would preserve the Union, but he also pretended that all Americans, both northerners and southerners, shared that goal. "While some of us may differ in political opinions, still we are all united in one feeling for the Union," Lincoln argued. "We all believe in the maintenance of the Union, of every star and every stripe of the glorious flag." He said nothing that could be interpreted as menacing toward the southern states. "There will be no bloodshed unless it is forced upon the government," the president-elect promised. "The government will not use force unless force is used against us."

In Columbus, Ohio, Lincoln assured a crowd that there was "nothing going wrong," but thoughtful Americans found it hard to see anything that was going right. They began to wonder whether Lincoln was indifferent to the danger the Union faced or was simply failing to comprehend the severity of the situation. Perhaps "Uncle Abe," as he was already known, really had no specific plan to deal with the secession crisis. Perhaps this naive, inexperienced Illinois lawyer would not be able to handle the job after all.

Lincoln was, in fact, buying time, hoping the Union would not deteriorate further before he took office. Then, with the power of the presidency, he intended to confront the Confederate challenge directly, using his inaugural address to outline a forceful policy toward the seceding states. He would assert that the Union was indissoluble, and that—even at the risk of war—he planned to reclaim the federal forts and arsenals in the South that the Confederate states had recently seized.

Back in Springfield, in a second-story room in his brother-in-law's store, Lincoln had written the original draft of this tough-minded inaugural message, keeping in front of him copies of the Constitution and Andrew Jackson's no-nonsense proclamation of 1833 against South Carolina's attempt to nullify federal law. Lincoln asked the publishers of the *Illinois Central Journal* to print four copies of the inaugural address for him, and then swore them to secrecy. He brought all the copies with him in a plain black satchel that he first entrusted to his seventeen-year-old son, Robert, without informing him of its contents. When the young man casually deposited the bag for safekeeping in a pile of nearly identical black satchels behind the desk in a hotel lobby in Indianapolis, Lincoln decided to keep it by his side for the rest of the trip.

In Washington, Lincoln showed the draft to a handful of experienced Republican Party leaders, several of whom recommended that he delete all references to the use of force and insert more conciliatory phrases. Reluctantly, he deferred to their judgment. Now, sitting in his suite at Willard's on the morning of his inauguration, Lincoln asked Robert to read him the speech aloud so he could hear it one last time. Always meticulous in his choice of words on public occasions, Lincoln—a notoriously poor extemporaneous speaker—wanted to make sure the address conveyed precisely the message he intended. It was printed in type slightly larger than normal to keep him from stumbling over any passage. Lincoln had even asked the printers to mark the draft for emphasis, with the typographical symbol of a fist and pointing finger in the margin of every paragraph that he felt might draw a reaction from the audience.

Washington: A Work in Progress

Downstairs, in Willard's renowned dining room and bar, regulars and guests had begun to gather for breakfast and gossip. Dozens of plain tables and chairs were wedged close together. There was no carpet, so conversation was constantly hindered by the screeching sound of chairs being shoved back and forth by the hotel's Negro servants, who served nearly 2,500 meals a day. Already the air inside the room was muggy and oppressive; the fact that many tourists from the Midwest seldom bathed did not improve the atmosphere. Spittoons abounded in strategic locations, but stains on the floor and walls testified to the poor aim of numerous guests. Still, only the most fastidious visitors complained. Besides the usual heavy meat and fish dishes, such as steak and onions and fried oysters, early morning diners at Willard's could feast on wild pigeon, pigs' feet, pâté de foie gras, robins on toast, and a variety of cakes and breads, all washed down by copious supplies of coffee or black tea.

Willard's, located at the corner of Fourteenth Street and Pennsylvania Avenue, was the most famous hotel in the city. The Willard brothers of Vermont had purchased the original building in 1847, refurbishing and expanding it into a sprawling rectangular block of rooms, six stories high and a hundred yards square. Every room, the proprietors boasted, featured running water, still a relatively rare commodity in Washington. Willard's was *the* place for Washington officials to dine and transact government business; cabinet officers, congressmen, and businessmen looking for lucrative government contracts came and went, and smoked and laughed in the hotel's public rooms. Nathaniel Hawthorne reported that "it may much more justly be called the center of Washington and the Union than . . . the Capitol, the White House, or the State Department."

Two blocks west of Willard's stood the White House, also known as the Executive Mansion. At the east end of Pennsylvania Avenue sat the Capitol, which was undergoing a prolonged process of renovation and expansion. In between, along the deteriorating cobblestones of the avenue, visitors found a mélange of shops, mansions, rooming houses, brothels, and squalid sheds, conforming to no particular style, some made out of marble, some of brick, and many of the cheapest plank timber.

Washington in 1861 was still a work in progress. At the turn of the century, the Virginia patrician John Randolph had described the capital as "a city of magnificent distances," but sixty years later few of the distances had been filled in. Washington remained, in the words of one British journalist, "all suburb and no city." Empty lots abounded. There were only a half dozen finished and functioning government buildings, including, on Fifteenth Street, the District's most impressive edifice, the Treasury building, in classic revival style. The State Department occupied a squat two-story redbrick structure hidden away a block behind the Executive Mansion.

Nearly all the city streets were unpaved clay or sand, which meant that Washington became a slough of nearly impassable mud in the spring and autumn, and a choking cloud of dust in the summer, when farmers drove herds of cattle through the downtown district to the stock pens near the unfinished Washington Monument. The federal government was still seeking contributions to complete this memorial to the nation's first president; meanwhile, the monument remained nothing more than a stubby shaft of white marble blocks with all the dignity, someone noted, "of a distillery smokestack."

Washington was also a pestilential city, particularly in the summertime, when the noxious combination of heat, humidity, and the occasional epidemic rendered the District nearly uninhabitable, and wealthy residents fled to vacation homes in the nearby countryside. The British government still considered Washington a hardship post and compensated its diplomatic representatives to the United States accordingly. In the absence of any sanitary services provided by the local government, garbage often lay strewn in the gutters, and dead cats floated in the canals. Hogs, geese, and dogs roamed wherever they wished. Since Congress had not yet appropriated sufficient funds for an aqueduct to bring fresh water from the nearby Potomac River, the city's 75,000 residents—61,000 whites, 11,000 free blacks, and 3,000 slaves—subsisted on water from local wells or springs in the Maryland hills. Mosquitoes swarmed from the District's swamps and creeks, particularly in the west end of town, just beyond the president's home.

Visitors agreed that Washington was a dreadful place. Ralph Waldo Emerson called it the "least attractive (to me) of cities," while Henry Adams, grandson of the nation's sixth president, dismissed it as a "rude colony" with "unfinished Greek temples for workrooms, and sloughs for roads." Frustrated with the lack of amenities in the still unfinished city, the British novelist Anthony Trollope complained about the distances between government offices, where "the country is wild, trackless, unbridged, uninhabited, and desolate." Even a young man from the rough western states, Congressman John Sherman of Ohio, found the capital an uninspiring sight. "It was an overgrown village," wrote Sherman, "with wide unpaved streets, with 61,000 inhabitants badly housed, hotels and boarding houses badly kept, and all depending more or less on low salaries, and employment by the government."

Lincoln's arrival on February 23 energized the city. Aside from a few carefully planned public appearances, the president-elect spent most of his waking hours greeting visitors who flocked to the parlor of his suite. Job-hunters clamoring for government positions, congressmen seeking control of federal patronage in their home states, reporters tracking down rumors, and curious bystanders merely desiring a closer look at the incoming president all clamored for his attention. Every room at Willard's was booked days before the inauguration; prospective Cabinet members who arrived in the city late had to find quarters in their friends' suites.

Washington's other hotels were equally crowded; visitors who could not find rooms anywhere wandered the streets at night or slept in one of the city's parks.

Cabinet Making

In the week before the inauguration, conversation at Willard's centered less on the breakup of the Union than on the composition of Lincoln's Cabinet. Certainly Lincoln spent more time conferring with Republican Party leaders over his Cabinet selections than negotiating with the Peace Conference of moderates from the border states, headed by former president John Tyler of Virginia, who were searching for a compromise solution to the secession crisis.

Washington insiders expected the inexperienced president-elect to rely heavily upon his advisers, so Lincoln's Cabinet choices were eagerly awaited as an indication of the policies he might pursue. Lincoln had drawn up a preliminary list of Cabinet candidates before he left Springfield, but he continued to juggle names and places right up to Inauguration Day, striving to find a balance among geographical regions, political philosophies, and rival personalities and factions within the Republican Party.

To placate the conservative eastern wing of the party, Lincoln offered the most prestigious Cabinet post—secretary of state—to Senator William Henry Seward of New York, the nation's best-known Republican. Seward, who had also served several terms as governor of New York, had been the front-runner for the Republican presidential nomination in 1860 until a coalition of his enemies derailed him; eight months later, the witty, urbane New Yorker remained incredulous that he had lost the nomination to "a little Illinois lawyer."

The diminutive, affable Seward was a familiar figure in Washington, with his sparkling blue eyes, unruly shock of fine straw-colored hair, prominent aquiline nose, ever-present cigar, and sallow complexion. He wore a worldly, distant expression that made him look, someone said, "like a wise macaw"; the impression was reinforced by a large head that looked badly out of place atop his long, slender neck. People were attracted to Seward by his easygoing manner, and few who knew Seward well disliked him. Yet something substantial appeared to be missing. A congressman from Massachusetts who admired Seward saw him as "an able, a specious and adroit and a very versatile man [who] escaped being really great. . . . He was, after all, as men instinctively felt, more a politician than a statesman."

Seward spent most of his political career in the Whig Party, which catered to the needs of businessmen, merchants, and commercial farmers. When the national Whig organization disintegrated in the early 1850s over the issue of the expansion of slavery into the western territories, Seward moved smoothly—and ahead of Lincoln—into the new Republican Party. In the North, he had a reputation as a moderate and an opportunist who preferred compromise to conflict. But southerners, taking his rhetoric at face value, viewed Seward as an extremist, largely because of his statements that the divergent cultures of North and South were leading the nation toward "an irrepressible conflict" between free white labor and slavery.

Insisting that the two opposing economic systems could not coexist, Seward proclaimed in 1858 that the United States "must and will, sooner or later, become either entirely a slave-holding nation or entirely a free-labor nation." To the South, this seemed a declaration of war against slavery, especially when combined with Seward's claim that there was "a higher law than the Constitution" regarding slavery—that is, a moral obligation to promote freedom, which overrode the legal protections that slaveholders enjoyed. So intensely did southerners detest Seward that Lincoln's Kentucky-born wife, Mary, objected violently to his appointment and spoke of him publicly as a "dirty abolition sneak."

Nothing could have been further from the truth. When Seward realized in the winter of 1860–1861 that the South was not bluffing, he became the leading Republican advocate of a negotiated solution to the secession crisis. Between Lincoln's election and his inauguration, Seward acted—on his own initiative—as the de facto head of the incoming administration in Washington, trying to reassure representatives of the remaining slave states and arrange a compromise to defuse the crisis.

Perhaps Congress could compensate slaveowners for runaway slaves, or promise never to interfere with slavery in the District of Columbia. Seward, like Lincoln, was buying time; once Lincoln was inaugurated and had been steered through the first few months of his administration without taking any dramatic action against slavery, Seward expected the South to react with strong pro-Union feelings. Then, he hoped, the secession movement would quietly disintegrate. One journalist who dined with Seward that winter reported that the senator openly depreciated the staying power of the secession movement. "Why, I myself, my brothers, and sisters, have been all Secessionists," Seward said. "We seceded from home when we were young, but we all went back to it sooner or later. These States will all come back in the same way."

To balance Seward's appointment, Lincoln offered the Treasury Department to Senator Salmon P. Chase of Ohio. Bitter rivals, Chase and Seward were total opposites: Seward was a former Whig from the East who was willing to make minor concessions on the slavery question, while Chase—a former Democrat from the Old Northwest—had become one of the nation's most outspoken antislavery politicians.

During four years as governor of Ohio and two more terms in the United States Senate, Chase supported voting rights for free Negroes and opposed the return of fugitive slaves to their southern owners. He was not, however, an abolitionist. Like most Republicans, Chase did not support the forced eradication of slavery in the South; his primary goal was to stop the spread of slavery into the western territories, to reserve them for white settlers. It was Chase who was credited with coining the slogan "Free Soil, Free Labor, Free Men," which became a rallying cry of the Republican Party in the 1850s.

Pompous, cold, and openly ambitious, Chase had been another of the leading contenders for the Republican presidential nomination in 1860, but his radical stance on slavery alienated party moderates. His lack of charisma further damaged his candidacy. Chase, however, never resigned himself to the loss of the nomination. Tall, with broad shoulders and handsome features, Chase certainly *looked* more like a president than Lincoln; his only disconcerting feature was a drooping right eyelid, the effect of a minor stroke. During the four-month interim between Lincoln's election and inauguration, Chase led the "iron-back" faction of Republicans, who opposed any concessions to the South. Alarmed at Seward's willingness to compromise, Chase's supporters pressured Lincoln to bring Chase into the Cabinet.

Lincoln knew he needed to offer a position to Chase—"Take him all in all," Lincoln told a visitor to Springfield in January, "he is the foremost man in the party"—but he also realized that Chase's ambition made him dangerously unpredictable. When Lincoln offered him the Treasury Department just before Inauguration Day, Chase hesitated, wondering whether he would improve his chances of gaining the White House by remaining in the Senate, where he could criticize the administration more freely. He finally accepted the appointment, but since his hard line against concessions to the South balanced Seward's conciliatory approach, observers still had no clear indication of the policy Lincoln would adopt.

None of Lincoln's remaining nominations provided a clearer insight. He offered the post of attorney general to Edward Bates, a well-known conservative and former Whig from the slave state of Missouri who shared Lincoln's strict-constructionist approach to the Constitution. To repay Pennsylvania for its support at the nominating convention, Lincoln named Senator Simon Cameron as secretary of war. A moderate on the issue of slavery, Cameron was an ex-Democrat whose name was synonymous with corruption and chicanery; someone once said that he "reeked with the stench of a thousand political bargains."

To bolster his support in the border slave states, Lincoln chose another former Democrat, Montgomery Blair of Maryland, as postmaster general. The Blair family had long been a power in Missouri politics; now Montgomery and his father, Francis Preston Blair (who had been a counselor to President Andrew Jackson thirty years earlier), lived on an estate in Silver Spring, Maryland, just outside the District of Columbia. Champions of the nonslaveowning whites of the upper South, the Blairs opposed any concessions to the seceding states. "Violence," insisted Montgomery, "is not to be met with peace." Equally adamant against compromise was Gideon Welles, the former Connecticut newspaper editor whom

Lincoln nominated as secretary of the navy, despite the fact that Welles had never been to sea. The final Cabinet post went to Representative Caleb Smith of Indiana, a political hack whom no one took seriously as secretary of the interior.

With Seward, Bates, and Cameron on one side, and Chase, Blair, and Welles on the other, Lincoln had assembled a querulous group of advisers who would have trouble agreeing on the time of day, let alone a course of action toward the South. Personal antagonism deepened the philosophical rifts. Chase despised Seward. Blair fought with everyone. No one trusted Cameron. Seward correctly predicted that this Cabinet would never work together harmoniously, but Lincoln knew it would provide him with advice from a variety of perspectives, leaving him free to follow whatever path he chose. All that remained was to have the Senate confirm Lincoln's nominees before congressmen left the wretched Washington climate for their spring and summer break.

Buchanan

By the middle of the morning, low gray clouds threatened rain on the inaugural parade and ceremonies. While Lincoln was dressing—in the same plain black suit he had worn for every formal occasion since he arrived in town—President James Buchanan was at the Capitol, signing last-minute bills passed by Congress in its rush to adjourn. It was fitting that Buchanan should end his presidency at the legislative end of Pennsylvania Avenue, for he had invariably looked to Congress to devise solutions to the sectional conflicts that were tearing the nation apart.

So had his predecessors. For forty years, ever since a bipartisan coalition of northern congressmen first objected to the expansion of slavery into western territories, legislative leaders had managed to reconcile the divergent interests of the North and South. In 1820, the Missouri Compromise balanced the admission of Missouri as a slave state with the admission of the free state of Maine, and established a line at 36° 30' through the rest of the Louisiana Purchase territory, prohibiting slavery north of that line. When the acquisition of new territories from Mexico in the 1840s threatened to upset the equilibrium between slave and free states, congressmen hammered out a series of deals known collectively as the Compromise of 1850, admitting California as a free state while giving southerners a more stringent federal Fugitive Slave Law that allowed them to pursue runaways onto northern soil. The question of whether to allow slavery in the territories of Utah and New Mexico was left up to their residents.

Yet these were only patchwork solutions to a deep and steadily widening division between northern and southern states. By the early 1850s the two sections had come to look upon themselves as distinct and separate societies, each with its own culture, ideals, and vision for the American future, and each hating the other. And the institution that best defined the contrast between them was human slavery.

All of the original thirteen colonies had permitted slavery during the seventeenth and eighteenth centuries. By 1805, however, every state north of the Mason-Dixon line had provided for the abolition of slavery, completely restricting the "domestic institution" to the South. There the development of the cotton gin in the early nineteenth century, accompanied by rapid expansion into the Gulf states, led to the emergence of a robust plantation economy that depended entirely upon slave labor.

Even though only one-fourth of whites in the South owned slaves, southerners came to view slavery as the indispensable cornerstone of their society. Negroes performed most of the menial labor in towns and cities, and all of the field work and domestic chores on plantations, allowing whites to devote their time to business interests and cultural pursuits. Work itself became demeaning. "Any man is a dog-goned fool to work," observed a planter in South Carolina, "when he can make a nigger work for him."

The result was a static, self-indulgent, seductive, and above all violent society. Masters might regard their slaves with affection, and persuade themselves that they were civilizing black heathens, but everyone knew the system rested upon the white man's power to end any Negro's life at any time. Both parties were transformed by the experience. White planters exercised tyrannical rule not only over their slaves but over women and poor whites as well; black slaves, realizing that nothing they did could ever change their fate, resorted to deceit, lying, and stealing to avoid the worst abuses of the system. "The whole commerce between master and slave is a perpetual exercise of the most boisterous passions," a southern slaveowner once wrote, "the most unremitting despotism on the one part, and degrading submission on the other."

As the black population in the Deep South expanded rapidly, southerners who had once expressed serious qualms about the morality of slavery came to agree that it could not safely be eliminated as long as millions of Negroes remained in the South. Increasingly they echoed a warning Thomas Jefferson issued shortly before his death: "We have the wolf by the ears, and we can neither hold him, nor safely let him go. Justice is in one scale, and self-preservation in the other."

Most northerners agreed. In the winter of 1861, only a vocal minority favored the immediate abolition of slavery in the South. Even those who opposed slavery on moral grounds assumed that Negroes could not easily or quickly make the leap from generations of bondage to the responsibilities of freedom. Nor did they believe that the government had the right to dispossess slaveowners of their property, even when that property took human form.

But if most northerners did not favor the immediate abolition of slavery in the South, they strongly opposed the *extension* of slavery, or policies designed to protect the institution. They were convinced that two centuries of human slavery had severely retarded the development of the southern states. After touring the South, Seward decided that the region offered only "an exhausted soil, old and decaying towns, wretchedly-neglected roads, and, in every respect, an absence of enterprise," As Harriet Beecher Stowe put it in 1852, in her best-selling novel *Uncle Tom's Cabin,* "It seemed as if everything had stopped growing, and was growing backwards."

That was not the future northerners desired for the territories, or for themselves. Northern society was based upon the assumption that every white man had an opportunity to be his own boss, as a farmer or businessman or craftsman. Even those who began at the bottom of the economic ladder could make their way to the top. If the path to wealth was blocked in an established community, a man could simply move to the western frontier and claim his own land, where his future would be limited only by his own effort and determination.

With their cheap land, the western territories served as a safety valve. But if slaveowners invaded the territories, the outlet would slam shut, depriving whites of their opportunities and leaving northern society to buckle under the strain of class divisions. On the other hand, southerners believed that slavery could not survive unless it were allowed to expand into fresh lands that could sustain new plantations and absorb the steadily increasing slave population. Since leaders of both sections viewed control of the western territories as the key to their future prosperity, the chance of negotiating another compromise seemed remote at best.

Not that Buchanan tried. At the end of his single term in the Executive Mansion, the sixty-nine-year-old Buchanan was exhausted. He had spent nearly three decades in national public life, as a Democratic congressman and senator from Pennsylvania, American minister to Great Britain and Russia, and secretary of state. After years of seeking the Democratic presidential nomination, Buchanan obtained the prize in 1856 only because he had the good fortune to be abroad while everyone else was choosing up sides on the issue of slavery. In a time of escalating tension, Buchanan was a safe candidate, a northerner whose best friends in Washington were southerners, a moderate who believed that the federal government should stay out of the quarrel over slavery in the territories.

Buchanan's moderation won him the election, but it doomed his presidency to failure when a series of shocks—from armed conflict between proslavery and free-soil raiders in the Kansas territory to John Brown's seizure of the government arsenal at Harpers Ferry—strengthened the hand of extremists on both sides. When Buchanan did take a stand, as in the dispute over Kansas, he sided with the southerners who dominated his Cabinet. By 1860, his administration's favoritism had created a backlash in the North, splintering the Democratic Party. That year the Democrats held separate conventions in North and South, each nominating its own candidate, virtually ensuring Lincoln's election.

Buchanan bequeathed Lincoln an empty federal treasury and severely depleted armed forces. His secretary of the treasury, Howell Cobb of Georgia, deliberately exhausted the federal government's reserves to render it powerless to wage war against the South. When Congress convened in December 1860—by which time Cobb had resigned to return to Georgia—there was not even enough money left to pay legislators their salary of eight dollars a day. Meanwhile, Secretary of War John B. Floyd of Virginia dispatched a substantial portion of the army's existing supplies of firearms and munitions to *southern* arsenals before he, too, resigned. Army units were scattered across the country, stationed predominantly in far western posts to guard against attacks by Indians, while the vessels of the tiny American navy (only forty-two ships) had been dispersed to foreign ports or southern harbors.

For decades southerners had dominated the upper echelons of the army. As the secession movement gathered momentum in the winter of 1860–1861, dozens of army officers stationed in the South resigned their commissions. Commanding officers surrendered their arsenals and forts without a fight to Confederate state militiamen or bands of armed southern citizens. For a brief period in December, the War Department left the nation's capital wholly without troops. Even at Lincoln's inauguration, Washington's defenses remained badly undermanned, because Buchanan feared that any gathering of military force might frighten Virginia into joining the Confederacy.

Whenever anyone asked his opinion, Buchanan insisted that states could not legally secede from the Union, but he also admitted that he saw no way to stop them. As the German-American newspaperman Carl Schurz put it, Buchanan "recoiled from active treason" but lacked "courage enough for active patriotism." When his southern advisers left the capital following Lincoln's election, Buchanan replaced them with northern Unionists, but the damage had been done.

In short, Buchanan and Congress had failed utterly to stem the tide of secession. Republican newspapers showered abuse upon the outgoing president, demanding that he resign or be impeached, or perhaps hanged as a traitor. "Old James Buchanan," wrote one New York critic, "stands lowest, I think, in the dirty catalog of treasonable mischief-makers. For without the excuse of bad Southern blood . . . he has somehow slid into the position of boss-traitor and master-devil of the gang."

Others spread the blame more widely. After visiting Washington early in 1861 and watching the nation's political leaders thrash about impotently, former army officer William Tecumseh Sherman washed his hands of the whole mess. "You have got things in a hell of a fix," Sherman told his congressman brother, "and you may get them out as you best can." To the New York attorney George Templeton Strong, the causes of the impending catastrophe ran even deeper. "We are a weak, divided, disgraced people, unable to maintain our national existence," Strong wrote. "The bird of our country is a debilitated chicken, disguised in eagle feathers. We have never been a nation; we are only an aggregate of communities, ready to fall apart at the first serious shock and without a centre of vigorous national life to keep us together."

One last shock remained for the weary Buchanan. Minutes before he left the Capitol on Inauguration Day to pick up Lincoln in the presidential carriage, Buchanan received a message from Fort Sumter, just outside of Charleston, South Carolina. Major Robert Anderson, the commander of Sumter—one of the two remaining southern forts still controlled by the federal government—estimated that he would need at least 20,000 reinforcements to hold his post against a Confederate assault. Buchanan sighed and consigned the report to his successor for a reply.

Procession

A few minutes after noon, Buchanan arrived at Willard's in the presidential carriage, an open barouche with a Negro driver. As he and Lincoln took their seats, a band outside the hotel began to play "Hail to the Chief." Lincoln, carrying his black silk stovepipe hat and a gold-headed ebony cane, sat next to Buchanan as they rode down Pennsylvania Avenue to the Capitol. At one point, Buchanan muttered something about how glad he was to be leaving the presidency and returning to his home in Pennsylvania, but there was little small talk between the two men for the rest of the short journey.

The skies over Washington had cleared again, although a gusty north-west wind was kicking up disagreeable swirls of thick yellow dust from the dry city streets. Few of the houses or shops along the parade route bore decorations to welcome the new president. The shouting crowds (esti-mated at nearly 10,000) on both sides of the wide avenue craned their necks for a view of Lincoln, but his lanky figure was largely hidden behind the mounted honor guard of regular army troops—wearing top hats and decorative sashes—that flanked the carriage. A cavalry officer who rode alongside Lincoln kept digging his spurs into his mount, deliberately mak-ing it and the other horses skittish so that potential assassins could not get a clear shot at the president-elect.

People were betting on the probability of an assassination attempt, of course, since gambling was one of Washington's leading industries. There were a few drunken rowdies who tried to obstruct the progress of the pro-cession, shouting insults at the marchers and cheering for the Confeder-acy. But the odds against anyone's drawing a bead on Lincoln had risen with General Scott's professed determination to protect his new com-mander in chief. Squads of cavalry guarded every side street along Penn-sylvania Avenue; platoons of militia stood at attention every hundred yards; infantry units with loaded weapons followed close behind the pres-idential carriage; and sharpshooters stood guard on rooftops and in the windows of strategically chosen buildings along the cobblestoned avenue. (A few windows along the route were shuttered tight, in silent protest against Lincoln's inauguration.) Special policemen with conspicuous badges circulated among the crowd to discourage troublemakers. Atop Capitol Hill waited General Scott—in a carriage, since he was too old, heavy, and arthritic to sit atop a horse—and two batteries of artillery.

One reporter complained that an American president was about to take the oath of office "surrounded and guarded not by the honest hearts of a happy people, but safely ensonced [sic] out of the people's reach, within a military cordon bristling with bayonets." "Evil was in the air, and I felt it," wrote Charles Francis Adams, Jr., grandson of the nation's sixth president. "The very knowledge of the military preparations going on all about me gave me . . . a feeling almost approaching fear." Congressman Sherman felt that the presence of so many troops in the capital seemed inauspicious; the sight of sharpshooters and howitzers and the sound of bugles and drums, Sherman noted, "united to produce a profound apprehension of evils yet to come."

When the presidential carriage reached the Capitol, with its white marble and stone staircases spattered irreverently with tobacco juice, Buchanan and Lincoln alighted and entered the building through a specially constructed tunnel with high boarded walls. The rest of the inaugural procession proceeded directly to the temporary platform erected on the recently completed east portico. Inside, where the regular session of Congress had just been gaveled to a close and a special session called to order, Representative George Julian watched Buchanan and Lincoln walk arm in arm into the Senate chamber and seat themselves in front of the desk of the vice president. The once portly figure of the outgoing president, Julian later recalled, "was so withered and bowed with age that in contrast with the towering form of his successor he seemed little more than half a man."

Other observers in the packed galleries disagreed. As the outgoing vice president, John C. Breckenridge, swore in his successor—the former senator Hannibal Hamlin of Maine (whose swarthy complexion had produced rumors in the South that he was a mulatto)—Adams kept watching Buchanan and Lincoln. In spite of Buchanan's one squinting eye and his oddly tilted neck, which inclined toward his left shoulder, Adams decided that "the outgoing President was undeniably the more presentable man of the two; his tall, large figure, and white head, looked well beside Mr. Lincoln's lank, angular form and hirsute face; and the dress of the President-elect"—that is, his black suit, without the old-fashioned standing collar and starched white choker that Buchanan wore—"did not indicate that knowledge of the proprieties of the place which was desirable."

Transfer of Power

After Vice President Hamlin took his oath of office, Lincoln and Buchanan walked together onto the platform by the east portico. Many in the crowd had never seen the incoming president. Their initial reaction was surprise that Lincoln was not as ugly as rumored. So many stories had circulated about Lincoln's unprepossessing appearance that observers typically were startled to find that he was not the "original orang-otang" or uncouth yokel portrayed in Democratic campaign propaganda. (Lincoln admitted on Election Day that he was lucky women couldn't vote; "otherwise," he joked, "the monstrous portraits of him which had been circulated during the canvass by friends as well as foes would surely defeat him.")

It was true that Lincoln was a westerner who moved awkwardly and appeared ill at ease on formal occasions. His remarkable proportions—six feet four inches tall but weighing only about 180 pounds—made his clothes seem not quite to fit. Lincoln's huge hands and feet added to the impression of gracelessness. As Carl Schurz noted, the president-elect "certainly did not present the appearance of a statesman as people usually picture it in their imagination." Cartoonists always had a field day with his thick black eyebrows, his shock of unruly black hair, his long sinewy neck, and his prominent nose in a narrow, deeply lined face.

In person, however, Lincoln's presence softened the severest aspects of his features. Walt Whitman saw Lincoln in New York shortly before the inauguration, and remembered "his perfect composure and coolness—his unusual and uncouth height, his dress of complete black, stovepipe hat push'd back on the head, dark-brown complexion, seam'd and wrinkled yet canny-looking face, black, bushy head of hair, disproportionately long neck, and his hands held behind him as he stood observing the people." The poet thought Lincoln "a hoosier Michel Angelo," with a face "so awful ugly it becomes beautiful, with its strange mouth, its deep cut, cris-cross lines, and its doughnut complexion."

Lincoln's appearance on the east portico may have reassured curious onlookers, but the scene behind him was a mess. The new cast-iron Capitol dome—a replacement for the original temporary wooden model—remained unfinished, its truncated form a counterpart of the incomplete Washington Monument at the other end of the avenue. A bare wooden derrick, supported by a web of steel ropes, rose like a black arm above the cupola of the Capitol. Scaffolding extended from the second story of the dome to the base. On the grounds nearby lay a jumble of construction materials, including blocks of marble and stone, assorted piles of lumber and a female figure grasping a wreath in one hand and a sword in the other.

Nearly 300 dignitaries crowded onto the inaugural platform. In the absence of any formal arrangements, it took Lincoln a few minutes to make his way through the crush of people to a small wooden canopy at the front. A brief period of confusion followed as politicians jostled for positions close to the president-elect. Senator Douglas, Lincoln's longtime political rival, found a place prominently near Lincoln, to demonstrate his support for the incoming administration. Buchanan sat slightly behind Lincoln, uttering deep, audible sighs throughout the proceedings. Beneath the platform but hidden from public view, fifty riflemen detailed by Scott to guard against bomb threats remained on alert.

Near Buchanan sat Roger Taney, chief justice of the United States, who came to administer the oath of office. Taney, a native of Maryland— a slave state—had survived a recent illness to celebrate his eighty-third birthday, and a reporter at the scene noted that the ancient, withered justice resembled "a galvanized corpse." He had administered the oath of office to presidents since 1836; Lincoln was the eighth chief executive he swore in.

No one in the crowd was more dedicated to southern values or to slavery than Taney. Although he had freed his own slaves decades earlier, Taney was convinced that slavery was the foundation of the southern way of life. He denounced northern antislavery agitators as assassins; at one point he threatened to refuse to administer the oath of office to Seward if the New Yorker won the presidency.

Taney's emotional commitment to slavery led him to overreach himself in writing the Dred Scott decision in 1857. Scott, a slave, sued for his freedom on the ground that he and his master had lived for several years in Illinois and the Minnesota territory, where slavery was legally forbidden. Taney rejected Scott's suit, but instead of simply upholding a lower court's decision, Taney and the southern majority on the Supreme Court issued a comprehensive ruling intended to bar Congress from prohibiting slavery in *any* territory. While he was at it, Taney declared that slaves had no right to bring suit in federal court; further, the decision asserted that the Constitution gave African-Americans *no* civil rights or legal protections.

Taney's ruling alarmed northerners because it appeared to open all free territories to the importation of slave labor, thereby reducing the opportunity for settlement of the West by free whites. Calling Taney's ruling a "burlesque upon judicial decisions," Lincoln charged that it "assailed, and sneered at . . . and torn" the noble ideals of the Declaration of Independence, the document that Lincoln held dearer than any other. Lincoln believed that the founding fathers had designed the Declaration to encourage "the progressive improvement in the condition of all men everywhere." Instead, the Court had reversed the process, taking rights away from Negroes and relegating them to a permanently inferior status.

Lincoln used the Dred Scott decision deftly in his unsuccessful bid for the United States Senate in 1858, suggesting to Illinois voters that the Supreme Court and Buchanan's Democratic Party planned to allow slave labor throughout the western territories, and eventually into the northern states as well. Two years later, northern voters decided to elect a Republican president who could gradually replace the pro-southern majority on the Supreme Court with antislavery justices.

No Force, No Retreat

Customarily the president-elect took the oath of office before making his inaugural address, but Lincoln reversed the order. He chose an old friend, Senator Edward D. Baker of Oregon, to introduce him. The two men had been schoolmates and had started their careers together as lawyers in Sangamon County, Illinois; an eloquent orator, Baker later moved to the West Coast and became one of Oregon's first senators. Although Baker was a Democrat, the two men remained so close that Lincoln named his second son Edward Baker Lincoln. (Never a robust child, the boy died at age four in 1850.)

At one-thirty, Baker presented Lincoln to the audience, which responded with cheers that struck observers as more respectful than enthusiastic. As Lincoln made his way to the small, rickety table that served as the podium, his face looked flushed, his lips compressed in determination. He bowed to acknowledge the cheers, then stood awkwardly for a moment, trying to decide where to put his new silk hat. Senator Douglas stepped forward gracefully, murmured, "Permit me, sir," and held the hat for the rest of the ceremony. Lincoln put on his steel-rimmed spectacles and arranged his manuscript on the table, using the golden head of his cane to keep the papers in place against the gusty wind.

He was obviously nervous, and seemed uncomfortable with the crowd so close behind him on the platform. But those who had never heard Lincoln speak in public were surprised at the power of his slightly high-pitched voice, which carried clearly and distinctly to the farthest reaches of his audience. Disdaining the ornate phrasing and classical delivery of the era's most popular eastern orators, Lincoln spoke in a direct, unpretentious, western style. Unlike most politicians of his day, he made few gestures as he spoke, partly because his movements were so awkward, but also because he wanted to focus attention on his carefully prepared script.

This was the moment the nation had been waiting for, when Lincoln would reveal his intentions toward the Confederacy and the southern states that remained in the Union. He began by trying to dispel the fears of southerners that a Republican administration in Washington would endanger their security or property—in other words, their slaves. "There has never been any reasonable cause for such apprehension," Lincoln insisted. Quoting from one of his previous speeches, Lincoln assured the South, "I have no purpose, directly or indirectly, to interfere with the institution of slavery in the States where it exists." He reminded his audience that the president had no constitutional power to abolish slavery, and he confirmed the right of each state "to order and control its own institutions according to its own judgment exclusively."

Lincoln added a promise that he would not expand his executive powers by interpreting the Constitution radically. He pledged to enforce the controversial Fugitive Slave Law; but Lincoln noted that the obligation to respect *all* federal statutes applied to the South as well—no section could ignore laws it did not like.

The president-elect then swung into the heart of his message. He was entering office under extraordinary circumstances: "A disruption of the Federal Union heretofore only menaced, is now formidably attempted." Convinced that "the Union of these States is perpetual," Lincoln could not ignore the threat. The southern interpretation of the Constitution as a nonbinding compact that could be ignored when any state chose to do so was both mistaken and illogical. "No government proper," he said, "ever had a provision in its organic law for its own termination." Besides, the Constitution expressly stated that it was designed to form a *more* perfect Union, not one that could be broken and therefore was *less* perfect than before.

It follows from these views that no State, upon its own motion, can lawfully get out of the Union,—that resolves and ordinances to that effect are legally void; and that acts of violence, within any State or States, against the authority of the United States, are insurrectionary or revolutionary, according to circumstances.

I therefore consider that, in view of the Constitution and the laws, the Union is unbroken; and, to the extent of my ability, I shall take care, as the Constitution itself expressly enjoins upon me, that the laws of the Union be faithfully executed in all the States.

So much for tolerating secession. Thus far Lincoln was on solid ground with public opinion in the North, which overwhelmingly supported the preservation of the Union. It was sharply divided over the use of force to prevent secession, however, so Lincoln promised that "there needs to be no bloodshed or violence; and there shall be none, unless it be forced upon the national authority."

Next, Lincoln raised his voice and, emphasizing every word distinctly, vowed that he would "hold, occupy, and possess the property, and places belonging to the government"—meaning Fort Sumter and Fort Pickens, the two military strongholds in the South still under federal control—and collect import duties and taxes in the southern states. "But beyond what may be necessary for these objects," Lincoln promised, "there will be no invasion—no using of force against, or among the people anywhere." He paused for a moment to allow the audience to take in the full meaning of his pledge. At that point, Senator Douglas nodded and murmured, "Good," and "No coercion," and then "Good again." Buchanan, on the other hand, seemed to have drifted off. For most of the address, the outgoing president occupied himself by squinting with his one good eye squarely at the toe of his right boot.

To conciliate the South, Lincoln even agreed not to send federal officials (other than revenue collectors) into states where the citizens appeared to be unusually hostile to the national government. "The course here indicated will be followed," Lincoln promised, "unless current events, and experience, shall show a modification, or change, to be proper." Nowhere, however, did Lincoln describe how he intended to carry out his pledge to collect import duties or hold the two remaining federal forts in the South without the use of force.

A few bystanders with southern sympathies began to drift away, but most of the crowd responded to the speech with polite applause. There was very little enthusiasm at any point, perhaps because Lincoln's straightforward style was not designed to evoke an emotional reaction. Instead, the audience seemed attentive and—for Americans—unusually respectful. At one point, a crash and a flurry of activity not far from Lincoln caused a moment of panic. A spectator had fallen from the breaking bough of a tree; the commotion threw Lincoln temporarily off balance.

Lincoln spent the last part of his address pleading for both northerners and southerners to display a spirit of compromise. The issue that divided them was clear: "One section of our country believes slavery is right, and ought to be extended, while the other believes it is wrong, and ought not to be extended." But secession, Lincoln argued, would actually make it harder for the South to preserve slavery. If the southern states tried to leave the Union, they would lose all their constitutional guarantees, and northerners would no longer be obligated to return fugitive slaves to disloyal owners. In other words, the South was safer inside the Union than without, and to prove his point Lincoln confirmed his willingness to support a recently proposed thirteenth amendment to the Constitution, which would specifically prohibit the federal government from interfering with slavery in states where it already existed.

Then Lincoln closed with a plea for a cooling-off period before either side took irreversible steps toward war. Again he promised that he would not initiate military action. "In *your* hands, my dissatisfied fellow country-men, and not in *mine,* is the momentous issue of civil war. The government will not assail *you.* You can have no conflict, without being yourselves the aggressors. *You* have no oath registered in Heaven to destroy the govern-ment, while *I* shall have the most solemn one to preserve, protect and de-fend it."

When Lincoln finished, Taney tottered forward in his black silk robe. As the chief justice held out to Lincoln a gilt-clasped Bible bound in cin-namon velvet, all those on the platform removed their hats. After Lincoln took the oath of office, the crowd gave its loudest cheer of the afternoon, and men flung their hats in the air. The batteries at the north end of the Capitol gave a thundering salute, answered by the rifle volleys of the mili-tia honor guard. The nation had its first Republican president.

A *Hand of Iron and a Velvet Glove*

Before the distinguished guests left the platform, reporters scurried to ob-tain their reactions to Lincoln's speech. "Well, I hardly know what he means," declared Senator Douglas. "Every point in the address is suscep-tible of a double construction; but I think he does not mean coercion." Buchanan brushed off all questions. "I cannot say what he means until I read his Inaugural," the former president snapped. "I cannot understand the secret meaning of the document."

Lincoln and Buchanan left the Capitol together and rode back to the White House in the presidential carriage. The rest of the inaugural pro-cession marched behind them, at times nearly lost to sight in the thick yellow dust kicked up by the carriage and the cavalry mounts alongside it. Along Pennsylvania Avenue, the crowd cheered with more exuberance than it had displayed all day. When the carriage reached the Executive Mansion, Lincoln invited his predecessor to spend the night as his guest, but Buchanan demurred. He shook hands with Lincoln and wished him luck, and then rode to the home of an old friend, Senator Robert Ould of Virginia.

Buchanan's work was not yet done. That evening, he met with his former Cabinet secretaries to discuss the latest dispatches from Fort Sumter. Before he left for his home in Pennsylvania the following morning, Buchanan and his advisers convened one last time at the War Department to draft a letter to Lincoln, summarizing the moves and countermoves of the federal government and South Carolina officials in their sparring over Fort Sumter.

Once Lincoln and Buchanan left Capitol Hill, Senator Charles Sumner of Massachusetts started to walk home along F Street, parallel to the parade route. There he met Charles Francis Adams, Jr., who had watched the ceremony from a ledge on the unfinished Senate wing of the Capitol. Sumner, one of the staunchest antislavery men in the Senate, applauded Lincoln's refusal to offer substantive concessions to the South. "I do not suppose Lincoln had it in his mind, if indeed he ever heard of it," he told Adams, "but the inaugural seems to me best described by Napoléon's simile of 'a hand of iron and a velvet glove.'"

As they walked on together, Sumner and Adams encountered General Scott, sitting in his carriage at one of the city's traffic circles, from which Scott could scan several intersecting streets. Although many visitors had relaxed after Lincoln was sworn in, Scott maintained his vigilance until the president returned to the White House. When Lincoln finally strode into the Executive Mansion, Scott relaxed and congratulated himself and his officers on a job well done. "Thank God," he sighed, "we now have a government."

Lincoln spent the evening of his inauguration at the White House fulfilling his ceremonial obligations. After the foreign diplomats in Washington paid their respects, the doors to the president's home were opened to the public. Since Lincoln had been sworn in, establishing a Republican order of succession in case of his death, security was not nearly as tight as it had been during the parade. A guard of United States marshals did, however, act as Lincoln's bodyguards, keeping any suspicious-looking strangers at a distance. After the president had greeted hundreds of visitors, the marshals cleared the rooms, and Lincoln—obviously worn out—retired to his private apartment on the second floor.

In a nearby tavern, a visiting New Yorker heard Senator Louis Wigfall of Texas, one of the most rabid secessionists in the city, proclaim his contempt for his southern friends. They had sworn to kill Lincoln, and now the Black Republican had been peaceably inaugurated. Wigfall muttered that he was "tempted to say he would have nothing more to do with such a damned set of humbugs."

2

THE WHITE MAN'S WAR

Most news traveled slowly in 1861. Even though 50,000 miles of telegraph wire crisscrossed the eastern half of the United States, rates were still so expensive that newspapers sent dispatches by telegraph only when they were of overriding interest. Lincoln's inaugural was one of those occasions. Within six hours, Americans from Maine to Mississippi were reading accounts of the president's speech. Reactions began to reach Washington the following day.

Lincoln had changed few minds. Editors of pro-Republican newspapers, many of whom viewed the secession movement as the work of a hotheaded minority in the Deep South, praised the inaugural address as statesmanlike, resolute yet patient. An editorial in the *New York Times* declared, "Mr. Lincoln's Inaugural Address . . . breathes the very spirit of kindness and conciliation, and relies upon justice and reflection, rather than force, for the preservation of the Federal Union." Lincoln's hometown newspaper, the *Springfield Republican,* concluded that the president had placed "the secession conspirators manifestly in the wrong. . . . They cannot take a single step without making treasonable war upon the government, which will only defend itself."

In Washington, Republican leaders were relieved that the president hadn't blundered. They interpreted his speech as supporting their several approaches to the secession crisis. Senator Henry Winter Davis of Maryland, a foe of concessions to the South, announced that he was "ready to stand on the President's position," while Charles Francis Adams, Jr., who favored a conciliatory policy, declared with a sigh of relief that the inaugural endorsed *his* stand.

Southerners ignored the conciliatory aspects of Lincoln's message. "His speech was just what was expected of him," decided a South Carolina schoolteacher, "stupid, ambiguous, vulgar, and insolent, and is everywhere considered a virtual declaration of war." The editor of the *Richmond Whig* denounced the "coercive policy of the inaugural," and warned that Lincoln's proposals to maintain the federal forts and collect federal revenue in the southern states "will meet with the stern and unyielding resistance of a united South." In North Carolina, the *Wilmington Herald* complained that "there is no mitigation of Lincoln's fanaticism in this inaugural address, and, painful as it may be to the American people, they might as well open their eyes to the solemn fact that war is inevitable."

Even though few Democratic newspapers in the North attacked Lincoln's policy, their editors confessed that they found the blend of firmness and conciliation bewildering. The *New York Herald* reprinted the address under the headline "The Country No Wiser than it was Before." "There is some plain talk in the address," acknowledged the *Providence Daily Post,* "but . . . it is immediately followed by obscurely stated qualifications."

Frederick Douglass, the leading spokesman for African-Americans in the North, shared the Democrats' objections. In his view, Lincoln had missed a golden opportunity to provide moral leadership. Instead, the president had delivered "a double-tongued document, capable of two constructions, [which] conceals rather than declares a definite policy." Lincoln's message also failed to inspire confidence on Wall Street; when trading resumed the day after the inauguration, prices on the New York Stock Exchange suffered another substantial decline in what was already a monthlong panic over secession.

But Lincoln had succeeded in buying time. The northern public still supported him, waiting to see what direction he would take. The special state conventions of the upper South took no action either. They kept watching Washington, poised to vote for secession if Lincoln ordered a military response to the Confederacy.

A Rude Awakening

Soon after returning from the inaugural ceremonies, Lincoln received Major Anderson's urgent letter from Charleston, South Carolina, warning that provisions at Fort Sumter would last only six weeks. Unless the government mounted a full-scale mission to defend or reinforce Sumter, Anderson—one of the few southern-born officers who had not abandoned their posts—said he would have no choice but to surrender.

Lincoln was stunned. Hours earlier, he had promised to "hold, occupy, and possess the property, and places belonging to the government" in the South, but there were only two such places left—Sumter and Fort Pickens, in Pensacola harbor. Before his inauguration, Lincoln asked General Scott to prepare plans to defend those forts, or retake them if necessary. If Lincoln allowed Sumter to fall without a shot, he would saddle his administration with an image of impotence from which it might never recover. Yet Lincoln had also pledged to refrain from "bloodshed or violence . . . unless it be forced upon the national authority," and there was no way to slip thousands of federal troops into Charleston harbor without provoking a hostile response from South Carolina.

It was a rude welcome to the White House, especially for a man who later admitted that he was at first "entirely ignorant not only of the duties, but of the manner of doing the business" of the presidency. When he walked into his office on the morning of March 5, Lincoln was alone. He inherited no executive staff, no bureaucracy to ease the transition to a new administration. The Senate had not yet approved his Cabinet (Chase still had not been formally notified of his appointment); neither had it given him permission to employ a private secretary. Nor could Lincoln turn to Congress for advice, since the members of the House were on their way out of town, and their colleagues in the Senate would depart quickly after confirming Lincoln's Cabinet appointments.

Lincoln rarely acted impulsively. He preferred to move cautiously, doing "what seemed best each day as each day came." Under the circumstances, he really had little choice. The government did not have 20,000 troops to reinforce Sumter, since the entire United States Army numbered a mere 16,000 regulars. Besides, Lincoln knew that only a minority of voters of the states still in the Union had elected him, and he was uncertain whether the northern public would support military action to retain Fort Sumter.

Congressional Republicans disagreed among themselves as to what Lincoln should do about Sumter. One bloc, led by Seward, preferred to abandon the fort to demonstrate the administration's peaceful intentions and persuade Virginia and the other states of the upper South to remain in the Union. A smaller faction insisted that the government reinforce the garrison as soon as possible, warning that any sign of retreat would be a public relations disaster for the party. A growing number of antislavery radicals—who feared that Lincoln might strike some "corrupt compromise" to keep slaveowners in the Union—wished to write off the South altogether and let the Confederate states secede, taking the curse of slavery with them.

Whatever their opinions about Sumter, a majority of northerners regarded the prospect of an armed conflict with the Confederate states with apprehension. "Nothing could possibly be so horrible," declared Senator Sumner, "or so wicked or so senseless as a war." Like Lincoln, the average northerner kept hoping that *something* would occur to avert violence. "We didn't know what," recalled Charles Francis Adams, Jr. "We couldn't even suggest a 'something'; but we clung to the childish belief all the same." As the possibility of war edged nearer, however, merchants in New York reported unprecedented sales of firearms to civilians.

To preserve his military options, Lincoln called Scott to his office on March 5 and directed him "to hold all these forts and make arrangements to reinforce them." Four days later, after the Senate had confirmed his Cabinet nominees, Lincoln met with his advisers. Everyone advocated holding onto Fort Pickens, which was still defensible, but only Montgomery Blair recommended reinforcing Sumter at the risk of war. One of the most pugnacious men in Washington, Blair yearned to confront the slaveowners, who he felt had long oppressed the poor whites of the southern states.

The rest of the Cabinet voted for peace. Cameron professed surprise that the question was even raised; he assumed everyone understood that the government would give up Sumter. Chase seemed uncertain. Seward led the argument for withdrawal. He had promised a delegation from Virginia that the administration would abandon the fort peacefully; deluded by wishful thinking, Seward still believed that if both sides could avoid bloodshed for the next few months, southern officials would realize that they could best safeguard their interests by staying in the Union. The president had encouraged Seward to explore this approach. Just before the inauguration, Lincoln offered to withdraw from Sumter if Virginia affirmed its loyalty to the Union. "Why not?" Lincoln asked. "If you will guarantee me the State of Virginia I shall remove the troops. A state for a fort is no bad business."

In the absence of a clear signal from Lincoln about his position—Cameron later complained that nothing was ever really decided at Cabinet meetings—the discussion around the large oak table in the president's office deteriorated. Lincoln sent his advisers on their way with a request for their written opinions on a proposal to provision Sumter by sea, without sending any troop reinforcements. The following day, March 10, Lincoln discovered that Scott had done nothing to develop plans to reinforce Sumter and Pickens. The president then repeated his order to Scott in writing.

When the Cabinet reconvened five days later (at the outset, there were no regularly scheduled meetings), only Blair and Chase supported a supply expedition to Sumter. Chase based his approval on the assumption that the action would not precipitate a war for which he knew the Union was woefully unprepared. The rest of the Cabinet confirmed its willingness to abandon Sumter. General Scott, who joined the meeting, agreed that since the fort could not be held in any case, "I now see no alternative but a surrender, in some weeks."

Still the president refused to make a final decision. Whenever he had faced a puzzling case in his law practice back in Springfield, Lincoln immersed himself in the details of the matter, trying to learn as much as he could. "I have seen him get a case and seem to be bewildered at first," recalled a longtime associate, "but he would go at it and after a while he would master it. He was very tenacious in his grasp of a thing that he once got hold of." Now Lincoln decided to send an old friend, Stephen Hurlbut (a native South Carolinian), to Charleston on a fact-finding mission to gauge public sentiment there.

While he awaited Hurlbut's return, Lincoln gave no hint of his intentions toward Sumter, even though the problem haunted him daily. "Of all the trials I have had since I came here, none begin to compare with those I had between the inauguration and the fall of Fort Sumter," he later admitted. "Could I have anticipated them, I would not have believed it possible to survive them." For the next four weeks, newspapers speculated constantly about the administration's intentions. One day the press was certain Lincoln would abandon Sumter; the next afternoon's newspapers carried excited predictions of war.

Interviews

As he wrestled with the problem of Fort Sumter, Lincoln devoted hours every day to the administrative headaches afflicting all incoming presidents. In the absence of a civil service system, the chief executive controlled appointments to thousands of federal jobs. Since the Republican Party had never been in power before, there was a rush of applications for positions. Congressmen, senators, and Cabinet officers petitioned the president to appoint their constituents and friends as postmasters, clerks, and diplomatic secretaries. Before he took office, Lincoln resolved to appoint only qualified applicants to government jobs, and so he tried to examine each candidate's record. To his surprise, he discovered that his Republican colleagues were recommending a number of men who were "physically, morally, and intellectually unfit" for government service.

Lincoln's attempts to sort out the applicants made him a prisoner in his own office. He was so inundated with job applications, Lincoln told a friend, "that he thought sometimes that the only way that he [could] escape from them would be to take a rope and hang himself on one of the trees in the lawn south of the president's house." "The clamor for offices is quite extraordinary," noted one reporter, and Senator Sumner claimed that the crowd of job-seekers in the city was as thick as "the buffaloes on the plains at the foot of the Rocky Mountains." Veteran Washingtonians were appalled by the rustic dress and lack of manners (and hygiene) of those who came from the midwest. "I had not noticed it before," wrote a journalist in his diary, "but certainly in all my long experience of Washington I have never seen such a swarm of uncouth beings."

Lincoln could hardly have avoided them. The president's three rooms of offices lay at one end of the second floor of the Executive Mansion, and his small, private bedchamber—which adjoined the larger bedroom his wife used—was at the other end. Each morning, Lincoln had only to walk to work down a corridor from bedroom to office, but the corridor filled quickly with men seeking a few moments of his time. The extraordinary security precautions for the inaugural evaporated in less than twenty-four hours. Anyone with sufficient patience and determination could obtain a private audience with the president, who scoffed at the possibility of assassination. Vice President Hamlin leaned far more toward abolition than Lincoln, so Lincoln knew that no southerner would kill him to make Hamlin president. "In that one alternative," the president joked, "I have an insurance on my life worth half the prairie-land in Illinois." Besides, he added, "if there were such a plot, and they wanted to get at me, no vigilance could keep them out."

Lincoln called the job-seekers a "hungry lot," and complained that their demands on his time made him feel "like a man letting lodgings at one end of his house, while the other end was on fire," but he continued to receive visitors nearly every day from nine in the morning until long after dark. "We scarcely have time to eat sleep or even breathe," complained presidential secretary John Nicolay. Visitors who expected a formal audience were sometimes puzzled by the style of the new president. "Those who visited the White House," recalled Carl Schurz, "saw there a man of unconventional manners, who, without the slightest effort to put on dignity, treated all men alike, much like old neighbors . . . who always seemed to have time for a homely talk and never to be in a hurry to press business, and who occasionally spoke about important affairs of State with the same nonchalance—I might say, almost irreverence—with which he might have discussed an every-day law case in his office at Springfield, Illinois."

Easterners were surprised to hear a president use such words as "thar," "ain't," "jes'," "kin," "heered," and "git." Nearly every visitor was treated to at least one of Lincoln's seemingly inexhaustible supply of stories (some of them off-color), delivered with gusto. A congressman from Indiana noted that when Lincoln told "a particularly good story, and the time came to laugh, he would sometimes throw his left foot across his right knee, and clenching his foot with both hands and bending forward, his whole frame seemed to be convulsed with the effort."

Lincoln's appearance continued to draw comments. "He is lank and hard-featured, among the ugliest white men I have seen," observed George Templeton Strong, who went on to describe the president as a "gorilla" with "the laugh of a yahoo." Yet by the time Strong left a conference at the Executive Mansion, he concluded that Lincoln was "a most sensible, straightforward, honest old codger" and the best American president since Andrew Jackson. "His evident integrity and simplicity of purpose would compensate for worse grammar than his," Strong decided, "and for even more intense provincialism and rusticity."

William Russell of the *London Times* paid an impromptu call upon Lincoln in the last week of March, in the company of Seward and an Italian diplomat. After waiting briefly in the president's spacious office, with its gilt chairs and imitation gold leaf ornaments, Russell got his first glimpse of Lincoln, who entered "with a shambling, loose, irregular, almost unsteady gait." Russell was struck by Lincoln's ill-fitting, wrinkled black suit ("which put one in mind of an undertaker's uniform at a funeral") and his prodigious hands and feet. He was even more impressed with the president's neighborly welcome. "He evidently controlled a desire to shake hands all round with everybody," Russell noted, "and smiled good-humoredly till he was suddenly brought up by the staid deportment of Mr. Seward." Lincoln greeted the Italian minister with formal diplomatic etiquette before turning to Russell:

Mr. Lincoln put out his hand in a very friendly manner, and said, "Mr. Russell, I am very glad to make your acquaintance, and to see you in this country. The *London Times* is one of the greatest powers in the world—in fact, I don't know anything which has more power, except perhaps the Mississippi. I am glad to know you as its minister." Conversation ensued for some minutes, which the President enlivened by two or three peculiar little sallies, and I left agreeably impressed with his shrewdness, humor, and natural sagacity.

By the end of March, Lincoln's old friend Orville Browning had seen enough. "You should not permit your time to be consumed, and your energies exhausted by personal applications for office," Browning told the president. The *New York Times* seconded the sentiment. Upon receiving news that Lincoln had fallen ill in the last week of March, the *Times* lamented that "Mr. Lincoln is evidently overtaxing his powers. It will be a miracle if, in six months, he is not either dead or dazed." (Actually, Lincoln had suffered an intense migraine attack, brought on by his constant worry about Fort Sumter.)

Impatient Republican leaders insisted that Lincoln stop spending his time on political appointments and foreign dignitaries, and instead devise a policy to meet the threat of secession. Senators who were convinced that Lincoln had "no fixed policy except to keep mum and see what end those seceding states will come to" spent the remainder of the special session trying to steer the president toward confrontation or compromise. To Congressman Sherman, the month following Lincoln's inauguration seemed "the darkest one in the history of the United States." "It was a time," Sherman noted, "of humiliation, timidity, and feebleness."

Collision

On March 27, Hurlbut returned from his presidential mission to South Carolina with bad news. Sentiment to rejoin the Union was dead there, and nearly everywhere else in the South as well. Confederate officials told him they demanded "unqualified recognition of absolute independence," and insisted that the federal government evacuate Fort Sumter *and* Fort Pickens. Unless Lincoln accepted the finality of secession, Hurlbut saw no alternative to civil war; there simply was no "policy which may be adopted by the Government [that] will prevent the possibility of armed collision."

One day later, General Scott confirmed Hurlbut's report by telling Lincoln that the only way to keep Virginia in the Union was to withdraw the federal garrisons from both Sumter and Pickens. Lincoln knew such a move would be political suicide. The president later confessed that Scott's cavalier willingness to abandon Pickens gave him "a cold shock," and raised doubts in his mind about Scott's judgment. Combined with Hurlbut's report, it also drove Lincoln to a decision.

After a sleepless night, Lincoln called his Cabinet together and announced that—against the recommendations of his military advisers—he was going to reinforce Fort Pickens and order a supply expedition to sail from New York to Fort Sumter, which now had only three weeks of provisions. Lincoln said he was acting for political and humanitarian reasons; he could not abandon the forts without reneging on his inaugural promises, nor could he allow the garrison at Sumter to be starved into submission. If South Carolina's artillery opened fire on Sumter or the ships, he could blame the Confederacy for starting a war.

This time the entire Cabinet, except Seward and Smith, voiced approval, although no one agreed with Lincoln's decision to give Governor Francis Pickens of South Carolina advance warning of the supply mission. Lincoln then sent an Army engineer, Montgomery C. Meigs, to carry his instructions to Scott.

Seward made one final attempt to persuade Lincoln to evacuate Sumter. On April 1, he dispatched a lengthy memorandum to the president from the State Department that included the tactless observation: "We are at the end of a month's administration, and yet without a policy either domestic or foreign." Seward then presumed to propose a policy. To keep the border states—especially Virginia, Kentucky, and Maryland—within the Union, Seward urged Lincoln to avoid discussing slavery in public for the foreseeable future, keeping the confrontation with the Confederacy focused solely upon the issue of *"Union or Disunion."* He could do this, Seward claimed, by abandoning Sumter while holding Pickens, and then perhaps distract everyone from the slavery controversy by picking a quarrel with Spain and France for interfering in Latin American affairs.

Seward had misjudged Lincoln. When he received the secretary's condescending memorandum, the president drafted a stinging rebuke. Although Lincoln tore up his reply before sending it (a tactic he frequently employed to let off steam), he subsequently met with Seward and let him know in no uncertain terms who was president. Whatever course he decided to follow on Sumter, Lincoln said, "*I must do it.*"

Even though Lincoln rejected Seward's advice on Sumter, he agreed that there was no need to raise the issue of slavery. The president was trying to keep his administration from being derailed by a problem that appeared to have no solution. Shortly after his election, Lincoln had compared his situation to the plight of an honest but unsophisticated Kentucky farmer who won an election for justice of the peace:

> The first case he was called upon to adjudicate was a criminal prosecution for the abuse of Negro slaves. Its merits being somewhat beyond his comprehension, he sought enlightenment (after hearing the evidence) in the statutes of the commonwealth and various handbooks for justices of the peace he had provided himself with on assuming the ermine [robes of office]. But his search for precedents proved in vain, and growing still more puzzled, he exclaimed at last, angrily, "I will be damned if I don't feel almost sorry for being elected, when the niggers is the first thing I have to attend to."

Several days after his meeting with Seward, Lincoln ordered the Sumter and Pickens expeditions to proceed. When the ships of the federal relief force approached Sumter at dawn on Friday, April 12, Charleston shore batteries began their bombardment. Thirty-six hours later, Major Anderson surrendered the fort to the Confederacy.

News of Sumter's fall reached Washington within a few hours. Northerners waited anxiously to see how the inexperienced president would handle the crisis. After visiting Lincoln for two hours on Sunday evening, Senator Stephen Douglas (who recommended hanging all traitors within forty-eight hours) told a friend not to worry. "I've known Mr. Lincoln a longer time than you have, or than the country has," Douglas said. "He'll come out right, and we will all stand by him." The following day, the president summoned Congress to a special session, to begin on July 4. To defend the Union—and particularly Washington—in the meantime, Lincoln called for 75,000 militiamen to serve for ninety days, the maximum period permitted by law.

Defending the Capital

In his call for troops, Lincoln made it clear that his only goal was to preserve "the honor, the integrity, and the existence of our National Union . . . and to redress wrongs already long enough endured." Nowhere in his public statements did the president attack slavery or discuss the possibility of emancipation. He went out of his way to assure southerners, and especially citizens of the slave states still in the Union, that "the utmost care will be observed . . . to avoid any devastation, any destruction of, or interference with, property"—meaning, of course, their slaves. Lincoln made the point even more strongly in private. When Senator Garrett Davis of Kentucky visited the Executive Mansion, he received Lincoln's guarantee that "he intended to make no attack, direct or indirect, upon the institutions or property of any state, but, on the contrary, would defend them to the full extent with which the Constitution and the laws of Congress have vested the president with the power."

Every state north of the Mason-Dixon line met Lincoln's call for volunteers with surprising enthusiasm. The attack upon Sumter dispelled the lethargy of March, unleashing a patriotic response in Republicans and Democrats alike. Thousands of men rushed to enlist. "The whole population, men, women, and children seem to be in the streets with Union favors and flags," reported a Harvard professor. Northern governors rapidly filled their quotas of volunteers, and then offered to raise twice as many regiments. Within forty-eight hours, the first wave of troops departed for Washington.

They arrived none too soon. Virginians viewed Lincoln's call for volunteers as the first step in an invasion of the Confederacy, and refused to send any troops to help the federal government. Following massive demonstrations of pro-Confederate sentiment in the streets of Richmond, delegates to the state's special convention voted on April 17 to secede and join the Confederacy. Virginia's departure from the Union immediately imperiled the nation's capital. Separated from rebel territory only by the Potomac River, Washington was an easy target for an assault across the Long Bridge from Virginia. At night, the city's residents could see the campfires of rebel soldiers on the south bank of the Potomac; Lincoln himself remarked that if he commanded the Confederate troops in Virginia, he would certainly capture Washington.

While they waited for reinforcements, federal authorities attempted to secure the city's public buildings and armories. They also organized an ad hoc defense force of local militiamen, government clerks, politicians (some of whom had served in the Mexican War), and western visitors in town to celebrate Lincoln's inauguration. Recently elected Senator Jim Lane from Kansas took command of an outfit that called itself the Kansas Warriors. Lane and his men were temporarily quartered in the East Room of the White House—partly to protect the president, and partly because there was no other suitable place to put them. Meanwhile, a former senator from Kentucky, Cassius Clay, organized his own band of soldiers with headquarters at Willard's Hotel.

Lincoln showed no sign of panic, but the tension became almost unbearable. One afternoon between Sumter's surrender and the arrival of the first northern troops, Lincoln was sitting alone in his office when he was overcome by a feeling of total helplessness. At once he heard a boom that sounded like cannon fire. Expecting his aides to rush in with word of a rebel attack upon the capital, Lincoln waited—but nothing happened. His servants swore they had heard nothing, and no Confederate force came storming through the city. So Lincoln walked by himself out of the Executive Mansion and kept walking until he reached the Arsenal. There was no one there, either, only open doors, stacked flintlock muskets inside, and no guard in sight. Everything was silent and still. On his way back to his office, Lincoln asked several passersby if they had heard anything resembling a cannon shot, but no one had.

On the evening of April 18, trains bearing several hundred untrained, unarmed soldiers from Pennsylvania pulled into Union Station. The Sixth Massachusetts militia regiment followed the next day, after surviving an assault by secessionist rowdies in Baltimore. Lincoln greeted the Massachusetts troops warmly. "If you had not arrived tonight," he told their commander, "we should have been in the hands of the rebels before morning."

Since the Senate had adjourned, the troops were bivouacked in the deserted Capitol building. They cooked bacon and coffee at the furnace fires in the basement, used Senate stationery to write letters home, and held mock sessions of Congress in the legislative chambers. "The scene was very novel," reported John Hay, Lincoln's junior secretary. "The contrast was very painful between the grey haired dignity that filled the Senate Chamber when I saw it last and the present throng of bright-looking Yankee boys, the most of them bearing the signs of New England rusticity in voice and manner, scattered over the desks chairs and galleries some loafing, many writing letters, slowly and with plough hardened hands."

For several days the entire city, reported Hay, was caught up in "a general tempest of enthusiastic excitement." It seemed as if everyone in Washington awaited the arrival of a relative or close friend from the North. At night the Massachusetts men drilled smartly along Pennsylvania Avenue; observers were impressed by the marked contrast between their polished performance and the ragged steps of the Pennsylvania troops. Fears that Confederate sympathizers might cut the rail lines from Maryland provoked a run on groceries. As housekeepers stockpiled provisions, prices skyrocketed—flour jumped all the way from $13 a bushel to $18, and cornmeal hit $2.50 a bushel. Anticipating the worst, Willard's reduced its menu to the bare essentials; only plain pound cake graced the hotel's table at teatime.

Border States

By the end of April, North Carolina, Tennessee, and Arkansas had followed Virginia's lead and joined the Confederacy. Although the four remaining slave states—Maryland, Missouri, Kentucky, and Delaware—stayed in the Union, at least for the time being, their governors refused Lincoln's request for troops.

For a few tense weeks, one or more of the border states appeared daily ready to secede. Sympathy for the Confederacy ran so high in Baltimore that the nervous governor of Maryland, Thomas Hicks, promised he would not allow any of the state's troops to be sent out of Maryland to fight the rebellion.

But Lincoln had no intention of letting Maryland secede. Its departure would have left the nation's capital an island surrounded by Confederate territory, completely isolated from the North. As Maryland's state legislators convened in Frederick on April 26 to debate secession, Lincoln approved contingency plans to seize the state's major cities by force—and suspend the writ of habeas corpus, if necessary—to quash any secession movement.

Lincoln was equally determined to keep Kentucky in the Union; to him, it was the strategic key to the war. Whoever controlled Kentucky dominated traffic on the Ohio River, one of the key arteries of the Midwest, and easily the best means of moving supplies and troops westward. Through the Cumberland and Tennessee River valleys, Kentucky also offered an invasion route into the heart of the Confederacy. "I think to lose Kentucky is nearly the same as to lose the whole game," Lincoln observed. "Kentucky gone, we can not hold Missouri, nor, as I think, Maryland. These all against us, and the job on our hands is too large for us."

Traditionally, Kentucky acted as a buffer between North and South. The late Senator Henry Clay, Lincoln's political hero, had played a key role in mediating sectional disputes over the expansion of slavery in 1820, 1833, and 1850. Sentimental attachment to the Union remained strong among Kentuckians, but sympathy for their southern brethren—and opposition to any attempt to coerce the South back into the Union—appeared equally powerful in the spring of 1861.

Missouri possessed the largest population and the greatest wealth of the four border slave states, but the state's real value lay in its strategic location. The Union needed Missouri—and especially the port and rail center of Saint Louis—to keep the Mississippi River open. The state also linked the North with the recently discovered silver and gold mines of the Rocky Mountain territories, which could provide enough hard currency to finance a war.

As a native of Kentucky, Lincoln felt he possessed insight into the character of southern Unionists. He was confident that the border states would remain in the Union so long as the federal government did not tamper with slavery. Yet the same wave of patriotic enthusiasm that swept over the North after Sumter also stimulated demands to eliminate slavery once and for all. Northerners who previously scorned abolition now began to view the emancipation of Negro slaves as a weapon to defeat the Confederacy and overthrow the southern planter aristocracy.

Emancipation Fever

Charles Sumner wasted no time in pressuring Lincoln to transform the secession crisis into a crusade against slavery. The patrician senator, one of the most cultured men in Washington, had long enjoyed a national reputation for scathing denunciations of southern society. One particularly vicious insult in 1856 had provoked Congressman Preston Brooks of South Carolina to assault Sumner on the floor of the Senate and beat him nearly to death with a cane. It took Sumner three and a half years to recover; Brooks was hailed as a hero throughout the South. When Sumner returned to active duty shortly before Lincoln's election, his desire to erase all traces of southern character from the Union had become an obsession. To Charles Francis Adams, Jr., who knew the senator well, Sumner seemed "an egotistical doctrinaire . . . devoid of hard common sense" who dwelt on the issue of slavery until "his friends at times feared for his sanity."

From the time Lincoln arrived in Washington, Sumner regarded him with suspicion. Lincoln was a recent convert to the antislavery crusade; Sumner would have preferred to welcome Chase to the Executive Mansion. He met the president-elect at Willard's during the last week in February and came away shaking his head in bewilderment. Sumner expected a president to embody the dignity of the American republic; Lincoln struck him as rude and uncultured. Lincoln's habit of peppering his conversation with amusing stories was completely lost on Sumner, who lacked any discernible sense of humor. Although he admired Lincoln's ability to delve straight into the heart of a problem, on the whole Sumner could not overcome his misgivings about the president's ability to handle the secession crisis.

When Sumner heard the news of South Carolina's bombardment of Fort Sumter, he hurried to the President's House to give Lincoln a lecture on recent history. The senator recalled that John Quincy Adams—an abolitionist during his postpresidential career in Congress—once declared that a president possessed the authority in wartime to eliminate slavery by proclamation. "I . . . told [Lincoln]," recalled Sumner, "that under the war power the right had come to him to emancipate the slaves."

In the weeks following the attack on Sumter, letters arrived daily at the White House urging the president to abolish slavery and enlist freed slaves into the Union armies. "Some of our northerners," Lincoln remarked coolly, "seem bewildered and dazzled by the excitement of the hour." A young commander of Massachusetts troops leaving Boston announced that he and his men were "going to free the slaves." Carl Schurz reported that thousands of Democrats who had never opposed slavery "are declaring that now is the time to remove the cause of all our woes. . . . What we could not have done in many lifetimes the madness and folly of the South has accomplished for us." Even Lincoln's old friend Orville Browning, known as a moderate on the issue of slavery, proposed a drastic scheme to put down the rebellion, establish a Negro republic in place of the "exterminated whites," and extend a federal protectorate over the freemen while they harvested cotton for northern textile mills.

The President's View

Such talk appalled Lincoln. Privately and publicly, the president insisted that the war should not be fought to free slaves. "The central idea pervading this struggle," Lincoln insisted, was not the emancipation of slaves but "whether in a free government the minority have the right to break up the government whenever they choose." The president realized that nearly 4 million Negro slaves within the Confederacy represented a potentially devastating weapon for the Union. "There exists in our case," he told John

Hay, "an instance of a vast and far reaching disturbing element, which the history of no other free nation will probably ever present." But Lincoln had no intention of employing that weapon yet. Sudden emancipation without adequate precautions, he feared, could lead to a racial war between southern whites and Negroes. Or, if freemen remained peacefully in the South, Lincoln worried that whites would force them into a permanent underclass—slavery without chains.

More than most northern politicians, Lincoln was willing to grant Negroes a measure of human dignity. "I must take into account the rights of the poor Negro," he once said. "If you do not like him, let him alone. If God gave him little, that little let him enjoy." Lincoln's fundamental objection to slavery was that it denied blacks the right to govern themselves and enjoy the fruits of their own labor. "We are all born with a mouth to eat and hands to work," he explained to an audience in Illinois in the mid-1850s, "that every man may eat the products of his own labor and be satisfied."

But Lincoln also knew how deep and widespread racial prejudice was in the North. "The colored man throughout this country was a despised man, a hated man," he admitted. Even many fervent opponents of slavery detested Negroes. "You loathe them as you would a snake or a toad, yet you are indignant at their wrongs," a southerner accused his New England cousin in *Uncle Tom's Cabin.* "You would not have them abused; but you don't want to have anything to do with them yourselves." A reporter in Washington once overheard Senator Benjamin Wade of Ohio, a leading antislavery radical, railing about too many "nigger" cooks in the capital; Wade complained that he had eaten meals "cooked by Niggers until I can smell and taste the Nigger all over."

Northerners blamed slavery for keeping Negroes in a childlike state of dependence, illiterate and submissive; but then they assumed that Negroes could not care for themselves. Such reasoning led northerners such as George Templeton Strong to condemn abolitionists as "false, foolish, wicked and unchristian" for urging emancipation with no one to take care of freed slaves. Whites' opinions of free Negroes in the North were only slightly more charitable. They discriminated against Negroes in employment, education, and housing, restricting them to menial jobs or reducing them to begging in the streets. After preventing Negroes from rising above poverty, whites argued that they lacked the ability to succeed in a competitive society.

White northerners who accepted prevailing racial stereotypes also believed that Negroes lacked sufficient independence and intelligence to participate in political affairs. (Many of the same arguments were used against granting voting rights to Irish immigrants.) "Until I can be satisfied that they are capable of enjoying and maintaining civil rights," declared Secretary of the Navy Gideon Welles, "I shall be opposed to their having and exercising in this country the privileges of freemen." If Negroes could not even defend their own freedom, how could they be trusted with the liberties of others? "Nature has set an impassable seal upon it," wrote Walt Whitman. "No race can ever remain slaves if they have it in them to become free. Why do the slave ships go to Africa only?"

In the first half of the nineteenth century, state legislatures in New York, New Jersey, Pennsylvania, and Connecticut took away Negroes' right to vote; and voters in Illinois, Indiana, Michigan, Maine, Iowa, and Wisconsin approved new constitutions that limited suffrage to whites. In Ohio, Negro males were permitted to vote only if they had "a greater visible admixture of white than colored blood." Legal discrimination did not end with voting. Several midwestern states, including Illinois, had "black codes" prohibiting Negroes from testifying in legal cases in which a white man was a party, or from suing to collect a debt from a white unless another white man testified on their behalf.

Negroes in the southern states had never experienced democracy or self-government; presumably, this made slaves even less prepared to vote responsibly if they were emancipated. Charles Sumner himself doubted that "a race, degraded for long generations under the iron heel of bondage, can be taught at once all the political duties of an American citizen."

Lincoln disapproved of the trend to limit Negroes' political rights; the American republic, he believed, was supposed to enable "the weak to grow stronger, the ignorant, wise, and all better, and happier together." As a realist, he accepted the legal distinctions between white and black

Americans, but he did not defend them. Asked about a law in Illinois forbidding intermarriage, he replied that "the law means nothing. I shall never marry a Negress, but I have no objection to anyone else doing so. If a white man wants to marry a Negro woman, let him do it—if the Negro woman can stand it."

Like nearly all white Americans, Lincoln assumed that the physical differences between the two races made social equality impossible. He argued, however, that Negroes deserved the same opportunity as whites to improve themselves, if they remained in the United States. For Lincoln, the ideal solution to the question of slavery was the gradual emancipation of slaves in a deliberate, measured manner—to ease the transition for whites and blacks alike—followed by the colonization of free Negroes in a suitable location in Central America. The separation of whites and Negroes, he believed, was essential to the welfare of both.

Few African-American leaders had any interest in colonization. Instead, they asked white Americans to accept responsibility for systematically dehumanizing Negroes for two hundred years. "Can [blacks] be expected to be scrupulously honest when they are continually, and have been forever, robbed of everything—time, labor, parents, children . . . even life itself?" asked an editorial in an African-American newspaper in San Francisco. But the crime went even deeper. "The enormity of your guilt, the immensity of the wrong does not appear in contemplating what you have made us," charged the editor of the *Anglo-African*, "but in the consideration of what you have prevented us from being."

Amateurs in Command

Within the Lincoln administration, there was no consensus on the best means of retrieving the Confederate states. Chase expected the Confederate experiment to collapse without a battle. Montgomery Blair suggested sending small bands of federal troops into the Confederacy to distribute guns to loyal Union men. Scott proposed a longer-term "Anaconda" strategy, to blockade the Atlantic ports and seize control of the Mississippi River, then slowly starve the Confederacy into submission.

Lincoln approved the blockade, but he also wanted action. The president suggested that once the new recruits secured Washington from rebel attack, Union troops should "go down to Charleston and pay her the little debt we are owing her."

The Confederate government's decision to move its capital to Richmond—150 miles south of Washington—gave Lincoln another option. If Union troops could capture the rebel capital quickly, dispelling southerners' belief in their military superiority, support for the Confederacy might melt away. So Lincoln told the northern public at the end of April that he would prosecute the war "with all the energy necessary to bring it to a successful termination." On May 3, he called for 42,000 three-year volunteers, increased the size of the regular army by ten regiments (about 23,000 men), and asked for an additional 18,000 sailors. The Confederate president, Jefferson Davis, responded five days later by declaring a state of war between the Confederacy and the United States.

Few northerners expected the rebellion to last long; Seward predicted that the Union would win in sixty or ninety days. Lincoln was less optimistic, and with good reason. No one at the War Department had devised a strategic plan to invade the Confederacy. Scott had no general staff to coordinate mobilization. The War Department's bureaucracy consisted of a handful of overworked clerks, headed by a Cabinet officer with a reputation for corruption. After mass resignations by southerners, the Union Army was left with only two senior officers who had ever commanded an army in combat. "What," asked Seward plaintively, "are we to do for generals?"

State and local authorities enlisted thousands of troops, but the recruits came in faster than the War Department could equip them. "Twenty-four hundred men in camp and less than half of them armed," complained Governor Oliver Morton of Indiana. "No officer here to muster troops into service. Not a pound of powder or a single ball sent us, or any sort of equipment." Most of the weapons that were available were over twenty years old. A shortage of drill sergeants forced the War Department to recall retired veterans of the Mexican War, who trained raw recruits with obsolete manuals of arms.

Coordination was virtually nonexistent between federal, state, and local officials, or volunteer organizations that decided to raise troops on their own. No one in Washington knew how many regiments existed, or where they were at any given time. Troops arrived in Washington in varying stages of readiness, wearing a bewildering array of uniforms—blue jackets, gray pants with bright green trim, purple or red shirts, black or red trousers.

Lincoln's slipshod administrative style made the confusion worse. Department heads were allowed to proceed independently; but without regular Cabinet meetings to resolve questions of jurisdiction, they kept stepping on one another's toes. Secretary of the Navy Welles complained of interference from Seward and Secretary of War Cameron. Chase meddled in recruiting campaigns and then grumbled that "everything goes in confused disorder. General Scott gives an order, Mr. Cameron gives another. Half of both are executed, neutralizing each other." Scott refused to confide in any civilians, including the president.

Lincoln involved himself in every aspect of the mobilization effort, directing troop movements, awarding military commissions to volunteers with political connections, arranging for the transport of gold from California to pay for the war, even scouring the Potomac with a telescope for signs of an invading rebel fleet. Senator Sumner was appalled by the president's intrusion into the minutiae of military preparations. "The difficulty with Mr. Lincoln," Sumner said, "is that he has no conception of his situation. And having no system in his composition he has undertaken to manage the whole thing as if he knew all about it."

Negroes who tried to enlist in the Union forces found the door barred. The regular army refused to accept them, and federal law enjoined Negroes from joining state militias. Nevertheless, meetings of Negroes in northern cities petitioned the national government for an opportunity to fight the Confederacy. Cameron refused. "I have to say that this Department has no intention to call into the service of the Government any colored soldiers," he told a black Washingtonian on April 29. Local officials were more blunt. "We want you damned niggers to keep out of this," police in Cincinnati informed a group of Negroes who sought to enlist. "This is a white man's war."

Contrabands

From the time militia regiments entered slave territory en route to Washington in April, the Union Army acted as a magnet for runaway slaves seeking asylum. When the first units of Massachusetts troops marched through Maryland, local slaves ran after them, begging for the chance to act as their servants. They obviously expected the soldiers to shelter them; one Negro who had purchased his own freedom told a Massachusetts volunteer, "If I had known you gemmen was a coming I'd a saved my money."

Runaway slaves in Maryland and the other border states put Lincoln in a bind. Orders to return fugitives to their owners would jeopardize support for the war in the antislavery strongholds of New England and the upper Midwest. But if the army protected runaways, the border states would object because it might encourage their own slaves to escape; besides, whites in the border states who did not own slaves had no desire to share the land with free Negroes.

Unwilling to choose either alternative, Lincoln permitted Union commanders to implement their own policies toward fugitive or captured slaves. At the start of the war, few regular Union Army generals favored emancipation, so they usually returned runaways to their masters. Some Union commanders permitted slaveowners' agents to search for fugitives behind their lines; others refused to allow any blacks to approach their lines. A few Union generals assumed that *all* Negroes whom they encountered were slaves, and occasionally free Negroes were delivered to slaveowners who claimed they were runaways.

A similar problem confronted Union commanders when the federal armies first ventured into Virginia. The portion of Virginia west of the Shenandoah Valley—the area that would break away from the rest of the state and become West Virginia in 1863—was a Unionist stronghold that had long resented eastern slaveowners' domination of state politics. At the end of May, Union volunteers led by generals George B. McClellan and William Rosecrans crossed the Ohio River to chase Confederate troops from the region and recapture the Baltimore and Ohio Railroad.

As he advanced through the mountainous territory, where there were few slaves anyway, McClellan promised residents that his troops would not encourage their property to escape. "We will, on the contrary, with an iron hand, crush any attempt at [slave] insurrection on their part," McClellan promised. "All your rights shall be religiously respected." Similarly, General Robert Patterson, an elderly army veteran commanding Union forces in the northern end of the Shenandoah Valley, instructed his soldiers on June 3 to guard the human property of loyal slaveowners and, "should occasion offer, at once suppress servile insurrection."

Lincoln did not object. He still expected Unionists in the upper South to rally to the national government—"It is my earnest hope," he said, "that as we advance, we shall find as many friends as foes"—and so he did not want Union troops to confirm the southerners' stereotype of "Lincoln's abolition hordes." Yet as one Union officer pointed out, it made little sense for northern troops in solidly Confederate territory to act "as a marshal's posse in catching runaway negroes to return them to their masters who were fighting us at the same time."

Eastern Virginia provided the first test case. When Virginia seceded, federal troops retained control of Fortress Monroe—the nation's largest fort—about a dozen miles outside of Norfolk. Located near the entrance to Chesapeake Bay, the fort could serve as a launching point for Union attacks on the coast of Virginia and North Carolina. To command Fortress Monroe, Cameron chose General Ben Butler, who had brought the first Massachusetts regiments to Washington in April. It seemed a safe appointment. A Democratic politician who condemned abolitionists as scoundrels, Butler had already pledged not to interfere with slavery as his Massachusetts troops marched across Maryland, and had offered to cooperate with Maryland officials in suppressing any slave insurrection.

Upon his arrival at Fortress Monroe on May 22, Butler learned that the Confederates were employing hundreds of slaves to build batteries from which to bombard the fort. A scouting expedition brought back three runaway slaves, who informed Butler that their master was preparing to send them south to construct coastal fortifications for the Confederate Army. Butler promptly declared the slaves contraband of war and confiscated them, as if they were crops, munitions, or livestock.

When a Virginian came to the fort and asked Butler to return the slaves, according to the terms of the Fugitive Slave Act, the general replied that the act did not apply to a state no longer in the Union. "You say you have seceded," Butler explained, "so you cannot consistently claim [the slaves]. I shall hold these negroes as contraband of war, since they are engaged in the construction of your battery and are claimed as your property."

News of Butler's action provoked a steady stream of runaway slaves to Fortress Monroe. Within three days, nearly sixty slaves had sought asylum. Butler confiscated them all and set them to work, keeping detailed records of their labor so the government could repay their masters if necessary. Meanwhile, he telegraphed the War Department for instructions. "Are these men, women, and children, slaves?" Butler asked. "Are they free?. . . What has been the effect of the rebellion and a state of war upon [their] status?" If they remained slaves, did they become the property of the army? And if they army did not want to keep them as slaves, did they become free?

No one knew where Lincoln stood on this issue. Just a day or two earlier, the president had received a message from McClellan, who assumed that *his* order *protecting* the rights of slaveowners reflected Lincoln's policy. When the Cabinet discussed Butler's questions, Lincoln again chose to dodge the issue. Seward, of course, supported the president; so did Chase, albeit reluctantly. "Until long after Sumter I clung to my old ideas of noninterference with slavery within the state limits," Chase later explained. "That the United States Government under the war powers might destroy slavery I never doubted. I only doubted the expediency of the enterprise."

Secretary of War Cameron informed Butler that the administration approved his actions because he had confiscated the slaves as a military necessity. Cameron ordered the general to follow a moderate course, neither encouraging slaves to run away nor returning fugitives to their Confederate masters if Butler felt they would be used against Union troops. The president would decide the slaves' permanent status at a later date.

Privately, Lincoln assured a friend that "the government neither should nor would send back to bondage such [runaway slaves] as came to our armies," but he issued no such order. Logically, he could not do so, because he refused to acknowledge that the Confederate states had left the Union. From the day he was elected, Lincoln insisted that no state had a legal right to secede. In his view, the conflict was not a war between nations, or even a clash between states and the national government, but a rebellion led by *individuals* against the federal government. Since Lincoln held that the Confederate states had never seceded, he felt an obligation to uphold the constitutional and legal rights of their loyal citizens, including the right to own slaves and have runaways returned to them. He would punish individual traitors; not entire states.

The Radicals

Congressmen returning to Washington at the end of June saw a city transformed by ten weeks of war. Strangers were everywhere. Trainloads of fresh recruits steamed into Union Station each day; some soldiers had tied pieces of rope to their musket barrels—nooses for bringing back prisoners from the South. Convoys of white-covered army wagons bumped through the dusty streets. Hotels were filled with businessmen seeking government contracts. Red-white-and-blue flags fluttered above Pennsylvania Avenue, and cannon rested in Lafayette Park, across from the White House. A lucky visitor might spot the president crossing the avenue, "striding like a crane in a bullrush swamp among the great blocks of marble, dressed in an oddly cut suit of grey, with a felt hat on the back of his head, wiping his face with a red pocket handkerchief."

Summer's oppressive heat and the odors from the overburdened sewers irritated everyone. Troop encampments spilled out of the downtown district, until the hills surrounding the city were covered with thousands of white army tents. Washington's eligible women enjoyed an endless supply of new suitors. Each night, the theaters were filled to capacity, and brothels enjoyed a booming business.

"Washington now, indeed, is the capital of the United States," declared one reporter. "But it is no longer the scene of beneficent legislation and of peaceful government. It is the representative of armed force engaged in war." The sounds of drilling troops and shouted commands echoed from dawn to dusk. Shopkeepers struggled to understand the accents of northern recruits, many of whom had recently emigrated from Germany or Ireland. After dark, soldiers in alleyways accosted passersby for spare change, and the night was filled with fireworks and random gunshots.

Runaway slaves from Virginia and Maryland were slipping into the capital at an increasing rate. They met a chilly reception. Military officials issued orders to keep fugitives from Maryland out of army camps, so runaways began crossing into Virginia to approach Washington from the south. The District police jailed Negroes who lacked sufficient documentation of their freedom. Anxious lest their property get lost in the confusion, many of Washington's slaveowners left town and headed south.

Still the nation waited impatiently for an advance into Confederate territory. Eighty days had passed since the attack on Sumter, with no combat except small skirmishes in western Virginia and Missouri. Pressure was mounting for a direct assault on the Confederate forces gathering at Manassas Junction, between Washington and Richmond, but General Irwin McDowell—whom Scott had appointed commander of the Grand Army of the Republic—insisted that his raw, ill-equipped troops were not yet ready.

Communication between Scott and civilian authorities remained poor. Lincoln complained that "Scott will not let us outsiders know anything of his plans." Excluded from conferences on strategy, the president occupied himself by reading texts on military strategy, trying out the latest weapons at his private rifle range in the park beyond the south lawn, and entertaining visitors to the Executive Mansion. When Carl Schurz, recently appointed American ambassador to Spain, met with Lincoln before departing for Madrid, he asked if he could bring his brother-in-law to the White House to shake the president's hand. "Certainly," replied Lincoln. "Bring him tomorrow around lunch time and lunch with me. I guess Mary will have something for us to eat."

The next day, Schurz and his brother-in-law (who was visiting from Prussia) dined alone with Lincoln, exchanging humorous stories and discussing European affairs. "As we left the White House," noted Schurz, "my companion could hardly find words to express his puzzled admiration for the man who, having risen from the bottom of the social ladder to one of the most exalted stations in the world, had remained so perfectly natural and so absolutely unconscious of how he appeared to others . . . and who bore himself with such genial sincerity and kindliness."

Lincoln's schedule filled up quickly once Congress returned. He had enjoyed a free hand for the past three months, but the start of the special session brought to Washington a host of Republican legislators determined to pursue their own agendas. Congressmen viewed themselves—not the president and the Cabinet—as the nation's true policymakers; the weak presidents of the 1850s had rarely challenged their authority.

Since few of the southern congressional delegations (who were overwhelmingly Democratic) remained in Washington, Republicans held a comfortable majority in both the House and Senate. Numerical superiority did not, however, encourage unity. The Republican Party still resembled a coalition of converts from other parties rather than a cohesive organization. On the party's right wing stood a group of senators who supported a war to restore the Union, but not to punish the South or reform southern society. This conservative bloc opposed both the expansion of slavery and the immediate forcible emancipation of the South's slaves. In the summer of 1861, these conservatives were Lincoln's natural allies, and he counted on them to support his measured response to the Confederate challenge.

Not so the extreme antislavery Republicans known as Radicals. At that time, the term "Radical" did not bear the association with anarchy that it acquired at the start of the twentieth century; these men were called Radicals for their determination to remake southern society from top to bottom in the northern image. They welcomed the war as an opportunity to eradicate the stain of slavery from the Union. From the start they urged Lincoln to wage a more aggressive military campaign.

Although the Radicals never enjoyed a majority in either house of Congress, seniority gave them control of several key committees. In the House, Thaddeus Stevens of Pennsylvania served as chairman of the Committee on Ways and Means, which oversaw government appropriations. One of the few American politicians who believed in racial equality, Stevens planned to pressure the president into using every available weapon to destroy the power of the southern "slaveocracy." Already the gaunt Pennsylvanian had denounced Secretary of State Seward for his willingness to compromise with the South to save the Union. "We have saved this Union so often," muttered Stevens, "that I am afraid we shall save it to death."

Radicals from Massachusetts headed two of the critical committees in the Senate. Charles Sumner served as chairman of the Foreign Relations Committee, and the state's junior senator, Henry Wilson—known as "the Natick cobbler" for his early days as a shoemaker—chaired Military Affairs. Far more congenial than Sumner, Wilson was equally consumed by a hatred of slavery. His enthusiasm led him to volunteer for a position on a Union general's staff, but after spending a day on horseback inspecting fortifications, riding nearly thirty miles, Wilson resigned his military post and spent the next week recovering in bed.

Both Sumner and Wilson distrusted Seward, and both considered Lincoln's Cabinet (with the exception of Chase) "a disgraceful surrender to the South." Other Radical leaders in the Senate included Benjamin Wade, who once offered to duel any southern congressman with squirrel rifles at thirty paces; Zachariah Chandler of Michigan, a former Detroit merchant whom Gideon Welles described as "steeped & steamed in whisky . . . coarse, vulgar, and reckless"; and Lyman Trumbull of Illinois, who already was furious with Lincoln for not granting him control of patronage in his home state.

From the beginning of the special session on July 4, Radical congressmen sought to use the Union armies to eradicate slavery. Representative Owen Lovejoy of Illinois took the first step by introducing a resolution that "it is no part of the duty of the soldiers of the United States to capture and return fugitive slaves"—a slap at commanders such as McClellan and Patterson, whom the Radicals denounced as "slave-catching generals." Since Lovejoy's resolution only expressed the sentiment of Congress and did not bind the army or the president, the House approved the measure almost unanimously.

In the Senate, Samuel Pomeroy of Kansas introduced a bill to instruct Lincoln to issue a proclamation providing for the immediate and unconditional emancipation of slaves in the states that had seceded. This was too big a step even for most Radicals, who realized that the northern public needed time to accept the idea of emancipation. They rallied instead behind Trumbull's proposal authorizing the army to confiscate all property in the Confederate states—specifically including slaves—that was actively employed in supporting the rebellion.

First Defeat

As Trumbull's confiscation bill made its way through Congress, Radicals joined the call for an invasion of Virginia. Suspicious of continued delay, Ben Wade furiously denounced everyone in authority as "incompetent or treacherous," and boasted that he could capture Richmond in a week with 10,000 troops. Trumbull introduced another resolution demanding that the government capture Richmond before the Confederate congress convened there on July 21. Newspapers took up the cry, "On to Richmond," even as they reported a lack of adequate transport, artillery, provisions, and discipline in the Union Army.

Scott knew the Grand Army was not ready for combat, but the northern public was impatient for action. "They think," scoffed William Russell of the *London Times*, "that the army is like a round of cannister which can be fired off whenever the match is applied." Lincoln needed no encouragement, for he had persuaded himself that one crushing victory would shatter the Confederates' morale and end the conflict. Besides, the original three-month enlistment period would expire soon, and Lincoln feared that further delay would cost him thousands of troops.

So Lincoln encouraged General McDowell—who, like almost every other officer in the Union Army, lacked combat experience—to advance with 40,000 soldiers on the rebel base at Manassas Junction, about twenty-five miles southwest of Washington. McDowell, a friend of Secretary of the Treasury Chase, still preferred to delay until his troops were better prepared for combat. He had scant respect for volunteers, or for political generals who knew little about tactics. "This is not an army," he warned Lincoln. "It will take a long time to make an army." Artillery was still in short supply. The Union cavalry, claimed one observer, consisted of "a few scarecrow-men, who would dissolve partnership with their steeds at their first serious combined movement." Nearly every unit wore a different uniform. There was no transport for reserve ammunition. And McDowell possessed no decent maps of the territory he would cross, nor any detailed knowledge about the whereabouts of the enemy.

But Lincoln kept prodding McDowell forward. "You are green, it is true," the president acknowledged, "but they are green, also; you are all green alike." On July 18, McDowell obediently left his headquarters at Alexandria and headed south. For three days, Washington waited. Rumors of Union victories kept rolling back to the capital; at one point, Charles Sumner jubilantly predicted that the army would be in Richmond by the weekend.

On Friday, July 19, Senator John J. Crittenden of Kentucky rose to introduce a joint resolution declaring that the federal government was *not* waging war for the "purpose of overthrowing or interfering with the rights or established institutions" of the Confederate states; instead, its only goal was "to defend and maintain the supremacy of the Constitution and to preserve the Union with all the dignity, equality, and rights of the several States unimpaired." As soon as these objects were attained, "the war ought to cease."

Crittenden timed his resolution to coincide with the anticipated battle at Manassas. If the Union armies won and the Confederacy collapsed, the nation would be restored with no change in the status of slavery. If McDowell lost, the war would continue for the sole objective of preserving the Union—the one goal that kept the North united. The vote in the House was delayed when Thaddeus Stevens objected on procedural grounds, but Crittenden planned to introduce the measure again on Monday.

McDowell reached Manassas on Sunday, July 21. Behind him trailed congressmen, government clerks, and socialites who had rented every available carriage and wagon in Washington. Bearing hampers filled with wine and picnic lunches sold at exorbitant prices by hotel keepers and chefs, they gathered on the hills overlooking a creek known as Bull Run to watch the ensuing battle. It was a lovely day. To the north, they could see militia units whose ninety-day enlistment had expired, marching back to Washington.

Once the battle began, spectators could barely make out anything through the dust and the shifting blue haze of smoke from the guns in the valley. "Are we really seeing a battle now?" someone asked. "Are they supposed to be fighting where all that smoke is going on?" McDowell found his plans foiled by the slow movement of his troops, who stopped at streams to drink or fill their canteens; when they finally encountered the rebels, the Union regiments were scattered and out of position. Still, the battle was a close-run affair for most of the day, until the arrival of fresh Confederate reserves late in the afternoon turned it into a rout.

News of the Union defeat reached Washington along the army's newly strung telegraph lines, several hours in advance of the retreating troops and panic-stricken spectators. Since Scott had assured Lincoln of victory, the debacle caught the president completely by surprise. He attended church that morning, then spent the afternoon at the White House, receiving optimistic dispatches from the front via the War Department's telegraph office. Late in the afternoon, Lincoln visited General Scott, who was taking a nap in his office. Again Scott reassured the president. Lincoln decided to go for his usual evening carriage ride, but at six o'clock Seward arrived at the Executive Mansion bearing the first intimations of disaster. After Lincoln heard the bad news, he went immediately to the War Department for confirmation, and then convened the Cabinet to spend the rest of the evening in Scott's office. "The fat is in the fire now," Lincoln's secretary John Nicolay wrote to his wife, "and we shall have to crow small until we can retrieve the disgrace somehow." Lincoln did not sleep at all that night.

Several blocks away, a secessionist shopkeeper and his wife rejoiced. "Believe me, it is the finger of the Almighty in it," the woman said. "Didn't he curse the niggers, and why should he take their part now with these Yankee Abolitionists, against true white men?"

3

A SEARCH FOR MIDDLE GROUND

A steady, driving rain fell on Washington the day after Manassas. All day, mud-soaked men trudged across the Long Bridge into the city, heading up Pennsylvania Avenue toward the Capitol. Soldiers from New York, Michigan, Minnesota, and Pennsylvania were jumbled together; many lacked shoes, coats, knapsacks, or weapons. To Frederick Law Olmsted, they seemed "a most woe-begone rabble, which had perhaps clothed itself with the garments of dead soldiers left on a hard-fought battle-field." "I'm going home," one soldier told a passing civilian. "I've had enough of fighting to last my lifetime." Others headed for the nearest liquor shops.

During the night, residents of Washington had expected the Confederates to follow their victory at Manassas by attacking the capital. In a rooming house near the War Department, a young Negro servant announced that he was leaving town. When a guest asked him why, he answered, "I 'spects, massa, the Seceshers soon be in here. I'm a free nigger; I must go, sar, afore de come cotch me." A clergyman who sympathized with the South headed for Richmond and left his cat in the basement of his house with three weeks' supply of food and water, assuming that the Confederate armies would capture Washington before the provisions ran out.

Hopes for a quick end to the rebellion vanished. Although Lincoln assured McDowell, "I have not lost a particle of confidence in you" ("I don't see why you should, Mr. President," McDowell replied), Lincoln had already sent a telegram at two o'clock that morning to General McClellan, ordering him to Washington to take charge of Union forces in the city. Later that day, Lincoln signed a bill calling for 500,000 three-year volunteers who would form the basis of McClellan's new force, the Army of the Potomac. Three days later, the president called for another 500,000 men.

McClellan arrived in the capital on July 26. Washington greeted him as its deliverer, the young Napoléon who had swept the rebels from the hills of western Virginia. Short and stocky, with close-cut dark hair and a thick mustache, McClellan looked even younger than his thirty-four years. He came with an impressive résumé: a graduate of West Point at nineteen, an engineer in the Mexican War who served with distinction, an American observer of European tactics in the Crimean War, and the author of a text on military strategy. He had resigned his commission in 1857 to accept a job as vice president of the Illinois Central Railroad, but he reenlisted after Sumter as a major general of Ohio volunteers.

McClellan's troops in Virginia adored him, and, in the summer of 1861, so did everyone else in Washington. "There is an indefinable air of success about him," wrote one observer, "and something of the 'man of destiny.'" Senators and congressmen lined up to shake his hand. "He has brains, looks as if he ought to have courage, and, I think, is altogether more than an ordinary man," decided Lincoln's friend Orville Browning. Fawning letters from an adoring public fed McClellan's ego. "By some strange operation of magic I seem to have become *the* power of the land," he wrote shortly after his arrival in the capital. "I almost think that were I to win some small success now I could become Dictator or anything else that might please me." After reviewing his new command, McClellan concluded that "God has placed a great work in my hands. . . . I was called to it; my previous life seems to have been unwittingly directed to this great end."

McClellan brought with him a deep-seated conviction that the war should be fought only to save the Union. A lifelong Democrat, he wanted no part of a crusade to abolish slavery, and he surrounded himself with a staff who shared his political views. In western Virginia, he had carried out his pledge not to interfere with the property of slaveowners. As long as he commanded the Army of the Potomac, McClellan would oppose any attempt to use the military as an instrument of emancipation.

A Fraying Coalition

On the day after Manassas, Representative Crittenden again introduced his resolution on the Union's war goals. This time it passed almost unanimously. Several days later, Senator Andrew Johnson of Tennessee submitted a similar measure to the Senate, where it was approved by a vote of 30 to 5. "I do not want to carry on this war for the purpose of subjugating the people of any State in any shape or form, and it is a false idea gotten up by bad men for bad purposes that it has ever been the purpose of any portion of the people of this country," declared Senator William Fessenden of Maine, a moderate who served as Republican leader in the Senate. "We have a purpose, and that is to defend the Constitution and the laws of this country, and to put down this revolt at any hazard."

Union soldiers agreed. They enlisted because they believed they were preserving "the Union, Constitution, and law," and maintaining the best government on earth. Viewing themselves as the heirs of the Revolutionary generation, which had suffered and died for liberty, they would repay their ancestors by risking their own lives in a patriotic cause. "We will be held responsible before God," wrote a New Jersey soldier, "if we don't do our part in helping to transmit this boon of civil & religious liberty down to succeeding generations."

The defeat at Manassas did not immediately disrupt the northern consensus on war goals, but it forced the North to consider a broader array of means to force the Confederate states back into the Union. One option, of course, was to encourage slave rebellions. On the same day that the House passed the Crittenden resolution, Vice President Hamlin, Senator Sumner, and Senator Chandler called on Lincoln and urged him to use his war powers to emancipate the Confederacy's slaves. Confederate officials already were employing thousands of slaves as teamsters, cooks, mill hands, miners, and labor gangs on roads and bridges. Without the benefit of slave labor behind the lines, Sumner predicted, the southern rebellion would collapse. Chandler suggested that a proclamation of emancipation would cause such fear and disorder in the South that the Confederacy would abandon the war.

Lincoln refused; the northern public, he said, was not ready to abolish slavery in the South. The president managed to convince Sumner that he was—in Sumner's words—"a deeply convinced and faithful antislavery man," but Hamlin, who was not involved at all in the administration's decision making, was less certain. "He was slow to move," the vice president recalled, "much slower than it seemed to us he should have been; much slower than I wanted him to be. . . . I urged him over and over again to act; but the time had not come, in his judgment."

Lincoln knew he had little to gain from raising the issue of slavery at that time, and much to lose. A presidential attack on slavery would splinter the northern consensus on war goals, strengthen secessionists in the border states, discourage Unionists in the Confederacy (whose numbers Lincoln consistently exaggerated), and embitter the South, making restoration of the Union more difficult.

In the aftermath of Manassas, the president's personal commitment to the antislavery cause wavered briefly. Something of a fatalist, Lincoln often believed he discerned the hand of God in events. The Union defeat and the prospect of a prolonged civil war did not bode well. When Orville Browning suggested that God would not bless the Union armies until the government struck a decisive blow against slavery, Lincoln gave an unexpected reply. "Browning," he said, "suppose God is against us in our view on the subject of slavery in this country and our method of dealing with it?"

Republicans in Congress did not hesitate to provide the administration with a new legal weapon against the rebellion. On August 6, 1861, Congress approved Senator Trumbull's confiscation bill, authorizing the federal government to seize and liberate slaves actively employed in the Confederate war effort. As a war measure, the Confiscation Act clearly served the Union's military interests, since the use of slave labor helped alleviate the South's relative shortage of white manpower—6 million compared with the North's 22 million. "There is no reason why the rebels should be allowed to take the field, and have their slaves at home to till the lands and provide them with food," argued one northern newspaper. "The very stomach of this rebellion," agreed Frederick Douglass, "is the negro in the condition of a slave."

Conservative Republicans could not refuse to support a measure presented in those terms, although they shied away from the apocalyptic prophecy of Thaddeus Stevens. "If their whole country must be laid waste, and made a desert, to save the Union from destruction, so let it be," proclaimed Stevens. "I would rather . . . reduce them to a condition where their whole country must be repeopled by a band of freemen than to see them perpetrate the destruction of this people through our agency."

Such Radical rhetoric strengthened the almost unanimous opposition of congressmen from the border states to Trumbull's bill. They remained suspicious of any measure that might encourage emancipation and endanger their own investment in slaves. Midwestern Democrats also opposed the Confiscation Act, fearing that their states could be overrun by freed slaves fleeing the Confederacy. The partisan nature of the vote marked the first split in the northern coalition—all but six Republicans in the House supported the Confiscation Act, while only three congressmen from border states or Democrats voted for it.

Trumbull's bill was only the first step. Congress adjourned a few days after passing the measure, but Radicals promised to agitate for the seizure of *all* rebel property when they returned to Washington in December. Although Lincoln dutifully promised to enforce the Confiscation Act, he allowed it to become a dead letter. With Congress out of town, Lincoln hoped for a season of grace before confronting the issue again.

Missouri Freedom

Trouble came unexpectedly soon. On August 30, General John C. Frémont, commander of Union forces in Missouri, issued a proclamation imposing martial law throughout the state, authorizing the confiscation of rebel property, and freeing the slaves of all citizens who actively supported the rebellion.

A self-promoting adventurer known as "the Pathfinder" for his exploits in crossing the Rocky Mountains in the 1840s, Frémont had built a political career as an antislavery crusader. His fame and the backing of the powerful Blair family won him the Republican Party's first presidential nomination in 1856. Frémont made a respectable showing among northern voters, but Republican leaders who wanted a moderate candidate did not seriously consider him again for the nomination four years later. Following the attack on Fort Sumter, Lincoln—acting on the Blairs' recommendation—made Frémont a major general and awarded him command of the Western Department (Kentucky, Illinois, Missouri, and all territory west of the Rocky Mountains), even though Frémont had never commanded as much as a regiment.

Soon after Frémont arrived in Saint Louis at the end of July, he began to display disturbing signs of incompetence. He complained about a lack of supplies from Washington. Instead of tracking down the rebel bands that roamed through Missouri, Frémont concentrated on fortifying Saint Louis against a phantom invasion. His corrupt staff siphoned off thousands of dollars worth of equipment while purchasing exorbitant quantities of guns and horses. Worse, Frémont feuded with Senator Frank Blair, Jr., Montgomery's brother, and then bought the Blair family's newspaper and turned it against the senator.

Recognizing that his command was in jeopardy, Frémont sought to divert attention from his failures by issuing an emancipation decree for Missouri, justifying it as a military necessity. He then set up his own "bureau of abolition" and devoted himself to drawing up "free papers" for slaves. Frémont expected his action to make him once more the darling of the antislavery movement, and it did. It also placed the president in an awkward position.

Unionists in Kentucky reacted vehemently to Frémont's proclamation. The news from Missouri, reported Senator Garrett Davis of Kentucky, "is most inopportune for the Union party." It fell upon the state's loyalists, he said, "with pretty much the effect of a bombshell. . . . There is a very general, almost a universal feeling in this State against this being or becoming a war against slavery." Joshua Speed, one of Lincoln's oldest and closest friends in the state, told the president that Frémont's "foolish proclamation will crush out any vestage [*sic*] of a union party in the state." "Frankly I say to you," Speed wrote in a separate note to Secretary Chase, "that it will ruin us." Upon learning that Frémont had freed slaves in Missouri, an entire company of Union volunteers in Kentucky reportedly threw down their guns and deserted.

Lincoln acted quickly to defuse the crisis. On September 2, he sent a message asking Frémont to modify his proclamation to conform to the Confiscation Act, which permitted the seizure of property only if it was used "for insurrectionary purposes." There was great danger, Lincoln explained, that a sweeping confiscation of *all* rebel property and the emancipation of *all* rebel slaves "will alarm our Southern Union friends, and turn them against us—perhaps ruin our rather fair prospect for Kentucky." Hoping to avoid a public dispute, Lincoln dispatched Montgomery Blair to Missouri to reason with the general.

Frémont refused to back down. In his reply to Lincoln on September 8, he predicted that his proclamation would devastate rebel resources in Missouri, and he urged the president to respect his judgment of local conditions. Frémont then sent his wife, Jessie Benton Frémont (the daughter of a former senator, Thomas Hart Benton), to Washington to argue with the president.

Lincoln received Mrs. Frémont shortly before midnight on the evening of September 10. It was not a pleasant meeting. The general's wife "taxed me so violently with many things," Lincoln later recalled, "that I had to exercise all the awkward tact I have to avoid quarreling with her." At one point, Jessie Frémont threatened the president by suggesting that her husband could establish his own government in Missouri. Lincoln abruptly cut her off. The general would have to back down. The war was being fought, Lincoln said, "for a great national idea, the Union, and . . . General Frémont should not have dragged the Negro into it."

Less than twenty-four hours later, Lincoln ordered Frémont to modify his proclamation. Unrepentant, Frémont immediately had two hundred copies of his original proclamation distributed throughout the North, to rouse public sentiment in his favor. Simultaneously, Lincoln gave the press his own order to Frémont of September 11. The initial reaction in the North favored Frémont overwhelmingly. His proclamation had clearly touched a nerve among vocal antislavery activists; after six months of ineffectual White House leadership and a dismal military performance in the East, *someone* had struck a blow at the rebellion.

"You have no idea of its electric effect upon all parts of the country," Senator Fessenden of Maine told a friend. "Men feel now as if there was something tangible and real in this contest." Scores of newspapers—Republican, independent, and even a few Democratic journals—sided with Frémont. In town halls and pulpits, angry antislavery speakers assailed Lincoln's "pigheaded stupidity" and organized protest rallies against the administration's "proslavery" policies. "No word describes popular sentiment but 'fury,' an attorney in Cincinnati wrote to Chase. "I have heard men of sense, such as are called Conservative, advocate the wildest steps, such as the impeachment of Mr. Lincoln, and the formation of a party to carry on the war irrespective of the President's and under Frémont."

Congressional Radicals joined the chorus. Senator James Grimes of Iowa praised Frémont's proclamation as "the only real noble and true thing done during this war." Senator Wade contemptuously described Lincoln as "poor white trash" and claimed that his decision to rescind Frémont's decree "could only come of one . . . educated in a slave State." Even Lincoln's old friend Orville Browning, chosen to fill the unexpired term of Stephen Douglas (who had died in June), told the president that "Frémont's proclamation was necessary and . . . has the full approval of all loyal citizens of the West and the North West."

Lincoln remained unmoved. He told Radical senators at a conference in the Executive Mansion that it was not yet time for emancipation: "This thunderbolt will keep." Despite the clamor over Frémont's proclamation, the president believed that a substantial segment of the northern public still opposed emancipation. "I think Sumner and the rest of you would upset our applecart altogether if you had your way," he told the Radicals. "We'll fetch 'em, just give us a little time. We didn't go into the war to put down slavery, but to put the flag back; and to act differently at this moment would, I have no doubt, not only weaken our cause, but smack of bad faith." Vindication of the president's view came a few weeks later, when the Massachusetts state Republican convention—perhaps the most Radical party organization in the North—defeated a resolution endorsing Frémont's proclamation.

In a letter to Senator Browning on September 22, Lincoln defended his actions in the Frémont affair. Everyone agreed that military officials could seize private property during wartime, but Lincoln felt that slaves presented a special case. If Frémont needed slaves, "he can seize them, and use them; but when the need is past, it is not for him to fix their permanent future condition." In the president's judgment, Frémont had exceeded the bounds of military necessity and violated Missouri slaveowners' property rights by extending his grant of freedom beyond the war.

"I cannot assume this reckless position," Lincoln concluded. "Can it be pretended that it is any longer the government of the U.S.—any government of Constitution and laws,—wherein a General, or a President, may make permanent rules of property by proclamation?" Lincoln predicted that Congress might eventually decide to free all rebel slaves, but in the meantime, the president refused to "expressly or impliedly seize and exercise the permanent legislative functions of the government."

Despite Frémont's insubordinate behavior, Lincoln did not immediately replace him but instead dispatched General David Hunter, an old friend from Illinois, to keep an eye on Frémont. In mid-October, a congressional investigating committee uncovered evidence that Frémont's staff had engaged in widespread fraud and corruption in awarding supply contracts. A president known as "Honest Abe"—whose campaign had criticized similar scandals in the Buchanan administration—could not afford accusations of profiteering. On October 24, Lincoln removed Frémont from command.

Frémont's dismissal gave his defenders one more chance to condemn Lincoln's cautious policy on slavery. "How many times," asked the New England poet James Russell Lowell, "are we to save Kentucky and lose our self-respect?" "It is said we must consult the border states," a Republican leader from Connecticut complained to Gideon Welles. "Permit me to say *damn* the border states. . . . A thousand Lincolns cannot stop the people from fighting slavery."

Reluctant Napoléon

McClellan spent August and September forging the Army of the Potomac into a more disciplined and confident military force. No general in either army rivaled his ability to organize and train troops. The ninety-day volunteers were replaced by 120,000 three-year recruits; observers noted that these new soldiers appeared to be in excellent physical condition. Working eighteen-hour days, McClellan dispelled the gloom of late July in a matter of weeks. By the middle of August, morale was higher than it had been before Manassas.

To provide a more orderly environment for his troops, McClellan set to work cleaning up Washington. He launched police sweeps through the taverns, arresting drunks and vagrants; persuaded Congress to prohibit the sale of liquor to soldiers; posted brigades to guard the approaches to the capital; ordered parades along Pennsylvania Avenue every day; and seemed to be in constant motion himself, riding through the city at a gallop each morning and evening, with his aides close behind. Earthworks bristling with hundreds of guns ringed Washington. Steadily increasing numbers of fugitive slaves, seeking freedom under the terms of the Confiscation Act, began to raise the population of blacks in the city. McClellan ordered the provost guard to arrest any Negroes who lacked proof of their freedom, lodging them in the Old Capitol prison. "The city," concluded the Polish refugee Count Adam Gurowski, "has a more martial look. . . . It seems that a young, strong hand holds the ribbons."

Perhaps. But after vowing to "crush the rebels in one campaign," McClellan refused to lead his army outside the capital parade grounds. By early October, critics began to ask when McClellan would invade Virginia. The same impatient demands for action that had sent McDowell prematurely to Manassas now fell upon McClellan. "I intend to be careful, and do as well as possible," McClellan assured Lincoln. "Don't let them hurry me, is all I ask." "You shall have your own way in the matter, I assure you," replied the president.

Lincoln professed complete trust in McClellan's judgment, but he never liked to rely on experts. So the president spent hours studying texts on military strategy, trying to understand interior and exterior lines, tactics, and all "the technical details of the art of slaying" while devising his own plan to invade Virginia. (He displayed a similar curiosity about the machinery of naval warfare, frequently visiting the Navy Yard to inspect the latest advances in maritime technology.) Late in the day, Lincoln often walked over to McClellan's house on the corner of Fifteenth and H Streets, across from Lafayette Park, to have "a chat with George" about troop movements, reconnaissance, and weapons such as the new repeating rifle that could shoot fifty balls a minute. Civilian visitors to McClellan's home found it hard to believe that the president came to McClellan, instead of summoning the general to the Executive Mansion.

In early October, William Russell of the *London Times* frequently saw Lincoln approaching the general's home, "armed with plans, papers, reports, recommendations, sometimes good-humored, never angry, occasionally dejected, and always a little fussy." One night, Russell reported, he was waiting in McClellan's parlor when Lincoln arrived wearing a navvy's cap and a suit that did not quite fit. "Well," the president asked McClellan's aide, "is George in?" "Yes, sir," the officer replied. "He's come back, but is lying down, very much fatigued. I'll send up, sir, and inform him you wish to see him." "Oh, no," Lincoln murmured. "I can wait."

Lincoln's deferential attitude, the adulation of the press, and the cheers of his soldiers fed McClellan's ego. McClellan dismissed General Scott as "a dotard or a traitor" and undermined the general's standing with Lincoln, until the feeble Scott finally retired on November 1. Lincoln hesitated before offering McClellan the position of general in chief, but McClellan assured him, "I can do it all."

McClellan privately derided the president, too, referring to him as "an idiot," "a well meaning baboon," "the *original gorilla*," and "an old stick—& of pretty poor timber at that." The general told his wife, "I can never regard him with feelings other than those of thorough contempt—for his mind, heart, & morality." McClellan thought even worse of the Cabinet members, calling them "some of the greatest geese I have ever seen. . . . I think Seward is the meanest of them all—a meddling, officious, incompetent little puppy. . . . Welles is weaker than the most garrulous old woman you were ever annoyed by . . . Bates an old fool." "It is sickening in the extreme," McClellan concluded, to "see the weakness and unfitness of the poor beings who control the destinies of this great country."

Occasionally McClellan overplayed his hand. One November evening, Lincoln, Seward, and Hay went to the general's house, only to learn that McClellan was attending a wedding. The president decided to wait. An hour later, McClellan returned, ignored his visitors—he walked right past the room where they were sitting—and went upstairs. Another thirty minutes passed. Lincoln told a servant to remind McClellan they were still waiting. Back came the answer that the general had retired for the evening. Lincoln acted as if he did not care, but afterward he rarely visited McClellan's home, preferring to meet at the general's headquarters or the Executive Mansion.

Meanwhile the pressure to invade Virginia mounted. "We want our army to kill somebody," explained a frustrated Republican from Maine. By the end of October, the Army of the Potomac totaled more than 150,000 men, compared with the 41,000 Confederates encamped at Manassas. Still McClellan refused to budge. His only venture out of the capital ended in disaster. On October 21, Union troops on a reconnaissance mission encountered a Confederate outpost at Ball's Bluff, about 15 miles south of Washington. An ill-advised attack on the entrenched rebel position cost the Union nearly a thousand casualties. Among the dead was Senator Edward Baker, Lincoln's old friend, who had enlisted as a colonel in the Army of the Potomac. The news of Baker's death staggered Lincoln; the president spent the night alone, pacing in his office, refusing to see or speak to anyone.

Ball's Bluff and the death of their colleague fed Radical senators' anger against McClellan. "I begin to despair of ever putting down this rebellion through the instrumentality of this administration," complained Wade. "They are blundering, cowardly and inefficient." Wade, Trumbull, and Chandler pressured Lincoln to order McClellan to advance, only to hear the president reply that "it would not do to disturb" the general.

Several Radical senators blamed McClellan's lethargy on his friendship with Democratic congressmen who wanted to restore the Union with a minimum of damage to the South. They knew that the general in chief opposed their plans to use the Army of the Potomac to emancipate Confederate slaves. "Help me to dodge the nigger," McClellan wrote to a friend that autumn, "we want nothing to do with him. *I* am fighting to preserve the integrity of the Union. . . . To gain that end we cannot afford to mix up the negro question."

Lincoln agreed, and continued to shield his commander from the Radicals. "You must not fight till you are ready," he instructed McClellan. Privately, however, Lincoln admitted that he was beginning "to believe [McClellan] will never get ready to fight." When the Army of the Potomac began building log huts for its winter quarters, it was clear that McClellan had no intention of leaving Washington before the end of the year.

Cracking Slavery

As the Union war effort in the East bogged down, doubts resurfaced about Lincoln's ability to direct a nation at war. The Confederate states seemed no closer to returning. The only Union military victory came from a naval attack on the Sea Islands along the coast of South Carolina. The navy wanted the islands as an operating base for the Union blockade fleet, and the Treasury Department needed the cotton grown on the islands to supply New England textile mills and bolster the northern economy. After a Union fleet bombarded the islands in November, rebel defenders fled, leaving behind 10,000 slaves.

It seemed a modest triumph. "The President has lost ground amazingly," wrote Senator Fessenden to a constituent. "[He] has lost all hold upon Congress, though no one doubts his personal integrity." "Lincoln means well," declared Zach Chandler, "but he has no force of character. He is surrounded by Old Fogy Army officers more than half of whom are downright traitors and the other one half sympathize with the South."

Lincoln bore the criticism politely. "Personally you [senators] are all very kind," he told Lot Morrill of Maine during a White House conference, "but I know we don't all agree as to what this administration should do, and how it ought to be done." He admitted that he still had no master plan to deal with the problems that beset the nation. "I confess I do not fully understand and foresee it all," he told Morrill. "But I am placed here where I am obliged to the best of my poor ability to deal with it. And that being the case, I can only go just as fast as I can see how to go."

The president's balancing act was growing more precarious. Each month, more northerners agreed with the clergyman Thomas W. Higginson of Massachusetts that "the idea of conquering rebellion without destroying slavery is only to be equalled by the idea of storming hell without disturbing the personal comfort of the devil." "I find everybody is an abolitionist in the war sense of that term," wrote Charles Hamlin, the vice president's eldest son, from his army camp. "And the sooner Congress puts the country on the record aright then the sooner we shall conquer."

At his post in Cairo, Illinois, Brigadier General Ulysses S. Grant discerned the shift in public sentiment. In November, Grant wrote to his father-in-law that northerners "do not want, nor will they want, to interfere with the institution"; they would cease to protect it, however, "unless the South shall return soon to their allegiance." Personally, Grant was willing to preserve slavery, since his wife still owned several slaves at their farm in Missouri. But he agreed that "if it is necessary that slavery should fall that the Republic may continue its existence, let slavery go." "In all this," Grant concluded, "I cannot but see the doom of slavery."

Every month, along the borders of the Confederacy, a thousand or more slaves fled their masters. Southerners began sending their slaves deeper into the interior to discourage them from trying to escape. Fears of Negro uprisings escalated. Confederate state legislatures passed laws designed to keep free blacks under constant surveillance; a few states even returned freedmen to slavery. In numerous southern communities, white citizens established vigilance committees or "committees of public safety" with regular armed patrols to discourage insurrections. One such committee in northern Alabama—sitting as an extralegal tribunal—heard testimony that local slaves believed "Lincoln is soon going to free them all, and they are everywhere making preparations to aid him when he makes his appearance." Slaves and free Negroes suspected of complicity in the alleged uprising were hanged ("like black birds," noted Mary Chesnut in her diary) or sentenced to prison for life.

Cameron's Bid

With no battles to report, northern newspapers filled their columns with accusations of scandals and corruption in the War Department. In the rush to buy equipment and supplies for half a million soldiers, the War Department's agents had ignored standard procedures and awarded contracts to unscrupulous merchants and political cronies without competitive bidding. Inferior merchandise purchased at exorbitant prices sat rotting in army camps: tainted meat, diseased horses, rotten blankets, antiquated muskets discarded by the Austrian government, and uniforms that disintegrated in the rain (transforming the cheap fabric known as "shoddy" into an adjective).

Haste and slipshod administration created much of the mess; graft accounted for the rest. Charges of fraud and waste were heard on Capitol Hill as early as June. When Congress asked Secretary of War Cameron for copies of supply contracts, he refused to comply. The House responded by establishing a special investigating committee whose hearings produced 1,109 pages of evidence of widespread mismanagement in the War Department.

Cameron's reputation as a corrupt machine politician made the accusations easy to believe. Bankers threatened to boycott the Treasury Department's loan issues until Lincoln found a new secretary of war. Even Chase, who was Cameron's closest ally in the Cabinet, condemned "the loose and unsystematic manner in which authority has been given irresponsible individuals . . . to raise troops, expend money and involve the government in debt." Although he was reluctant to dismiss Cameron (whose younger brother had died at Bull Run) and add to the impression of chaos within the War Department, Lincoln privately began dropping hints that Cameron should start looking for another job.

Cameron would not go quietly. He, too, had been a candidate for the

Republican nomination in 1860, and still harbored presidential ambitions. Before Lincoln could force him out, Cameron decided to break with the president and identify himself publicly with the rising demand for emancipation. Even more boldly, he chose to reverse his previous stand and endorse the arming of fugitive slaves who reached Union lines.

In mid-October, Cameron issued orders to General Thomas Sherman, commander of the federal troops in the Sea Islands, instructing him to employ runaway slaves "as you deem most beneficial to the service." It was time, Cameron declared, to use "every means which God has placed in our hands," including arming fugitive slaves. At a party in Washington on the evening of November 19, Cameron again endorsed using freed slaves in combat. His comments made headline news in the *New York Times* the following day.

Without consulting Lincoln, Cameron inserted a passage into the War Department's annual report for 1861 stating that it was "as clearly a right of the Government to arm slaves, when it may become necessary, as it is to use gun-powder taken from the enemy." When the government printer showed Lincoln the War Department's report, the president was appalled. "This will never do!" he exclaimed. "General Cameron must take no such responsibility. That is a question that belongs exclusively to me." Lincoln was even more disturbed when he learned that Cameron had distributed advance copies of the report to the press without submitting it for his approval.

At the next Cabinet meeting, Lincoln—pacing restlessly back and forth—reproached Cameron for contradicting administration policy. He demanded that Cameron recall all copies of the report and delete the offending passage. Cameron complied, but several newspapers had already obtained the original text. They subsequently published both versions, so readers could see the changes Lincoln had imposed.

Most northerners were not yet ready to use freed slaves to fight white southerners, and so Lincoln's censorship of Cameron's report did not provoke as much of a public outcry as his revocation of Frémont's emancipation decree. Still, abolitionists hailed Cameron and proclaimed that he stood "head & shoulders above the President & all the Cabinet beside." His patience exhausted, Lincoln began searching for a replacement for

Cameron. Meanwhile, the president sent an addendum, in his own handwriting, to Cameron's orders to General Sherman in South Carolina. The use of freed slaves by the Union Army, he wrote, should not under any circumstances include "a general arming of them for military service."

The Cost of Freedom

Congress assembled for its regular session on December 2. On the first day, Thaddeus Stevens introduced a resolution asking Lincoln to emancipate "all slaves who leave their masters, or who shall aid in quelling rebellion." Stevens's resolution went considerably beyond the Confiscation Act by emancipating *all* fugitive slaves, and by virtually inviting slaves to rise up against their masters. In the Senate, Trumbull gave notice that he would introduce a similar measure to confiscate all rebel property and emancipate all slaves in the Confederate states. The *New York Times* estimated that half the congressmen in both houses now favored military emancipation; "the slave question," its editors predicted, "is likely to occupy the most prominent part in congressional discussion and action this session."

Lincoln responded to the rising pressure for emancipation in his first annual message to Congress on December 3. The theme of his message—which, following accepted practice, was read to the assembled legislators by a clerk—was that the conflict remained a war to restore the Union, and nothing more.

The president began by claiming that he had fulfilled the promise of his inaugural address by keeping "the integrity of the Union paramount as the primary object of the contest on our part, leaving all questions which are not of vital military importance"—including emancipation—"to the more deliberate action of the legislature." If Congress wished to free the Confederacy's slaves, it must take responsibility for the consequences. "I have been anxious and careful," Lincoln assured the congressmen, "to ensure that the conflict shall not degenerate into a violent and remorseless revolutionary struggle." In his only concession to the emancipation movement, the president granted freedom to all fugitive slaves in Union Army camps and acknowledged that the government would be responsible for their welfare.

Lincoln recognized that the war was slowly destroying slavery by arousing northerners' feelings in favor of emancipation, and by encouraging slaves to flee to the Union for protection and freedom. Slavery, he said, "has received a mortal wound."

As a practical matter, the erosion of slavery in the Confederate states inevitably exerted pressure on the border states as well. To soften the impact, Lincoln proposed that slaveholders in the border states transfer control over their slaves to the federal government in lieu of taxes. The government would then colonize the Negroes "at some place, or places, in a climate congenial to them." "It might be well to consider, too," Lincoln added, "whether the free colored people already in the United States could not, so far as individuals may desire, be included in such colonization." Perhaps they could be dispatched to the recently independent republics of Haiti and Liberia, with whom Lincoln intended to open diplomatic relations. "The emigration of colored men," Lincoln reminded the assembled congressmen, "leaves additional room for white men remaining or coming here."

Lincoln was no sudden convert to colonization. Montgomery Blair, the postmaster general, had been encouraging Lincoln's interest because the Blair family had long sought to expel the nation's entire black population to Central or South America. Blair defended these plans as the best means of preventing free Negroes from inundating the western territories, while reassuring southerners that the national government did not intend "to set negroes free among them to be their equals and consequently their rulers when they are numerous."

Although none of the Blairs' elaborate and expensive schemes ever generated much support in Congress (whose members were reluctant to send several million productive laborers out of the country) or among Negroes, Lincoln already had approved a feasibility study of their latest proposal to establish a colony of freed slaves on the Panamanian isthmus, along a body of water known as the Chiquiri Lagoon. A businessman in Philadelphia named Ambrose W. Thompson owned the rights to a two-thousand-acre tract of land at the lagoon, which reportedly was suitable for growing cotton. None of the Cabinet officers except Blair expressed any interest in the project, but Lincoln's commitment to encouraging free blacks to leave the United States remained so strong that the *New York Times* claimed that, "the President will approve no measure of emancipation not embracing colonization."

To keep his options open, Lincoln vowed at the end of his annual message to employ "all indispensable means"—including emancipation—to preserve the Union. Clearly, however, his plan to accept freedmen in lieu of taxes and his endorsement of colonization were attempts to encourage gradual change and minimize the disruptive effects of emancipation. To ease the economic burden on American slaveowners—whose investment in human property, based on contemporary prices for slaves, totaled nearly $3 billion—Lincoln also was willing to approve financial compensation for owners who voluntarily freed their slaves. Behind the scenes, Lincoln was working with a congressman from Delaware, George Fisher, to develop a model plan for gradual, compensated emancipation in that state. Lincoln chose Delaware as a test case because the release of its relatively small slave population (slightly more than 1,500) was unlikely to create serious problems.

Lincoln and Fisher devised two plans: one would free every slave in Delaware by 1867; the other would draw out emancipation until 1893. Lincoln preferred the more gradual plan, largely because it would help calm whites' anxieties about free Negroes in their midst. The federal government would pay Delaware slaveholders $500, in the form of 6 percent bonds over a period of thirty-one years, for each slave owned in 1860.

Lincoln hoped that his plan would cement the border states to the Union by removing the one institution that linked them with the Confederacy. Once the Confederates recognized that they had no chance of luring the border states away, the rebellion might collapse. As the president pointed out, the expense of compensating Delaware's slaveowners would be negligible compared with the cost of a continued war. "I am satisfied," Lincoln concluded, "that this is the cheapest and most humane way of ending the war."

In the first week of December, Fisher circulated the proposal among the pro-Union members of the Delaware legislature, keeping Lincoln's involvement a secret. Lincoln also discussed the plan with Charles Sumner, who was sufficiently impressed to set aside his opposition to compensating slaveowners for the loss of their property. "Never should any question of money be allowed to interfere with human freedom," conceded Sumner.

Lincoln told Sumner that "the only difference between you and me on this subject is a difference of a month or six weeks in time," but that was not true. Congress was moving faster than the president toward emancipation. On December 4, Republican congressmen gave Lincoln their negative reply to his moderate proposals. When Representative Crittenden sought to reaffirm congressional sentiment by introducing the same resolution the House had passed in July—declaring that the war was being fought only to preserve the Union and defend the Constitution—a solid bloc of Republicans voted against it, sending it down to defeat.

At a caucus of Republican congressional leaders later that week, Thaddeus Stevens denounced Lincoln's cautious approach toward emancipation. Perhaps the party had been deceived when Lincoln's backers touted him as an antislavery man, Stevens suggested. The Radicals converted their distrust of Lincoln into action on December 9, when they persuaded their colleagues to approve the establishment of a joint congressional committee to investigate the administration's conduct of the war.

By the end of the year, the fate of slavery had begun to split opinion in the North. Debates over the wisdom and timing of emancipation divided the Cabinet, Congress, the army, and the public. In an editorial supporting Lincoln's reluctance to attack slavery, the *New York Times* argued that "no greater disaster could happen to us than *the destruction of that unanimity of public sentiment* which has thus far been our strength in the struggle for the Constitution and the Union. . . . *The time for the safe and successful treatment of the Slavery question*, in its broadest aspects, *has not yet come.*"

A growing number of northerners disagreed. In a letter to Secretary of the Treasury Chase, the owner of the *Cincinnati Gazette* reported that antislavery demonstrators in southern Ohio were burning Lincoln in effigy. The attorney George Templeton Strong, who had never supported abolition, observed growing support in New York City for "an opposition party, founded on anti-slavery feeling stronger than that of the Administration." In his *New York Tribune,* Horace Greeley proposed a new policy for the Union: "Notify the slaveholders frankly that they may have thirty or sixty days more in which to lay down their arms and return to loyalty; but if they shall continue to defy the National authority and menace the National existence after the expiration of that term, their slaves shall, as a matter of inexorable public policy . . . be proclaimed free."

Analyzing the American conflict from Vienna, Karl Marx concluded that the war eventually would force Lincoln to destroy slavery. "The long and short of the business seems to me to be that a war of this kind must be conducted on revolutionary lines, while the Yankees have so far been trying to conduct it constitutionally," Marx wrote to Friedrich Engels. "In my opinion all this will take another turn. In the end the North will make war seriously, adopt revolutionary methods and throw over the domination of the border slave statesmen. A single Negro regiment would have a remarkable effect on Southern nerves. . . ."

Harriet Tubman envisioned a similar outcome, although for different reasons. "God won't let Massa Linkum beat de South till he do de right ting," the former slave said in the last days of 1861:

Massa Linkum he great man, and I'se poor nigger; but dis nigger can tell Massa Linkum how to save de money and de young men. He do it by setting de niggers free. S'pose dar was awfu' big snake down dar, on de floor. He bite you. Folks all skeered, cause you die. You send for doctor to cut de bite; but snake he rolled up dar, and while doctor dwine it, he bite you agin. De doctor cut out dat bite; but while he dwine it, de snake he spring up and bite you agin, and so he keep dwine, till you kill him. Dat's what Massa Linkum orter know.

4

LONG ROUTE TO FREEDOM

By nine o'clock on the first morning of 1862, eager sightseers filled the streets and sidewalks around the White House. The president and his wife were hosting their New Year's Day reception, an annual social ritual imported from New York. It was a beautiful morning, one of the warmest January days anyone could remember, but the crowds who lined Pennsylvania Avenue had spent a restless night. A continuous thundering of artillery coming from the Virginia side of the Potomac sounded like the prelude to a Confederate attack on the city; some regular Union troops stood at the ready all night long.

At ten o'clock on New Year's morning, the entire diplomatic corps in Washington and various high-ranking government officials—including senators, justices of the Supreme Court, and members of the Cabinet—began arriving at the Executive Mansion to call on the president. A deputation of the city police also appeared, joined by an assortment of military officers, resplendent in their dress uniforms. "If our soldiers could prove as useful as they are ornamental," commented one reporter, "nothing more could be desired of them." General McClellan, however, did not attend the reception; he had contracted typhoid fever a week earlier and was still confined to his bed.

When guards opened the gates to the public at noon, there was an unseemly rush for the reception room as men jostled one another for position. Once inside, however, they adopted a more respectful demeanor. Visitors moved rapidly through the receiving line, shaking hands with the president, Mrs. Lincoln, and several local officials before they were ushered into a hall where the Marine Band played patriotic airs. There was a brief opportunity for free food and drink—the new carpets were covered with cloth as a precaution—and a concert by the Hutchinson Family, popular abolitionist minstrels from New Hampshire whom General McClellan had banned from Union Army camps. By a little after two o'clock the crowd had vanished, and the doors were closed. Only later did Senator Browning realize that a pickpocket had stolen his wallet during the reception.

Reporters wrote that the crush of curiosity seekers at the President's House was "the greatest jam ever witnessed on any similar occasion," but swarms of people were everywhere in Washington in early 1862. Since Lincoln's inauguration, the city's population had jumped to more than 100,000, an increase of nearly 40 percent. It was the first time in Washington's history that the city had been crowded for more than a few months at a time. Many of the newcomers were troops stationed temporarily in the capital. Wherever one went, noted the British actress Fanny Kemble, "the sound of drums and trumpets and artillery practicing never ceased." Along with soldiers came con men, gamblers, counterfeiters, embalmers, and special correspondents from the major metropolitan dailies, as well as showmen: actors, singers, and prizefighters. Prostitutes arrived from cities as far away as Chicago; when General Joseph Hooker sought to restrict the bordellos to one part of town, the whores became known as "Joe Hooker's Division," or simply "hookers."

"Politicians of every grade, adventurers of either sex, inventors of all sorts of military appliances, and simple citizens, good and bad, flocked thither in great numbers," wrote the abolitionist author Julia Ward Howe. Every vacant house in a respectable neighborhood was rented or sold. Hundreds of newly hired government clerks crammed themselves into already overcrowded boardinghouse bedrooms. There were hospitals, too, and men and women searching for relatives who had been reported wounded or missing. Tourists came to visit the battlefield at Manassas, scavenging the landscape for lost soldiers' keepsakes to take home as souvenirs. Fugitive slaves slipped into the city in increasing numbers, especially after Secretary of State Seward ordered McClellan to stop arresting Negroes who lacked documents to prove that they were free. City officials restricted Negro immigrants to the malaria-ridden lowlands known as "Murder Bay" by the Chesapeake and Ohio Canal, or to Negro Hill on North Tenth Street, a safe distance from the respectable parts of town.

Fears that Confederate forces would cut the city's supply lines kept prices of almost all consumer items exorbitantly high. As one longtime Washingtonian noted, the city paid a cost for producing nothing but politics; everything had to be imported, and the army often commandeered the sole single-track railway to Baltimore. Shortages of civilian goods inevitably followed. Besides, the capital's freight depot was a jumbled mass of goods that had been dumped there and shoved aside to make way for the next incoming shipments.

General Frémont was in Washington that winter, seeking a new military appointment. Horace Greeley was there, too, as one of the featured speakers in the first lecture series ever sponsored by the Smithsonian Institution. Most of the guest lecturers were abolitionists, although a representative of the Smithsonian announced before each speech that the institution did not necessarily endorse the sentiments of the speaker. When Greeley appeared before a crowded auditorium on the evening of January 3, he was flanked on the platform by distinguished government officials, including President Lincoln, Secretary of the Treasury Chase, and several Radical congressmen. Greeley spent most of his speech encouraging the government to destroy slavery and confiscate all Confederate property; "Rebels," he said, "have no right to own anything." Each time Greeley called for drastic retaliation against the Confederacy, the audience clapped enthusiastically. The loudest cheer came when he mentioned the name of Frémont. At the end of the address, Lincoln turned to Congressman George Julian and whispered that he wanted to take Greeley's manuscript home with him "and carefully read it over some Sunday."

Throughout the North, abolitionist speakers were drawing larger crowds than ever, and critics who used to mock the antislavery crusaders now viewed them with respect. "Peculiar circumstances," reported the *New York Times*, were giving abolitionist rallies "an importance that has hitherto not been theirs." Newspaper editorials kept steady pressure on Lincoln to use emancipation as a weapon against the Confederacy. "Our nation is on the brink of ruin," warned Joseph Medill, editor of the *Chicago Tribune*. "Mr. Lincoln, for God's sake and your Country's sake rise to the realization . . . that this is a Slave-holders rebellion."

In the Union armies, increasing numbers of volunteers from all parts of the North were joining the emancipation cause; by January 1862, it seemed that nearly half of the northern troops favored abolition, at least as a practical measure. A typical comment came from an Iowan who wrote, "I believe that Slavery (the worst of all curses) was the sole cause of this Rebellion, and until this cause is removed and slavery abolished, the rebellion will continue to exist."

Personal contact with runaways or abandoned slaves in western Virginia or South Carolina's Sea Islands fed the Union soldiers' outrage against the southern institution. "I thought I hated slavery as much as possible before I came here," wrote a recruit from Pennsylvania who heard the story of a brutal whipping, "but here, where I can see some of its workings, I am more than ever convinced of the cruelty and unhumanity of the system."

Experience with slavery also reinforced Union troops' determination not to return runaways to their masters, even in the border states. When a slaveowner in Maryland came into a Union camp outside Annapolis to reclaim a slave, soldiers roughed him up. An officer who watched the scuffle believed that if the slaveowner had persisted, "he would have lost his life in this Negro Hunt. As it was he got well frightened, & I presume will think twice before he goes into a Camp of northern Soldiers to reclaim biped property."

Not all Union soldiers favored emancipation, of course. Many agreed with a recruit from New York who argued that "we must first conquer & then its time enough to talk about the *dam'd niggers*." And some of those who helped liberate slaves were not particularly concerned about the ultimate fate of the freed Negroes. One Union lieutenant who protected "a runaway nigger" admitted, "I don't care a damn for the darkies."

Numerous army officials who advocated the use of black troops viewed Negroes as little more than cannon fodder. "For my part," announced an officer stationed in South Carolina, "I make bold to stay that I am not so fastidious as to object to a negro being food for powder and I would arm every man of them." Governor Israel Washburn of Maine agreed. "Why have our rulers so little regard for the true & brave white men of the north?" asked Washburn. "Will they continue to sacrifice them? Why will they refuse to save them by employing black men? . . . Why are our leaders unwilling that Sambo should save white boys?"

Radical congressmen understood that the mere presence of Union armies in slave territory tended to dissolve slavery, but there was still no sign that McClellan intended to take his troops out of Washington once he recovered from his illness. Convinced that the Union war effort was being sabotaged by the incompetence—and perhaps treason—of the army's top leadership, the Radicals pursued their military opponents through the special investigative Joint Committee on the Conduct of the War, chaired by Benjamin Wade, perhaps the most aggressive Radical in the Senate and an early candidate for the Republican presidential nomination of 1864. Ultimately, Republican legislators intended to force army officials to relinquish direction of the war to Congress.

The existence of the Joint Committee also reflected a lack of confidence in Lincoln's leadership. Senator Fessenden gibed that "if the President had his wife's will and would use it rightly, our affairs would look much better." Attorney General Bates agreed. "The Prest. is an excellent man, and, in the main wise," Bates wrote in his diary at the end of 1861, "but he lacks *will* and *purpose*, and, I greatly fear he has not *the power to command*." Members of the Joint Committee made the same point at a series of meetings with Lincoln at the turn of the new year. During one conference at the Executive Mansion, Wade exploded with frustration. "Mr. President," he shouted, "you are murdering your country by inches in consequence of the inactivity of the military and the want of a distinct policy in regard to slavery."

Yet even an inactive army required money. Chase was trying to contain inflation by financing the war through loans and minimal tax increases, but unprecedented war expenditures had drained the nation's gold and silver reserves by the beginning of 1862. Government bonds were trading considerably below par value. On the last day of 1861, banks in New York, Boston, and Philadelphia suspended payments of bank notes in gold and silver, forcing the federal government to do likewise. With the treasury nearly empty, Chase had no choice but to ask Congress to start funding the war through increased taxes and paper currency.

Lincoln was as frustrated as anyone. McClellan would not confide in him, and when Lincoln went to the general's house for a briefing, McClellan refused to see him. Cabinet members, too, were growing restless. An inconclusive meeting on the afternoon of January 10 left an exasperated Bates complaining about "great negligence, ignorance and lack of preparation and forethought. Nothing is ready. McClellan is still sick, and nobody knew his plans, if he have any."

After the Cabinet departed, Lincoln asked Quartermaster General Montgomery Meigs to stay a moment longer. "General," he asked, "what shall I do? The people are impatient; Chase has no money, and he tells me he can raise no more; the General of the Army has typhoid fever. The bottom is out of the tub. What shall I do?"

That evening, the president called several key advisers together: Seward, Chase, General McDowell, and General William B. Franklin, one of McClellan's confidants. Lincoln admitted that he was "in great distress" over the continuing inactivity of the Army of the Potomac, and he wanted McDowell and Franklin to tell him whether the army could soon launch an advance into Virginia. "If something was not soon done," the president concluded grimly, "the bottom would be out of the whole affair, and if General McClellan did not want to use the army, he would like to borrow it, provided he could see how it could be made to do something." After spending hours of his spare time reading every text on military strategy he could find, Lincoln even considered leading the Army of the Potomac into battle himself.

McDowell recommended an advance upon Manassas—which was Lincoln's preferred strategy—and Franklin reluctantly concurred, but the following day Postmaster General Blair and General Meigs protested that another direct attack on the Confederate forces would produce only a repeat of the disaster at Bull Run. Suspecting a conspiracy to undermine his authority, McClellan finally appeared at the Executive Mansion on January 13. He refused to tell the president when or where he intended to advance. "If I tell him my plans," McClellan whispered to Meigs, "they will be in the *New York Herald* tomorrow morning. He can't keep a secret." When Chase asked him directly "what he intended doing with his army, and when he intended doing it," McClellan again demurred, explaining that "in military matters the fewer persons who were knowing of them the better." Pretending to accept McClellan's assurances that he had a definite timetable for an invasion of Virginia, Lincoln adjourned the meeting.

Enter Stanton

By the time McClellan left the President's House on the afternoon of January 13, Simon Cameron was no longer a member of the Cabinet. For the past month, Lincoln had been searching for a graceful way to ease Cameron out of the administration. When the American minister to Russia, former Senator Cassius Clay, expressed a desire to return to the United States, Lincoln decided to replace Clay with Cameron. He pretended that Cameron had requested the change. In return, Lincoln allowed Cameron to resign instead of being dismissed. Few in Washington mourned Cameron when he departed for Moscow; Thaddeus Stevens cynically advised the czar to lock up his valuables at night.

Reporters attributed Cameron's exodus to his vocal support of emancipation and Negro troops. As Cameron's replacement, Lincoln chose Edwin M. Stanton, a Democrat from Ohio best known for his service as attorney general in the final months of the Buchanan administration. A distinguished lawyer with little experience in elective politics, Stanton had come to Washington several years earlier to defend Congressman Dan Sickles of New York after Sickles shot and killed his wife's lover, the Washington socialite Philip Barton Key. Stanton won Sickles an acquittal; most of those who applauded him did not yet know that Stanton was also brilliant at backstairs intrigues. Observers viewed his selection as an attempt by Lincoln to maintain northerners' bipartisan consensus on the war by giving pro-war Democrats a voice in the Cabinet.

Stanton accepted the Cabinet post despite his unflattering opinion of the president. Six years earlier, Lincoln and Stanton had served together on a legal team in a suit involving patent infringement. As lead attorney, Stanton—who enjoyed far more prestige than Lincoln in legal circles—had completely ignored the westerner, dismissing him as "that damned long armed Ape" who "does not know any thing and can do you no good." Lincoln's election to the presidency had not substantially altered Stanton's judgment. A reporter who encountered Stanton in Washington during the week before Lincoln's inauguration was surprised to hear him denounce the president-elect in vehement terms, describing Lincoln as "a low, cunning clown." "It is impossible to be more bitter and malignant than he is," the journalist concluded. "Every word was a suppressed and a very ill-suppressed sneer."

After the inauguration, Stanton continued to privately denounce Lincoln's "painful imbecility" while he publicly supported the war effort. A master at ingratiating himself with men in authority, Stanton entered office with the recommendation of both Seward and Chase. The Joint Committee on the Conduct of the War also approved his appointment, even though Stanton had grown very close to McClellan after McClellan assumed command of the Army of the Potomac. Stanton had served Cameron as well, as a legal adviser on War Department business. Lincoln did not know that Stanton had secretly authored the paragraph in Cameron's annual report endorsing the arming of freed slaves.

But Stanton was bright, capable, furiously energetic, honest in public affairs, and utterly dedicated to the Union cause. Lincoln hired him to shake up the War Department's sluggish bureaucracy, and as soon as he accepted the post on January 20, Stanton set to work. He reformed the department's purchasing procedures to make competitive bidding mandatory, hired more than fifty additional staff members, secured funds to expand and modernize the War Department's offices, launched an audit of supply contracts, returned (without payment) thousands of dollars worth of defective materials, canceled other orders, and threatened to sue negligent contractors.

A short, barrel-chested man, Stanton liked to intimidate his subordinates and anyone else who walked into his second-floor office at the War Department, overlooking the Executive Mansion. He wore a "perpetually irritable look," possessed a high-strung temperament, and suffered from asthma and violent mood swings. Since Stanton lacked time to exercise, his doctors recommended that he stand behind his desk when he greeted visitors. The effect added to Stanton's intimidating presence, with his flowing, ragged beard streaked with white; his balding head whose sparse strands of long hair were swept back and curled around his ears; and his dark, thick eyebrows arched above heavy-lidded eyes and gold-rimmed spectacles. "He would lean his arm on the desk, settle his spectacles, and wait for people to come and state their business," wrote one observer, "a peppery little man who looked as though he had not slept well, and as if it would not give him much pain to refuse your most urgent request."

Newspaper correspondents hated Stanton because he censored war news, rewarded his favorite reporters with tidbits of inside information, and punished journalists who criticized the government. As far as Stanton was concerned, negative articles constituted treason. Soon after he took control of the War Department, Stanton ordered the arrest of a *New York Tribune* reporter as a Confederate spy; the reporter was detained without trial for three months at Fort McHenry in Baltimore.

Lincoln treated the press quite differently. Although he granted few formal interviews, he went out of his way to cultivate friendly relations with reporters. Journalists were always welcome at the White House and Lincoln frequently interrupted conferences to answer a visiting reporter's question or confirm or deny a rumor. "You gentlemen of the press seem to be pretty much like soldiers, who have to go wherever sent, whatever may be the dangers or difficulties in the way," Lincoln told a reporter for the *New York Herald*. "God forbid I should by any rudeness of speech or manner, make your duties any harder than they are. . . . The press has no better friend than I am—no one who is more ready to acknowledge . . . its tremendous power for both good and evil."

Since Stanton was a Democrat and a confidant of McClellan, Washington insiders assumed that he opposed abolition. As he witnessed the rising public support for emancipation in the first nine months of the war, however, Stanton began to modify his views. During his confirmation hearings, he managed to persuade observers of widely divergent views that he was on their side. Samuel Barlow, a wealthy Democratic lawyer from New York, swore that Stanton was "as firm a Democrat as I know." Speaking for moderate Republicans, Senator Fessenden asserted that Stanton "is just the man we want" because "we agree on every point . . . the conduct of the war, the negro question, and everything else." Senator Trumbull, on the other hand, claimed that Radical congressmen "who have conversed with him, say he is fully up to all they could ask."

Stanton's vigorous administrative style infused life into the Union war effort. "As soon as I can get the machinery of the office working, the rats cleared out, and the rat holes stopped, we shall *move*," he assured a subordinate. Stanton's impatience soon found a target in the Army of the Potomac and his former idol McClellan. "This army has got to fight or run away," Stanton snapped, "and while men are striving nobly in the West, the champagne and oyster suppers on the Potomac must be stopped." Privately, Stanton told the journalist Charles Dana that thus far "we have had no war. We have not even been playing war. . . . Instead of an army stuck in the mud of the Potomac, we should have . . . one hundred thousand men thrusting upon Nashville and sweeping rebellion and treason out of Kentucky with fire & sword."

Two Steps Forward

Lincoln agreed that McClellan must move his army forward as soon as possible. On January 27, under heavy pressure from Congress and the public to force McClellan to attack, Lincoln finally issued his General War Order No. 1, directing all Union land and naval forces to begin an advance on or before February 22. Four days later, the president specifically ordered the Army of the Potomac to undertake an overland advance toward Richmond by way of Manassas.

McClellan objected. In a twenty-two-page memorandum to Stanton, he argued that the Confederate defenses in front of Manassas remained too strong for a frontal assault. Instead, McClellan proposed to take his army down the Rappahannock River to Urbanna—east of Richmond—and attack the Confederate capital from that direction.

Lincoln had more than a few doubts. McClellan's plan was too elaborate, too expensive, and too slow; besides, it would remove the Army of the Potomac as the shield that protected Washington from a Confederate attack. Nevertheless, Lincoln deferred to his general in chief's judgment, although rumors spread through the army camps that McClellan would lose his job if he did not soon deliver a victory.

No troops were going anywhere for the next several weeks anyway. Constant cold rain and drizzle had made the roads of Washington and northern Virginia impassable. "Mud, mud," wrote Corporal Elisha Hunt Rhodes in his diary. "I am thinking of starting a steamboat line to run on Penn. Avenue between our office and the Capitol." The only way to travel around Washington was on horseback, and even that was treacherous in the thick, persistent fog.

As McClellan completed his preparations for the Urbanna expedition, news came from the West that a Union naval expedition of four ironclads and three wooden gunboats had forced the Confederates to evacuate a key defensive stronghold—Fort Henry on the Tennessee River—on February 6. Eleven days later, Union forces under the command of General Grant captured an even more critical rebel position, Fort Donelson, about 12 miles away on the Cumberland River. In the process, Grant's troops captured more than 12,000 Confederate prisoners.

Union forces now controlled the Tennessee and Cumberland rivers, which provided an excellent avenue for an invasion; one writer described them as "a double-barreled shotgun" leveled at the heart of the Confederacy. For the rest of the war, Union armies would dominate Kentucky and Tennessee. The Confederate commander Albert Sidney Johnston had lost nearly a third of his forces. With two more Union armies under the command of General Don Carlos Buell and General John Pope converging on him from the north and west, Johnston was forced to evacuate his troops from Nashville, whose ironworks made it one of the major industrial centers of the South. Many of Nashville's leading citizens fled as well; when a northern journalist arrived at the city's premier hotel, he was greeted only by a Negro servant who welcomed him with a smile, saying, "Massa done gone souf."

Meanwhile, off the coast of North Carolina, an amphibious Union expedition led by General Ambrose Burnside captured Roanoke Island on February 7. The island—site of Walter Raleigh's ill-fated "lost colony" nearly 300 years earlier—provided the Union navy with a base to attack the rest of North Carolina's Atlantic ports. It would take the Union blockade fleet less than three months to shut down nearly all of the state's harbors. Burnside's victory at Roanoke also opened a back door to Norfolk and its naval yard, and raised the possibility of a two-pronged attack on the Confederate Army in Virginia.

Starved for victories, northern newspaper editors overreacted to the reports from North Carolina and the Tennessee Valley. Henry Raymond, editor of the *New York Times*, declared that he could now see the end of the rebellion: "After this, it certainly cannot be materially postponed. The monster is already clutched and in his death struggle."

Except that McClellan still had not budged. By the end of February, members of the Joint Committee on the Conduct of the War were out of patience. Senator Wilson charged that McClellan appeared "to be more anxious to catch negros than to catch rebels." Senator Wade accused the general of "infernal, unmitigated cowardice"; at least, Wade suggested, McClellan should secure Washington's lines of communication by clearing the rebels out of Harpers Ferry (which they had held since the war began), and reopening the Baltimore and Ohio Railroad to Union traffic. McClellan replied that he was already planning to do precisely that, and then advance through the Shenandoah Valley to Winchester, Virginia.

McClellan's troops got as far as Harpers Ferry, but the specially built barges that McClellan sent to transport artillery and wagons up the Chesapeake and Ohio Canal proved too wide for the canal locks. Unwilling to move farther without his heavy guns, McClellan decided to abandon the attack upon Winchester.

A member of McClellan's staff went to the White House to give Lincoln the bad news. He found the president alone in his office. McClellan had called off the advance, the officer explained, because the pontoon trains were not ready. "Why in ——— ain't they ready?" Lincoln demanded. Flustered, the officer retreated without answering. Lincoln turned back to his desk and began writing furiously, at twice his normal speed. A secretary later claimed that he never saw Lincoln "so really angry, so out of all patience," as when he heard the news from Harpers Ferry.

Lincoln called for McClellan's chief of staff, General Randolph Marcy (who also was McClellan's father-in-law), and demanded to know why McClellan did not know ahead of time that the boats were too wide for the canal locks. "I am no engineer," Lincoln fumed, "but it seems to me that if I wished to know whether a boat would go through a hole or a lock, common sense would teach me to go and measure it." The president added that he was "almost despairing at these results":

> Everything seems to fail. The general impression is daily gaining ground that the General does not intend to do anything. By a failure like this we lose all the prestige we gained by the capture of Fort Donelson. I am grievously disappointed—almost in despair.

Crossing the River

Lincoln's mood was not improved by constant agitation over slavery from Radicals in Congress and newspaper editorials. Every week, congressmen in both houses presented petitions from their constituents urging the president to free the Confederacy's slaves. The Joint Committee on the Conduct of the War took a break from denouncing McClellan to allow General Frémont to testify in defense of his Missouri emancipation proclamation, and Republican members praised Frémont's willingness to attack slavery.

Senator Trumbull introduced a second confiscation bill, tougher than the first, providing for the seizure of rebel property and the emancipation of Confederate slaves. In the House, Representative Thomas Eliot of Massachusetts offered a resolution calling on Lincoln to issue an order of general emancipation "whenever such action should be demanded by military necessities." Thaddeus Stevens submitted a bill to enlist 150,000 Negro troops in the Union ranks, and then delivered an impassioned plea for emancipation, arguing that the Union would never defeat the rebellion until it had freed the Confederacy's slaves. (Stevens hastened to reassure his colleagues that the freed Negroes would not invade the North because the northern climate was too cold for them.)

Carl Schurz conducted an informal poll of congressmen and found that most Republicans wanted the administration to adopt "a stronger and more openly pronounced anti-slavery policy." During a private meeting at the White House, Schurz urged the president to heed the growing sentiment for emancipation. Lincoln replied that he believed most northerners still opposed emancipation. "Would not the cry of 'abolition war,' such as might be occasioned by a distinct anti-slavery policy, tend to disunite those forces, and thus weaken the Union cause?" the president asked. To help him gauge the public's attitude, Lincoln asked Schurz to tour the North to sample opinion.

On January 29, George Templeton Strong and his colleagues on the New York Sanitary Commission—established to improve conditions at Union Army camps—called on Lincoln at the White House. Their business with the president did not take long, but Lincoln seemed eager to sit and talk with them about other matters. During the conversation, someone asked the president about the rising pressure for emancipation. "Wa-al," Lincoln replied, "that reminds me of a party of Methodist parsons that was travelling in Illinois when I was a boy thar, and had a branch to cross that was pretty bad—ugly to cross, ye know, because the waters was up. And they got considerin' and discussin' how they should git across it, and they talked about it for two hours, and one on 'em thought they had ought to cross one way when they got there, and another another way, and they got quarrelin' about it, till at last an old brother put in, and he says, says he, 'Brethren, this here talk ain't no use. I never cross a river until I come to it.'"

But the river was coming to Lincoln. As Union troops advanced, the number of runaway slaves increased dramatically. General Grant's advance through Kentucky and Tennessee brought hundreds of fugitive slaves into his camp. In the absence of orders from either Lincoln or Stanton, Grant was uncertain what to do with the contrabands. Several months earlier, his commanding officer, General Henry Wager Halleck, had issued orders to keep fugitive slaves out of the Union lines. Halleck feared that the Negroes were acting as Confederate spies, gathering information about the strength of Union troops and then reporting back to their rebel masters.

Halleck's views mattered little, though; individual officers followed their own preferences in dealing with runaways. William Tecumseh Sherman told one of his subordinates that it was "better to keep the negroes out of your camp altogether, unless you brought them along with the regiment." But another officer in the West granted asylum to runaway slaves, declaring, "I have no faith in Kentucky's loyalty, therefore have no great desire to protect her pet institution, slavery." Grant tried to walk a middle path by refusing to allow slaveowners to search his camp for fugitives, while prohibiting his own troops from forcibly emancipating slaves.

A more urgent situation existed in South Carolina's Sea Islands. There, nearly 10,000 former slaves abandoned by their masters received little comfort from Union Army commanders, who generally ignored them; by January, many of the Negroes were starving or seriously ill. They seemed to be the government's responsibility, but no federal department stepped forward to claim them. Abolitionists who wanted to use the freedmen as a test case—to prove that newly freed Negroes who were properly educated could survive on their own and lead productive lives— petitioned Secretary of the Treasury Chase to take up their cause. Motivated as much by the North's need for cotton as by humanitarian concerns, he agreed to launch the experiment.

Chase sent an attorney from Massachusetts named Edward Pierce to look into the situation on the islands. A personal friend of both Chase and Senator Sumner, Pierce had previously served with General Butler at Fortress Monroe, an experience that led him to write an article for the November 1861 issue of the *Atlantic Monthly* in which he praised the abilities of the contrabands. In response to the question, "Will the people of African descent work for a living?" Pierce reported that the Negroes at Fortress Monroe were eager to learn to read, and displayed a willingness to work as hard as whites if they were encouraged by the promise of payment. Pierce added that he believed the freedmen would make "good and responsible soldiers."

After spending several weeks in the Sea Islands, Pierce delivered his initial report to Chase on February 3. "The Negroes on the islands already had begun to awaken from the deadening impact of slavery," he wrote. But since they still needed white men to guide them through the transition to freedom, Pierce recommended the appointment of government superintendents to oversee the larger plantations and enforce "a paternal discipline" over the Negro workers. Privately, Pierce urged Chase to authorize the recruitment of teachers and ministers to educate the freedmen.

At Chase's suggestion, Pierce went to the Executive Mansion to discuss his report. Lincoln reacted with uncharacteristic gruffness. After a few minutes of Pierce's presentation, the president snapped that "he ought not to be troubled with such details." He complained that "there seemed to be a great itching to get Negroes within our lines," and the bothersome issue of contrabands was causing him trouble in Congress. The president grudgingly authorized Chase to give Pierce "such instructions in regard to Port Royal contrabands as may seem judicious," but Lincoln did not encourage the experiment. Neither did the congressmen whom Pierce met. Most of them, Pierce decided, were reluctant to address a question with such unforeseeable consequences for American society.

A week after his meeting with Pierce, Lincoln held a brief conference with General Butler, who was leading 1,500 troops to Louisiana to participate in a joint army-naval expedition to capture New Orleans. Butler noticed that Lincoln seemed distracted; two days earlier, the president's ten-year-old son, Willie, had died of a fever.

"Good-bye, General," Lincoln said. "Get into New Orleans if you can, and the backbone of the rebellion will be broken. It is of more importance than anything else that can now be done; but don't interfere with the slavery question, as Frémont has done at St. Louis."

"May I arm the negroes?" Butler asked.

"Not yet," Lincoln answered. "Not yet."

A Gradual Freedom

On the morning of March 6, Lincoln summoned Senator Sumner to the White House. The two men had developed a fruitful working relationship; Lincoln flattered Sumner by consulting him on foreign affairs and slavery, and the senator provided Lincoln with a sounding board for his proposals to Congress. Yet nearly a year after they met, Sumner remained bewildered by the president's manner and his cautious approach to emancipation. One of Sumner's friends often saw the senator pacing back and forth restlessly in his rooms, with his hands uplifted to heaven. "I pray that the President may be right in delaying," he said. "But I am afraid, I am almost sure, he is not. I trust his fidelity, but I cannot understand him."

After Sumner arrived on the morning of the sixth, Lincoln informed him that he wanted to read him a message he had prepared for Congress. "I want to know how you like it," Lincoln said. "I am going to send it in today." The president then read aloud a proposal to provide federal funds to any state that adopted a plan for the "gradual abolishment of slavery." Sumner was stunned. It was the first time an American president had asked Congress to adopt any emancipation measure. Although Sumner found some of the president's prose a bit clumsy ("aboriginal," he called it), the senator was so overcome that he kept reading the message over and over again until the president pried the manuscript away.

Lincoln aimed his proposal at the congressmen from border states, designing it to protect their states from the financial effects of the steady dissolution of slavery that had already begun. The plan was based on the president's conviction that since slavery was "the disease of the entire nation . . . all must share the suffering of its removal." Accordingly, the federal government would compensate slaveowners in any state that agreed to adopt a program of gradual emancipation. Lincoln admitted that he had not considered plans to free any slaves immediately. "In my judgment," he noted in the message, "gradual, and not sudden emancipation, is better for all."

Nor would the president force the border states to adopt his plan. As he had insisted since his election, the federal government had no authority to interfere with slavery within the states; "absolute control of the subject" remained with the citizens of each state. If any of the Union slave states did approve a program of gradual emancipation, however, Lincoln predicted that it would shorten the war significantly by disabusing Confederate officials of any hope that the border states would join the rebellion to protect slavery. "To deprive them of this hope, substantially ends the rebellion," Lincoln argued, "and the initiation of emancipation completely deprives them of it."

Lincoln concluded his message with a thinly veiled warning to border-state congressmen. Although he continued to resist immediate and forcible emancipation, he had pledged in his first annual message to employ "all indispensable means" to preserve the Union. If the rebellion continued, Lincoln noted, "the war must also continue; and it is impossible to foresee all the incidents, which may attend and all the ruin which may follow it."

Moderate Republicans greeted Lincoln's proposal warmly. The *Daily Alta California* in San Francisco called it "just the right thing, at the right time, and in the right place." The *New York Times*'s editor, Henry Raymond, described the president's plan as "a masterpiece of practical wisdom and sound policy."

Radical congressmen, though, denounced the president's message as a pale substitute for immediate emancipation. In the House, Thaddeus Stevens condemned it as "the most diluted milk-and-water-gruel proposition that was ever given to the American nation." Representative John Hickman of Pennsylvania charged that Lincoln's plan was "rather an excuse for non-action than an avowed determination to act." Outside Congress, Count Adam Gurowski dismissed the president's initiative as nothing more than a sop designed to forestall further criticism from abolitionists. "Every concession made by the President to the enemies of slavery has only one aim," Gurowski scoffed. "It is to mollify their urgent demands by throwing to them small crumbs, as one tries to mollify a boisterous and hungry dog."

Lincoln hoped the border-state congressmen would recognize the value of his proposal, but for several days they failed to respond at all.

Fearing that the legislators misunderstood his motives, Lincoln asked Montgomery Blair to invite a delegation from the border states to the Executive Mansion on March 10.

When the congressmen arrived, Lincoln assured them that he was trying to protect their interests in the midst of a difficult situation. Slavery was crumbling as a result of the war. "Immense armies were in the field," he said, "and must continue in the field as long as the war lasts." Wherever Union troops advanced through slave territory, they would inevitably attract runaway slaves. Already Union armies in Kentucky were employing contrabands to build wagon roads and fortifications; as the army's need for labor grew, so would the temptation to hold on to fugitive slaves or even recruit them.

As president, Lincoln found himself torn between the demands of antislavery activists to protect runaways, and Union slaveholders who insisted that the army return their property. Those slaveowners' complaints, Lincoln said, were "numerous, loud, and deep," and had become "a serious annoyance to him and embarrassing to the progress of the war." They irritated the rest of the northern public and kept alive the Confederates' hopes that the border states would join the rebellion. If the border states wanted to save the Union and their own financial interests, the president concluded, they should consider his proposal "in the same patriotic spirit in which it was made."

Still skeptical, the congressmen peppered Lincoln with questions. Was this measure a prelude to a program of general emancipation? Would the government colonize the former slaves after they were freed? What were the chances that Congress would appropriate sufficient funds for the program? At one point, someone asked the president directly how he felt about slavery. Lincoln replied that

> he did not pretend to disguise his antislavery feeling; that he thought it was wrong and should continue to think so; but that was not the question we had to deal with now. Slavery existed, and that, too, as well by the act of the North as of the South; and in any scheme to get rid of it, the North, as well as the South, was morally bound to do its full and equal share.

Nothing was accomplished. In the ensuing congressional debate, no legislator from a border state supported Lincoln's proposal. "I reject it now; I utterly spit at it and despise it," snorted Representative William H. Wadsworth of Kentucky. "Emancipation in the cotton States is simply an absurdity. . . . There is not enough power in the world to compel it to be done."

Congress eventually approved the president's plan by a wide margin, but almost entirely along party lines. Few Democrats favored the measure, and every congressman from Kentucky, Maryland, Missouri, and Delaware voted against it.

At least, Lincoln told Carl Schurz, his message had made it clear "what would inevitably come if the war continued." His proposal "was, perhaps, the last of the kind"; if the border states refused it, "theirs was the responsibility." There was none of the usual humor in Lincoln's face when he added, "an awful responsibility either way."

McClellan Moves

William Russell, the *London Times*'s correspondent, returned to Washington in early March after an extended visit to New York. He found affairs "very much as I had left them; the army recovering from the effect of the winter's sickness and losses, animated by the victories of their comrades in Western fields, and by the hope that the ever-coming tomorrow would see them in the field at last."

McClellan still had not budged. "What are you waiting for, Tardy George?" asked the lyrics of a popular song. Members of the Joint Committee on the Conduct of the War suspected that the Army of the Potomac was frozen less by the snow, frost, and mud that beset Washington than by McClellan's disloyalty. Rumors circulated that McClellan was a Confederate sympathizer, and that his plan to take his army on the circuitous route down the Rappahannock to Urbanna was actually a plot "conceived with the traitorous intent of . . . giving over to the enemy the capital and the government, thus left defenceless."

Since Lincoln no longer visited McClellan's headquarters, he summoned the general to the Executive Mansion on March 8 to answer this accusation. McClellan furiously denied the charge. He brought his twelve division commanders to the White House so that Lincoln and Stanton could question them individually on the merits of the Urbanna plan. When eight of the twelve supported McClellan, Lincoln allowed the general to proceed, although he still harbored grave reservations. "Going down the Bay in search of a field, instead of fighting at or near Manassas," Lincoln told McClellan, "was only shifting, and not surmounting, a difficulty . . . We would find the same enemy, and the same, or equal, intrenchments, at either place."

Before the day ended, the president issued General War Order No. 2, which divided the Army of the Potomac—now reaching an unwieldy size—into four corps. After consulting with congressional leaders, Lincoln personally named the four corps commanders; three of them opposed McClellan's Urbanna plan. The same evening, Lincoln wrote and issued General War Order No. 3, demanding that McClellan launch his advance by March 18, but forbidding the Army of the Potomac to leave Washington without leaving the capital "entirely secure."

Lincoln's sinking confidence in McClellan reached bottom the following day. Discerning McClellan's intention to outflank him, the Confederate general Joseph Johnston had stealthily withdrawn his forces southward from Manassas. As Union troops marched into the deserted town on March 9 in a pouring rain, singing "John Brown's Hymn," they discovered that the defenses that had paralyzed McClellan for months were mostly "Quaker guns," logs painted to look like artillery. It had all been a sham. For months, McClellan had insisted that the rebel defenders at Manassas numbered at least 100,000; evidence at the scene indicated there had been considerably less than half that number.

Lincoln was furious. "Old Abe is mad," reported Senator Chandler gleefully, "and the war will now go on." At a Cabinet meeting, Stanton announced that McClellan had been deliberately withholding information from him. The general, Stanton said, refused to tell him his plans. Moreover, the army's internal affairs reportedly were in a mess. Stanton said that a recent investigation had uncovered "great ignorance, negligence and lack of order and subordination—and reckless extravagance."

On the evening of March 11, Lincoln convened his top advisers—Stanton, Seward, and Chase—and announced that since McClellan was taking the field at the head of the Army of the Potomac, the president was relieving him of his duties as general in chief. Lincoln claimed it was a painful decision, but under the circumstances he thought he was doing McClellan "a very great kindness in permitting him to retain command of the Army of the Potomac, and giving him an opportunity to retrieve his errors."

For the time being, there would be no general in chief, only commanders of three separate departments, all of whom reported directly to Stanton. McClellan became commander of the Department of the Potomac. Lincoln consolidated the Union armies in the Mississippi Valley into the Department of the Mississippi, under the command of General Henry Halleck, who had taken the credit for capturing Forts Henry and Donelson. To satisfy the Radicals, the president awarded General Frémont command of the Mountain Department, in eastern Kentucky and Tennessee.

McClellan learned of his demotion from an aide, who read Lincoln's order in the *National Intelligencer*. The general accepted the action without a public protest. "I shall work just as cheerfully as ever before," he assured the president. Still, McClellan concluded that the politicians were conspiring against him. "The less I see of Washington," he decided, "the better."

Johnston's retreat from Manassas forced McClellan to alter his plans. Since the Confederate Army now blocked the path between Urbanna and Richmond, McClellan proposed to transport the Army of the Potomac all the way down Chesapeake Bay to Fortress Monroe, and then fight his way up the Virginia peninsula, using the Union navy to secure his supply line.

Lincoln still believed that McClellan should advance directly on Richmond, forcing a confrontation with the Confederate armies. The key to victory, in his view, was the destruction of the rebel forces, not the capture of the capital. Nevertheless, the president was not prepared to overrule McClellan and bear the responsibility if his own plan failed. So he allowed McClellan to proceed as long as the general left 40,000 troops behind to protect Washington.

On March 17, the Army of the Potomac—with more than 120,000 men, accompanied by 300 cannons, over 1,000 wagons, and 15,000 animals loaded onto 400 ships—began its journey down the Potomac River. "The Army is in magnificent spirits, & I think are half glad that I now belong to them alone," McClellan wrote to a friend. "*The President is all right,*" the general concluded generously. "He is my strongest friend."

Lincoln subsequently admitted to Senator Sumner that he let McClellan depart "very much against my judgment." Sumner was not pleased to hear it; McClellan, he believed, was an "utter incompetent."

Slavery and Diplomacy

When reports of Lincoln's message to Congress recommending gradual, compensated emancipation reached Europe in the middle of March, northern diplomats rejoiced. "The recommendation," wrote William Dayton, the American consul in Paris, "has made a most favorable impression in Europe. It is almost universally looked upon as the 'beginning of the end,' and that is much, although the end may be distant."

From the start of the war, the Lincoln administration's diplomatic representatives in Europe—many of whom were well-known antislavery activists—had urged the president to adopt a more aggressive policy against slavery. "It is my profound conviction," wrote Carl Schurz from Madrid, "that as soon as the war becomes distinctly one for and against slavery, public opinion [in Europe] will be so strongly, so overwhelmingly in our favor, that, in spite of commercial interests or secret spites, no European government will dare to place itself, by declaration or act, upon the side of a universally condemned institution."

Even before the attack on Fort Sumter, Confederate agents had been negotiating with European governments to purchase military supplies and obtain assistance in breaking the Union blockade, and ultimately diplomatic recognition. They hoped especially for help from Great Britain, then the strongest naval power in the world. Confederate officials knew that the Lancashire textile industry, which employed nearly 20 percent of British factory workers, relied almost exclusively on American cotton; they believed they could coerce Britain into recognizing the South's independence by withholding the cotton that fueled British prosperity.

Their hopes rose when the British cabinet, headed by Viscount Palmerston, declared its neutrality in the American conflict in May 1861. Palmerston's decision allowed both sides to purchase arms and obtain loans from private sources in Great Britain; since the Confederacy lacked sufficient factories to produce its own weapons, British neutrality clearly proved a boon to the South.

Palmerston's government decided not to intervene forcibly in the American conflict, however. "They who in quarrels interpose," quoted Palmerston, "will often get a bloody nose." The Confederates' calculations of King Cotton's power failed to reckon with the vast stockpiles of raw materials already in British warehouses at the start of the war, which kept textile mills running at full speed through 1861. Nor did Confederate officials fully comprehend the depth of antislavery feeling in Britain. The British government had abolished slavery in its empire thirty years earlier, and even the English aristocracy—so contemptuous of moneygrubbing Yankee society—balked at supporting what the Duke of Argyll called "the *Scoundrelism* of the South."

But Lincoln's refusal to define the war as a conflict to abolish slavery blurred the distinction between North and South in European eyes. The North's moral advantage eroded further when Secretary of State Seward specifically ordered American diplomats in Europe not to raise the issue of slavery or emancipation with their host governments.

By early 1862, American diplomats were warning Seward that the Union's failure to publicly embrace emancipation risked the loss of foreign support for their cause. The initial overwhelmingly pro-Union reaction of the Italian people had faded, wrote the American envoy in Turin, and "unless we soon place ourselves in a position to appeal to some other principle than that of mere legal right, we shall find ourselves altogether friendless." William Dayton warned Seward that the French monarch, Louis-Napoléon, was seriously considering intervention to help the Confederacy achieve its independence, even though the French people over-whelmingly opposed slavery. Carl Schurz resigned as minister to Madrid and hurried home to plead personally with Lincoln to put the war "upon a higher moral basis, and therefore give us the control of public opinion in Europe." Cassius Clay had earlier left his post in Moscow to provide Lincoln with similar advice.

Confederate propaganda took full advantage of the Union government's reluctance to discuss slavery. Southern agents in Paris insisted that both the Union and the Confederacy favored the perpetuation of slavery. In February 1862, Charles Francis Adams, the United States ambassador to Great Britain, warned Seward that several Confederate diplomats in London were hinting that their government would inaugurate a program of gradual emancipation after it gained its independence. British newspaper editors who sympathized with the Confederacy gave the rumor wide circulation.

Seward refused to alter his policy. In a lengthy note to Adams, he replied angrily that he still saw no reason why the Union government should explicitly proclaim its opposition to slavery. "Although the war has not been waged against slavery," Seward wrote, anyone could see that a victory for the North would weaken the institution. Already Union armies were acting as "an emancipation crusade," encouraging slaves to free themselves. "To proclaim the crusade is unnecessary," he added, "and it would even be inexpedient, because it would deprive us of the needful and legitimate support of the friends of the Union who are not opposed to slavery, but who prefer Union without slavery to disunion with slavery."

An attempt to promote emancipation, Seward warned, might provoke slave revolts in the South. "Does France or does Great Britain want to see a social revolution here, with all its horrors, like the slave revolution in Santo Domingo?" he asked. Better to trust in the victory of Union armies to eradicate slavery on a piecemeal basis, Seward suggested. With McClellan and the Army of the Potomac finally en route to Norfolk, and General Halleck's troops descending both banks of the Mississippi, the secretary of state felt confident that "the insurrectionary government must very soon fall and disappear."

Even without a declaration of emancipation, news of the victories at Fort Henry and Fort Donelson strengthened the Union cause in Britain. "Nowhere has the condition of the western campaign been productive of better effects than in this country," reported Ambassador Adams on March 21. "People are changing their notions of the power of the country to meet such a trial." European observers who read about McClellan's expedition down the Potomac marveled at the immense size of the Union armies mobilized in March 1862. "As our swarm of armies strike deeper and deeper into the South," confirmed Henry Adams, the ambassador's younger son, "the contest is beginning to take to Europeans proportions of grandeur and perfection like nothing of which they ever heard or read."

Manassas Redux

McClellan reached Fortress Monroe on April 2. He left behind in Washington a growing chorus of critics. "The outcry opened against General McClellan, since the enemy's retreat from Manassas, is really terrible, and almost universal," wrote Nathaniel Hawthorne. Secretary of War Stanton, who met twice with the Joint Committee on the Conduct of the War during this time, declared McClellan "a dead failure" and told Senator Orville Browning that the general ought to have been removed long ago. After members of the Joint Committee toured the deserted Confederate defenses at Manassas, "they were certain," reported Congressman George Julian, "that [McClellan's] heart was not in the work."

Browning asked Lincoln if he harbored any doubts about McClellan's patriotism. The president replied that he had no reason to do so, yet he believed McClellan "was not sufficiently energetic and aggressive in his measures." McClellan could prepare well for a battle, Lincoln said, "but as the hour for action approached, he became nervous and oppressed with the responsibility and hesitated to meet the crisis."

The Manassas scenario repeated itself when McClellan approached the rebel defenses at Yorktown, at the southern tip of the Virginia peninsula. The Confederate commander, General John Magruder, had only about 13,000 men, against the 55,000 Union troops that already had

landed outside Yorktown. To fool McClellan into thinking he faced superior numbers, Magruder kept his troops marching constantly from one
spot on the defensive line to another, showing themselves at every opportunity, and shifting their artillery as noisily as possible.

McClellan hesitated. Deprived of General McDowell's entire division,
(which Lincoln kept in the Washington area), and another 10,000 men
detached to reinforce Frémont's army in the mountains, McClellan felt
too weak to attack. So he dug in for a lengthy siege.

"The little Napoleon sits trembling before the handful of men at Yorktown," mocked the president's secretary, John Hay, "afraid either to fight
or run." Lincoln could not hide his impatience. "I think it is the precise
time for you to strike a blow," Lincoln telegraphed to McClellan on April
9. Further delay would permit the rebels to reinforce their forces and
strengthen their defenses. "And once more," Lincoln warned, "let me tell
you, it is indispensable to *you* that *you* strike a blow. *I* am powerless to help
this."

> You will do me the justice to remember I always insisted, that going
> down the Bay in search of a field, instead of fighting at or near Man-
> assas, was only shifting, and not surmounting, a difficulty—that we
> would find the same enemy, and the same, or equal, entrenchments,
> at either place. The country will not fail to note—is now noting—that
> the present hesitation to move upon an intrenched enemy, is but the
> story of Manassas repeated.

McClellan told his wife that the president had instructed him to
"break the enemy's lines" without delay. "I was much tempted to reply,"
McClellan confessed, "that he had better come & do it himself."

So the siege continued. Meanwhile, news came from the west of the
terrible battle of Shiloh, where a Confederate army caught General Grant
unaware. Union casualties in the two-day battle surpassed 13,000, more
than double the total of all the previous battles since the war began. Northerners who had lauded Grant for capturing Fort Henry and Fort Donelson
now denounced him as a butcher. Rumors began to circulate that Grant

had returned to his prewar drinking habits. Lincoln refused to listen. "I can't spare this man," he told a visitor to the White House. "He fights."

And so, complained Horace Greeley, "we shuffle and trifle on, and let the Union go to ruin."

Freedom in the Capital

Radical Republican congressmen viewed McClellan's peninsula campaign with mixed emotions. On one hand, they relished the opportunity to defeat a rebel army in battle, to redeem the disgrace of Manassas. If the Army of the Potomac could push north to Richmond and capture the Confederate capital, the rebellion might collapse.

Yet the Radicals did not want McClellan, a Democrat, to receive credit for the decisive victory. Nor did they wish the conflict to end with slavery still intact. They knew that the war represented their best chance to attain emancipation. They also feared that Lincoln—who they believed was "too easy and amiable, and . . . misled by the malign influence of Kentucky counselors"—would accept a negotiated peace restoring the Confederate states to the Union while allowing them to retain slavery. "Patch up a compromise now, leaving the germ of evil, and it will soon again overrun the whole South, even if you free three-fourths of the slaves," warned Thaddeus Stevens in the House. "Your peace would be a curse. You would have expended countless treasures and untold lives in vain."

"Our accounts say that at Washington the contest is getting very bitter," reported Henry Adams from London. "The men who lead the extreme Abolitionists are a rancorous set. They have done their worst . . . to over-ride the Administration rough-shod." Day after day, Stevens and his Radical colleagues descended on the White House to urge Lincoln to free the slaves. "Stevens, Sumner, and Wilson, simply haunt me with their importunities for a Proclamation of Emancipation," Lincoln told Senator John Henderson of Missouri. "Wherever I go and whatever way I turn, they are on my trail, and still in my heart, I have the deep conviction that the hour has not yet come." It reminded him, he said, of an incident in his childhood, when he and his schoolmates were reading passages from the Bible:

Our lesson one day was the story of the Israelites who were thrown into the fiery furnace and delivered by the hand of the Lord without so much as the smell of fire upon their garments.

It fell to one little fellow to read the verses in which occurred for the first time in the chapter the names of Shadrach, Meshach, and Abednego. Little Bud stumbled on Shadrach, floundered on Meshach, and went all to pieces on Abednego. Instantly the hand of the master dealt him a cuff on the side of the head and left him wailing and blubbering, as the next boy in line took up the reading.

But before the girl at the end of the line had done reading, he had subsided into sniffles and finally become quiet. His blunders and disgrace were forgotten by the others of the class until his turn was approaching to read again. Then like a thunderclap out of a clear sky, he set up a wail which alarmed even the master, who with rather unusual gentleness, asked what was the matter now. Pointing with a shaking finger at the verse which a few moments later, would fall to him to read, Bud managed to quaver out, "Look there, marster, there comes them same damn three fellows again!"

Congress could not free the slaves in any state, but it did possess authority to legislate for the District of Columbia and the western territories. For years, abolitionists had denounced the presence of slavery and public slave markets in the nation's capital. In 1862, there were still nearly 3,000 slaves in Washington, most of whom were household servants, many with more than a trace of white blood. The local government's practice of lodging itinerant contrabands in the appallingly unsanitary conditions of the local jail further fueled the Radicals' outrage.

In early March, Congress took up a bill to abolish slavery in the District of Columbia. Introduced by Senator Wilson, the measure provided payment to loyal owners of $300 per slave, provided they freed their property within ninety days; after that time, they would receive no compensation. At Lincoln's request, the Senate added a rider offering steamship tickets to any freed slaves who wished to emigrate to Haiti or Liberia.

Radicals made no secret of their intention to use emancipation in the capital as a springboard to abolition throughout the South. To end the war, Senator Sumner predicted, slavery "must be suppressed at every cost, and if its suppression here [in the District of Columbia] endangers slavery elsewhere, there will be a new motive for determined action."

Residents of Washington fought the measure with petitions and letters. Local newspapers published editorials denouncing the bill; both the *Washington Star* and the *Intelligencer* argued that immediate emancipation would impose an unfair tax burden on residents to care for Negroes who could not cope with the demands of freedom. Besides, argued the *Star*, $300 per slave was a grossly inadequate price.

Washington's mayor and board of aldermen pleaded with Congress not to pass the bill. They feared it would make the capital, located between the slaveholding states of Maryland and Virginia, "an asylum for free negroes, a population undesirable in every American community, and which it has been deemed necessary to exclude altogether from some even of the non-slaveholding states." If that happened, Washington would become "a hell on earth for the white man." Congressional galleries, they predicted, would be filled with Negroes, making them unfit for white women.

As Wilson's bill neared a vote in the Senate in late March 1862, the president informed Horace Greeley that he favored the abolition of slavery in the capital but wanted to reserve for himself "the time and manner of doing it." He also disliked the threatening tone of the Radicals' legislation and some of the accompanying speeches in Congress. "If I were to suggest anything," Lincoln told Greeley, "it would be that as the North are already for the measure, we should urge it *persuasively,* and not *menacingly,* upon the South."

Congress ignored his advice. After rejecting the Democrats' proposed amendments, Congress approved the District emancipation bill on April 12—the anniversary of the Confederate attack on Fort Sumter. The vote followed party lines closely: more than 95 percent of Republicans voted for the measure, while over 90 percent of Democrats opposed it.

Lincoln was not entirely satisfied with the bill. "It should have been for gradual emancipation," he told Senator Browning. "Now families would at once be deprived of cooks, stable boys, etc., and they of their protectors without any provision for them." The president told Congress that the provisions for compensation and colonization pleased him—"I am so far behind the Sumner lighthouse," Lincoln admitted, "that I will stick to my old colonization hobby"—but he suggested that the government could save money be reducing the payment for less valuable slaves, including infants and insane persons.

Lincoln agreed to approve the measure, but he waited two days before signing it. A former government official, he explained, "had two family servants with him who were sickly and who would not be benefited by freedom." The official had gone to the White House to request a brief delay so he could get his slaves out of the city, and Lincoln obliged him.

"Lincoln has signed the Emancipation Bill," wrote George Templeton Strong in his diary. "Only the damndest of 'damned abolitionists' dreamed of such a thing a year ago. Perhaps the name of abolitionist will be less disgraceful a year hence. . . . The federal government is now clear of all connection with slaveholding."

In Washington, a free Negro went to tell a slave woman that the government had set her free. He found her with another slave, "talking relative to the Bill expressing doubts of its passage & when I entered they perceived that something was ahead and immediately asked me 'Whats the news?'. The Districts free says I pulling out the 'National Republican' and reading its editorial when I had finished the chambermaid left the room sobbing for joy. The slave woman clapped her hands and shouted, left the house saying 'let me go and tell my husband that Jesus has done all things well.' . . . Were I a drinker I would go on a Jolly spree today but as a Christian I can but kneel in prayer and bless God for the privilege I've enjoyed this day."

Washington's provost marshal, General William Doster, watched the exodus of slaveowners from the District. They seemed to him "like a master whose house is burning and carries his furniture from room to room, unable to comprehend the system as doomed and bound to go down." Military authorities had orders to prevent the forcible removal of slaves, and many Negroes simply refused to accompany their masters out of town. Their owners attempted to persuade them to go on a visit to Baltimore or across the Anacostia River into Maryland. Some who succeeded later lost their investment—and any chance at compensation—when their slaves escaped back into the District and freedom.

Numerous slaveowners who remained in Washington persuaded their Negroes to remain as servants, working for wages. Other freed Negroes joined army officers as cooks or valets; a smaller number, willing to forgo the guarantee of governmental protection, headed north. Life for freedmen in the District improved several weeks later when Congress forced the repeal of the most repressive aspects of the city's black codes, permitting Negroes to operate their own businesses and testify in local courts.

Contrabands who had worked all their lives as field hands on southern plantations possessed few marketable skills, however. To help them survive, and to protect the community from "irresponsible" and uneducated Negroes, white Washingtonians founded the Freedmen's Relief Association, dedicated to providing ex-slaves with "clothing, temporary homes, and employment, and, as far as possible, to teach them to read and write, and bring them under moral influences." In May, Congress passed a law requiring officials in Washington and Georgetown to establish public schools for Negro children. They were supposed to fund the schools by taxing property owned by Negroes, but since all the local tax revenues were collected into a single fund, officials could give the Negro schools as much or as little as they wished.

"I trust I am not dreaming," Frederick Douglass told Senator Sumner upon hearing that slavery in Washington was dead. An editorial in the newspaper *Anglo-African* proclaimed that Americans "can now hold up their heads when interrogated as to what the Federal Government is fighting for, and answer, 'There, look at our Capital and see what we have fought for.'"

But some observers noticed signs of a backlash among moderates in Congress. His Radical colleagues, complained Senator Fessenden, were "so much engaged in 'abolishing slavery under the war power,' in 'confiscating the property of rebels,' and . . . purchasing negroes in the border states, that practical measures have lost their interest. I am getting to be considered a 'conservative'; pretty soon I shall be a pro-slavery member."

5

LINCOLN'S TIGHTROPE

General McClellan besieged Yorktown for four weeks. Determined to avoid the errors of overly aggressive European commanders he had witnessed as an official American observer during the Crimean campaigns nearly a decade earlier, McClellan spent long hours meticulously directing the placement of artillery and the construction of earthworks. The thoroughness of the Union activity amazed the Confederate general Joe Johnston, who knew how weak the rebel defenses were. "No one but McClellan," Johnston muttered, "could have hesitated to attack."

McClellan would not be hurried. "I feel that the fate of a nation depends upon me," he wrote to his wife on May 3. McClellan's plans called for the siege to conclude with a spectacular bombardment by his heavy guns, scheduled to begin on May 5. But before the artillery barrage began, Johnston ordered the Confederate forces to evacuate Yorktown.

McClellan failed to cut them off. An unexpected attack by the rebel rearguard at Williamsburg threw him off balance, and by the time McClellan recovered, heavy rains made the roads impassable. So he paused again and telegraphed Washington for reinforcements.

In Richmond, Confederate officials began to panic. They knew the Army of the Potomac significantly outnumbered Johnston's forces, and

President Jefferson Davis had no more confidence in Johnston's abilities than Lincoln had in McClellan. Domestic problems were mounting, too. Confederate currency was depreciating rapidly; the congress in Richmond was preparing to invoke martial law and conscription; and there seemed to be little hope of relief from abroad. Critics sniped at Davis, who quarreled publicly with both Johnston and General Pierre Beauregard.

"We have reached a very dark hour," wrote one reporter in Richmond. Fearing an imminent Union attack on the capital, gentlemen sent their wives and children out of the city, and the government transported many of its official records to safer locations in the Deep South. Morale among Confederate troops sank as Yankees proved they were not the cowards southerners had expected. "The romance of the thing is entirely worn off," complained a rebel soldier in the Shenandoah Valley, "not only with myself but with the whole army."

Lincoln had his own worries. Except for the capture of New Orleans—the largest and richest city in the Confederacy—by General Ben Butler and Admiral David Farragut on April 25, Union armies seemed to have stalled on all fronts. The president could not sleep well at night. He was losing weight, and Browning reported that Lincoln looked "weary, care-worn and troubled." A doctor visiting the White House advised the president not to neglect his health. "Well," Lincoln replied, "I cannot take my vittles regular. I kind o' just browze round."

To escape the pressures of Washington and obtain a firsthand view of conditions on the Virginia peninsula, Lincoln accepted Stanton's suggestion that they take a brief excursion to Fortress Monroe. On the evening of May 5, the two men, along with Secretary of the Treasury Chase and a navy escort, set sail in a revenue cutter down the Potomac River. Arriving at the fort twenty-four hours later, Lincoln discovered that the local commander, General John Wool (who was nearly eighty years old), had recently ignored a promising opportunity to capture the city of Norfolk.

So Lincoln and his two Cabinet officers scanned the maps and planned an amphibious attack on the city. After ordering a bombardment of Norfolk, the three men took a tugboat and scouted out possible landing sites. At one point Lincoln stepped out of the boat onto Virginia soil and strolled for a few minutes along the Atlantic beach. The following day, Union troops waded ashore and captured Norfolk, although most of the rebel defenders were already gone. "So has ended a brilliant week's campaign of the President," boasted Chase to his daughter in Washington.

South Carolina Freedmen

Charles Francis Adams, Jr., spent the spring of 1862 on Port Royal Island—one of South Carolina's Sea Islands—as a cavalry officer in a Massachusetts regiment. The island, he wrote to his brother in England, was "naturally one of the most delightful places in the world," particularly in springtime. Mockingbirds, hares, wild pigeons, quail, duck, and plover seemed to start from every field; swamps contained alligators, huge turtles, and exotic snakes.

"One can ride indefinitely over this island and never exhaust its infinite cross-roads and out-of-the-way plantations," continued Adams, "but you cannot ride fifteen minutes in any direction, however new, without stumbling over the two great facts of the day, pickets and contrabands." The future of the 10,000 former slaves on the Sea Islands remained unsettled, but Adams was certain of one thing: "Here, in this little island, all around us, has begun the solution of this tremendous 'nigger' question."

Private philanthropic organizations, such as the American Missionary Association and the New York Freedmen's Relief Association, were enlisting eager northern volunteers to minister to the physical and spiritual needs of the freedmen of Port Royal. Many of the recruits were college or divinity students, or well-educated young women, devoted to demonstrating the superiority of free labor over slavery. They knew that the government had not decided the future of slavery in the Sea Islands, but they hoped that by educating freedmen and training them to be independent, they would make it more difficult to return Negroes to slavery.

The first wave of missionaries arrived at Port Royal in March 1862. Their initial impressions of Port Royal and their Negro charges were not generous. One noted the absence of even primitive machinery, such as windmills to grind corn; all labor was performed by Negro hands. "Slavery is written upon the shore, the trees, the sky, the air," wrote his wife. "There steals over you the feeling that you are passing under a great cloud of accumulated wrongs in which you are mysteriously implicated, the vague feeling that you yourself have done something awful, somewhere in the past. . . . "

Contact with Negroes elicited such descriptions as "sly," "docile and submissive," and "wretched and stupid enough"; one young teacher from Boston saw them as "a race of stunted, misshapen children" whose only counterparts in white society were the Irish immigrants back home. Adams shared this judgment. The Negroes, he wrote, "are just such as the white has made them and as we have heard them described. They are intelligent enough, but their intelligence too often takes the form of low cunning. They lie and steal and are fearfully lazy; but they will work for money and indeed are anxious to get work. . . . They are not brave, and they are not fierce—these qualities the white man took out of them generations ago, and in taking them deprived the African of the capacity for freedom. . . . They are indolent, shiftless, unable to take care of themselves and plundered by every comer—in short, they are slaves. For the present they must be provided for."

Agents appointed by the Treasury Department organized the freedmen into work gangs, setting them to plant and tend the cotton fields as they had done under their southern masters; even the antebellum prohibition against traveling from one plantation to another without a permit was retained. At the end of April, the freedmen received a small cash payment for their labor, although government officials withheld part of their wages to ensure that they would continue to work in the fields.

Behind all the regulations and restrictions lay an assumption by civilian and military authorities that the Negroes could not yet be trusted to live on their own. Nevertheless, the introduction of more efficient methods of production was breaking down the antiquated reliance upon manual labor. Adams feared the transition would render the freedmen irrelevant.

"My impression from what I see," he reported, "is that Emancipation as a Government measure would be a terrible calamity to the blacks as a race; that rapid emancipation as the result of an economic revolution destroying their value as agricultural machines would be a calamity, though less severe; and finally, that the only transition to freedom absolutely beneficial to them as a race would be one proportioned in length to the length of their captivity. . . . The blacks must be cared for or they will perish, and who is to care for them when they cease to be of value?"

Major General David Hunter offered an answer. In March, Secretary of War Stanton appointed Hunter—a West Point graduate from Illinois—commander of the Department of the South, which consisted of the coastal areas of Florida, Georgia, and South Carolina under Union control, including the Sea Islands. Hunter had served as one of Lincoln's bodyguards on his preinaugural train ride from Springfield to Washington, and as Frémont's replacement after the imbroglio over emancipation in Missouri. Following Cameron's dismissal from the Cabinet, Hunter cultivated a close relationship with Stanton; one reporter characterized him as a "hanger-on at Washington, doing dirty jobs for the War Department."

Hunter never hid his support for emancipation and the use of freed slaves as troops. "It is time slavery had its quietus," Hunter insisted in a letter of December 9, 1861, to Senator Trumbull. "We have been trifling long enough."

In a private conference with Stanton before leaving for South Carolina, Hunter made it clear that he wished to strike a blow for freedom. "Please let me have my own way on the subject of slavery," he pleaded. "The administration will not be responsible. I alone will bear the blame; you can censure me, arrest me, dismiss me, hang me if you will, but permit me to make my mark in such a way as to be remembered by friend and foe."

On April 13, about two weeks after arriving at Port Royal, Hunter clarified the status of the Sea Islands contrabands by declaring that all Negroes formerly held as slaves by rebel masters "are hereby confiscated and declared free." Lincoln did not object; Hunter's action fell within the spirit, if not the letter, of the Confiscation Act.

Hunter then began recruiting former slaves into a special army unit known as the First South Carolina Volunteers. He planned to take the Negro troops to Hilton Head, where the army would outfit them in distinctive dark blue jackets and scarlet pants (which Stanton purchased from France on short notice), although they would not receive weapons.

Stanton knew of Hunter's intentions; so did Senator Sumner, who remarked that "this looks in the right direction."

But the freedmen proved reluctant to enlist, partly because they were unsure of the army's plans for them. Even if they did join the service, missionaries doubted that the Negroes would ever make decent soldiers. "I don't believe you could make soldiers of these men at all," reported one. "They are afraid, and they know it." Another white teacher decided that "Negroes—plantation negroes, at least—will never make soldiers in one generation. Five white men could put a [Negro] regiment to flight."

Hunter decided to try his experiment anyway, but first he needed to encourage potential recruits. Without consulting Lincoln, the general issued a proclamation on May 9 emancipating every slave in South Carolina, Georgia, and Florida. Hunter explained that the three states were under martial law, and since "slavery and martial law in a free country are altogether incompatible," all slaves in his Department were declared "forever free"—and eligible for military service.

He defended his proclamation on the grounds of military necessity. Hunter told Senator Fessenden, whose son served on Hunter's staff, that he saw no reason why the army should not use Negro guards instead of white troops to patrol cotton plantations; besides, an emancipation decree would encourage slaves to flee and deprive the rebels of a vital labor supply behind the lines.

Hunter kept his edict secret for three days, so the freedmen could not flee before his recruiting officers arrived. Early on the morning of May 12, companies of Union troops fanned out across the Sea Islands, spreading the good news and encouraging every able-bodied newly freed Negro male to join the army. They offered free plugs of tobacco and half-dollar pieces to recruits, but few freedmen volunteered. A rumor spread among the terrified Negroes that the army was planning to send them to Cuba to be sold into slavery again. Sometimes an entire plantation's workers sought refuge in the woods, but to no avail. According to Edward Pierce, Union soldiers took many men from the cotton fields at gunpoint, without giving them a chance to retrieve their personal belongings.

In Washington, Lincoln and his Cabinet turned a blind eye to

Hunter's formation of the First South Carolina Volunteers. Lincoln did not ignore Hunter's emancipation edict, however. The president refused to allow any military official to usurp his authority on emancipation. On May 17, the president sent a curt reply to Chase: "No commanding general shall do such a thing, upon *my* responsibility, without consulting me." In his public statement (written with Stanton) rescinding Hunter's order, Lincoln explained that he had not known of Hunter's proclamation in advance, nor had he authorized anyone to free any slaves.

It was possible, Lincoln added, that the president—as commander in chief—might possess the authority to emancipate the slaves of any states in order to preserve the Union. That was a question, he said, "which, under my responsibility, I reserve to myself, and which I can not feel justified in leaving to the decision of commanders in the field."

The rest of Lincoln's public statement was a plea to border-state congressmen to reconsider their rejection of his gradual, compensated emancipation plan of March 6. The implication was clear. The war was killing slavery; already one could see a "strong tendency to a total disruption of society in the South." If the conflict continued, the pressure for sudden, forcible emancipation would grow, and Lincoln admitted that he could not withstand it indefinitely.

Some Radical congressmen, including Thaddeus Stevens, assailed Lincoln for revoking Hunter's proclamation. The nineteen-year-old abolitionist orator Anna Dickinson, who drew immense crowds wherever she spoke, charged that the president was "not so far from [being] a slave catcher after all."

Yet other antislavery spokesmen rejoiced that the president at last publicly acknowledged and accepted the imminent death of slavery. "Let no one be discouraged nor alienated because of this Presidential step," declared Horace Greeley in an editorial in the *New York Tribune* on May 20. If border-state congressmen continued to reject Lincoln's proposal, Greeley wrote, "they and the whole country may know what to expect. 'The stars in their courses fight against' Slavery, and its doom is sure."

Senator Grimes delivered the same message to his colleagues. The long-awaited hour of emancipation, Grimes predicted, was finally on the horizon—"protracted by the obstinacy and stupidity of rulers it may be, but come it will nevertheless."

Fair Oaks

On May 23, the Army of the Potomac stood within seven miles of Richmond. "Our progress has been slow," McClellan admitted to General Ambrose Burnside, "but that is due to ignorance of the country (we have to feel our way everywhere; the maps are worthless), [and] the narrowness, small number, and condition of the roads, which become impassable for trains after a day's rain, of which we have had a great deal."

McClellan continued to overestimate the strength of the enemy. "All accounts report their numbers as greatly exceeding our own," he telegraphed to Lincoln, even though the Army of the Potomac actually numbered nearly 100,000 men, while the Confederate general Joe Johnston could count on only 65,000. So McClellan continued to beg Lincoln for reinforcements, especially to restore McDowell's forces to his command. "That effort," McClellan argued, "would do more to protect Washington than his whole force can possibly do anywhere else in the field."

Still, McClellan was in good spirits. His steady advance up the Virginia peninsula was exerting pressure on the rebel forces. The Confederate congress prepared to evacuate the capital, and Jefferson Davis sent his family out of the city. In Washington, the House of Representatives passed a resolution—sponsored by the abolitionist Owen Lovejoy—praising the general "for the display of those high military qualities which secure important results with but little sacrifice of human life."

Like many northerners, McClellan assumed that the capture of Richmond would essentially end the rebellion. Already Stanton had suspended recruiting to preserve the government's dwindling funds. And McClellan knew that if the war ended soon, it would end with slavery intact, especially since Lincoln had revoked General Hunter's emancipation decree.

As McClellan crept northward, McDowell's army moved south from Washington toward Richmond, always prepared—on Lincoln's orders—to defend the capital against a sudden Confederate assault. On May 23,

Lincoln rode down to Fredericksburg to confer with McDowell. While he was there, General George Meade commended the president for rescinding Hunter's order. "I am trying to do my duty," Lincoln replied, "but no one can imagine what influences are brought to bear on me."

Lincoln left McDowell's camp at dusk that evening. By the time he returned to Washington, news had reached the capital that the Confederate general Thomas "Stonewall" Jackson had routed a Union force at Front Royal, in western Virginia, and was advancing rapidly through the Shenandoah Valley.

Stanton and Lincoln both assumed that Jackson intended to make an all-out assault on Washington; the capital, concluded Stanton, "is the only object now worth a desperate throw." Someone started a rumor that the entire Confederate Army was marching toward Washington. Newsboys ran through the streets of the city the next day shouting the headline, "Washington in danger!" As 4,000 home guards and local militiamen— many lacking ammunition—mustered for action, Stanton sent telegrams to officials in Maryland and Pennsylvania, pleading for reinforcements.

Major B. B. French, who was responsible for the security of Washington's public buildings, refused to panic, whiling away the time playing euchre or relaxing in his garden. But Lincoln lost his nerve. The president telegraphed McDowell to suspend his movement against Richmond and send 20,000 troops to support Frémont in the Shenandoah Valley. On May 25, Lincoln informed McClellan that he had withdrawn the bulk of McDowell's forces from the Fredericksburg area. "I think the time is near," the anxious president told McClellan, "when you must either attack Richmond or give up the job and come to the defence of Washington."

McClellan did neither. Railing against the nervous civilian authorities in Washington ("It is perfectly sickening to deal with such people," he muttered), the general refused to allow either Lincoln or Jackson to distract him from his methodical advance against Richmond. "The net is quietly closing," McClellan wrote to his wife on May 26, "& some fish will soon be caught."

Five days later, Johnston surprised McClellan with a sudden strike against his left wing. In the ensuing battle of Fair Oaks, Confederate casualties (6,100 dead or wounded) exceeded Union losses (5,000), a rare occurrence in the eastern theater. Poor tactical decisions by both commanders contributed to the high casualty figures, but the disparity in losses was primarily due to the Army of the Potomac's superior equipment—specifically, newly acquired Springfield rifles with four times the range of the Confederate troops' smoothbore muskets.

Shaken by the loss of life, McClellan mourned "the sickening sight of the battlefield, with its mangled corpses & poor suffering wounded." Once again, he telegraphed Washington for reinforcements. Having recovered from the brief invasion scare, Lincoln promised to send McClellan as many troops as he could spare for a final push toward Richmond.

A Capital Summer

In the first days of June, thousands of Union casualties from Fair Oaks—many of whom had lain on the swampy shores of the James River for up to forty-eight hours with no medical attention—passed through Washington on their way to hospitals farther north. Most of the capital's limited medical facilities for troops were makeshift affairs, tents or buildings hurriedly converted from other uses. Construction had recently begun on numerous military hospitals, but until they were completed, military authorities had to house sick and wounded soldiers in churches, schools, the halls of the Capitol, the city's insane asylum, and Robert E. Lee's deserted mansion in Alexandria.

When Walt Whitman arrived in Washington, he saw wounded men billeted in the Patent Office, lying between display cases filled with scale models of mechanical inventions. It was, Whitman noted, "a curious scene, especially at night when lit up. The glass cases, the beds, the sick, the gallery above, and the marble pavement under foot—the suffering and the fortitude to bear it in various degrees—occasionally, from some, the groan that could not be repress'd." At night, Negroes drove carts loaded with dead soldiers to the city's cemeteries.

Rebel prisoners were lodged in the Old Capitol jail, where local officials had recently housed contraband Negroes. On the corner of Pennsylvania and Fifteenth Street, Hammack's Restaurant displayed one of the Confederate wooden "Quaker guns" from Manassas. A jewelry store nearby exhibited the "bulletproof" vest of a dead southern soldier; sightseers could detect the small hole where a minié ball had pierced the steel. Enterprising Washington merchants sold Confederate banknotes as souvenirs, which city residents predicted might soon be more valuable than northern currency.

Prices of consumer goods in Washington continued to rise, especially the cost of fresh fish, since fishermen were reluctant to venture past the Confederate artillery that dominated the lower Potomac. Gold and silver coins had disappeared from circulation, hoarded by speculators. The national government's paper money—known as greenbacks—provided the most stable medium of exchange, but northern cities also issued their own banknotes in small denominations. Merchants viewed these notes with skepticism and placed strict limits on the amount of change they would give customers who used large-denomination state notes. Recently, Congress had approved postage stamps as legal tender, but Washingtonians found the small, sticky stamps messy and inconvenient.

In other ways, though, the war benefited Washington. To enhance the city's appearance and encourage a patriotic spirit, Congress appropriated thousands of dollars to complete the Treasury Building, expand the War Department and Navy Department buildings, and repair and renovate the Capitol basement after Union troops finished using its furnaces as a bakery. Judiciary Square, on the north side of Pennsylvania Avenue, received a much-needed face-lift. Construction recommenced on the aqueduct to the Potomac over Rock Creek.

Washington was losing its outward layer of southern gentility; efficiency became the new watchword. A recently completed street railway ran along Pennsylvania Avenue, with iron tracks creasing the middle of the boulevard from the Capitol to the redbrick State Department building on Seventeenth Street. In the summer, residents rode in long open cars; for cooler weather, officials of the Washington and Georgetown Street Railroad Company purchased closed cars with velvet seats and damask curtains. The company underestimated the demand for the new service, however, and in the early summer of 1862, many cars were crowded beyond capacity. Initially restricted to white passengers, the cars were opened to Negro riders after Senator Sumner pushed through Congress legislation barring discrimination on the line. A conductor who tried to prevent the Negro abolitionist Sojourner Truth from riding the streetcar line was fired and later arrested.

In June, the federal government established an agency to supervise Washington's growing population of fugitive slaves, now numbering nearly 3,000. Headquartered in an old army barracks at Twelfth and O Streets in the northern part of the city, the agency provided contrabands with passes that guaranteed them military protection against arrest as runaways. It also hired able-bodied male Negroes to work—for forty cents a day—on local street repairs, at the army's corrals, or in army hospitals. Although northern businessmen frequently sent requests for cheap labor, the head of the agency, Reverend D. B. Nichols, reported that "not one in a hundred" of the contrabands could be persuaded to go north. Still, nearly all of the Negroes—most of whom were former field slaves—were willing to work on local projects, although few saved their earnings. They were, Nichols concluded, "a docile people."

White Washingtonians aimed to keep them subservient, especially after Congress forced repeal of the city's black codes. In the summer of 1862, a congressional committee discovered that in the absence of slavery in the nation's capital, white prejudice against Negroes grew stronger. Whites were quick to file criminal complaints against Negroes, especially for theft, and gangs of white thugs attacked Negroes with increasing frequency.

As the summer heat returned to Washington, the president's family deserted the city for the more congenial climate of Maryland. On a hilltop two and a half miles north of the city stood the Soldiers' Home, a large stone building that sheltered disabled homeless Union veterans. At this elevation the air was considerably purer than the noxious vapors of the Potomac flats.

Beginning in 1862, Mrs. Lincoln and her nine-year-old son, Tad, spent most of their summers in one of the two-story Gothic-style stone cottages on the grounds of the Soldiers' Home, previously reserved for military officials. The president worked at the Executive Mansion during the day, and then left for Maryland around sunset, often riding in an open barouche escorted by a special company of cavalry with drawn sabers who remained on guard outside his cottage during the night. He returned to the city early in the morning. When the press of business kept him at the White House overnight, Lincoln typically sent out to Willard's for a light dinner.

Some in Washington feared that the president's security arrangements left much to be desired. "To my unsophisticated judgment," noted the reporter Noah Brooks of the *Sacramento Daily Union*, "nothing seems easier than a sudden cavalry raid from the Maryland side of the fortifications, past the few small forts, to seize the President of the United States, lug him from his 'chased couch,' and carry him off as a hostage worth having."

Throughout the summer, Lincoln received a steady stream of visitors to the Executive Mansion. On June 20, a delegation of Quakers presented the president with a petition imploring him to issue an emancipation decree. Lincoln replied that a presidential proclamation would be practically useless. "Such a decree surely could not be more binding upon the South than the Constitution," he told them, "and that cannot be enforced in that part of the country now. Would a proclamation of freedom be any more effective?"

The Quakers left Lincoln with a prayer that God might show him a way to free the slaves and preserve the nation. Suddenly solemn, Lincoln assured his visitors he was "deeply sensible of his need of Divine assistance." Sometimes, Lincoln added, he thought that "perhaps he might be an instrument in God's hands of accomplishing a great work, and he certainly was not unwilling to be."

Before Congress adjourned for the summer, it approved a measure abolishing slavery in the national territories, thereby resolving the issue that had torn the nation apart in the first place. In the lobby of Willard's hotel, Senator Chandler publicly denounced General McClellan as a coward and a liar. (Observers noticed that Chandler seemed to be quite drunk—"a bad habit," remarked Attorney General Bates, "that has lately crept upon him.")

Abolitionists throughout the North echoed Chandler's sentiments.

Anna Dickinson repeatedly called McClellan an enemy of liberty and warned that the longer the war lasted, the greater influence military officials would have over the civil government. At antislavery rallies, audiences sang their new anthem, the "Battle Hymn of the Republic," written by Julia Ward Howe and recently published in the *Atlantic Monthly*, whose editor paid Howe five dollars for the poem.

In the last week of June, Lincoln traveled to West Point to consult with General Scott, now retired. The meeting touched off rumors that McClellan was dead, or that he had "lost his mind and gone crazy with anxiety and excitement." Northerners continued to hope that the Army of the Potomac's slow but steady advance up the Virginia peninsula would end in the capture of Richmond, but Senator Wade cherished no such illusions. The Union, Wade decided, was swiftly going to hell.

Seven Days

In Richmond, Confederate critics doubted that their new commander—General Robert E. Lee, who assumed command after Joe Johnston was wounded at Fair Oaks—could stop McClellan. Lee's record did not encourage optimism. Known primarily as an engineer and staff officer, he had failed to hold western Virginia against McClellan in the summer of 1861, leading one Richmond newspaper to refer to him as "Evacuating Lee." A subsequent brief assignment to South Carolina resulted in no victories, only the redesign of several coastal forts.

Southern observers noticed that General Lee, like McClellan, seemed reluctant to risk his troops in battle. Lee reinforced the popular impression when he put his soldiers to work strengthening Richmond's defenses. As his men expanded the perimeter of earthworks around the city, they began calling Lee the "King of Spades." But Lee also raised morale by improving the rations of men who had been living on spoiled meat, and by issuing decent uniforms to replace the threadbare motley of his troops. In the space of several weeks, he welded the loose-knit coalition of divisions he had inherited into an efficient, coordinated force that he named the Army of Northern Virginia.

All the while, Lee took McClellan's measure. Throughout the war, Lee's insight into the psychology of opposing generals, combined with a willingness to employ unorthodox, unpredictable strategies himself, would give him a significant advantage over numerically superior Union forces. The cautious advance of the Army of the Potomac made it clear that McClellan did not intend to attack Lee's forces. Instead, McClellan planned to lay siege to Richmond, counting on his heavy artillery to pound the enemy into submission.

Lee knew that if he allowed McClellan to move his siege guns into position, he would never dislodge the superior Union force, and Richmond would be lost. Besides, a second Union army was again preparing to advance upon the Confederate capital from the north.

Frustrated by McClellan's excessive caution, Lincoln had combined the commands of Generals McDowell, Frémont, and Banks to form a new force, the Army of Virginia, led by General John Pope. Pope's recent victories at the battles of Island No. 10 and Corinth in the West had earned him a reputation for aggressiveness—a trait Lincoln longed for in a commander. There was a personal connection as well. Lincoln knew Pope's father, a judge in Illinois, from his own days as a lawyer in Springfield; Pope himself had been part of the entourage that accompanied Lincoln from Illinois to Washington in early 1861.

Postmaster General Blair warned the president not to trust John Pope. Pope's father was "a flatterer, a deceiver, a liar and a trickster," claimed Blair, "all the Popes are so." There was even a saying among Union troops: "as big a liar as John Pope." Lincoln dismissed such criticisms as irrelevant. "A liar," the president observed, "might be brave and have skill as an officer."

On June 24, General Pope arrived in Washington and began ingratiating himself with Radical Republican congressmen. An outspoken opponent of slavery, Pope told members of the Joint Committee on the Conduct of the War that he yearned to launch an offensive against the rebel armies. Impressed, the legislators pressured Lincoln to award Pope the command of all Union forces in the East.

At a dinner party with Secretary of the Treasury Chase, Pope announced that he favored "the most rigorous measures" in prosecuting the war. "Slavery must perish," Pope insisted. According to Chase, Pope said he favored "using every instrument which could be brought to bear against the enemy, and while he did not speak of a general arming of the slaves as soldiers, he advocated their use as laborers . . . and in any way in which their services could be made useful without impairing the general tone of the service."

Lincoln initially expected Pope to capture Manassas while the bulk of the Confederate Army in Virginia was still between McClellan and Richmond. Then Pope, with his 56,000 troops, could advance toward the Confederate capital from the west and north. McClellan, meanwhile, would continue to advance up the peninsula. Lincoln hoped to catch the rebel forces in a vise, smashing them between the two Union armies.

But Lee frustrated Lincoln's plans by attacking first. On June 26, Confederate troops suddenly struck an isolated Union corps on McClellan's right flank, north of the Chickahominy River, near Mechanicsville. It was the first example of Lee's willingness to flout the conventions of orthodox warfare and accept breathtaking risks.

McClellan never saw the blow coming. Lee, he thought, was "*too* cautious and weak under grave responsibility—personally brave and energetic . . . [yet] likely to be timid and irresolute in action."

Both sides suffered heavy losses the following day during savage fighting at Gaines's Mill, but only McClellan lost his nerve. Shortly after ten o'clock that evening, he ordered the Army of the Potomac to retreat. As usual, McClellan blamed the administration for leaving him to face an enemy who possessed "vastly superior numbers." "The Govt has not sustained this Army," he telegraphed to Stanton early on June 28. "If you do not do so now the game is lost. If I save this Army now I tell you plainly that I owe no thanks to you or any other persons in Washington—you have done your best to sacrifice this Army." When McClellan's insubordinate message reached Washington, the telegraph operator in the War Department carried it to his superior, who ordered the final sentence deleted before either Stanton or Lincoln saw it.

Even though McClellan remained in the rear directing the Union withdrawal, the retreat threatened to degenerate into chaos. Several thousand Union supply wagons, more than a hundred artillery guns, nearly 15,000 horses and mules, and 2,500 cattle all were funneled into a few inadequate roads leading south along the peninsula, between the James and the Chickahominy. As the Union troops crossed the battlefield of Fair Oaks, where they had fought four weeks earlier, they found corpses from the previous encounter only partially buried, exposed to the elements.

Along the way, Lee kept pounding the Army of the Potomac. In seven days of fighting, Union soldiers held their own against repeated Confederate assaults, exacting a fearsome toll on their rebel tormentors. At one point, General Edwin Sumner flatly refused to retreat, shouting, "I never leave a victorious field!" until McClellan threatened to remove him from command. On the morning of July 1, General Philip Kearney—a cavalry officer who had lost an arm in the Mexican War—recommended that the Union armies take advantage of the heavy Confederate losses by launching a counteroffensive. He told his staff that McClellan's defensive strategy could "only be prompted by cowardice or treason."

Even though Confederate losses outnumbered the Union casualties, McClellan insisted that the Army of the Potomac continue its southward descent. It did not halt until July 2, when it reached Harrison's Landing, where McClellan nestled his troops under the protection of Union gunboats on the James.

"It is considered generally that McClellan has been completely outwitted," wrote a Union colonel, Francis Barlow. "I think the whole army feels that it was left to take care of itself and was saved only by its own brave fighting." Union troops tried to burn their supply depots as they retreated, to keep them out of rebel hands, but the Confederates managed to capture 30,000 rifles and pistols and 50 cannons, along with more than 6,000 prisoners.

"I did not expect this would be the result of our campaign," mourned Sergeant Elisha Hunt Rhodes, "but I suppose it is all right. We have marched night and day, and no one will know how much the Army has suffered. No sleep, scant food, and tired almost to death."

During the Seven Days' fighting, Lincoln spent many hours in Stanton's office in the War Department, lying on a sofa as he waited for the latest reports from the telegraph office on the second floor. General Pope acted as the president's unofficial military adviser, analyzing the latest news from the front and taking every opportunity to criticize McClellan's cautious strategy.

Northerners searched newspapers anxiously for reports of the fighting, but bulletins from the War Department were slow and sketchy—always a bad sign. "We cannot make out exactly what's coming," complained George Templeton Strong, "but it has the walk of a defeat and a very bad one." The final tally of Union losses was nearly 16,000 men and millions of dollars worth of materiel. Lee's army suffered over 20,000 casualties, but he had saved Richmond.

Lincoln's Cabinet was united in its denunciation of McClellan. Describing the general as an "imbecile, a coward, [and] a traitor," Chase declared that if he were commander in chief, he would order McClellan shot. Stanton wondered aloud whether the general ever intended to capture the Confederate capital; according to Stanton, General George Armstrong Custer heard a prominent Democratic congressman say that "it is not on our books that McClellan shall take Richmond." Perhaps McClellan deliberately stalled and then retreated, so he could blame the administration for lack of support and earn votes for McClellan's Democratic allies in the autumn congressional elections.

Secretary of the Navy Welles concluded that McClellan "wishes to outgeneral the Rebels but not to kill and destroy them." "It was notorious that he hesitated, doubted, had no self-reliance, any definite and determined plan, and audacity to act," wrote Welles. "In short, he was not a fighting general."

Publicly less critical than his Cabinet, Lincoln instructed McClellan to "maintain your ground if you can, but save the army at all events, even if you fall back to Fort Monroe. We still have strength enough in the country, and will bring it out." While the Army of the Potomac was still retreating, the president issued a call for 300,000 new troops, to launch another assault on Richmond. "I expect to maintain this contest until successful," Lincoln declared, "or till I die, or am conquered, or my term expires, or Congress or the country forsakes me."

First Draft

McClellan's failure to capture Richmond did not surprise Lincoln; the president had expressed reservations about the peninsula campaign from the start. But he was stunned when McClellan's chief of staff, General Marcy, came to Washington to warn Stanton that without reinforcements, the Army of the Potomac might need to surrender. "General," Lincoln replied grimly, "I understand you have used the word 'capitulate'; that is a word not to be used in connection with our army."

The Union setbacks in Virginia persuaded Lincoln to take the first tentative step toward emancipation. "Things had gone on from bad to worse," Lincoln later recalled, " until I felt that we had reached the end of our rope on the plan of operations we had been pursuing; that we had about played our last card, and must change our tactics, or lose the game. I now determined upon the adoption of the emancipation policy; and, without consultation with, or the knowledge of the Cabinet, I prepared the original draft of the proclamation."

Lincoln composed his initial draft in the telegraph room of the War Department. He found it a congenial place to work, a sanctuary from the constant press of visitors to the White House. By this time, the president had struck up friendships with the telegraph operators, who listened patiently to his stories as he waited for incoming dispatches.

On a morning in late June, Lincoln asked Captain Thomas T. Eckert, the officer in charge, for a sheet of paper "to write something special." He sat down at Eckert's desk, looking onto Pennsylvania Avenue. "He would look out of the window a while, and then put his pen to paper," Eckert noted, "but he did not write much at once. He would study between times and when he had made up his mind he would put down a line or two, and then sit quiet for a few minutes. After a time he would resume his writing . . . ." By the time he left the telegraph room, Lincoln had written less than a full page. He gave the long sheet of foolscap to Eckert and asked him to put it in a locked desk without showing it to anyone.

When he returned the following day, Lincoln resumed writing. The draft proceeded slowly; the president repeatedly revised the text, leaving question marks in the margin of passages he wished to revisit. On some days, he added only one or two lines.

Before Congress adjourned for the summer, Lincoln decided to obtain Vice President Hamlin's reaction to his manuscript. On the day Hamlin was scheduled to leave for Maine, Lincoln surprised him with an invitation to dine that evening. "I want you to go with me to the Soldiers' Home tonight," he said. "I have something to show you."

After dinner, the president took some papers from his pocket. "Hamlin," he explained, "you have often urged me to issue a proclamation of emancipation. I am about to do it. I have it here, and you will be the first person to see it." Lincoln read the proclamation aloud several times. Hamlin later recalled that he made several minor suggestions, which Lincoln seemed willing to accept. The president, Hamlin noticed, "was much moved at the step he was taking."

Independence Day

Washingtonians celebrated a sober Fourth of July. Thousands of sick and wounded Union soldiers from the Virginia peninsula—some dying—lay in makeshift hospital beds around the city. Many churches could not ring their bells to celebrate the holiday because of the wounded men lying on the floors underneath.

Senator Sumner suggested that Lincoln make Independence Day "more sacred and historic than ever" by issuing an emancipation proclamation. "You need more men, not only at the North, but at the South, in the rear of the Rebels," Sumner argued. "You need the slaves."

Lincoln demurred, calling emancipation "too big a lick." "I would do it," the president added, "if I were not afraid that half the officers would fling down their arms and . . . three more states would rise—Kentucky, Maryland, Missouri." Besides, Lincoln feared that a presidential decree would accomplish nothing in the South. "Wait," he advised Sumner. "Time is essential."

On the banks of the James River, General McClellan released an Independence Day message to the Army of the Potomac. "Your achievements of the last ten days have illustrated the valor and endurance of the American Soldier!" McClellan told his troops. "Attacked by vastly superior forces, and without hope of reinforcements, you have . . . in every conflict beaten back your foes with enormous slaughter."

As military bands played and artillery fired salutes to mark the holiday, McClellan ordered his exhausted soldiers to construct a line of forts to protect their front, stretching for three miles from the James inland. "Rest is what we want now," wrote Sergeant Elisha Rhodes, "and I hope we shall get it. I could sleep for a week. The weather is very hot, but we have moved our camp to a wood where we get the shade. This is a queer 4th of July, but we have not forgotten that it is our national birthday, and a salute has been fired. We expect to have something to eat before long."

At one point along the front, pickets from the Union and Confederate armies faced each other across a field of ripe blackberries. To celebrate the holiday, they agreed not to fire at one another. Instead, they put down their weapons and went out into the field where, according to a rebel lieutenant, they "gathered berries together and talked over the fight, traded tobacco and coffee and exchanged newspapers as peacefully and kindly as if they had not been engaged for the last seven days in butchering one another."

In a holiday speech in New York, Frederick Douglass denounced General McClellan as "either a cold blooded Traitor, or . . . an unmitigated military Imposter." Douglass also had harsh words for Lincoln. The president, Douglass charged, was attempting to "shield and protect" slavery, "to reconstruct the union on the old and corrupting basis of compromise, by which slavery shall retain all the power that it ever had."

Meanwhile, Vice President Hamlin told an audience in Bangor, Maine, that they could trust Lincoln to do the right thing about slavery. "The time will come," Hamlin declared, "when Federal bayonets shall not protect rebel property, and the work of putting down the rebellion will be done in earnest."

"My belief is unshaken that the end of this conflict is to topple down the edifice of slavery," wrote Ambassador Charles Francis Adams from London. "Perhaps we are not yet ready to come up to that work, and the madness of the resistance is the instrument in the hands of Divine Providence to drive us to it."

Harrison's Landing

Before Lincoln decided whether to replace McClellan, he wanted a first-hand view of the Army of the Potomac. So he left Washington on the evening of July 7, arriving at Harrison's Landing on the steamer *Ariel* late the following day. As he reviewed the troops by moonlight, the president was pleasantly surprised; most soldiers had returned to their units, and they were in better condition than McClellan had led him to believe. Sickness, though, was rampant. Almost one in every four soldiers, excluding the wounded, was suffering from malaria, typhoid, or dysentery.

The troops were genuinely glad to see Lincoln. His presence, wrote one lieutenant, "seemed to infuse new ardor into the dispirited army." A soldier from New York wrote that McClellan's popularity with the men "will never measure 1/100th part of Honest Abe's. Such cheers as greeted him never tickled the ears of Napoleon in his palmiest days." There was laughter, too, especially when the president's long legs threatened to "become entangled with those of the horse . . . and both come down together." Lincoln's attempt to salute the troops while controlling his high-strung horse only emphasized his habitual awkwardness. "That arm with which he drew the rein, in its angles and position resembled the hind leg of a grasshopper—the hand before, the elbow away back over the horse's tail," wrote one observer. "But the boys liked him. In fact his popularity with the army is and has been universal."

Lincoln told the soldiers he had spent sleepless nights worrying about their condition, "but after what he had seen and heard, he would go back to Washington, satisfied that it was all right with the army of the Potomac." He added that he was sure they would never give up until they captured Richmond.

In a private conference, Lincoln asked McClellan if he could safely withdraw the army from the James and return to northern Virginia. McClellan protested that he wished to remain on the peninsula and resume his advance on Richmond. Three of the Army of the Potomac's five corps commanders supported McClellan.

Before Lincoln left on the morning of July 9, McClellan handed him a lengthy document. The president glanced at it and saw that it contained McClellan's confidential advice on how to win the war. "All right," Lincoln replied, and slipped the memorandum into his pocket.

McClellan's letter was an attempt to persuade Lincoln to continue to wage the war along conservative lines. Fearing that the president would yield to the rising power of the Radicals in Congress, McClellan suggested to his wife that the outcome of the Seven Days' Battle may have been a blessing in disguise. "If I had succeeded in taking Richmond now," he wrote, "the fanatics of the North might have been too powerful & reunion impossible."

In his letter to Lincoln, McClellan implored the president to seize full control of the war effort and prosecute it "upon the highest principles known to Christian Civilization." Neither wholesale confiscation of rebel property nor the "forcible abolition of slavery should be contemplated for a moment," McClellan argued; only a moderate policy toward slavery would elicit sufficient recruits to win the war. "A declaration of radical views, especially upon slavery," McClellan concluded, "will rapidly disintegrate our present Armies."

McClellan was only partly correct. In July 1862, the debate within the Union armies over emancipation was heating up. Many of McClellan's officers—especially Democrats—remained opposed to both emancipation and the "black Republicans" in Washington. "If anyone thinks that this army is fighting to free the Negro," wrote an Irish sergeant in a Massachusetts company, "they are terribly mistaken."

In the aftermath of the Seven Days' Battle, however, an increasing number of Union soldiers voiced their willingness to treat the rebels as harshly as necessary. "The tendency of public opinion in the army is very radical," reported one recruit from Illinois. "You cannot be too ultra for the soldiers."

"Slavery must be cleaned out," proclaimed an officer from Wisconsin. "The only way to put down this rebellion is to hurt the instigators and abettors of it." A chaplain in an Ohio regiment agreed that "this thing of guarding rebel property when the owner is in the field fighting us is played out. That is the sentiment of every private soldier in the army."

Enter "Old Brains"

A day after Lincoln left Harrison's Landing, McClellan told his wife that the president's manner at their parting made him uneasy. "It seemed that of a man about to do something of which he was much ashamed," the general wrote.

When Lincoln returned to Washington on the evening of July 10, he showed McClellan's letter to the Cabinet. Predictably, Chase and Stanton recommended that Lincoln dismiss the general. This time the president agreed.

Lincoln offered the command of the Army of the Potomac to General Burnside, McClellan's loyal subordinate. Burnside refused. Until he could find a better candidate, Lincoln decided to keep McClellan in command, but he abandoned any hope that McClellan could ever defeat the rebellion. The following day, the president appointed General Henry Halleck as general in chief of all the Union armies, and ordered him to report to Washington at once.

A short, paunchy man with a broad, high forehead, a dark complexion, and bulging eyes, Halleck was known as "Old Brains" for his intellectual approach toward war. He had written several treatises on military science; one of his texts, *Elements of Military Art and Science*, published in 1846, became required reading at West Point. Early in the war, Lincoln selected Halleck to command the Department of the West. When Lincoln and Stanton restructured the Union armies in March 1862, they had awarded him command of the consolidated Department of the Mississippi.

During the winter of 1861–1862, Lincoln borrowed several of Halleck's works from the Library of Congress to teach himself the basics of military strategy. His respect for Halleck's knowledge, combined with the victories of Union troops in the West—for which Halleck received more credit than he deserved—convinced Lincoln that the general could provide the sort of professional leadership the Union armies had lacked since he dismissed McClellan as general in chief.

Everyone acknowledged Halleck's ability to manage and coordinate an army, but there was something unpleasantly cold about him. Halleck accepted his appointment without enthusiasm, fearing entanglement in the "political hell" of the capital. Despite Lincoln's urgings ("I am very anxious—almost impatient—to have you here," the president telegraphed), Halleck wrapped up his affairs in the West slowly, not arriving in the capital until almost two weeks later. Lincoln and Stanton immediately pressed him to replace McClellan, but Halleck demurred. McClellan, who harbored hopes of resuming the command of all Union armies himself, did not learn of Halleck's promotion until he read it in an evening newspaper on July 20.

Congressional Confiscation

Before McClellan's retreat down the Virginia peninsula, the Radicals' campaign in Congress to punish the South by confiscating rebel property—including slaves—had stalled. Lincoln remained the main barrier. After Congress abolished slavery in the District of Columbia and the territories, Representative George Julian submitted a bill to repeal the Fugitive Slave Acts of 1793 and 1850, but the measure died when the president refused to support it.

Radical leaders saw no evidence that Lincoln intended to modify his opposition to emancipation anytime soon. Thaddeus Stevens was convinced that the president—"as honest a man as there is in the world," but "too easy and amiable"—was being misled "by the malign influence of Kentucky counsellors." General James Wadsworth, one of the leading military advocates of emancipation, visited Lincoln and came away doubting that the president would ever free the slaves. "The President is not with us; has no Anti-slavery instincts," Wadsworth told a reporter for the *New York Tribune*. "If emancipation comes at all," he added, "it will be from the rebels, or in consequence of their protracting the war."

But McClellan's failure to capture Richmond revived the second Confiscation Act, introduced by Senator Trumbull in December 1861. Designed to "punish treason and rebellion," the original draft of the bill gave federal courts authority to seize and confiscate all property within the Confederate states. After a sixty-day grace period, the slaves of any southerner who continued to support the rebellion could be emancipated by the courts. Union army officers were forbidden to return runaway slaves to their masters until a court hearing determined whether the slaveowner was loyal. To keep freed slaves from disturbing white society, the bill also appropriated $500,000 to establish Negro colonies outside the United States. Finally, the Confiscation Act authorized the president "to employ as many persons of African descent as he may deem necessary and proper" in the Union armies.

When Congress began debating the second Confiscation Act in March 1862, Radical legislators and their allies made it clear that they intended to use the bill to remake southern society by destroying the economic and political power of the plantation owners who provoked secession. "Treason must be made odious, and traitors must be punished and impoverished," insisted Senator Andrew Johnson of Tennessee, a longtime foe of southern aristocrats. "Their great plantations must be seized, and divided into small farms, and sold to honest and industrious men."

Thaddeus Stevens proposed selling the confiscated property of the rebels to pay the costs of the war and provide cheap land for Union veterans. Abolitionist spokesmen outside Congress concurred. "Let me confiscate the land of the South, and put it into the hands of the negroes and white men who have fought for it," argued Wendell Phillips, "and . . . I have planted a union sure to grow as an acorn to become an oak."

Led by Senator Fessenden, moderate and conservative Republicans worked to soften the harshest provisions of Trumbull's bill. But the failure of the peninsula campaign persuaded a majority of Republican congressmen that drastic measures—including emancipation—were now essential to win the war.

"You can form no conception of the change of opinion here as to the Negro question," John Sherman wrote to his brother. Sherman claimed that his Republican colleagues were now convinced that the rebellion must be "subdued—conquered—by confiscation—by the employment of their slaves—by terror—energy—audacity—rather than by conciliation." Even Senator Fessenden reluctantly decided to support the Confiscation Act, although he complained that "it would have been better not to legislate upon the subject of confiscation at all."

On July 12, four days before Congress was scheduled to adjourn for the summer, the Senate gave preliminary approval to the Confiscation Act. That same day, Lincoln invited congressmen from the border states to the White House for a private meeting. Reading from a prepared statement, the president pleaded with them once more to accept his proposal for gradual, compensated emancipation. Sumner recalled that Lincoln's "whole soul was occupied" with this plan. "In familiar intercourse, with him, I remember nothing more touching than the earnestness and completeness with which he embraced this idea."

Lincoln assured the congressmen that no state government need emancipate any slaves immediately. All he sought was "a *decision* at once to emancipate *gradually*." Then state officials could prolong and smooth the transition from slavery to freedom.

He pointed out that passage of the Confiscation Act demonstrated the strength of the rising abolitionist tide in Congress. The presidency, Lincoln suggested, was the only safeguard remaining for the property rights of slaveowners in the border states. But Lincoln warned that he could not indefinitely withstand the public pressure for emancipation. His revocation of General Hunter's emancipation decree had antagonized powerful northern antislavery elements—including many men "whose support the country cannot afford to lose"—and he might not be able to risk such a fight again.

McClellan's failure to capture Richmond meant that the war would probably continue for years. Already Union armies were moving back and forth through the border states; their presence inevitably encouraged slaves to flee their owners. "If the war continue long, as it must," Lincoln noted, "the institution in your states will be extinguished by mere friction and abrasion—by the mere incidents of the war. It will be gone, and you will have nothing valuable in lieu of it."

Lincoln reminded his guests that a large part of their slaves' value had already disappeared. "How much better for you, and for your people," he suggested, "to take the step which, at once, shortens the war, and secures substantial compensation for that which is sure to be wholly lost in any other event."

Few congressmen welcomed Lincoln's advice. "I regard the whole thing," said one of Kentucky's senators, "as full of arsenic, sugar-coated." As the legislators left the White House, Lincoln felt certain they would do nothing; they later voted overwhelmingly against even considering the president's proposal. Lincoln later confessed that during these days, "I was as nearly inconsolable as I could be and live."

Trial Balloon

The next day, July 13, was a Sunday. Late that morning, Lincoln left the White House in the presidential carriage to attend the funeral of Secretary of War Stanton's infant son, who had died several days earlier. Lincoln headed first for Seward's redbrick townhouse on Lafayette Park, across Pennsylvania Avenue from the Executive Mansion, to pick up the secretary of state. Then he told the driver to stop at Secretary of the Navy Welles's house, just a few steps away at the corner of Lafayette Square and Sixteenth Street.

Welles—whom Washington reporters dubbed "Marie Antoinette" for his supposed facial resemblance to the French queen—noticed that the president seemed to be unusually grim. En route to the church, Lincoln suddenly announced that if the war did not end soon, he was planning to issue an emancipation proclamation. It was the first time Welles had ever heard the president speak in favor of emancipation.

Startled, Seward and Welles listened as Lincoln admitted that he remained reluctant "to meddle with this question, around which there were thrown constitutional safeguards, and on which the whole southern mind was sensitive." According to Welles, Lincoln said that he had tried "various expedients to escape issuing an executive order emancipating the slaves, the last and only alternative, but it was forced upon him by the rebels themselves. He saw no escape. Turn which way he would, this disturbing element which caused the war rose up against us, and it was an insuperable obstacle to peace."

Lincoln's unsuccessful interview with the border-state congressmen the day before was the final straw. He now believed "that it was a military necessity absolutely essential for the salvation of the Union, that we must free the slaves or be ourselves subdued." Lincoln added that he had not yet raised the subject with anyone else; he wanted the reactions of the two Cabinet officers first.

Seward replied cautiously that he needed to give the matter further thought. He assured Lincoln that the rebellion justified a presidential emancipation decree; whether it was expedient or necessary was another question.

Welles was too surprised by the abrupt shift in the president's thinking to do anything more than support Seward's opinion. "Until this time, in all our previous interviews," Welles later wrote in his diary, "whenever the question of emancipation or the mitigation of slavery had been in any way alluded to, [Lincoln] had been prompt and emphatic in denouncing any interference by the General Government with the subject." But the failure of McClellan's peninsula campaign impelled the president "to adopt extraordinary measures to preserve the national existence."

Lincoln returned to the subject several times during the carriage ride. When he left Welles and Seward after the funeral, Lincoln asked them to give the matter special attention over the next several days, because he was "earnest in the conviction that something must be done."

Later that afternoon, Lincoln met with two Radical Republican congressmen from Illinois: Owen Lovejoy—a personal friend—and Isaac Arnold. Recently Lovejoy had assured an audience at Cooper's Union in New York that Lincoln was moving, albeit slowly, toward emancipation. If the president "does not drive as fast as I would," Lovejoy claimed, "he is on the right road, and it is only a question of time."

Seeking to delay further congressional initiatives against slavery, Lincoln explained to Lovejoy and Arnold how difficult it was to keep the Republican Party united on the emancipation issue. Perhaps, Lincoln suggested, the Radicals might temper their rhetoric and give him more time to lobby the border-state congressmen. If they agreed to accept his program of gradual emancipation, it might end the rebellion and doom slavery everywhere in the United States. "How I wish the border states would accept my proposition," Lincoln said. "Then you, Lovejoy, and you, Arnold, and all of us, would not have lived in vain!"

A Threatened Veto

On Monday, July 14, Senator Browning brought a copy of the Confiscation Act to the Executive Mansion. Browning—who opposed the measure on the grounds that it violated the constitutional rights of southern property owners as well as the rules of "civilized warfare"—urged Lincoln to veto the bill. Otherwise, he warned, Lincoln would face "dangerous & fatal dissatisfaction" in the Union Army.

Lincoln needed no urging. He had already stated that he would veto the Confiscation Act unless Congress made substantive changes. Lincoln demanded that the bill's penalties apply only to southerners who supported the rebellion *after* the measure was passed, and that the confiscation of rebel estates must not extend "beyond the lives of the guilty parties."

Lincoln was most disturbed by Congress's attempt to enact legislation emancipating slaves. "It is startling to say that congress can free a slave within a state," he remarked. "Congress has no power over slavery in the states and so much of it [slavery] as remains after the war is over . . . must be left to the exclusive control of the states where it may exist."

As a practical matter, Lincoln was willing to grant freedom to slaves who escaped to Union lines, but he opposed attempts to induce them to flee their masters. "They come now faster than we can provide for them, and are becoming an embarrassment to the government," he told Browning. In Louisiana, so many Negroes flocked to the Union camps that military officials were overwhelmed. One general complained that his camp was swamped with "plantation carts, filled with negro women and children, with their effects; and . . . I have no rations to issue to them. I have a great many more negroes in my camp now than I have whites."

By communicating his objections to Congress before legislators voted on the bill, Lincoln broke long-standing traditional restraints on presidential power. Congressional leaders chastised Lincoln for interfering in the legislative process. "The President cannot lay down and fix the principles upon which a war shall be conducted," insisted Senator Wade. "It is for Congress to lay down the rules and regulations by which the Executive shall be governed in conducting a war."

Representative George Julian claimed that Lincoln's threat to veto the Confiscation Act earned him more enmity on Capitol Hill than anything else the president had ever done. Even the moderate Fessenden reproached Lincoln. The president's threat to veto the bill, he claimed, "will disappoint, and I fear will dishearten the country. Well, we have what we bargained for, a Splitter of rails, and have no right to complain."

To a clergyman who visited him one evening at the Soldiers' Home, Lincoln explained his refusal to immediately emancipate slaves of Confederates—or approve any drastic punishment of southern landowners—until he had exhausted all other options. Slavery, the president observed, "has shaped nearly everything that enters into what we call government. It is as much northern as it is southern . . . It is wrong, a great evil indeed, but the South is no more responsible for the wrong done to the African race than is the North."

Lincoln then walked over to his visitor and put his hand on the back of the minister's head. "Here is a tumor," he said, "drawing upon the vitality of your body."

You must be rid of it or it will destroy your life. Now we bring in three physicians to have a consultation over this tumor. All agree at once that it must be removed, but each one has his own opinion of the proper course to be pursued. One wants to poultice it and sweat it and so evaporate it. Another is positive that it should be taken out at once, that it should be cut and pulled out, even at the risk of the patient's life. But the third doctor says, "Gentlemen, I differ from you both as to the treatment proposed. My advice is to prepare the patient for the operation before venturing on it. He must be depleted and the amount of his blood diminished." Now, my opinion is that the third doctor is about right.

Lincoln antagonized congressional leaders further by asking them to approve a bill—which he had drafted—to use government bonds to compensate slaveholders in any state that abolished slavery. The legislators were irritated by Lincoln's apparent presumption that Congress would approve a measure submitted by the executive. Accordingly, they referred the bill to a select House committee on emancipation, where it died.

Congressional leaders doubted that Lincoln would veto the Confiscation Act, but on July 15, Lincoln bluntly warned them to remain in Washington in case he returned the bill "with objections." With Congress scheduled to adjourn the following day, legislators had to accept Lincoln's revisions or lose the Confiscation Act until the next session. Before the bill came up for a final vote on July 17, Republican leaders modified the provisions to which Lincoln objected most strenuously. Congress then approved the measure.

Lincoln signed the Confiscation Act, but subsequently sent the text of his veto message to Congress anyway. Although he agreed that Confederates deserved to lose their property, the president explained that "the severest justice may not always be the best policy." Drastic legislation against rebel civilians might embitter the South and prolong the rebellion. "Would it not be wise to place a power of remission somewhere," he suggested, "so that these persons may know they have something to lose by persisting, and something to save by desisting?"

Public reaction made it clear that most northerners did not share Lincoln's moderation. In the wake of McClellan's military failures, the prospect of seizing rebel property lifted northerners' morale. "The government," wrote George Templeton Strong approvingly, "seems waking up to the duty of dealing more vigorously with rebellion by acts of emancipation and confiscation."

Confidence in the president, however, appeared to be waning. Derisive comments about the "gorilla ape" in the Executive Mansion had long since disappeared from polite northern society, but many still doubted

Lincoln's abilities as a leader. "Everything he does reminds me of an old lady," noted one of Walt Whitman's friends. A critic in New York complained that the administration "does not lead the people; the people has to . . . shove the government forward to every vigorous step."

Abolitionists crowed that they had been right about Lincoln all along. "Not a spark of genius has he," insisted Henry Ward Beecher, "not an element for leadership. Not one particle of heroic enthusiasm." William Lloyd Garrison declared that Lincoln was "nothing better than a wet rag" at the head of a "stumbling, halting, prevaricating, irresolute, weak, [and] besotted" administration.

"The simple truth is," wrote Senator Fessenden, "there was never such a shambling half-and-half set of incapables collected in one government since the world began." Apparently the northern financial community agreed. The New York stock market slumped badly in early July. Union finances were a disaster. The Treasury was nearly $36 million behind in payments to troops and contractors, with only $50 million in Treasury notes on hand. Unless the army or the administration could inspire confidence in a Union victory, Secretary of the Treasury Chase foresaw either national bankruptcy or runaway inflation from additional issues of paper currency.

Balancing on the Tightrope

"The great phenomenon of the year is the terrible intensity which this [emancipation] resolution has acquired," observed the *Boston Advertiser*, an antiabolitionist business journal. "A year ago men might have faltered at the thought of proceeding to this extremity," but now "they are in great measure prepared for it."

Throughout July, Republican officials pressured Lincoln to enforce the Confiscation Act and allow Negroes to serve in the Union armies. "The time has come for the adoption of more decisive measures," argued Governor Richard Yates of Illinois. "Blows must be struck at the vital parts of the rebellion."

Yet some northerners feared that mounting demands for revenge would loose uncontrollable forces. "If we succeed in our attempt at sub-jugation," wrote Charles Francis Adams, Jr., to his father in London, "I see only an immense territory and a savage and ignorant populace to be held down by force, the enigma of slavery to be settled by us somehow, right or wrong, and, most dangerous of all, a spirit of blind, revengeful fanaticism in the North." Adams feared that unless Lincoln could restrain the Radi-cal Republicans, Sumner and his colleagues would "bankrupt the nation, jeopard all liberty by immense standing armies, debauch the morality of the nation by war, and undermine all our republican foundations to effect the immediate destruction of the institution of slavery."

Lincoln shared Adams's concerns. He tried to explain his position to a group of forty prominent citizens from Boston who came to the White House that summer to present a petition urging him to abolish slavery.

When they finished, Lincoln sat thoughtfully for a few moments. Throwing a long leg over the corner of a table in front of him, he finally asked whether they remembered the famous circus performer Blondin, who had walked a tightrope across Niagara Falls several years earlier.

Of course, they replied. "Suppose," Lincoln continued, "that all the material values in this great country of ours, from the Atlantic to the Pa-cific—its wealth, its prosperity, its achievements in the present and its hopes for the future, could all have been concentrated, and given to Blondin to carry over that awful crossing and that their preservation should have depended upon his ability to somehow get them across to the other side." And suppose, he said to the spokesman of the group,

> that everything you yourself held dearest in the world, the safety of your family, and the security of your home also depended upon his crossing, and suppose you had been standing upon the shore when he was going over, as he was carefully feeling his way along and balanc-ing his pole with all his most delicate skill over the thundering cataract, would you have shouted to him "Blondin, a step to the right!" "Blondin, a step to the left!" or would you have stood there speechless, and held your breath and prayed to the Almighty to guide and help him safely through the trial?

Without waiting to hear the president explain the point of his story, the Bostonians glanced at one another and then, bidding Lincoln good day, stalked silently out of the room.

An Unexpected Presidential Message

Early on the morning of Monday, July 21, Lincoln sent messengers to the homes of his Cabinet officers, calling them to a special meeting at ten o'clock that morning. It was an unusual request. Since Lincoln preferred to deal with the executive departments separately, the Cabinet seldom discussed substantive issues as a whole.

By ten o'clock everyone except Postmaster General Blair had arrived at the Executive Mansion. Dispensing with the usual preliminaries, Lincoln blurted out that he was prepared "to take some definitive steps in respect to military action and slavery." But instead of telling the Cabinet about his proposed emancipation proclamation, the president spent the meeting reviewing several executive orders he was issuing to implement the Confiscation Act.

None aroused much controversy. The first order authorized Union army commanders in Confederate territory to confiscate civilian property when such action "may be necessary or convenient," a policy General Pope was already implementing in northern Virginia.

Lincoln's second order endorsed the use of Negroes as laborers in Union army camps, but the president made it clear that he still opposed arming Negroes to fight white rebels. The third order provided compensation for loyal slaveowners whose Negroes were confiscated, and the fourth recommended that the government colonize freed slaves in Central America.

When the Cabinet reconvened on Tuesday afternoon, Lincoln announced that he was now willing to allow the army to recruit free Negroes and fugitive slaves of disloyal owners, and arm them "for purely defensive purposes." Then the president declared that he had decided to issue an executive order of emancipation.

There was a brief moment of silence while the news sank in. "I said to the Cabinet that I had resolved upon this step," Lincoln recalled, "and had not called them together to ask their advice, but to lay the subject-matter of a proclamation before them; suggestions as to which would be in order, after they had heard it read."

Lincoln was reluctant to free the South's slaves forcibly, and this shone through in the language and structure of the draft proclamation. It began by citing the Confiscation Act of July 17 as legal justification for an emancipation decree. Pursuant to that act, the president gave rebel slave-owners sixty days "to return to their proper allegiance to the United States." To encourage Confederates to abandon the rebellion, Lincoln said that he intended to submit to Congress yet another bill for gradual, compensated emancipation.

If the rebellion continued, however, Lincoln promised to use his authority as commander in chief to issue an emancipation proclamation on January 1, 1863, "as a fit and necessary measure." On that date, "all persons held as slaves within any state or states, wherein the constitutional authority of the United States shall not then be practically recognized, submitted to, and maintained, shall then, thenceforward, and forever, be free."

A Lack of Enthusiasm

Reactions among the Cabinet members were mixed. Stanton—who scrawled on a piece of notepaper that "the measure goes beyond anything I have recommended"—urged Lincoln to issue the proclamation immediately, to deprive the rebels of a vital source of labor.

Attorney General Edward Bates, perhaps the most conservative member of the Cabinet, approved the proclamation as long as it was coupled with a proposal for colonization of freed slaves. Without the deportation of Negroes, Bates foresaw disaster. Welles's notes of the meeting revealed that the attorney general "dreaded any step which should be taken to bring about social equality between the two races. The effect, he said, would be to degrade the whites without elevating the blacks. Demoralization, vice and misery would follow."

Postmaster General Blair opposed the proclamation. Although he favored emancipation, Blair believed Lincoln's draft was an ill-timed political blunder that would cost the Republican Party scores of congressional seats in the fall elections. Secretary of the Interior Caleb Smith of Indiana, steeped in the anti-Negro prejudice of the lower Midwest, agreed with Blair. If Lincoln issued the proclamation, Smith warned, he would resign "and go home and attack the administration." The threat did not disturb Lincoln. A political lightweight, Smith had already decided to resign because he enjoyed scant influence in the Cabinet.

Gideon Welles remained silent. A disciple of states' rights and limited presidential authority, Welles privately considered Lincoln's proclamation "an arbitrary and despotic measure in the cause of freedom." For the moment, Welles kept his opinion to himself.

Treasury Secretary Chase reacted cooly. Determined to obtain the Republican presidential nomination in 1864, Chase feared that an emancipation proclamation might allow Lincoln to preempt him on the slavery issue, which Chase considered his special provenance.

So Chase said he felt emancipation would proceed more smoothly if it were achieved gradually by Union Army commanders, who could decide when the moment was right to free slaves within each district. Military emancipation, Chase argued, could be effected "more quietly" than a presidential proclamation, thereby avoiding the dangers of redoubled white support for the rebellion and "depredation and massacre" by vengeful southern Negroes.

Lincoln's continued advocacy of gradual, compensated emancipation and colonization also struck Chase as unworthy. "How much better," Chase later wrote in his diary, "would be a manly protest against prejudice against color! And a wise effort to give freemen homes in America."

None of these reactions made much impression on Lincoln until Seward weighed in with a plea for delay. The timing of emancipation was wrong, he argued. If the president had advocated an end to slavery at the start of the war, emancipation might have seemed a moral act. But if Lincoln freed the Confederacy's slaves while Union armies were retreating on all fronts, the administration's critics would view emancipation as an admission of weakness, "the last measure of an exhausted government, a cry for help; the government stretching forth its hands to Ethiopia, instead of Ethiopia stretching forth her hands to the government." As Lincoln later put it, Seward feared that a proclamation would sound like "our last *shriek*, on the retreat."

Since slavery provided the cotton for the mills of Britain and France, Seward argued that emancipation might also provoke European nations into recognizing the Confederacy or intervening on the rebels' behalf. Already British stockpiles of raw cotton had fallen by nearly 70 percent from their prewar level, and the situation in France was nearly as bad. To Seward, the logic seemed simple. English textile mills depended on southern cotton; southern cotton plantations depended on slave labor. If Lincoln freed the slaves, it might take southern planters sixty years to develop alternative sources of labor.

Seward urged Lincoln to wait for a more propitious moment—when volunteer reinforcements filled the northern armies and Union victories persuaded European powers that the South could not win.

Lincoln decided to heed Seward's advice. He set his proclamation aside, storing the draft in his desk drawer. From time to time the president would take it out and make minor revisions, touching up a line here and there, as he awaited a Union victory.

6

TO SAVE THE UNION

On the Sea Islands, General Hunter's experiment with Negro troops was nearing its end. Because the War Department refused to acknowledge their existence, the First South Carolina Volunteers had drawn no pay since they enlisted. Nor could they train with firearms, since the president still prohibited Negro soldiers from bearing weapons.

Morale slumped and desertions rose, until Hunter was forced to station white guards around the perimeter of the Negro camps. Moreover, the white troops remained unenthusiastic about the prospect of Negro troops. When Hunter conceded defeat and announced on August 10 that he was disbanding all but one company of the First South Carolina Volunteers, nearby white soldiers cheered. One officer concluded that Hunter's failure was illustrative of "those blunders which have distinguished all [of] our experiments on slavery throughout this war."

> We have had declarations of emancipation ingeniously framed so as not to free a slave and yet to thoroughly concentrate and inflame our enemy. We have wrangled over arming the slaves before the slaves showed any disposition to use the arms, and when we have never had

in our lives 5000 of them who could bear arms. Why could not fanatics be silent and let Providence work for awhile.

Even after Congress repealed the ban on Negro troops in state militias in mid-July, northern opinion remained ambivalent about the use of Negroes as soldiers. The editors of *Harper's Weekly* estimated that most Americans in 1862 "entertained a notion that it was unworthy of a civilized or a Christian nation to use in war soldiers whose skin was not white."

Representatives of the border states feared that Negroes would use their weapons first against white civilians. "Place arms in the hands of these human gorillas to murder their masters and violate their wives and daughters," warned one congressman, "and you will have a war such as was never witnessed in the worst days of the French Revolution, and horrors never exceeded in San Domingo."

Many northerners—including President Lincoln—assumed that Negro troops would flee at the first sound of cannon. Others felt that the use of Negroes in combat represented an admission of cowardice on the part of whites. "Certainly we hope we may never have to confess to the world that the United States Government has to seek an ally in the negro to regain its authority," declared an editorial in the *Milwaukee Sentinel*. "We don't want to fight alongside with the nigger," agreed a recruit from New York. "We think we are a too superior race for that."

Radical congressmen disagreed. For several months, the Joint Committee on the Conduct of the War had gathered testimony from army officials on the value of fugitive slaves as spies and laborers, and their potential as combat troops. On July 19, committee members published a summary of their findings in the form of an "Address to the Loyal People of the United States" in the *New York Tribune*, urging the administration to employ Negroes in a wide range of military capacities—to transform, in Sumner's words, "the rear-guard of the rebellion . . . into the advance guard of the Union."

"I would raise a hundred thousand of them to-morrow and have them drilled," declared Thaddeus Stevens. "History tells us that they make the best and most docile soldiers in the world. They are not barbarians in nature. They are a people as well calculated to be humanized as any other."

Vice President Hamlin probably reflected northerners' opinion more accurately when he told a Union rally in Bangor in July that "we want to save, as much as possible, our men, [even] if it is done by men a little blacker than myself." Governor Samuel Kirkwood of Iowa put the matter more baldly when he voiced a desire to see "some dead niggers as well as dead white men." "For my part," confessed a Union army officer in South Carolina, "I make bold to say that I am not so fastidious as to object to a negro being food for powder and I would arm every one of them."

Already Union commanders in the South were employing former slaves in nearly every capacity except combat. "I have no hobby of my own with regard to the Negro, either to effect his freedom or to continue his bondage," General Grant acknowledged. "I am using them as teamsters, hospital attendants, company cooks and so forth, thus saving soldiers to carry the musket. I don't know what is to become of these poor people in the end, but it weakens the enemy to take them from them." In Kentucky, Union gunboats raided the plantations of rebels and loyalists alike, carrying off slaves to help build military railroads, fortifications, and wagon roads.

Upon occupying New Orleans in May 1862, General Ben Butler initially rejected the services of a regiment of free Negro soldiers raised by Confederate authorities. Believing that Negroes were "horrified of firearms," Butler dismissed the idea of enlisting them in the Union ranks. "These people act like savages," he sniffed, "and slavery has made them so." When General John Phelps, an abolitionist, proposed to raise three regiments from the fugitive slaves who fled to his lines, Butler concluded, "Phelps has gone crazy. . . . I told him he must set the negroes to work and not drill them. . . . I have sent the whole matter to the President."

Butler reversed his stance after a Confederate counteroffensive recaptured Baton Rouge and threatened Union control of New Orleans in early August. Since the War Department could not send him the white reinforcements he requested, Butler decided to accept one regiment of free Negroes and two more regiments of fugitive slaves, and combine them all into a "Free Colored Brigade."

"These men will be good soldiers," claimed George Denison, who was serving as federal customs collector in New Orleans. "Most of them are a very light color, and, I believe, will make good soldiers." Yet Butler planned to use them only for fatigue duty and to garrison unhealthy positions around New Orleans. Beneath the surface, Butler shared the assumption that Negroes remained savages capable of frightening violence. When someone informed Butler that Britain and France were contemplating diplomatic recognition of the Confederacy, the general answered with a warning: "Let England or France try it, and I'll be damned if I don't arm every negro in the South, and make them cut the throat of every man, woman, and child in it. I'll make them lay the whole countryside waste with fire and sword, and leave it desolate!"

In Kansas, Senator Jim Lane and abolitionist leaders began recruiting Negro troops in the summer of 1862. "I am receiving negroes under the late act of Congress," Lane telegraphed the War Department on August 5. "Is there any objection?" Although Lane later claimed that Lincoln had given him oral authority to enlist Negroes, Stanton wired back that "regiments of persons of African descent can only be raised upon express and special authority of the President."

Like Hunter, Lane found free Negroes reluctant to enlist. To augment the ranks of free Negro troops, Lane accepted former slaves liberated by raids into Missouri. "Give them a fair chance," Lane pleaded, "put arms in their hands, and they will do the balance of the fighting in this war." Still, Lane took the precaution of training his Negro troops apart from skeptical white Union soldiers. "With one exception," observed a local journalist, "there is not a Kansas regiment from which [the Negro soldiers] would not have as much to fear as from the rebels."

Such prejudice confirmed Lincoln's objections to arming Negroes. "It would produce dangerous and fatal dissatisfaction in our army," the president assured Senator Browning, "and do more injury than good."

When a delegation of Republicans from Indiana came to the White House on August 4, offering to raise two Negro combat regiments, the president refused their help. He would employ "all colored men offered as laborers," Lincoln explained, but he would not promise to make them soldiers. He feared that arming Negroes "would turn 50,000 bayonets from the loyal Border States against us," and possibly lead Kentucky to secede. The westerners pressed him until Lincoln lost his temper. "Gentlemen," he replied, "you have my decision. I have made my mind up deliberately and mean to adhere to it. . . . If the people are dissatisfied, I will resign and let Mr. Hamlin try it."

End of a Campaign

At the end of July 1862, Union armies in the West were on the defensive. Instead of advancing farther into Confederate territory, General Halleck divided the Union forces to protect their recent gains. But the Union lacked sufficient manpower to safeguard every strategic point, and concentrated Confederate attacks overwhelmed the dispersed northern armies. General Braxton Bragg recaptured Chattanooga and headed north for Kentucky. Baton Rouge fell to the rebels while Grant stood idly in northern Mississippi, awaiting further orders.

In the east, Halleck chose to gather the Union forces for another advance on Richmond. On August 3, the general in chief ordered McClellan to withdraw his army from the peninsula and bring it north to join Pope's Army of Virginia. McClellan protested. "Here, directly in front of this army, is the heart of the rebellion," he wired Halleck. "It is here that all our resources should be collected to strike the blow which will determine the fate of the nation."

"I find the forces divided, and I wish to unite them," Halleck replied. "If you or anyone else had presented a better plan I certainly should have adopted it. But all of your plans require reinforcements, which it is impossible to give you."

Still camped east of Richmond, between the Confederate capital and the Army of the Potomac, Lee watched McClellan slowly transfer his forces northward to join Pope's Army of Virginia. Lee knew that he could not withstand the combined force of the two Union armies. He would have to lure Pope into a battle before the bulk of McClellan's troops arrived.

Lincoln, meanwhile, ordered Pope not to risk a battle unless he was certain of destroying the rebel armies. Another defeat in northern Virginia, Lincoln feared, "would be a greater nuisance than several victories would abate."

Emancipation Debate

Passage of the Confiscation Act did not resolve the debate over emancipation in Congress. The bill itself freed no slaves; it permitted confiscation of slaves only after federal courts declared their owners guilty of treason, and no federal courts were operating in the South. So antislavery activists maintained their pressure on legislators and the president to liberate the Confederacy's slaves.

Even moderate journals in the North began to urge immediate emancipation. The *National Intelligencer*, an old-line Washington newspaper known for its paternalistic attitude toward Negroes, urged Lincoln on July 31 to transform the Confiscation Act into an emancipation decree. Freeing the slaves would strike at "the stomach of the rebellion," the editors argued, by depriving the Confederate Army of labor behind the lines. "If hominy be wanting can the Southern Confederacy expect to thrive?"

Numerous northern soldiers and government officials who saw first-hand the effects of slavery on southern society concluded that the institution had to be destroyed—as much for the sake of southern whites as the Negroes themselves. "The more I see of slavery in all its enormity the more I am satisfied that it is a curse to our country," wrote one Union colonel in Tennessee. "Outside the towns in the South the people are a century behind the free states." "The institution of slavery is as much a curse to the whites as the blacks and kills industry and improvements of every kind," observed another Union soldier in the South. "Slavery has deadened all enterprise and prosperity."

General Butler underwent the same conversion as he grew more familiar with the institution. As one observer noted, Butler "began to see that this is not an armed rebellion, but a great social and political revolution; that, sooner or later, the character and habits of the whole people must be reformed . . . by organizing free, compensated and honest labor." By August, Butler had destroyed Louisiana's "black codes," and he stopped returning fugitive slaves to loyal owners.

At the same time, however, prejudice against Negroes was rising among white northerners. Some whites blamed Negroes for causing the war, as if slavery were the fault of the slaves themselves. Other whites, particularly Irish immigrants living in northern cities, feared that freed slaves might migrate north and compete with them as a source of cheap labor.

"There is but one thing, sir, that we want here," announced an Ohioan to a visiting journalist, "and that is to get rid of the niggers." A lecturer for the American Anti-Slavery Society reported that denunciations of Negroes "were never more common in my hearing. Many Republicans unite with Democrats in cursing the 'niggers,' and in declaring that the slaves, if possibly emancipated by the war, must be removed from the country."

"We may as well look this prejudice in the face as a disturbing element in the way of emancipation," noted the editors of one Anglo-African newspaper. To thousands of white northerners, "setting black men free to be the equals of white men in the slave States is something more dreadful than rebellion or secession, or even a dismembered union."

When several state governments found it necessary to institute conscription in the summer of 1862, anti-Negro riots broke out among immigrant and southern-born communities in Pennsylvania, Indiana, and Ohio, where protestors insisted that "we won't fight to free the nigger." Before the summer ended, more violent demonstrations against Negroes erupted in Cincinnati and New York.

Doubts and Threats

Throughout August, Lincoln gave the northern public no sign that he intended to issue an emancipation decree. As he awaited a Union victory, the president sought to allay his doubts about the wisdom of emancipation.

Meanwhile, not even the oppressive heat and humidity of Washington in midsummer stemmed the constant stream of visitors to the White House. "The crowd continually increases instead of diminishing," complained John Hay. One guest, an Indian agent, brought Lincoln a gorgeously embroidered pair of Indian moccasins; when he put them on, the president's face broke into a huge grin.

In early August, Lincoln called his old friend Leonard Swett to the Executive Mansion. Together, they reviewed the president's recent correspondence about slavery, defining the arguments for and against emancipation. Swett departed with the definite impression that Lincoln "will issue no proclamation emancipating negroes."

Yet Lincoln did not hesitate to employ the *threat* of emancipation to encourage southern whites to return to the Union. His warnings to the residents of Union-occupied southern Louisiana were particularly blunt. When a special State Department agent reported in late July that rumors of impending emancipation had quashed whatever Unionist sentiment existed in that region, Lincoln replied that Louisianans could still rejoin the Union "upon the old terms"—retaining slavery, at least temporarily. If they persisted in their rebellion, however, they could expect the president to use every weapon at his command. "What I *cannot* do, of course I *will* not do," wrote the president, "but it may as well be understood, once for all, that I shall not surrender this game leaving any available card unplayed."

In a note to a loyalist in Louisiana on July 28, Lincoln admitted that he had delayed emancipation as long as possible, trying to buy time for southern slaveholders to accept gradual, compensated emancipation. But he could no longer protect them and still win the war. "The truth is, that what is done, and omitted, about slaves, is done and omitted on the same military necessity," the president concluded.

Several days later, Lincoln told the financier August Belmont, a leading New York Democrat, that "this government cannot much longer play a game in which it stakes all, and its enemies stake nothing." Confederate leaders, Lincoln added, "must understand that they cannot experiment for ten years trying to destroy the government, and if they fail still come back into the Union unhurt. If they expect in any contingency to ever have the Union as it was . . . 'Now is the time.'"

Colonization: A Final Request

"I do not think that . . . the *government* has any *purpose* to get rid of slavery," announced the abolitionist Wendell Phillips in a speech in New York on August 1. "On the contrary, I think the present purpose of the government . . . is to end the war and save slavery." In a letter to Senator Sumner, Phillips charged that "Lincoln is doing twice as much today to break this Union as [Jefferson] Davis is. We are paying thousands of lives & millions of dollars as penalty for having a *timid* and *ignorant* President, all the more injurious because *honest*."

To the abolitionist orator Anna Dickinson, Lincoln seemed nothing more than "an Ass . . . for the Slave Power to ride." Frederick Douglass compared Lincoln unfavorably to the inept James Buchanan. "I do not hesitate to say," Douglass continued, "that whatever may have been his intentions, the action of President Lincoln has been calculated in a marked and decided way to shield and protect [slavery] form the very blows which its horrible crimes have loudly and persistently invited."

Lincoln refused to reply to these attacks. With emancipation an imminent possibility (if Pope should defeat Lee), the president faced the vexing problem of how to fit more than 3 million free Negroes into American society.

Assuming that whites would not grant equal rights to Negroes, Lincoln still hoped that freed slaves might serve as the vanguard in a government-sponsored colonization project. To coordinate the administration's colonization efforts, Lincoln appointed the Reverend James Mitchell of Indiana as commissioner of emigration in the Department of the Interior.

A bipartisan majority in Congress supported the president's initiatives, authorizing $600,000 to investigate various colonization prospects. Most legislators did not take these schemes seriously—one Republican congressman dismissed them as "a damn humbug"—but they hoped that proposals for colonization would allay whites' anxieties about increased numbers of free Negroes.

One venture already was under way. Between 1861 and 1862, over 2,000 American Negroes emigrated to Haiti. Unfortunately, the Haitian project suffered from mismanagement and unrealistic expectations. After months of battling disease, an inhospitable climate, impoverished soil, and a backward economy, most of the surviving emigrants returned to the United States wholly disillusioned.

Still, Lincoln saw no viable alternative to colonization. Hoping to persuade prominent Negroes to publicly endorse the concept of colonization, Lincoln received a delegation of Negro leaders at the White House on August 14, 1862.

For nearly an hour Lincoln spoke without giving his guests a chance to respond. Emigration, he insisted, would provide Negroes with enhanced economic opportunities. "You and we are different races," the president said. "We have between us a broader difference than exists between almost any other two races. Whether it is right or wrong I need not discuss, but this physical difference is a great disadvantage to us both, as I think your race suffer very greatly, many of them by living among us, while ours suffer from your presence. In a word we suffer on each side. If this is admitted, it affords a reason at least why we should be separated."

There was no place in the United States, Lincoln continued, where white Americans treated Negroes as equals. "Go where you are treated the best," he said, "and the ban is still upon you." The civil war had only exacerbated whites' prejudices. "See our present condition," he told them, "the country engaged in war!—our white men cutting one another's throats, none knowing how far it will extend; and then consider what we know to be the truth. But for your race among us there could not be war, although many men engaged on either side do not care for you one way or the other."

If his guests endorsed one of his colonization schemes for Central America, Lincoln predicted, they "would open a wide door for many to be made free." Both races would benefit by reducing tension between whites and blacks, Lincoln claimed, and the Union could be restored more quickly.

When the president finished, the delegation's chairman replied curtly that he and his colleagues would send their reply to the Executive Mansion. A few Negro spokesmen applauded Lincoln's plan, but an overwhelming number of Negroes in the North rejected it. "This is our country as much as it is yours, and we will not leave it," a Negro in Philadelphia wrote to Lincoln. "Pray tell us," asked an outraged Negro in New Jersey, "is our right to a home in this country less than your own, Mr. Lincoln? Must I crush out my cherished hopes and aspirations, abandon my home, and become a pander to the mean and selfish spirit that oppresses me?" Infuriated by the racist implications of Lincoln's speech, Frederick Douglass dismissed it as the words of "an itinerant Colonization lecturer, showing all his inconsistencies, his pride of race and blood, his contempt for Negroes and his canting hypocrisy."

A Sense of Foreboding

By the middle of August, General Lee was planning an assault upon Pope's Army of Virginia, encamped south of Manassas between the Rapidan and the Rappahannock. Despite the fact that Lee had 15,000 fewer men, the Confederate commander intended to divide his forces and launch a surprise attack from two directions, trapping Pope in the "V" formed by the two rivers.

Recognizing the danger, Pope withdrew behind the Rappahannock on August 18. Soon he received a message from Halleck: "Stand firm on that line until I can help you . . . Dispute every inch of ground, and fight like the devil till we can reinforce you. Forty-eight hours more and we can make you strong enough."

Burnside's troops arrived, but most of McClellan's force remained on the peninsula. McClellan claimed that he lacked enough transports to move his men. When Halleck urged him to hurry his troops to join Pope, McClellan promised to "faithfully carry out the new programme." Yet McClellan privately swore that "it will take a long time to embark this army & have it ready for action on the banks of the Potomac."

Even when McClellan's troops were on their way, Lincoln took no comfort from the news. "Now I am to have a sweat of five or six days," the president sighed. "The Confederates will strive to gather on Pope before McClellan can get around, and his first corps is not in the Potomac yet."

Union First

"Do you remember," Horace Greeley wrote to Senator Sumner, "that old theological book containing this: 'Chapter One—Hell; Chapter Two—Hell Continued.' Well, that gives a hint of the way Old Abe *ought to be* talked to in this crisis." Impatient for a presidential emancipation proclamation, Greeley vowed to chastise Lincoln continuously in the editorials of the *New York Tribune* "till the Government toes the mark on the Slavery question."

In an open letter to Lincoln published on August 20, Greeley accused the president of failing to enforce the Confiscation Act of 1862. The northern people demanded emancipation, he insisted. "There is not one disinterested, determined, intelligent champion of the Union cause who does not feel that all attempts to put down the Rebellion and at the same time uphold its inciting cause [i.e., slavery] are preposterous and futile."

Two days later, Lincoln responded to Greeley in his own open letter. The president made it clear that the preservation of the Union remained his primary concern, as it had been since Inauguration Day.

"I would save the Union," Lincoln wrote. "I would save it the shortest way under the Constitution. The sooner the national authority can be restored, the nearer the Union will be 'the Union as it was'"—in other words, a Union *with* slavery.

"If there be those who would not save the Union, unless they could at the same time *save* slavery," Lincoln continued, "I do not agree with them. If there be those who would not save the Union unless they could at the same time *destroy* slavery, I do not agree with them. My paramount object in this struggle is to save the Union, and is not either to save or to destroy slavery. If I could save the Union without freeing *any* slave I would do it, and if I could save it by freeing *all* the slaves I would do it, and if I could save it by freeing some and leaving others alone I would also do that. What I do about slavery, and the colored race, I do because I believe it helps to save the Union; and what I forbear, I forbear because I do *not* believe it would help to save the Union. I shall do *less* whenever I shall believe what I am doing hurts the cause, and I shall do *more* whenever I shall believe doing more will help the cause. I shall try to correct errors when shown to be errors; and I shall adopt new views so fast as they shall appear to be true views."

Following Greeley's publication of Lincoln's letter on August 25, moderate Republican politicians and editors seconded the president's sentiments. "He could not have said anything more satisfactory to the country in general," noted the *New York Times*. Nevertheless, Greeley continued to assail the president in the *Tribune*. Finally Lincoln invited the editor to come to Washington to discuss the matter in person. When Greeley arrived at the Executive Mansion, Lincoln asked what he had done to provoke the hostility of the *Tribune*.

"You should issue a proclamation abolishing slavery," Greeley replied.

"Suppose I do that," Lincoln said. "There are now 20,000 of our muskets on the shoulders of Kentuckians, who are bravely fighting our battles. Every one of them will be thrown down or carried over to the rebels."

"Let them do it," Greeley snapped. "The cause of the Union will be stronger if Kentucky should secede with the rest than it is now."

"Oh," Lincoln answered, "I can't think that!"

Second Manassas

In the last week of August, Charles Francis Adams, Jr., checked into Willard's Hotel in Washington. While his Massachusetts regiment received orders to reinforce the Army of Virginia, Adams had been offered a position on General Pope's staff.

After spending a few days in the capital, Adams was inclined to refuse the offer. There was too much jealousy and infighting among the Union generals and the civilian leadership. Lincoln's advisers—especially Stanton and Chase—still distrusted McClellan; McClellan and his coterie despised Pope; and no one respected Halleck. "The air of this city seems thick with treachery," wrote Adams to his father. "Our army seems in danger of utter demoralization and I have not since the war began felt such a tug on my nerves as today in Washington. Everything is ripe for a terrible panic."

On August 27, General Stonewall Jackson attacked Pope's supply depot at Manassas. The rebels took everything they could carry or eat and destroyed the rest. By the time Pope realized what had happened, Jackson was gone, and Pope spent the night trying to find him.

When Pope finally found the elusive rebels, he ordered a vigorous attack at dawn on August 29. Assuming that he had caught Jackson in a trap, Pope sent a triumphant telegram to Washington anticipating the destruction of the Confederate army. On the same battlefield by Bull Run that had witnessed the first major battle of the war thirteen months earlier, wave after wave of Union infantrymen smashed into the rebel defenders. The Confederate lines held; nevertheless, Pope wired Stanton that "our troops behaved splendidly," and he expected to pursue and defeat the enemy in the morning. By that time, however, Lee had brought the rest of his army to Jackson's side.

Meanwhile, McClellan finally arrived in Alexandria with the remaining three corps of the Army of the Potomac. Halleck ordered him to send two corps at once to reinforce Pope. McClellan demurred, claiming to have received reports that a Confederate force of 120,000 men had slipped behind Pope and was heading for Washington.

Lincoln spent most of August 29 in the War Department's telegraph office, awaiting news from Bull Run. While Pope's troops were assaulting the Confederate lines at Manassas, Lincoln wired McClellan for his advice on their next move. McClellan suggested that they "leave Pope to get out of his scrape & at once use all our means to make the Capital perfectly safe." When he read McClellan's reply, Lincoln's temper exploded. A reporter for the *New York Tribune* later wrote that he had never seen the president "so wrathful as last night against George."

As Lincoln and John Hay rode together from the Soldiers' Home to the White House the following morning, Lincoln told Hay about McClellan's erratic conduct, including his determination to keep one of his corps from advancing to Pope's support, despite Halleck's direct order. "It really seemed to him that McC wanted Pope defeated," Hay noted. "The President seemed to think him a little crazy."

Shortly after noon on Saturday, August 30, Pope—still unaware that Lee had reinforced Jackson—sent his Union troops straight into the jaws of a Confederate vise. Rebel artillery pounded the unsuspecting Union lines; as the northern troops staggered and fell back, Confederate reserves advanced at a run. By nightfall the Union army was in full retreat, fleeing northward toward Washington, burning freight cars full of supplies and munitions along the way.

"It's another Bull Run, sir. It's another Bull Run!" reported one stunned Union general. Pope's initial reports to Washington displayed no sense of panic. "We have had a terrific battle again today," he wired Halleck that evening. "The troops are in good heart, and marched off the field without the least hurry or confusion. . . . Do not be uneasy. We will hold our own here."

But Pope's troops understood the magnitude of their defeat, and they blamed the outcome squarely on their commander. "Open sneering at General Pope was heard on all sides," reported one Union veteran as they trudged sullenly through the mud toward Washington under a cold, soaking rain. The Union ranks were jumbled in disorder, with half-formed regiments—some with guns and some without—and stragglers drifting away, and wagons wrecked and abandoned. "Everyone you met had an unwashed, sleepy, downcast aspect," noted an officer, "and looked as if he would like to hide his head somewhere from all the world."

Washingtonians could hear the sound of cannon, could smell the gunpowder from Manassas. Confident of victory, Lincoln dined early that evening with Stanton and Hay. Shortly before eight o'clock, a messenger brought word to the White House that Pope was retreating. Lincoln turned sadly to Hay. "Well, John, we are whipped again, I am afraid."

As a strong wind cleared the skies over Washington the following day, Lincoln learned that most of the Army of Virginia was still intact, and that the Confederate Army, too, had suffered heavy casualties. This news, Hay noted, put the president "in a singularly defiant tone of mind."

Despite Pope's losses, Lincoln expected the Union troops to regain the offensive. "We must hurt this enemy," he insisted over and over again. "We must whip these people now. Pope must fight them, [and] if they are too strong for him he can gradually retire to these fortifications."

Time, however, only discouraged Pope. Each day he grew more convinced that his army was on the verge of disintegration. On the morning of

September 1, he recommended that the Army of Virginia withdraw to Washington to "avoid great disaster." Shortly afterward, Pope asked Halleck "whether you feel secure about Washington should this army be destroyed?" "Unless something can be done to restore tone to this army," Pope warned, "it will melt away before you know it."

Alarmed, Stanton took the precaution of distributing arms to government clerks, organizing them into militia companies. Washington's saloons were shut down, and vital War Department documents were packed up for shipment to New York. Halleck, meanwhile, sent a telegram to McClellan: "I beg of you to assist me in this crisis with your ability and experience. I am utterly tired out."

McClellan Returns

As wounded Union soldiers staggered into the capital, Pope blamed his defeat on McClellan's refusal to come to his aid. Stanton agreed. With Chase's encouragement, the secretary of war drafted a petition to the president charging McClellan with insubordination and incompetence, insisting that he be dismissed to prevent "the destruction of our armies, the protraction of the war, the waste of our national resources, and the overthrow of the government." Attorney General Bates agreed to sign Stanton's petition, as did Secretary of the Interior Smith. Welles refused, suggesting that they discuss the matter with Lincoln instead of presenting him with an ultimatum. Chase replied that mere "conversations amounted . . . to but little with the President on subjects of this importance. Argument was useless. It was like throwing water on a duck's back."

In the meantime, Halleck convinced Lincoln that Pope's army was thoroughly demoralized and might be incapable of defending Washington. So, on the morning of September 2, Lincoln and Halleck visited McClellan at breakfast and offered him command of the Union troops in and around Washington—uniting the remnants of the Army of Virginia with the Army of the Potomac. "A terrible and thankless task," McClellan wrote to his wife. "I only consent to take it for my country's sake & with the humble hope that God has called me to it—how I pray that he may support me."

When Lincoln arrived at a Cabinet meeting that afternoon, Bates noted that "he seemed wrung by the bitterest anguish." The president admitted that "he felt almost ready to hang himself." Then he announced that he had approved Halleck's request to restore McClellan to command, at least until the general prepared the Army of the Potomac to fight again. "I must have McClellan to reorganize the army and bring it out of chaos," Lincoln said. No Union general could organize an army more effectively, and Lincoln could trust McClellan to fight capably on the defensive. Besides, he added, "McClellan has the army with him."

Stunned, every member of the Cabinet—including Postmaster General Blair, who was the only one still on reasonably good terms with McClellan—insisted that Lincoln was making a serious mistake. "I cannot but feel that giving command to McClellan is equivalent to giving Washington to the rebels," argued Chase.

His advisers' unanimous opposition to McClellan deepened Lincoln's distress. Yet he claimed he had no choice. "The order is mine," Lincoln replied, "and I will be responsible for it to the country." Privately, he agreed that McClellan "has acted badly in this matter, but we must use what tools we have. There is no man in the army who can man these fortifications and lick these troops of ours into shape half as well as he." McClellan was "too useful just now to sacrifice," Lincoln told Hay. "If he can't fight himself, he excels in making others ready to fight." Besides, the appointment of McClellan might conciliate moderate Democrats and help preserve the splintering northern pro-war coalition.

Although he blamed McClellan for the defeat at Manassas, Lincoln relegated the unfortunate Pope to Minnesota to subdue fractious Indian tribes. He sent McDowell, twice disgraced, to California. Neither general saw Washington again before the war ended.

Upon his return to the capital in early September, Seward confessed that the intense hostility between McClellan and Pope surprised and saddened him. "What is the use of growing old?" he asked a young friend.

"You learn something of men and things but never until too late to use it. I have only just now found out what military jealousy is."

Meditation

Alone in his office, Lincoln struggled to find a reason why the North could not quell the rebellion. Although he was not an outwardly religious man, Lincoln possessed a deep sense of fatalism; now he thought he discerned the hand of God in the recent Union defeats.

"The will of God prevails," Lincoln wrote as he turned the matter over in his mind. "In great contests each party claims to act in accordance with the will of God. Both *may* be, and one *must* be wrong. God can not be *for*, and *against* the same thing at the same time. In the present civil war it is quite possible that God's purpose is something different from the purpose of either party."

Yet Lincoln did not know what God wanted him to do about slavery. During the days after the second battle of Manassas, the president's private secretaries claimed that "his mind was burdened with the weightiest question of his life"—whether or not to emancipate the South's slaves.

"I am almost ready to say this is probably true—that God wills this contest, and wills that it shall not end yet," the president continued. "By his mere quiet power, on the minds of the now contestants, He could have either *saved* or *destroyed* the Union without a human contest. Yet the contest began. And having begun He could give the final victory to either side any day. Yet the contest proceeds."

Invasion

General Lee crossed the Potomac River with nearly 55,000 Confederate troops on September 4. He planned to sever Washington's rail connections to the Midwest by destroying key bridges and aqueducts, and then lure the Army of the Potomac from the capital and strike it far away from its base of supplies. His own starving troops—sick of subsisting on green corn and apples—could live off the rich produce of western Maryland's farms, and perhaps garner support from proslavery Marylanders, whom Lee expected to rise up in support of the Confederate invasion.

Meanwhile, Virginia would gain a respite from six months of constant warfare. Although Lee realized that his army lacked sufficient supplies and transportation to sustain an invasion, he decided to advance anyway. By the autumn of 1862, northern factories were producing war materiel in increasing quantities, and Lee knew that the South could not win a war of attrition. "We cannot afford to be idle," Lee concluded, "and though weaker than our opponents in men and military equipments, must endeavor to harass them if we cannot destroy them."

By invading the North, officials in Richmond also hoped to persuade Britain and France to recognize the Confederacy. Following the second Union defeat at Manassas—which one British cabinet member deemed "a very complete smashing"—Prime Minister Palmerston told Lord Russell that a decision by Great Britain to recognize the Confederacy hinged upon Lee's invasion of Maryland. "If the Federals sustain a great defeat," Palmerston said, "they may be at once ready for mediation, and the iron should be struck while it is hot."

Even without foreign help, the presence of a rebel army on Union soil might induce the northern public to abandon the fight. Already some northern Democrats were suggesting that moderates on both sides could patch up their differences. One antiwar New Yorker foresaw a compromise peace arranged by a coalition of Confederates and conservative Union generals who would "turn out Lincoln and his 'Black Republicans' and use their respective armies to enforce their decision North and South and reestablish the Union and the Constitution."

Lincoln, on the other hand, viewed Lee's invasion of Maryland as an opportunity to lure the rebels into a trap and regain the offensive. "We could end the war by allowing the enemy to go to Harrisburg and Philadelphia," the president suggested. Once the Confederate Army advanced too far from its supply base in Virginia, Union forces could turn and destroy it.

Such a patient course would have been political suicide. Already, news of Confederate troops on Union soil was renewing doubts about Lincoln's leadership. The expenditure of millions of dollars and thousands of lives over the past eighteen months seemed to have accomplished nothing. "Disgust with our present government is certainly universal," reported George Templeton Strong. "Even Lincoln himself has gone down at last, like all our popular idols of the last eighteen months. . . . It is impossible to resist the conviction that he is unequal to his place."

By failing to find a competent general and stick with him, Lincoln created an impression of indecisiveness. "This changing from McClellan to Pope, and from Pope to McClellan, creates distrust and uncertainty," noted a Republican from Ohio. Other critics dismissed the president as nothing more than a ribald jokester. "Tale-telling and jesting illy suit the hour and become the man in whose hands the destiny of a great nation is trembling," declared one of Chicago's leading Methodist clergymen. Strong agreed; Lincoln's "only special gift," he wrote, "is fertility of smutty stories."

In early September, a convention of Republicans in Massachusetts refused to pass a vote of confidence in the Lincoln administration; it did, however, approve a resolution that "slavery should be exterminated." Governor John Andrew of Massachusetts was so convinced of Lincoln's incompetence that he scheduled an emergency meeting of all northern governors for late September at Altoona, Pennsylvania. Andrew claimed that his goal was "if possible to save the Prest. from the infamy of ruining his country," but he really wanted to wrest control of the war effort from the president.

Radicals in Congress also wished to push Lincoln aside and direct the war themselves. Senator Chandler, who felt that the president was being "bullied by those traitor generals," felt it imperative to act before McClellan and his lieutenants launched a coup and established a military dictatorship. In the House, Thaddeus Stevens insisted that only the Radical Republican leadership possessed "sufficient grasp of mind and sufficient moral courage, to treat this as a radical revolution, and remodel our institutions"—including the emancipation of southern slaves and "the desolation of the South."

Salmon Chase doubted that Lincoln would ever free himself of the influence of his friends from the border states. "The truth," thought Chase, "is that the President with the most honest intentions in the world, and a naturally clear judgment and a true, unselfish patriotism, has yielded so much to Border State and negrophobic counsels that he now finds it difficult to arrest his own descent towards the most fatal concessions. He has already separated himself from the great body of the party which elected him; distrusts most those who most represent its spirit; and waits—For what?"

Conservatives, meanwhile, feared that Lincoln might succumb to the Radicals' persistent demands and widen the war to include emancipation, in an effort to increase public support. Lincoln's old friend Orville Browning begged him not to destroy the bipartisan pro-war coalition by giving in to those "few very radical and extreme men who can think, nor talk, nor dream of any thing but the negro." Blaming the recent Union defeats on "the most sinister" influence of Stanton and Chase, Senator Garrett Davis of Kentucky urged the president to dismiss the two Cabinet officials before they further damaged the Union cause.

During the next several weeks, Lincoln was besieged by visitors and petitions arguing for or against emancipation, many assuring him that God was on their side. Lincoln shrugged aside such claims. "I hope it will not be irreverent for me to say, that if it is probable that God would reveal his will to others, on a point so connected with my duty, it might be supposed he would reveal it directly to me," he said to one group of guests. "*And if I can learn what it is,*" the president added, "*I will do it!*"

Final Arguments

On September 13, Lincoln met with a delegation of church leaders from Illinois who came to the Executive Mansion to urge him to free the Confederacy's slaves. He assured them that the difficulty of subduing the rebellion had cured him of any legal or constitutional objections about issuing an emancipation proclamation. "As commander-in-chief of the army and navy, in time of war," he explained, "I suppose I have a right to take any measure which may best subdue the enemy." He also had shed any fear that southern Negroes, suddenly freed, might rise up and slaughter their former masters.

Instead, Lincoln said that he now viewed emancipation primarily as "a practical war measure," which he could employ "according to the advantages or disadvantages it may offer to the suppression of the rebellion."

With Confederate troops advancing through northern territory, however, he feared that any emancipation decree would earn the federal government nothing but ridicule. "What *good* would a proclamation of emancipation from me do," Lincoln asked, "especially as we are now situated? I do not want to issue a document that the whole world will see must necessarily be inoperative, like the Pope's bull against the comet!"

Besides, the federal government was not prepared to cope with massive numbers of runaway slaves who might be inspired by a presidential proclamation to desert their masters. "*What should we do with them*?" Lincoln asked. "How can we feed and care for such a multitude?"

Lincoln admitted that emancipation probably would help the Union cause in Europe, but he was less sanguine about public reaction in the northern states. "It would help *somewhat* at the North," he told the ministers, "though not so much, I fear, as you and those you represent imagine."

Nor did Lincoln underestimate the opposition to emancipation that still existed in the border states. He feared that a premature declaration of emancipation might drive those states into the arms of the Confederacy. Lincoln also doubted that Negro soldiers would contribute much to the Union war effort. "If we were to arm them, I fear that in a few weeks the arms would be in the hands of the rebels," he confessed, "and indeed thus far we have not had arms enough to equip our white troops."

As his guests prepared to leave, Lincoln assured them that his doubts did not mean he had decided not to issue an emancipation decree. "I can assure you that the subject is on my mind, by day and night, more than any other. Whatever shall appear to be God's will I will do."

Decision

As Lee's army occupied the town of Frederick, Maryland, and Confederate scouts penetrated into southern Pennsylvania, Lincoln reached a decision. "When the rebel army was at Frederick," he later recalled, "I determined, as soon as it should be driven out of Maryland, to issue a Proclamation of Emancipation such as I thought most likely to be useful. I said nothing to any one; but I made the promise to myself and—to my Maker."

Antietam Creek

Within a week after McClellan assumed command of the Army of the Potomac, it was clear that the Union troops were not nearly as demoralized as Lincoln and Halleck feared. As Lee marched through western Maryland, Lincoln asked General Ambrose Burnside to take command of the army and smash the Confederate invaders. Loyal to McClellan, Burnside refused.

So McClellan led more than 80,000 Union soldiers into Maryland on September 7, using his troops to shield Washington from Lee's army. He carried with him Lincoln's repeated admonitions to "find and hurt this enemy now." But McClellan maintained a leisurely pace, covering less than 6 miles a day. Even at the head of this vast army—if the men and wagons were stretched out in line, they would have covered 50 miles—McClellan imagined that Lee's army outnumbered him. On September 11, he asked Lincoln for 25,000 reinforcements. "I am for sending you all that can be spared," Lincoln replied, dispatching General Fitz-John Porter with 21,000 men, and rushing Pennsylvania militiamen across the border. "I hope others can follow Porter very soon," the president wired McClellan.

Once the rebels cut the Baltimore and Ohio rail line to Washington, Lee expected the Union garrison of 11,500 men at Harpers Ferry to withdraw, but Halleck failed to issue the order. With this Union force still behind him, commanding a key point along the Potomac, Lee decided to divide his forces again, sending Stonewall Jackson to western Virginia and General A. P. Hill to compel the garrison at Harpers Ferry to surrender before rejoining the main Confederate Army.

On the morning of September 13, a Union soldier found a copy of Lee's orders, wrapped around three cigars, lying in a field on a farm outside of Frederick. The papers were brought to McClellan later that day. Now McClellan knew that he outnumbered the Confederates, and that his enemy was divided, with Lee's depleted army less than a day's march away.

"There never was a general so fruitlessly favored by fortune as McClellan," wrote Hay and Nicolay. Although an immediate Union assault on Lee would have resembled, in their words, "a fight between a man blindfolded and one having use of his eyes," McClellan maintained his patient, methodical pace.

That evening, a group of officers on McClellan's staff devised a plan to march to Washington and intimidate Lincoln, Stanton, and Halleck—whom they called "the old women at Washington"—into ending the war. Regarding Lincoln with contempt and Stanton with hatred, the officers believed that if they forced the president to abandon any plans to interfere with slavery, the Union could be restored without further bloodshed. McClellan apparently knew nothing of their plot.

Early the following day, Union troops attacked an outnumbered Confederate force at South Mountain. By nightfall, they had forced their way through one gap. McClellan was jubilant. "It has been a glorious victory," he informed Halleck. "I am hurrying everything forward to endeavor to press their retreat to the utmost."

"Destroy the rebel army, if possible," Lincoln urged McClellan. "God bless you, and all with you." But still McClellan dawdled. "Time," observed one Confederate commander, "was of no especial importance to him."

On September 15, the Union garrison at Harpers Ferry surrendered. By now, Lee—encamped at Sharpsburg, Maryland—realized that McClellan knew the Confederate forces were dangerously divided. Lee urged Hill to return at once. Jackson, too, hurried eastward with his division.

McClellan spent September 15 arraying his army along Antietam Creek, a mile away from Sharpsburg. Even though he outnumbered the enemy by nearly 30,000 men, McClellan made no move toward the rebel armies that day.

Nor did he attack the following day. By the time the battle of Antietam began on the morning of September 17, a substantial portion of Jackson's men had reached Sharpsburg. The remainder arrived that afternoon.

Still, McClellan enjoyed nearly a two-to-one superiority in numbers at the start of the day. Lee's army held the higher ground, and while a lack of equipment kept them from digging entrenchments, the Confederate troops took up strong defensive positions behind stone walls, rocks, clumps of trees, and—in the center of the rebel line—a sunken farm road.

Nearly 100,000 men were wedged into a compact field, leaving scant room for maneuvering. Little maneuvering was attempted on either side. At daylight, McClellan threw the first Union corps, led by General Joe Hooker (McDowell's replacement), against the Confederate left. "In a second the air was full of the hiss of bullets and the hurtle of grapeshot," recalled one northern soldier. "The mental strain was so great that I saw at that moment . . . the whole landscape turned slightly red."

After a Confederate counterattack devastated Hooker's corps, McClellan sent another wave against the rebel left. "In less time than it takes to tell it," reported a colonel from Massachusetts, "the ground was strewn with the bodies of the dead and wounded. Nearly two thousand were disabled in a moment."

By failing to commit overwhelming numbers along the entire line at once, McClellan afforded Lee time to shift men from his right to withstand the staggered Union assault. Shortly before noon, a third Union corps slammed into the Confederate left. "There was nothing of it but sheer, persistent, brutal slaughter," recalled one horrified observer. In some places, Confederate and Union soldiers stood only fifty paces apart, firing at one another. "The men are loading and firing with demoniacal fury, and shouting and laughing hysterically," reported a Union officer. At midday, the brunt of the fighting shifted to the center, where the sheer weight of Union manpower and artillery fire finally broke the rebel line.

At 1:45 in the afternoon, McClellan took time to draft a telegram to his wife: "We are in the midst of the most terrible battle of the age." Already 12,000 men lay dead or wounded in cornfields, woodland, or the bloody sunken lane. McClellan still possessed sufficient reserves to turn the battle into a rout. "Lee's army was ruined," confessed one southern officer, "and the end of the Confederacy was in sight." But McClellan—believing that Lee, too, was holding thousands of men in reserve—refused to commit his reinforcements. Instead, Burnside belatedly launched an attack against the Confederate right, driving it back, grudgingly, until A. P. Hill arrived with his division to halt the Union advance.

By nightfall, Union troops had gained nearly a mile of ground. The Army of the Potomac suffered 12,000 casualties, nearly one-sixth of its entire force. Confederate losses totaled 11,000—one-fourth of Lee's army. "Who can tell, who can even imagine, the horrors of such a night," wondered an officer from Massachusetts, looking over the field of wounded men, "while the unconscious stars shone down, and the unconscious river went rippling by?"

McClellan convened his corps commanders to decide whether to resume the attack the following day. Three of them—Burnside, Hooker, and General William B. Franklin—favored a renewed offensive. But the appalling Union losses brought "the cold fit" upon McClellan once again. Anticipating a Confederate counterattack, he decided to hold his ground and begged Halleck to "send all the troops you can, by the most expeditious route."

Lee wanted desperately to remain at Sharpsburg, but his generals counseled retreat. "Where is the splendid division you had this morning?" Lee asked General John Hood. "They are lying on the field," Hood replied, "where you sent them." After waiting a full day, almost daring McClellan to resume the battle, Lee ordered a withdrawal. On the evening of September 18, in a pouring rain, the exhausted Confederate Army—dispirited and disordered by numerous stragglers—marched down narrow roads to the only Potomac ford and recrossed the river into Virginia. "This," Lee wrote to President Jefferson Davis, "is a woful condition of affairs."

Nearly all the Confederate troops were back on southern soil before McClellan realized they were gone. Jubilant that his army would not have to face a Confederate attack, McClellan informed Halleck on the morning of September 19 that "our victory was complete. The enemy is driven back into Virginia. Maryland & Penna. are now safe."

McClellan's soldiers did not share his exultation. "Why did we not attack them and drive them into the river?" asked Elisha Hunt Rhodes. "I do not understand these things. But then I am only a boy."

"If McClellan had only attacked again early Thursday morning [September 18], we could have driven them into the river or captured them," insisted another Union officer. "It was one of the supreme moments when by daring something, the destiny of the nation might have been changed."

After pressing McClellan repeatedly to crush the Confederate Army, Lincoln was stunned to hear that the rebel force had escaped. He had given McClellan every available soldier, a force nearly twice the size of the enemy, and still McClellan had achieved little more than a draw. Reporters in Washington speculated that McClellan allowed Lee to escape because he did not *want* to destroy the Confederate Army and open the way to abolition and a Radical revolution in the South. The president's only public comment was that McClellan was "well educated but very cautious." Privately, Lincoln later told Hay that he had heard reports of a Union officer saying "they did not mean to gain any decisive victory but to keep things running on so that they, the army, might manage things to suit themselves."

Emancipation

Antietam resolved Lincoln's thoughts on several critical issues. McClellan's failure to crush Lee's army meant that the war would continue for months, possibly years. If McClellan remained in command of the Union armies in the East, the North would probably never win a decisive victory. Yet McClellan remained the hero of a substantial segment of northern Democrats and conservative Republicans who wanted to restore the Union without abolishing slavery. With the autumn congressional elections approaching, Lincoln could not afford to dismiss McClellan.

But Lincoln also knew that a majority of Republicans in Congress now favored emancipation, at least as a military measure to weaken the Confederacy. Moreover, Radicals were threatening to withhold appropriations for military supplies unless Lincoln adopted a stronger antislavery policy and removed conservative generals from command. According to the editor of the moderate *National Intelligencer*, the president believed that "if he did not keep the Radical portion of his party at his back he could not long be sure of keeping an army at the front."

At the same time, Lincoln needed to keep control of the war from the Radicals, whose zeal for remaking the South would sabotage his plans to reunite the nation quickly once the rebellion ended. "My idea of this war,"

Lincoln explained to a reporter from New York, "is that it should always have a peace in its belly."

Lincoln spent most of the weekend after Antietam at the Soldiers' Home revising his draft of the Emancipation Proclamation. He returned to Washington on Sunday, passing wagons bringing thousands of wounded Union soldiers from Sharpsburg. All of the city's long, low white army hospital buildings and tents were full. Since Congress was in recess until December, military officials set up several thousand cots in the halls of the Capitol to handle the overflow of casualties.

On Monday morning, Lincoln sent State Department messengers to call Cabinet members to the Executive Mansion. When he met them at noon, the president appeared to be in a jocular mood. He began by reading aloud from the humorist Artemus Ward's latest book. The story concerned a visit to Utica of a showman with wax figures of Jesus and his disciples at the Last Supper. Outraged by the inclusion of Judas Iscariot in the scene, "a big burly feller" promptly assaulted the offending statue, "stoving in" Judas's head to prove that the renegade disciple "can't show hisself in Utiky with impunerty by a darn site." Everyone chuckled except the dour Stanton and Chase, of whom Lincoln once said that it would take a surgical operation to get a joke into his head.

"Gentlemen," Lincoln asked, "Why don't you laugh? With the frightful strain that is upon me night and day, if I did not laugh I should die, and you need this medicine as much as I do."

Putting Ward's book aside, the president came to the point. "I have, as you are aware, thought a great deal about the relation of this war to slavery," Lincoln said. The subject had dominated his thoughts ever since they discussed an emancipation proclamation two months earlier. "I have thought all along that the time for acting on it might very probably come," the president continued. "I think the time has come now."

He knew the circumstances were not ideal. "I wish," he said, "it were a better time. I wish we were in a better condition. The action of the army against the rebels has not been quite what I should have best liked." But the Confederate Army no longer threatened Union territory, and "the time for the annunciation of the emancipation policy could be no longer delayed." Many of his closest friends and supporters demanded the proclamation, and Lincoln believed that opinion in the North would sustain it as a military measure.

Hesitating briefly, the president added in a low voice that he also had promised God he would do it. Startled to hear Lincoln make a religious reference, Chase—sitting at the president's right hand—asked Lincoln to repeat it. "I made a solemn vow before God," Lincoln said, "that if General Lee was driven back from Pennsylvania, I would crown the result by the declaration of freedom to the slaves."

Emancipation was his decision alone, the president continued. He was not seeking his Cabinet officers' consent to issue a proclamation; he sought their advice only on wording and style. (It was a habit Lincoln frequently indulged in. "I can always tell more about a thing after I've heard it read aloud and know how it sounds," he said on another occasion. "What I want is an audience. Nothing sounds the same when there isn't anybody to hear it and find fault with it.")

Before he began reading, Lincoln admitted that he was not the ideal choice to play the role of emancipator. "I know very well that many others might, in this matter, as in others, do better than I can," he said. Nevertheless, the president believed he still retained more national support than any politician in Washington. "I am here," Lincoln concluded. "I must do the best I can, and bear the responsibility of taking the course which I feel I ought to take."

Lincoln then read his revised proclamation to the Cabinet, pausing occasionally to explain specific passages. A calm, reasoned document, it contained no outrage or condemnation of slavery, no call for a moral crusade.

In Lincoln's view, the chief executive alone possessed the power to emancipate slaves, and only as an emergency measure undertaken during a time of rebellion. To emphasize this point, Lincoln began the proclamation with the simple words: "By the President of the United States of America." For the rest of the document, he referred to himself as "Commander-in-Chief of the Army and Navy." Congressional Radicals could hardly criticize Lincoln's exercise of expanded executive powers in pursuit of a goal they so often had urged upon him.

Next came the title: "A Proclamation." No explanation, no subtitle.

Lincoln spent the first paragraph confirming, in cautious legalistic language, that his primary goal remained the restoration of the Union—"the constitutional relation between the United States, and each of the states, and the people thereof, in which that relation is, or may be suspended, or disturbed."

In the second paragraph, Lincoln outlined his plans to submit another proposal for compensated, voluntary emancipation to the next session of Congress. He would provide funds to any state in the Union that agreed to adopt plans for either immediate or gradual emancipation. To protect himself against charges that he was violating southern slaveowners' property rights, Lincoln extended the offer to any Confederate state that returned to the Union.

Knowing that whites feared the presence of large numbers of free blacks in their midst, Lincoln closed the second paragraph with a pledge to continue his efforts "to colonize persons of African descent upon this continent, or elsewhere." Negroes, he argued, would benefit by increased economic and political opportunities outside the United States, but Lincoln gave no indication that he intended to ask the freed slaves whether they wished to be colonized or not.

Not until the third paragraph did Lincoln mention freedom. Then he declared that on January 1, 1863, "all persons as slaves within any state, or designated part of a state, the people whereof shall be in rebellion against the United States shall be then, thenceforward, and forever free." Lincoln promised that as long as he was president, "the executive government of the United States, including the military and naval authorities thereof, will . . . recognize such persons as being free." Because he understood that his proclamation would not, by itself, physically deliver any slave from bondage, Lincoln added a pledge that no United States civilian or military official would take any action "to repress such persons, or any of them, in any efforts they may make for their actual freedom."

And so the slaves were freed—or were they? Here was no ringing declaration of human liberty, no phrases to inspire, no call to action. Instead, Lincoln bestowed freedom on more than 3 million individuals through words so carefully chosen that they threatened to obscure the impact of the proclamation.

The president's edict applied only to slaves in states still in rebellion against the federal government on January 1, 1863. Although Lincoln knew that no Confederate state was likely to return to the Union in the next three months, he nonetheless left the avenue open, making the proclamation a conditional grant of freedom.

Its effectiveness also depended on the support of Congress and the federal judiciary, since Lincoln could commit neither the legislative nor the judicial branch to emancipation. The presence of a Republican majority in Congress made it highly unlikely that either the House or Senate would overturn the proclamation, but the courts could modify or severely restrict its effects. Lincoln's decision to limit presidential support for emancipation to the life of his own administration reflected the same conservative interpretation of his executive powers, as if he were still feeling his way through a constitutional brier patch. Lincoln doubted that the federal government would ever return slaves to bondage once they were freed, but his decision to justify emancipation through the president's implied war powers opened up the possibility that slavery could be reinstituted once the rebellion ended.

After the president read the crucial third paragraph, Seward interrupted and suggested that Lincoln commit the executive branch to recognizing *and maintaining* the freedom of the former slaves. Lincoln replied that he had decided against adding such a phrase for practical reasons. "It was not my way to promise what I was not entirely *sure* that I could perform," Lincoln explained, "and I was not prepared to say that I thought we were exactly able to 'maintain' this."

Returning to his proclamation, Lincoln outlined the procedure by which he would determine which states remained in rebellion on January 1. The key test was whether a state was "in good faith represented in the Congress of the United States, by members chosen thereto, at elections wherein a majority of the qualified voters of such state shall have participated." These criteria exempted Tennessee from the proclamation, since Senator Andrew Johnson retained his seat despite the secession of the state government and the departure from Washington of all of Tennessee's other congressional representatives.

Most of the last sections of the proclamation cited the legal and political precedents for emancipation, specifically the second Confiscation Act and Congress's article of war of March 13, 1862, prohibiting any United States military personnel from returning fugitive slaves. Lincoln simply cut out the relevant passages from published copies of these acts and pasted them in the appropriate place in his manuscript.

He concluded by ordering all Union military officials to fulfill their duties under the Second Confiscation Act, while reassuring loyal slaveowners in the Confederate states that they would be compensated for the loss of any slaves liberated by the federal government.

When the president finished, Seward immediately gave his blessing to the proclamation. He still believed, however, that the president should strengthen it by committing the government to maintaining the freed slaves' liberty. Moreover, Seward recommended that the document omit "all reference to the act being sustained [only] during the incumbency of the present President."

Chase seconded Seward's suggestions and criticized the proclamation for its fainthearted support of Negro liberty. "The Proclamation does not, indeed, mark out exactly the course I should myself prefer," observed Chase. Though it galled him to see Lincoln gain credit for emancipation, he could hardly oppose the spirit of the proclamation.

After several other Cabinet members expressed their approval of Seward's revisions, Lincoln agreed to make the changes. Seward then offered one more suggestion. Anticipating an attempt to remove freed slaves forcibly from the United States, Seward asked Lincoln to add a phrase making any colonization project dependent upon the consent of the Negroes. Once again the entire Cabinet agreed, and Lincoln amended the proclamation accordingly.

No one questioned the justice of emancipation, or the president's legal authority to free the slaves. Only Postmaster General Montgomery Blair advocated delay. Blair feared that the proclamation would give Democrats "a club . . . to beat the Administration" and would cost the Republican

Party thousands of votes in the congressional elections scheduled to occur over the next six weeks. He also anticipated resistance to the proclamation within the army, and he worried that it might finally push the border states into secession.

Lincoln replied that he could defer no longer to the border states. Nor could he afford to conciliate northern Democrats at the risk of alienating moderate Republicans. "The difficulty," Lincoln explained, "was as great not to act as to act." Besides, he added, the Democrats' clubs "would be used against us take what course we might."

At the end of the meeting, Secretary of the Interior Smith walked out of the room with Blair and muttered under his breath that "if the President carried out that policy, he might count on losing Indiana" in the fall elections.

Several hours after the Cabinet meeting, the president and Secretary of State Seward signed the preliminary emancipation proclamation, and the Government Printing Office began preparing copies for distribution. Several hundred copies were dispatched to newspapers across the North. Fifteen thousand more went to the army, to be read to the troops two days later.

By the President of the
United States of America
A Proclamation.

I, Abraham Lincoln, President of the United States of America, and Commander-in-Chief of the Army and Navy thereof, do hereby proclaim and declare that hereafter, as heretofore, the war will be prosecuted for the object of practically restoring the constitutional relation between the United States, and each of the states, and the people thereof, in which states that relation is, or may be suspended, or disturbed.

That it is my purpose, upon the next meeting of Congress to again recommend the adoption of a practical measure tendering pecuniary aid to the free acceptance or rejection of all slave-states, so called, the people whereof may not then be in rebellion against the United

States, and which states, may then have voluntarily adopted, or thereafter may voluntarily adopt, immediate, or gradual abolishment of slavery within their respective limits; and that the effort to colonize persons of African descent, with their consent, upon this continent, or elsewhere, with the previously obtained consent of the Governments existing there, will be continued.

That on the first day of January in the year of our Lord, one thousand eight hundred and sixty-three, all persons held as slaves within any state, or designated part of a state, the people whereof shall be in rebellion against the United States shall be then, thenceforward, and forever free; and the executive government of the United States, including the military and naval authority thereof, will recognize and maintain the freedom of such persons, and will do no act or acts to repress such persons, or any of them, in any efforts they may make for their actual freedom.

That the executive will, on the first day of January aforesaid, by proclamation, designate the States, and part of states, if any, in which the people thereof respectively, shall then be in rebellion against the United States; and the fact that any state, or the people thereof shall, on that day be, in good faith represented in the Congress of the United States, by members chosen thereto, at elections wherein a majority of the qualified voters of such state shall have participated, shall, in the absence of strong countervailing testimony, be deemed conclusive evidence that such state and the people thereof, are not then in rebellion against the United States.

That attention is hereby called to an Act of Congress entitled "An act to make an additional Article of War" approved March 13, 1862, and which act is in the words and figures following:

Be it enacted by the Senate and House of Representatives of the United States of America in Congress assembled, That hereafter the following shall be promulgated as an additional article of war for the government of the army of the United States, and shall be obeyed and observed as such:

Article—. All officers or persons in the military or naval service of the United States are prohibited from employing any of the forces under their respective commands for the purpose of returning fugitives from service or labor, who may have escaped from any persons to whom such service or labor is claimed to be due, and any officer who shall be found guilty by a court-martial of violating this article shall be dismissed from the service.

Section 2. *And it be further enacted,* That this act shall take effect from and after its passage.

Also to the ninth and tenth sections of an act entitled "An Act to suppress Insurrection, to punish Treason and Rebellion, to seize and confiscate property of rebels, and for other purposes," approved July 17, 1862, and which sections are in the words and figures following:

Sec. 9. *And be it further enacted,* That all slaves of persons who shall hereafter be engaged in rebellion against the government of the United States, or who shall in any way give aid or comfort thereto, escaping from such persons and taking refuge within the lines of the army; and all slaves captured from such persons or deserted by them and coming under the control of the government of the United States; and all slaves of such persons found *on* (or) being within any place occupied by rebel forces and afterwards occupied by the forces of the United States, shall be deemed captives of war, and shall be forever free of their servitude and not again held as slaves.

Sec. 10. *And be it further enacted,* That no slave escaping into any State, territory, or the District of Columbia, from any other State, shall be delivered up, or in any way impeded or hindered of his liberty, except for crime, or some offence against the laws, unless the person claiming such fugitive shall first make oath that the person to whom the labor or service of such fugitive is alleged to be due is his lawful owner, and has not borne arms against the United States in the present rebellion, nor in any way given aid and comfort thereto; and no person engaged in the military or naval service of the United States shall, under any pretence whatever, assume to decide on the validity of the claim of any person to the service or labor of any other person, or surrender up any such person to the claimant, on pain of being dismissed from the service.

And I do hereby enjoin upon and order all persons engaged in the military and naval service of the United States to observe, obey, and enforce, within their respective sphere of service, the act, and sections above recited.

And the executive will in due time recommend that all citizens of the United States who shall have remained loyal thereto throughout the rebellion, shall (upon the restoration of the constitutional relation between the United States, and their respective states, and people, if that relation shall have been suspended or disturbed) be compensated for all losses by acts of the United States, including the loss of slaves.

In witness thereof, I have hereunto set my hand, and caused the seal of the United States to be affixed.

Done at the City of Washington, this twenty second day of September, in the year of our Lord, one thousand, eight hundred and sixty two, and sixty two, [sic] and of the Independence of the United States, the eighty seventh.

By the President: ABRAHAM LINCOLN
    WILLIAM H. SEWARD,   Secretary of State

7

A HUNDRED DAYS

Newspapers across the country printed copies of Lincoln's proclamation on Tuesday, September 23. That evening, a group of Washingtonians marched down Pennsylvania Avenue to serenade the president. Lincoln refused to greet them. When Hay pressed him, he relented and walked onto the balcony of the White House.

Lincoln told them he hoped he had not made a mistake in issuing his emancipation message. "No mistake," someone called out from the crowd. "You've made no mistakes yet." "Go ahead," shouted someone else, "you're right."

"What I did," Lincoln said, "I did after very full deliberation, and under a very heavy and solemn sense of responsibility." The serenaders applauded; there were cheers of "Good, good" and "Bless you."

"I shall make no attempt on this occasion to sustain what I have done or said by any comment," the president continued. "It is now for the country and the world to pass judgment on it, and, may be, take action upon it. I will say no more upon this subject. In my position I am environed with difficulties."

As Lincoln anticipated, his emancipation proclamation received a mixed reception in the North. When Hay offered to summarize the press reaction, Lincoln demurred. He had studied the proclamation longer than any newspaper editors, the president told Hay. He could learn nothing from them.

Abolitionists celebrated the emancipation message with torchlight parades, bonfires, and jubilant rallies. "God bless Abraham Lincoln!" exclaimed a headline in the *New York Tribune*. After months of vilifying the president for his refusal to attack slavery, Frederick Douglass rejoiced that he had lived to witness "this righteous decree." Ralph Waldo Emerson forgave "every mistake, every delay," and predicted that the North would rally around the proclamation.

Congressional Radicals were less enthusiastic. Most either refused to comment on Lincoln's message or praised it grudgingly. "The President may be a fool," wrote one congressman, "but see what he has done. He may have no policy. But he has given us one."

Legislative leaders objected, however, to Lincoln's claim that a president possessed the authority to emancipate the Confederacy's slaves. During a train ride to Washington, Senator Fessenden complained to a colleague that "the President, as President, had nothing to do with the condition of the negro." As commander in chief, Fessenden said, Lincoln "should simply have said that on the first of January he would direct his [Generals] to seize all the negroes they could reach in the insurrectionary districts." But the president's proclamation—which Fessenden felt was "very unfortunately worded"—"did not and could not affect the status of a single negro."

At the Republican governors' conference in Altoona, Pennsylvania, news of Lincoln's message and the Confederate retreat from Maryland derailed the movement to dictate policy to the president. On September 26, the state executives went to Washington to assure Lincoln of their support. All but one joined in endorsing the emancipation decree as "a measure of justice, humanity, and sound policy." Privately, Governor John Andrew of Massachusetts described the president's message as "a poor *document,* but a mighty *act.*"

Many northerners outside of abolitionist circles welcomed Lincoln's proclamation as a practical wartime measure. They expected it to weaken the Confederacy by encouraging slaves to desert their masters. Instead of providing strength to the Confederate states, argued an editorial in the *New York Times*, slavery would henceforth prove "an element of weakness," leading to the "total destruction" of the South, "when we make such use of it and its victims as lies in our power."

Some northerners who supported emancipation echoed Lincoln's anxieties about the ability of freed slaves to survive if they were suddenly given their freedom. "Immediate and absolute emancipation would benefit neither whites nor blacks," insisted the editors of the *Alta California* of San Francisco. "To be a blessing instead of a curse it must be gradual in its operations. The first duty of the Government will be to teach the negroes self-reliance, and that can only be done by a gradual slackening of the reins."

Since the proclamation freed only slaves outside the reach of the Union armies, other northerners dismissed it as a futile gesture—in the words of Elizabeth Blair, the postmaster general's sister, "a paper pronunciamento and of no practical result." When someone asked Secretary of State Seward why the administration had issued "so useless and mischievous a thing," Seward recounted the story of a Revolutionary War patriot who insisted upon erecting a liberty pole even after the war against Britain had been won. Asked why he needed to put up a pole when he was already free, the patriot replied, "What is liberty without a pole?" So it was with the president and his abolitionist supporters, Seward noted. What is war, he asked cynically, without a proclamation?

Worse, some northern critics foresaw a *longer* war now that Lincoln had threatened the Confederacy with the destruction of slavery. The editors of the antiadministration *New York Express* predicted that the proclamation would encourage enlistment in the South, adding as many as 300,000 soldiers to the Confederate cause. An editorial in the *Chicago Times* charged that it would make a peace based on compromise impossible. "If utter desperation had not before seized the people of the rebel States, as a consequence of the abolition and confiscation measures of the Congress at Washington, it will seize them now," predicted the *Times*. General Halleck responded that the events of the past year had already transformed the war into a life-and-death struggle. "There is now no pos-

'sible hope of reconciliation," Halleck insisted. "We must conquer the rebels or be conquered by them."

In the border states, Lincoln's message met with nearly universal condemnation. The *Louisville Journal* termed it "a gigantic usurpation, unrelieved by the promise of a solitary advantage." A number of Lincoln's longtime political allies in Kentucky broke with him over emancipation, and the Union Party in that state disavowed the proclamation to distance itself from the administration. In Tennessee, Unionists denounced "the atrocity and barbarism of Mr. Lincoln's proclamation," which they considered "treachery to the Union men of the South."

Midwestern opponents of the proclamation raised the specter of several million free Negroes fleeing Alabama, Mississippi, and Louisiana for Ohio, Indiana, and Illinois. Anti-Negro feeling in the region was on the rise; only a few months earlier, the Ohio state legislature had defeated by only two votes a motion to remove all Negroes already residing in the state. Even Senator Browning, Lincoln's longtime friend, attacked the proclamation as "unfortunate" and refused to discuss the issue with the president.

News of the proclamation coincided with Secretary of War Stanton's decision to transport into Illinois dozens of runaway slaves who had sought shelter in Union army camps. By September 1862, the number of contrabands in the Midwest threatened to overwhelm the army's relief efforts, leading Stanton to order the release of contraband women and children to civilian authorities, who would try to provide them with employment in the North. When the first wave of freed slaves arrived in Illinois farm communities seeking work, Democrats charged that the administration was attempting to "Africanize" the state. "This," they argued, "is but the beginning of the results we may expect from the emancipation policy inaugurated by the Republicans."

More than anything else, conservatives feared that Lincoln's proclamation—especially his pledge that the federal government would do nothing to repress slaves "in any efforts they may make for their actual freedom"— would encourage slave revolts in the South. In their platform for the upcoming congressional elections, New York Democrats condemned the proclamation as "a proposal for the butchery of women and children, for scenes of lust and rapine, and of arson and murder."

Fear of a slave uprising naturally loomed largest in the South. One Confederate Army officer declared that Lincoln's proclamation marked "the crowning act of the series of black and diabolical transactions which have marked the entire course of his administration . . . a most infamous attempt to incite flight, murder, and rapine on the part of our slave population." Charging that Lincoln was "as black of soul as the vilest of the train whose behests he is obeying," the editors of the *Richmond Enquirer* accused the president of condemning "the Southern Confederacy to the Direst destruction that can befall a people."

"I cannot make up my mind to fight for such an accursed doctrine as that of a servile insurrection," wrote General George McClellan to his wife. "It is too infamous." Among McClellan's faithful subordinates in the Army of the Potomac, Lincoln's emancipation message reportedly evoked "disgust, discontent, and expression of disloyalty" to the president. This "absurd proclamation of a political coward," claimed General Fitz-John Porter, would "tend only to prolong the war by rousing the bitter feelings of the South—and causing unity of action among them—while the reverse with us."

After canvassing his friends for advice, McClellan eventually agreed to "submit to the Presdt's proclamation & quietly continue doing my duty as a soldier." On October 7—two weeks after Lincoln had issued the proclamation—McClellan distributed the president's message to his troops, reminding them that the army was duty bound to support the civilian authorities. McClellan added that "the remedy for political error if any are committed" could be found "in the action of the people at the polls."

Union soldiers' reactions to the proclamation were as varied as the northern civilian population. "Abraham 'has gone and done it' at last," an enthusiastic corporal from Minnesota wrote. "Yesterday will be a day hallowed in the hearts of millions of the people of these United States, & also by the friends of liberty and humanity the *world* over." An antislavery sergeant from Iowa was equally certain that "the God of battle will be with us . . . now that we are fighting for Liberty and Union and not Union and

Slavery." "Nothing should stand in the way of the Union," agreed a private in the Army of the Potomac. "Niggers, nor anything else."

Yet in the autumn of 1862 there seemed to be nearly as many Union soldiers who were unwilling to fight and die for emancipation. A private in the Fifth Maryland regiment declared that he was "sick and tired" of fighting, since "it really seems to me, that we are not fighting for our *country*, but for the freedom of the negroes." "I don't want to fire another shot for the negroes," wrote a soldier in an artillery unit from New York, "and I wish all the abolitionists were in hell."

In Britain, Lincoln's proclamation failed to impress the leaders of the government or the press. Noting the "very strange nature" of the proclamation, the foreign minister, Lord Russell, observed with disappointment that it contained "no declaration of a principle adverse to slavery." Lincoln's refusal to extend emancipation to the Union slave states confused Britons. "The principle asserted," wrote the editor of the *London Spectator*, "is not that a human being cannot justly own another, but that he cannot own him unless he is loyal to the United States." "Where he has no power Mr. LINCOLN will set the negroes free," scoffed an editorial in the *Times* of London. "Where he regains power he will consider them as slaves."

Critics and supporters alike expected the proclamation to spark a revolution in southern society if the Union won the war. The editors of the *New York Times* anticipated "nothing less than the utter extermination of the slaveholding aristocracy of the Cotton States, and an entire reorganization of society."

Salmon Chase welcomed the prospect. At a gathering of Union generals and Republican party leaders at his home on the evening of September 23, the secretary of the treasury declared that the southern rebellion "was a most wonderful history of an insanity of a class that the world had ever seen. If the Slaveholders had staid in the Union they might have kept the life in their institution for many years to come . . . What no party and no public feeling in the North could ever have hoped to touch they had madly placed in the very path of destruction." Observing Chase and his friends, John Hay felt that they "all seemed to feel a sort of new and exhilarated life," as if Lincoln's proclamation "had freed them as well as the slaves. They gleefully and merrily called each other and themselves abolitionists, and seemed to enjoy the novel sensation of appropriating that horrible name."

But northern business journals worried that the destruction of slavery would cripple the North's economy by depriving factories of essential raw materials produced by slave labor. European businessmen dependent upon southern cotton shared this fear. An even darker view of the future came from General William Tecumseh Sherman. Convinced that "the two races cannot live in harmony save as master and slave," Sherman insisted that "when the Negroes are liberated they or their masters must perish. They cannot exist together except in their [present] relationship."

A Reluctant Emancipator

Several days after issuing his emancipation message, the president met with the former congressman Edward Stanly, whom he had appointed military governor of North Carolina. Stunned by Lincoln's proclamation, which he considered a betrayal of southern Unionists, Stanly had resigned his post and hurried to Washington to confer with the president.

Lincoln explained to Stanly that he had issued the proclamation "to prevent the Radicals from openly embarrassing the government in the conduct of the war." If he had not embraced emancipation, Lincoln said, congressional Radicals might have withheld military supplies, "leaving the whole land in anarchy." According to Stanly, "Mr. Lincoln said that he had prayed to the Almighty to save him from this necessity, adopting the very language of the Saviour, 'If it be possible, let this cup pass from me,' but the prayer had not been answered."

The president later admitted that his proclamation "was followed by dark and doubtful days." Even though he never expected the proclamation to have any immediate effect on the Confederacy, Lincoln told Vice President Hamlin on September 28 that he had hoped for "instantaneous" benefits from the North. Instead, after six days the New York stock market continued to decline, and enlistments slowed. "This, looked soberly in the face, is not very satisfactory," noted Lincoln drily. "We have fewer troops in the field at the end of six days than we had at the beginning—the attrition among the old outnumbering the addition by the new. The North responds to the proclamation sufficiently in breath; but breath alone kills no rebels."

When a delegation of clergymen visited the White House to congratulate him on the proclamation, Lincoln told them a story about a farmer who sold a neighbor a calf, claiming that it was a unique five-legged creature. It turned out that the calf really had only four legs, and the neighbor took the case to court, where the farmer insisted that the animal's tail was a fifth leg. But the decision of the judge was that calling the tail a leg, did not make it a leg, Lincoln said. And calling his proclamation an emancipation measure, the president acknowledged, actually freed no slaves.

In a conversation with a friend in the Interior Department in late September, Lincoln played down his role in destroying slavery. "The foundations of slavery have been cracked by the war, by the rebels," the president insisted, "and the masonry of the machine is in their own hands. . . . They have held its fate, and can't complain."

Lincoln acknowledged, however, that if he issued the final emancipation decree on January 1, 1863, he would irrevocably transform the nature of the conflict. "From the expiration of the 'days of grace,'" Lincoln predicted, "the character of the war will be changed. It will be one of subjugation and extermination. . . . The [old] South is to be destroyed and replaced by new propositions and ideas."

Lincoln dismissed the possibility that his proclamation would provoke slave insurrections, but he still expected Negroes to recognize that their interests would be better served by leaving the United States. At a meeting the day after the proclamation was published, the president again asked his Cabinet to consider the best way to promote the colonization of free blacks. According to Representative George Julian, Lincoln "wished it distinctly understood that the deportation of the slaves was, in his mind, inseparably connected" with emancipation. It was quite possible, Julian claimed, that if Lincoln had known that none of the proposed colonization schemes would prove feasible, he might not have issued his emancipation proclamation. Lincoln seemed so certain the free Negroes would emigrate that he told a friend in late 1862 that he expected the South to return to an apprentice system to fill its labor needs after the war.

Within days, slaves in the South heard of the president's proclamation, either through the "grapevine" telegraph or by overhearing conversations among whites. They eagerly awaited the advent of Union troops to make freedom a reality. "Early one morning," remembered Booker T. Washington years later, "I was awakened by my mother kneeling over her children and fervently praying that Lincoln and his armies might be successful."

Even though many slaveowners tried to protect their investment by moving into the interior of the Confederacy, an increasing number of slaves fled their masters or simply stopped working. Annoyed at the insubordination of his slaves, one planter in Mississippi claimed to see "gloom and despondency on the countenance of all property holders. We fear the Negroes are demoralized and lost for further use." In Alabama, the mistress of a plantation complained that her slaves would no longer perform even routine chores: "They say they are free."

Autumn Lull

To counter the impression that he had cast his lot with the Radicals by issuing an emancipation proclamation, Lincoln retained McClellan at the head of the Army of the Potomac. "I kept McClellan in command after I had expected that he would win victories," Lincoln explained to a reporter, "simply because I knew that his dismissal would provoke popular indignation and shake the faith of the people in the final success of the war."

Lincoln also feared that McClellan was more popular with the army than he was. Besides, he had no viable candidate to replace Little Mac. But McClellan's position remained tenuous. Suspecting that the general "was playing false—that he did not want to hurt the enemy," Lincoln elected to give McClellan one final test. "I saw how he could intercept the enemy on the way to Richmond," the president later said. "I determined to make that test. If he let them get away I would remove him."

On October 1, Lincoln visited McClellan at Harpers Ferry. An officer saw the president arrive at the general's headquarters unceremoniously in an ambulance, "with his long legs doubled up so that his knees almost struck his chin." Lincoln seemed distracted and distant during his stay. He neglected to exchange the usual pleasantries with individual soldiers while reviewing the troops. Early the following morning he asked Ozias M. Hatch, an old friend from Illinois, to accompany him to a hill that overlooked the camp. "Hatch, Hatch," Lincoln asked as they gazed down upon the white tents below. "What is all this?"

"Why Mr. Lincoln," Hatch replied, "this is the Army of the Potomac." Lincoln shook his head. "No, Hatch, no," he said. "That is a mistake. It is only General McClellan's bodyguard."

Before he left, Lincoln urged McClellan to follow Lee across the Potomac as soon as possible. Since his visit had convinced him that the troops would support him against any challenge by McClellan, Lincoln put his request in the form of an order five days later.

McClellan resisted. He told Halleck that he still lacked sufficient equipment—especially shoes and horses—to advance. He also refused to move beyond the safety of his rail supply line. Meanwhile, the Confederate general Jeb Stuart carried out a lightning raid into Pennsylvania, riding entirely around the Army of the Potomac and escaping into Virginia without retaliation.

Impatient, Lincoln poked another sharp stick under McClellan's ribs. "Are you not over cautious when you assume that you can not do what the enemy is constantly doing?" Lincoln asked on October 13. "I say 'try'; if we never try, we shall never succeed. . . . It is all easy if our troops march as well as the enemy; and is it unmanly to say they can not do it."

Still McClellan refused to budge. Stanton insisted that Lincoln fire McClellan. Lincoln hesitated; Stanton nearly resigned in frustration. On October 24, McClellan complained that he could not advance because his horses were "absolutely broken down from fatigue." Lincoln shot back a sarcastic reply: "Will you pardon me for asking what the horses of your army have done since the battle of Antietam that fatigue anything?"

By the end of October, when McClellan finally began moving his army across the Potomac, Lee was comfortably ensconced at Culpepper, between Richmond and the Army of the Potomac.

Palmerston's Postponement

To William Gladstone, British chancellor of the exchequer, it seemed clear that the Union could never quash the rebellion. In a speech on October 7, Gladstone announced—without the approval of the rest of Palmerston's Cabinet—that the Confederacy had proved its ability to maintain its independence and therefore deserved diplomatic recognition. "There is no doubt that Jefferson Davis and other leaders of the South have made an army," Gladstone insisted. "They are making, it appears, a navy. And they have made what is more than either; they have made a nation."

Appalled by the carnage on the American battlefields, painfully aware of the economic damage the conflict had wrought in Britain, and certain that the war would not end soon, Foreign Minister Lord Russell proposed an armistice between North and South. Louis-Napoléon quickly seconded Russell's suggestion.

Prime Minister Palmerston, however, heard other voices outside his Cabinet. Lincoln's preliminary emancipation proclamation transformed the nature of the American conflict for the British public; after September 1862, it was clear that support for the Confederacy represented support for human slavery. The hostile reaction to Gladstone's speech of October 7, particularly among the strongly abolitionist British middle and working classes, persuaded Palmerston to delay any thought of intervening on behalf of the Confederacy or even of attempting mediation.

"We must continue to be lookers-on," the prime minister informed Russell in late October, "till the war shall have taken a more decided turn."

November Verdict

As the autumn elections approached, many Democrats sought to make the vote a referendum on emancipation. In Ohio, Indiana, and Illinois, Democratic candidates warned voters that millions of free Negroes were prepared to invade their states, driving down wages and throwing whites out of work. In Ohio, a Democratic speaker recommended as a platform "the Constitution as it is, the Union as it was, *and the Niggers where they are*."

"I told you so," exclaimed one Democratic candidate after another. "Can't you see this is an Abolition war and nothing else?" Surveying the Republicans' prospects for November, Lincoln's longtime political adviser Judge David Davis noted drily that "the Proclamation has not worked the wonders that were anticipated."

New York was a case in point. Antislavery activists rejected the advice of moderates and secured the nomination of a veteran abolitionist, General James S. Wadsworth, as the Republican gubernatorial candidate. Democrats successfully painted Wadsworth as an extremist, "a malignant Abolition disorganizer." The Democratic candidate, Horatio Seymour, linked Wadsworth with the Lincoln administration and suggested that "if it be true that slavery must be abolished to save this Union, then the people of the South should be allowed to withdraw themselves from the government which cannot give them the protection guaranteed by its terms."

At the end of October, guests at the President's House noticed that Lincoln appeared to be "literally bending under the weight of his burdens." His wartime political coalition was breaking apart. McClellan continued to drag his feet; in the west, General Don Carlos Buell—who also opposed emancipation—refused to challenge the Confederate forces in eastern Tennessee. One member of a women's delegation who called on Lincoln noted that his "introverted look and his half-staggering gait were like those of a man walking in sleep"; the president's face showed "the ravages which care, anxiety, and overwork had wrought."

A British Quaker who came to Washington to preach and pray for the president found Lincoln in a fatalistic mood. "We are indeed going through a great trial—a fiery trial," he told his visitor. "If I had had my way, this war would never have commenced; If I had been allowed my way this war would have been ended before this, but we find it still continues; and we must believe that He permits it for some wise purpose of his own, mysterious and unknown to us."

In New England, the heartland of abolitionism, Lincoln's Emancipation Proclamation strengthened the Republican cause at the ballot box.

Elsewhere, though, it damaged Republican candidates. In the first week of November, Democrats captured control of the congressional delegations of Ohio, Indiana, New York, Pennsylvania, and Illinois. The Speaker of the House of Representatives, Galusha Grow, was defeated, as was Seward's longtime political ally Roscoe Conkling, and the president's close friend Leonard Swett, who sought Lincoln's former congressional seat in Illinois. After a bitter campaign, Seymour defeated Wadsworth in the New York gubernatorial race by a comfortable margin.

Overall, the Democratic presence in the House rose from forty-four seats to seventy-five, slicing the Republican majority to eighteen. Even though the Republicans gained five seats in the Senate and kept control of most northern state legislatures, a headline in the *New York Times* pronounced the election results a stunning "Vote of Want of Confidence" in the Lincoln administration. "Abolition Slaughtered," declared a newspaper in Indiana.

Angry Republicans blamed the president for the party's defeats. "It was not your fault that we were not *all* beaten," complained Congressman J. K. Moorhead of Pittsburgh, who added bitterly that a number of his colleagues in Pennsylvania "would be glad to hear some morning that you had been found hanging from the post of a lamp at the door of the White House."

"You need not be surprised to find that the suggestion has been executed any morning," answered Lincoln. "The violent preliminaries to such an event would not surprise me."

Opposition to the administration's policies extended far beyond emancipation, however. Inflation, rising taxes, the army's failure to crush the rebellion, the imposition of conscription, and especially Lincoln's decision in late September to suspend the writ of habeas corpus and arrest the most vocal critics of the war also fed voters' discontent.

Surprised by the extent of the Republican losses, Lincoln said that he felt "somewhat like that boy in Kentucky who stubbed his toe while running to see his sweetheart. The boy said he was too big to cry, and far too badly hurt to laugh." He tried to blame the defeats on Democratic demagoguery and the disloyalty of conservative Republican newspapers, but he acknowledged that emancipation, combined with the ineffective prosecution of the war, had alienated numerous voters.

Exit McClellan

Radicals in Congress preferred to blame Republican losses on Lincoln's failure to adopt stronger antislavery policies. Anxious lest the election returns lead Lincoln to relapse into his conservative ways, they launched a campaign to oust Secretary of State Seward, whom they blamed for Lincoln's reluctance to attack slavery.

Lincoln refused to dismiss Seward, whose counsel and friendship he valued more than any other Cabinet member's. But with the elections behind him, Lincoln finally felt sufficiently secure to dismiss McClellan as commander of the Army of the Potomac. He had "tried long enough to bore with an auger too dull to take hold," the president told Postmaster General Blair.

Lincoln named General Ambrose Burnside to replace McClellan. One of the few Union generals to win battles in the east, Burnside had twice earlier declined the command of the Army of the Potomac. A former tailor and a graduate of West Point, Burnside certainly looked like a soldier: tall, muscular, with dark eyes, and thick whiskers on his cheeks that became known to the public as "sideburns." His victories along the coast of Virginia and North Carolina recommended him to Lincoln. Burnside, however, believed himself unfit for this position, and he wept when he accepted the command.

To spur the western army into action, Lincoln ousted the dilatory Buell and promoted General William S. Rosecrans to lead the reorganized Army of the Cumberland. Unlike McClellan and Buell, who were Democrats, Burnside and Rosecrans were neutral in political affairs, even though Burnside remained a loyal admirer of McClellan.

McClellan's dismissal sent shock waves through the Union ranks. "This has been a sad day for the Army of the Potomac," wrote Elisha Rhodes in his diary. "General McClellan has been relieved from command and has left us." "Little Mac has gone," mourned another officer, "and my heart and hopes have gone with him."

In the North, editorials divided along partisan lines, but southerners accurately gauged McClellan's legacy. "How fortunate for us that he was chosen chief of the Yankee army!" proclaimed the *Richmond Whig*. "The

Yankees might have taken Richmond after the battle of Seven Pines, when our forces were in confusion," had McClellan not delayed. "After the battle of Antietam the same."

Privately, McClellan muttered that "they have made a great mistake—alas for my poor country." His friends urged him to refuse to recognize Lincoln's order and "throw the infernal scoundrels into the Potomac," but McClellan departed gracefully. "In parting from you I cannot express the love and gratitude I bear for you," he told his troops in a written farewell on November 10. "The glory you have achieved, our mutual perils & fatigues, the graves of our comrades fallen in battle & by disease . . . unite us still by an indissoluble tie."

After spending a day or two briefing Burnside, McClellan boarded a train in Warrenton, Virginia, to take him north. As soldiers thronged around his railroad car, pleading with him to stay, McClellan asked them to "stand by General Burnside as you have stood by me, and all will be well." He passed through Washington without stopping. Meanwhile, Democratic Party officials began to boost McClellan as a candidate for the presidential election of 1864.

Negro Troops Take the Field

In New Orleans, General Benjamin Butler continued to recruit free Negroes and runaway slaves into the Louisiana Native Guards. By the second week of November, Butler commanded three Negro regiments, an assortment of skilled artisans and former field hands. Two of the regiments had already been mustered into the United States Army, as the Union's first Negro units of the war. "Recruits come in faster than they can be provided for," reported Samuel Denison to his uncle, Secretary of the Treasury Chase. "They learn more quickly than white soldiers, and will certainly fight, when the proper time comes."

Butler armed the Negro troops without the approval of the War Department and put them through basic training at a Union camp 4 miles north of New Orleans. He might have raised several more regiments had he possessed an adequate supply of weapons. For the time being, Butler limited the Negroes' duties to outpost duty and guarding railroads and kept them under close supervision by white officers. Still, Denison noted that "they have done well, and accomplished all that has been given them to do."

In Kansas, General Jim Lane was drilling two regiments of Negro soldiers despite opposition from local whites. Although the War Department refused to recognize the Kansas (Colored) Volunteer Infantry, Lane gave his Negro troops—known as "Zouaves d'Afrique" for their distinctive scarlet pantaloons—rifles in the autumn of 1862 and permitted them to fight against rebel guerrillas in Kansas and Missouri.

On the Sea Islands, General Rufus Saxon, the military governor, received authorization from the War Department to begin recruiting five regiments of Negro troops, with white officers, to guard nearby plantations. On November 7, the First South Carolina Volunteers were mustered into the United States Army. Stanton awarded command of the unit to Massachusetts abolitionist Thomas Wentworth Higginson. After an initial review of his troops, Higginson decided that "it needs but a few days to show the absurdity of doubting the equal military availability of these people, as compared to whites."

Confederate military authorities responded by publishing a "Black Flag order," condemning to death armed Negroes in Union uniforms. Captured white officers of Negro troops were to be tried and executed as felons. "Just think how infamous it is that our gentlemen should have to go out and fight niggers," complained one furious woman in South Carolina, "and that every nigger they shoot is a thousand dollars out of their own pockets! Was there ever anything so outrageous?"

In November, rebel raiders on one of the Sea Islands captured and hanged four Negroes of the First South Carolina Volunteers.

Midgets and Money

Legislators returning to Washington for the final session of the Thirty-seventh Congress found a bustling and prosperous city. By the end of the year, the capital's civilian population soared to 120,000. With nearly 500 new arrivals at Union Station every day, the throngs of businessmen, lobbyists, military officers, and office seekers reportedly brought the proprietors of Willard's Hotel more than $30,000 profit in 1862. Tavern keepers and restaurateurs flourished; the city's income from liquor license fees increased fivefold over what it had been in 1860. Tailors, blacksmiths, and other skilled workmen could easily make $3.50 per day. Each day dockworkers unloaded massive shiploads of army supplies—lumber, hay, potatoes, and coal—and loaded them into wagons and transports for the main camp of the Army of the Potomac in northern Virginia.

At night, Washingtonians flocked to see P. T. Barnum's midgets, including General Tom Thumb and his wife, who stayed at Willard's while the circus was in town. ("She is very beautiful," noted one admirer, "I understand only thirty inches tall, he thirty-two.") Lincoln invited another of Barnum's midgets, Commodore Nutt, to the White House to sing "Columbia, the Gem of the Ocean" for the Cabinet. But there were no public concerts on the mall; Mrs. Lincoln's ban on performances following the death of her son Willie remained in effect.

Since the military order prohibiting the sale of liquor after 9:30 P.M. proved unenforceable, Provost Marshall General Wadsworth—recently defeated in the gubernatorial election in New York—reopened Washington's bars. Delighted citizens drank a toast to the old general's health. A reporter for the *Washington Star* determined that there were 3,900 prostitutes in the city—2,300 whites and 1,600 Negroes. To deter petty crime, city officials hung red placards reading PICKPOCKET and THIEF upon miscreants, and marched them through the streets to the accompaniment of fifes and drums.

"Washington is just now lively beyond all precedent," reported a correspondent for the *Chicago Times:*

Three theaters, two circuses, and two hybrid places of amusement . . . beside a dozen smaller places of enjoyment, are in full blast, and are nightly jammed to repletion. Hacks by the hundreds, filled with pleasure-seeking parties, are incessantly dashing hither and thither; gaily dressed equestrians canter about the avenues, and dense crowds of happy, richly-dressed pedestrians throng the sidewalks at all hours. . . . The gigantic war affects people as little as if it were being waged between the Hotentots [sic] and Senegambians.

But in the daylight, Washingtonians could not avoid the sight of crippled soldiers on crutches, or the scores of white hospital buildings and tents about the city. Besides the massive Armory Square Hospital, situated between the Smithsonian Institution and the Maryland Avenue docks, there were Stanton Hospital on New Jersey Avenue, Judiciary Square Hospital, Harewood Hospital near the Soldiers' Home, Columbian Hospital on the site of Columbia College, and Douglas Hospital, consisting of the elegant residences formerly occupied by Senators Stephen Douglas, Henry Rice, and John C. Breckenridge along I Street.

Military authorities commandeered private homes, churches, cavalry barracks, schools, hotels, seminaries (including Georgetown College), and warehouses to shelter their wounded. Nearly half the federal office buildings in the city were converted into temporary hospitals; so was the former home of the British ambassador, off Washington Circle. Conditions in most of these structures were so appallingly unsanitary that local residents formed a relief society to petition for reforms. More effective were the efforts of the United States Sanitary Commission, based in New York—a scientific board led by Dr. Henry Bellows, a Unitarian minister; the landscape architect Frederick Law Olmsted; and George Templeton Strong.

By the time Congress reconvened, all the wounded had been removed from the Capitol. The rooms were cleaned; the exterior sparkled with a fresh coat of white paint. A derrick stood ready to raise the massive white columns into position along the Senate and House wings, although Thomas Crawford's statue Armed Freedom remained grounded on the Capitol lawn.

At the end of November, the journalist Noah Brooks arrived in Washington from California. Having met Lincoln as a "happy-faced Springfield lawyer" in Illinois in 1856, Brooks noticed immediately the change in the president's appearance when he saw Lincoln at a Sunday service at the New York Avenue Presbyterian Church. "His hair is grizzled, his gait more stooping, his countenance sallow," Brooks noted, "and there is a sunken, deathly look about the large, cavernous eyes, which is saddening to those who see there the marks of care and anxiety."

Yet Brooks also witnessed the warm reception that the other worshipers afforded the president. "He inspires that feeling by his personal presence as much as by his acts, and as he moves down the church aisle, recognizing, with a cheerful nod, his friends on either side, his homely face lighted with a smile, there is an involuntary expression of respect on every face, and men, who would scorn to 'toady' to any President, look with commiserating admiration on that tall, mourning figure."

Death of Gradual Emancipation

During the lull between the elections in November and the return of Congress, Lincoln devoted much of his time to drafting his second annual message. With slightly more than a month remaining before his self-imposed deadline for the final emancipation proclamation, Lincoln planned to use the speech to make a last plea for gradual, compensated emancipation.

Visiting his old friend at the White House near the end of November, Judge David Davis thought Lincoln looked "weary and care worn," but still optimistic about the success of his plan. The president apparently had convinced himself that if Congress approved bond issues to pay for emancipated slaves, the governments of Maryland, Kentucky, Missouri, and Delaware would accept the terms. "Mr. Lincoln's whole soul is absorbed in his plan of remunerative emancipation," Davis reported, "and he thinks if Congress don't fail him that the problem [of slavery] is solved."

On December 1, John Nicolay carried Lincoln's message to Capitol Hill, where a clerk read it to Congress. To end the war, Lincoln argued, the government must abolish slavery. "Without slavery the rebellion could never have existed," the president contended. "Without slavery it could not continue." Recognizing the division within the Republican Party over the timing and means of emancipation, Lincoln proposed a plan of "mutual concessions," consisting of three constitutional amendments.

Lincoln's first amendment proposed that any slave state—including states in the Confederacy—that abolished slavery before the year 1900 would receive government bonds to replace the value of its slaves. The schedule of payments would be tied to the pace of emancipation. Emphasizing the gradual nature of this plan, Lincoln claimed that it would spare both races from "the evils of sudden derangement—in fact, from the necessity of any derangement." It would also protect freedmen from "the vagrant destitution which must largely attend immediate emancipation in localities where their numbers are very great."

The president dismissed complaints from abolitionists who opposed government payments to slaveholders. Again he emphasized that the South was not solely responsible for the introduction of human slavery into North America. "And when it is remembered how unhesitatingly we all use cotton and sugar, and share the profits of dealing in them, it may not be quite safe to say, that the south has been more responsible than the north for its continuance."

Lincoln's second amendment was designed to protect Negroes who had freed themselves during the war. Since it would be "impracticable" to return these people to bondage, he recommended that Congress explicitly state that "all slaves who shall have enjoyed actual freedom by the chances of the war, at any time before the end of the rebellion, shall be forever free." The president's proposal would provide compensation for loyal slaveowners whose slaves had run away or been confiscated.

The third amendment would authorize Congress to provide funds to colonize former slaves "with their own consent, at any place or places without the United States." If a substantial number of freedmen agreed to leave the country, the decline in the labor supply would raise the value of white labor. But even if colonization failed, the president claimed, the presence of free Negroes would not harm white workers. If the freedmen remained where they were, "they jostle no white laborers; if they leave their old places, they leave them open to white laborers."

Lincoln also rejected the popular argument that emancipation would lead Negroes to breed more prolifically, threatening to overwhelm whites by sheer force of numbers. "Are they not already in the land," he asked. "Will liberation make them any more numerous? Equally distributed among the whites of the whole country, there would be but one colored to seven whites. Could the one, in any way, greatly disturb the seven?"

Once slavery was eliminated, Lincoln believed, Negroes would have less reason to flee the South. Hence he suggested that white northerners who feared a massive influx of freedmen into their region ought to support emancipation as a means of keeping Negroes in the South.

Lincoln's message concluded with a call for a farsighted solution to the problem of emancipation:

> Is it doubted, then, that the plan I propose, if adopted, would shorten the war, and thus lessen its expenditure of money and of blood? . . . The dogmas of the quiet past, are inadequate to the stormy present. The occasion is piled high with difficulty, and we must rise to the occasion. As our case is new, so we must think anew, and act anew. We must disenthrall ourselves, and then we shall save our country.
>
> Fellow citizens, we cannot escape history. . . . In *giving* freedom to the *slave,* we *assure* freedom to the *free*—honorable alike in what we give, and what we preserve. We shall nobly save, or meanly lose, the last best, hope of earth.

Conservatives joined the Radicals in denouncing Lincoln's scheme for gradual emancipation. Senator Browning confessed that he was surprised "by the hallucination the President seems to be laboring under that Congress can suppress the rebellion by adopting his plan of compensated emancipation."

"We have always admired the President as a joker," commented the editor of the *New York Herald,* "but we never imagined that he could so aptly blend exquisite humor and practical common sense in an official document." Other newspapers simply ignored the president's proposal.

Before Lincoln submitted his annual message, Chase told him that Congress would never pass any plan involving compensated emancipation. The president's proposed amendments never reached a decisive vote in either house, and Lincoln never raised the subject again.

The middle ground had disappeared. Congressional Democrats assailed the president's proposed emancipation proclamation for "its suddenness, its utter contempt for the Constitution, its imperial pretension, [and] the thorough upheaving of the whole social organization which it decreed." Their resolution denouncing the proclamation as "a high crime against the Constitution" worthy of impeachment was defeated on a straight party-line vote. The House—also along party lines—then approved a Republican motion endorsing emancipation and a bill authorizing $600,000 to colonize freed slaves in Central America.

Delay

"It snowed yesterday," wrote John Nicolay from Washington on December 7, "and last night froze up tight and fast. I pity the poor soldiers who had to do guard and picket duty last night."

Under heavy pressure from the administration and the northern public to attack the rebels before winter, General Burnside led the Army of the Potomac to the banks of the Rappahannock River, across from Fredericksburg. Burnside hoped to cross the river quickly and take Lee by surprise, but bureaucratic bungling delayed the arrival of pontoon bridges from Harpers Ferry. By the time the pontoons were in place in early December, heavy rains swelled the river and turned the roads to a quagmire.

Lee used the delay to array his forces on the hills overlooking the town, on the other side of the Rappahannock. Confederate authorities advised Fredericksburg's residents to flee. "I never saw a more pitiful procession than they made trudging through the deep snow," reported a soldier from Virginia. "Some had a Bible and a toothbrush in one hand, a picked chicken and a bag of flour in the other. Where they were going we could not tell, and I doubt if they could."

On paper, Burnside enjoyed a formidable advantage, with 120,000 men to Lee's 73,000, but northern civilians had learned to treat military statistics with skepticism. Too many of those listed as available for action were stragglers and deserters. "There was never an army in the world . . . of which so small a percentage could be got into battle," Lincoln told Frederick Law Olmsted. "Order the army to march to any place! Why it's jes' like *shovellin' fleas.*" When a woman asked the president why he didn't order stragglers to be shot, Lincoln gave her a curious look. "Oh, I ca-an't do *that,* you know."

"It's an army of lions we have," commented one New Yorker, "with a sheep for commander-in-chief."

Darkest Days

Union artillery began bombarding Fredericksburg on December 11. By sundown, federal troops controlled the city, but not the hills known as Marye's Heights, where Lee's forces waited.

At noon on Saturday, December 13, Burnside ordered the first wave of Union infantry to charge across several hundred yards of open plain and ravines toward Marye's Heights. Four ranks of Confederate sharpshooters, protected by a stone wall 1,200 feet long, relentlessly mowed them down.

Entire brigades were devastated within ten minutes. "Above us . . . within speaking distance was line after line of earthworks filled with rebels, while above them was the artillery vomiting fire and death incessantly," reported a sixteen-year-old private from Maine. "The ground was covered with guns, blankets, haversacks and canteens, while . . . dead comrades were lying grim and ghastly around us."

All afternoon, Burnside kept sending new waves of infantry forward. "It can hardly be in human nature for men to show more valor," observed one reporter, "or generals to manifest less judgment."

"There has been enough blood shed to satisfy any reasonable man," commented General Hooker, "and it is time to quit." But not even darkness stopped the slaughter. The firing finally stopped around eight o'clock in the evening. No Union soldier ever reached the stone wall.

Hundreds of wounded men spent the night trapped on the freezing ground under a bitterly cold wind, with the northern lights flickering in the sky. "My first battle is over and I saw nearly all of it," wrote a Union drummer boy. "I saw wounded men brought in by the hundred and dead men lying stark on the field, and then I saw our army retreat to the very place they started from. . . . I came out here sanguine as any one, but I have seen enough, and I am satisfied that we never can whip the South."

In thirty-six hours, Burnside lost more than 12,000 men, more than twice the number of Confederate casualties. As the magnitude of the disaster became apparent, Burnside broke down and wept. "Oh those men! Oh those men!" he cried, pointing toward the field where the Union dead and wounded lay. "Those men over there! I am thinking of them all the time!"

Morale in the Army of the Potomac was shattered, and public confidence in the Lincoln administration plummeted to an all-time low. The people of the North, wrote the editors of *Harper's Weekly,* "have borne, silently and grimly, imbecility, treachery, failure, privation, loss of friends, but they cannot be expected to suffer that such massacres as this at Fredericksburg shall be repeated."

Republican leaders renewed their demand for the use of Negro troops. Governor Israel Washburn of Maine told Vice President Hamlin that he was sick and tired of sacrificing white troops to free Negro slaves. "The men cannot be raised North, at least, so long as the present policy remains," Washburn wrote. "Disloyalty is growing rampant even in New England."

Many northerners began to doubt that the Lincoln administration could win the war. "The general indignation is fast growing revolutionary," noted an attorney in New York. "A year ago we laughed at the Honest Old Abe's grotesque genial Western jocosities, but they nauseate us now. If these things go on, we shall have pressure on him to resign and make way for Hamlin."

Some critics suggested a military dictator to crush the rebellion. Others feared that the midwestern states, sick of the fighting, might break off and form their own separate nation. In Washington, Judge David Davis observed "a growing dread that we will be unsuccessful in Virginia. . . . The feeling is increasing that we can't conquer the South." The rate of desertions rose alarmingly, until 80,000 soldiers were missing from the Union muster rolls. "The Army of the Potomac," Halleck declared, "has ceased to exist."

Chase's Gamble

For a few days, Lincoln sank into depression. "We are now on the brink of destruction," he told Browning. "It appears the Almighty is against us, and

I can hardly see a ray of hope." But the president never considered surrender. When Judge Davis visited him on December 16, Lincoln told his former campaign manager a story of old Mother Partington.

"You know the old lady lived on the sea beach," Lincoln said, "and one time a big storm came up and the waves began to rise till the water began to come in under her cabin door. She got a broom and went to sweeping it out. But the water rose higher and higher; to her knees; to her waist; at last to her chin. But she kept on sweeping and exclaiming, 'I'll keep on sweeping as long as the broom lasts and we will see whether the storm or the broom will last the longest!' And that is the way with me."

Republican senators had other ideas. "The President is a weak man," charged Senator Chandler, "too weak for the occasion and those fool or traitor generals are wasting time and yet more precious blood in indecisive battles and delays." Senator Fessenden complained that "folly, stupidity, and wickedness rule the hour. The President gives no hope of improvement, and Seward still rules him."

On December 17, a council of Republican senators—secretly encouraged by Secretary of the Treasury Chase—approved a resolution demanding that Lincoln purge the army and Cabinet of anyone who did not share their enthusiasm for an all-out war effort, including emancipation. Once again, their primary target was Seward, since Chase had assured them that the president listened to no one but the secretary of state.

The following evening, members of the council met with Lincoln and urged him to dismiss Seward and pay more attention to the advice of Chase and Stanton. Learning of the senators' demands, Seward offered to resign to save the president further embarrassment. "They may do as they please about me," he said, "but they shall not put the President in a false position on my account." Lincoln tried to change Seward's mind, but the secretary of state remained adamant. Rumors of a massive Cabinet shakeup swept through Washington. "The feeling is everywhere of exultation at the prospect of getting rid of the whole Cabinet," reported a correspondent from New York. "There is no exception to this in Congress or anywhere else."

One journalist noted that the president "is awfully shaken." To another reporter, Lincoln admitted that "if there was any worse hell than he had been in for two days, he would like to know it."

"They wish to get rid of me," Lincoln told Browning, "and I am sometimes half disposed to gratify them."

He did not. Instead, Lincoln confronted Chase and his congressional allies at a follow-up meeting the next evening. He told the senators that they were thinking more of *their* plans than *his* benefit. Turning to his Cabinet members, the president asked them to confirm that even though he did not always have time for lengthy discussions of routine matters, he usually discussed all major policy decisions with them. All—including Chase—agreed.

Lincoln then announced that he had no intention of reorganizing his Cabinet, unless Seward and Chase resigned together. "If one goes, the other must," the president insisted; "they must hunt in couples." Otherwise, he feared, the administration would tilt too far toward the Radicals.

Several hours later, a subdued Chase tendered his resignation. With a satisfied laugh, Lincoln filed it away in his desk drawer with Seward's letter. "Now I have the biggest half of the hog," he said. "I can dispose of this subject now." The following day, Lincoln told the Cabinet that he had no intention of abandoning old friends. He kept both Seward and Chase in the Cabinet for the time being, but no one in Washington doubted that the president was master of his administration.

Holidays

To mark the Christmas holidays, volunteer women decked Washington's military hospitals with evergreens. Mrs. Lincoln and Mrs. Caleb Smith—whose husband had recently resigned as secretary of the interior to return to Indiana as a circuit court judge—led a drive to donate provisions for the wounded soldiers' Christmas dinners. Republican legislators, including Senator Sumner, toured the wards, encouraging the scarred and maimed men.

Despite the lingering gloom from Fredericksburg, Washingtonians attended the theater and opera in record numbers that winter. At Ford's Athenaeum on Tenth Street, the new National Theater on E Street, and the venerable Washington Theatre on C Street, the city's resident stock companies—augmented by visiting stars—presented varied fare: *Macbeth, Othello, The French Spy, Pocohontas,* and the melodramatic *Six Degrees of Crime,* featuring "INTEMPERANCE, LICENTIOUSNESS, GAMBLING, THEFT, MURDER, AND THE SCAFFOLD." Patrons seated in the rear of theaters were advised to protect themselves from the streams of tobacco juice emanating from those seated around them.

Late in December, Ford's Athenaeum Theater caught fire. While the city's first steam-powered fire engine spun its wheels helplessly in the mud on the corner of Pennsylvania and Thirteenth Street, the theater burned to the ground. With the backing of local businessmen, John T. Ford—a native of Baltimore known for his Democratic sympathies—announced plans to build a new, modern playhouse (complete with fire hydrants and hoses) on the same site. With 2,400 seats, it would be twice the size of the old theater, highlighted by luxurious private boxes at both ends of the balcony, and a special double box for the president.

Smallpox, a plague in Negro sections of the city since the war began, was spreading throughout the capital. The city's primitive sanitary system broke down completely under the pressure of a burgeoning population. Heaps of night soil in open pits littered the grounds of military hospitals, and carcasses of mules and horses lay half buried near the government corrals on Nineteenth Street.

"I was never in such a place for *smells,*" an army wife complained to her mother. "What should you think if all the slops from sleeping rooms were thrown either into the gutters or alley. Here there are no sewers, no cess pools or vaults for any purpose in the yards." An investigation by local authorities revealed that the Washington Canal—little more than a "shallow open sewer"—and the "miasmatic swamp" near the President's House remained dangerous health hazards.

Prices of consumer goods continued to rise. A survey revealed that the cost of rent, food, and fuel in Washington averaged $1,333 per year, compared with $940 in Baltimore. Much to the disgust of Walt Whitman, the price of a glass of beer reached 38 cents. But at least the city's residents felt safe. Forty-eight forts now protected Washington from Confederate attack, augmented by a 15-mile-long barricade of logs that stretched from the eastern branch of the Potomac to Chain Bridge.

Mississippi Freedmen

From his headquarters north of Vicksburg, Mississippi, General Grant reported that so many runaway slaves were flocking to his camps that his troops could not advance. Grant put the Negroes to work, employing able-bodied men as cooks and teamsters, and using women and children to pick cotton in abandoned nearby plantations.

"At once," Grant reported, "the freedmen became self-sustaining." Government officials did not pay them their wages directly. Instead, the War Department channeled their earnings into a fund that provided them with food, clothing, and shelter. In return, the government obtained much-needed supplies of cotton.

Just before Christmas, Confederate raiders severed Grant's supply line, forcing him to abandon his siege of Vicksburg. As he retreated into Tennessee, Grant discovered that his troops could survive on the food they appropriated from civilians along the way. "It showed that we could have subsisted off the country for two months," he wrote. Both Grant and General William Tecumseh Sherman, who tried and failed to capture Vicksburg on December 29, would remember the lesson.

Within the Confederacy, nerves frayed as the date of the emancipation proclamation neared. On December 30, news reached New York of an incident in Charleston, South Carolina, in which local authorities hanged nineteen slaves for insubordination. The draconian nature of the punishment demonstrated the depth of southerners' fears that the proclamation would incite a slave rebellion. As yet, however, no violent slave uprisings had occurred anywhere in the Confederacy.

Waiting

In the last week of December, Democratic newspapers predicted that the president would renege on his promise and refuse to issue the emancipation proclamation on January 1. Senator Browning sent an envoy to the White House to persuade his old friend to modify or delay his proclamation.

Lincoln refused. If he should fail to issue his proclamation, Lincoln said, "there would be a rebellion in the north." Even though he confessed that the proclamation "would not make a single negro free beyond our military reach," the president said that he felt "a great impulse moving me to do justice to five or six millions of people."

"I have studied that matter well, my mind is made up," Lincoln told another visitor. "*It must be done. I am driven to it.* There is no other way out of our troubles."

"The President is occupied on the Proclamation," Charles Sumner wrote in his diary on Christmas Day, 1862. "He will stand firm. He said to me that it was hard to drive him from a position which he had once taken." Lincoln also told Sumner of his plans "to employ African troops to hold the Mississippi River and other posts in the warm climates, so that our white soldiers may be employed elsewhere."

Three days later, Sumner returned to the subject with mounting excitement. "The President says he would not stop the Proclamation if he could, and he could not if he would," Sumner exclaimed. "Hallelujah!"

Final Changes

On the last three days of the year, Lincoln convened his Cabinet three times. At the first meeting, on December 29, Lincoln read aloud his draft of the final Emancipation Proclamation, written entirely on his own.

After he finished, Lincoln asked his Cabinet officers for their comments. Only Chase replied. He objected to Lincoln's decision to exempt portions of Confederate states (primarily Louisiana and Virginia) where Union troops were already in control. Such a distinction, Chase claimed, would create administrative headaches and clashes between federal and state authorities.

Lincoln replied that he could not accept Chase's suggestion. He could justify the proclamation only as a military measure during a time of rebellion; otherwise, the Constitution prohibited him from interfering with the property of American citizens.

When the Cabinet met again the following evening, Lincoln distributed printed copies of the draft proclamation for comments. Still anxious lest the message encourage slave uprisings, Seward recommended that Lincoln strengthen the language of the proclamation to "command and require" the freedmen to avoid violence, instead of merely "enjoining" them to do so.

Attorney General Bates, who objected to the proclamation's expansion of presidential power, argued that emancipation must be presented as a *war measure,* not a law or declaration of principle "for the future guidance of others." The conservative Missourian wanted to make it clear that Congress or the courts could overturn the proclamation once the war ended.

Bates also proposed that the president delete the promise that freed slaves would be welcomed into the Union Army. Despite the vehemence of Bates's objections, Lincoln decided not to incorporate his suggestions into the message.

On New Year's Eve, at the final Cabinet meeting of 1862, Chase and Postmaster General Blair recommended several more last-minute changes to the proclamation. Like Seward, Blair wanted stronger language to discourage slave uprisings. Chase, too, desired to avoid the appearance of encouraging slave rebellions. He suggested that Lincoln insert a phrase "not encouraging or countenancing . . . any disorderly or licentious conduct."

At the same time, Chase proposed a statement of moral principle at the end of the proclamation: "And upon this act, sincerely believed to be an act of justice warranted by the Constitution, and of duty demanded by the circumstances of the country, I invoke the considerate judgment of Mankind and the gracious favor of Almighty God."

After considering his advisers' comments, Lincoln made his final revisions before retiring for the evening.

New Year's Eve

On the banks of the Rappahannock outside Fredericksburg, the Army of the Potomac marked the holidays with packages from home filled with turkeys, ducks, geese, pickles, preserves, and mince pies. Even though liquor was officially banned from the camps, soldiers managed to smuggle in flasks of wine and whiskey to toast the new year. "The year has not amounted to much as far as the war is concerned," wrote Sergeant Elisha Hunt Rhodes, "but we hope for the best and feel sure that in the end the Union will be restored. Good bye, 1862."

Within Fredericksburg, Confederate soldiers found no more cause to celebrate. "I was in hope I would get a letter to enliven the day," admitted a lieutenant from North Carolina who foraged on the deserted battlefield for an overcoat, boots, and cap. "There was no gaiety in the camp at all."

Throughout the Confederacy, supplies of food and clothing were running low under the pressure of war and the Union blockade. Prices rose 10 percent each month. "There were no sugar or coffee or tea," recalled a ten-year-old girl in Bladensfield, Virginia, "no new calicos or cotton. There were no men to keep the stores . . . they had all gone to the war." To extend their provisions, southern women toasted rye and mixed it with coffee, or brewed ground acorns, chickory, or pumpkin seeds instead.

On Sixth Street in Washington, a Negro named Edward Jones was attacked by a white crowd during the night for allegedly insulting a white woman. The police arrested Jones just before the mob could lynch him.

At a gathering of Negroes just outside Washington, former slaves eagerly awaited the dawn, and the president's proclamation. One contraband recalled the day his daughter was sold. "Now no more of that," he said. "They can't sell my wife and children anymore—bless the Lord."

8

EMANCIPATION

New Year's Day, 1863, dawned chilly and gray in Washington. A storm the night before had left the unpaved streets full of slush and mud, treacherous for the worshipers heading home from watch meetings in the Methodist churches. Around two in the morning, a gang of white toughs touched off a brawl on Capitol Hill by assaulting Negroes on their way home from a church service.

Lincoln rose early and walked across the hall to his office around eight o'clock. He began to make corrections to the official copy of his Emancipation Proclamation, but he was interrupted by General Burnside, who came to Washington to complain that his officers were plotting against him. Without their confidence, he felt he must resign as commander of the Army of the Potomac. Burnside suggested that Halleck and Stanton, too, should step down for their part in the Fredericksburg debacle. Not yet willing to replace Burnside, Lincoln persuaded the general to return to his headquarters in northern Virgina.

At ten o'clock, Lincoln went downstairs for the traditional New Year's reception. By this time the sky was clearing, and the temperature began rising steadily. Throughout the city, similar receptions were taking place at Willard's and the National Hotel, and at the homes of congressmen and

Washington socialites. "Anyone who behaves himself," noted a journalist from California, "can go and see them at home."

As usual, Lincoln spent the first hour greeting the diplomatic corps and the members of his Cabinet (most of whom subsequently departed to host receptions of their own), followed at eleven o'clock by army and navy officers in full-dress uniforms and a company of veterans of the War of 1812, known as the Old Defenders, wearing cockades on their hats.

At noon, the military guards opened the gates of the Executive Mansion to ordinary citizens who wanted to wish "the Pres.," as they called him, a happy New Year. ("With a sincere hope," suggested one observer, "that it might be happier than his last two years have been.") The crush was overwhelming. Women's bonnets were wrecked, angry men threatened to punch one another, and one congressman had his coattail torn off.

Once inside the door, guests formed a well-behaved single line as they listened to tunes played by the Marine Band. Marshal Ward Hill Lamon, who still served as Lincoln's bodyguard, introduced each visitor to the president. The correspondent Noah Brooks saw the president, "his heavy eyes brightening," greet everyone by name, offer a compliment to the visitor's home state, and shake his or her hand vigorously. Mary Lincoln—dressed in black velvet—stood by her husband's side, but she seemed preoccupied, still mourning Willie.

Around one o'clock, Lincoln left the reception and returned to his office, where he met Secretary of State Seward and Seward's son, Fred, who served as assistant secretary of state. Seward had brought the official, engrossed copy of the Emancipation Proclamation for Lincoln's signature. Fewer than a dozen people were present in the president's office; most of them had come out of curiosity and perhaps a sense of history.

"I never, in my life, felt more certain that I was doing right," the president said quietly, "than I do in signing this paper." Taking up a gold pen supplied by Senator Sumner—donated by one of his constituents—Lincoln started to sign his name. But his hand was shaking so badly that he had to put down the pen.

After a moment Lincoln picked it up again, and then once more set it down. He explained to Seward that he had been shaking hands for several hours, and his right arm was stiff and numb. "Now, this signature is one that will be closely examined," the president added, "and if they find my hand trembled, they will say 'he had some compunctions.' But, anyway, it is going to be done."

So Lincoln picked up the pen and quickly signed his name. Looking up, he smiled and said, "That will do." (The pen was subsequently returned to Sumner's constituent, a writer in Massachusetts, as a souvenir.) Later that evening, friends told Lincoln that his signature still looked tremulous. "Three hours' hand-shaking," he explained, "is not calculated to improve a man's chirography." The president added that he had no regrets about his decision to issue the proclamation. "The South had fair warning," he said, "that if they did not return to their duty, I should strike at this pillar of their strength. The promise must be kept, and I shall never recall one word."

Like Lincoln's preliminary edict a hundred days earlier, the final proclamation began by acknowledging that the measure was solely the president's responsibility. It recalled his warning in September that an emancipation decree would be issued on January 1 if the rebellion continued. In fact, the official draft of the proclamation contained two paragraphs clipped and pasted from a State Department copy of the preliminary proclamation, to save the time and effort of recopying.

In the fourth paragraph, Lincoln defined the proclamation as "a fit and necessary measure" to suppress the southern rebellion. There followed a list of the areas that would be affected by the proclamation—all the states that had seceded in 1861, except Tennessee, the Union-occupied areas of Virginia and Louisiana, and the recently formed state of West Virginia.

More than halfway through the document, Lincoln arrived at the heart of the proclamation: "And by virtue of the power, and for the purpose aforesaid, I do order and declare that all persons held as slaves within said designated States, and parts of States, are, and henceforward shall be free; and that the Executive government of the United States, including the military and naval authorities thereof, will recognize and maintain the freedom of said persons." In the preliminary proclamation, Lincoln used the term "forever free"; the final document dropped the word "forever."

Following Chase's suggestion, Lincoln removed from the previous version his promise not to hinder the former slaves' bids for "their actual freedom." And even though his language was not as strong as Seward's, Lincoln cautioned freed slaves "to abstain from all violence, unless in necessary self-defense; and I recommend to them that, in all cases when allowed, they labor faithfully for reasonable wages." Rejecting Attorney General Bates's advice, the president promised that the federal government would welcome freed slaves into the military, although only "to garrison forts, positions, stations, and other places, and to man vessels of all sorts in said service."

Finally, at the end of the proclamation, Lincoln inserted the phrase suggested by Chase, the sole note of morality in the document: "And upon this act, sincerely believed to be an act of justice, warranted by the Constitution, *upon military necessity* [Lincoln's addition], I invoke the considerate judgment of mankind, and the gracious favor of Almighty God." At the bottom of the document, Lincoln and Seward affixed their signatures, accompanied by the Great Seal of the United States.

Although Karl Marx would later compare the Emancipation Proclamation to a summons sent by one country lawyer to another, Lincoln deliberately employed cautious, legalistic language to protect freedom if anyone challenged the proclamation in court.

That evening, Lincoln walked to the telegraph office at the War Department to hear the latest news from Tennessee, where General Rosecrans was engaged in a fierce battle at Stones River. The president sat in his usual chair and put up his feet on a nearby table to relax.

After a few minutes, Lincoln embarked upon a story from his days as a lawyer in Illinois, but he stopped when he came to a judge whose name he could not recall. He started again, but then paused and ran his fingers through his disheveled hair. "I wish I could remember that name," he said. When one of the telegraph operators, who had known Lincoln in Illinois, prompted him with the judge's name, Lincoln gave a surprised shout. "Why, yes, that's the name," he exclaimed. "Do you know him?" The president then recalled to the others in the room how the operator had taught him the mysteries of the telegraph when they first met.

Before Lincoln departed, the operators began to send the text of the Emancipation Proclamation over the telegraph wires.

January 1, 1863

By the President of the
United States of America:
A Proclamation.

Whereas, on the twentysecond day of September, in the year of our Lord one thousand eight hundred and sixty two, a proclamation was issued by the President of the United States, containing, among other things, the following, towit:

"That on the first day of January, in the year of our Lord one thousand eight hundred and sixty-three, all persons held as slaves within any State or designated part of a State, the people whereof shall then be in rebellion against the United States, shall be then, thenceforward, and forever free; and the Executive Government of the United States, including the military and naval authority thereof, will recognize and maintain the freedom of such persons, and will do no act or acts to repress such persons, or any of them, in any efforts they may make for their actual freedom.

"That the Executive will, on the first day of January aforesaid, by proclamation, designate the States and parts of States, if any, in which the people thereof, shall on that day be, in good faith, represented in the Congress of the United States by members chosen thereto at elections wherein a majority of the qualified voters of such State shall have participated, shall, in the absence of strong countervailing testimony, be deemed conclusive evidence that such State, and the people thereof, are not then in rebellion against the United States."

Now, therefore I, Abraham Lincoln, President of the United States, by virtue of the power in me vested as Commander-in-Chief, of the Army and Navy of the United States in time of actual armed rebellion against authority and government of the United States, and as a fit and necessary war measure for suppressing said rebellion, do, on this first day of January, in the year of our Lord one thousand eight hundred and sixty three, and in accordance with my purpose so to do publicly proclaimed for the full period of one hundred days, from the day first above mentioned, order and designate as the States and parts of States wherein the people thereof respectively, are this day in rebellion against the United States, the following, towit:

Arkansas, Texas, Louisiana, (except the Parishes of St. Bernard, Plaquemines, Jefferson, St. Johns, St. Charles, St. James[,] Ascension, Assumption, Terrebonne, Lafourche, St. Mary, St. Martin, and Orleans, including the City of New-Orleans) Mississippi, Alabama, Florida, Georgia, South-Carolina, North-Carolina, and Virginia, (except the fortyeight counties designated as West Virginia, and also the counties of Berkley, Accomac, Northampton, Elizabeth-City, York, Princess Ann, and Norfolk, including the cities of Norfolk & Portsmouth[)]; and which excepted parts are, for the present, left precisely as if this proclamation were not issued.

And by virtue of the power, and for the purpose aforesaid, I do order and declare that all persons held as slaves within said designated States, and parts of States, are, and henceforward shall be free; and that the Executive government of the United States, including the military and naval authorities thereof, will recognize and maintain the freedom of said persons.

And I hereby enjoin upon the people so declared to be free to abstain from all violence, unless in necessary self-defense; and I recommend to them that, in all cases when allowed, they labor faithfully for reasonable wages.

And I further declare and make known, that such persons of suitable condition, will be received into the armed service of the United States to garrison forts, positions, stations, and other places, and to man vessels of all sorts in said service.

And upon this act, sincerely believed to be an act of justice, warranted by the Constitution, upon military necessity, I invoke the considerate judgment of mankind, and the gracious favor of Almighty God.

In witness whereof, I have hereunto set my hand and caused the seal of the United States to be affixed.

Done at the city of Washington, this first day of January, in the year of our Lord one thousand eight hundred and sixtythree, and of the Independence of the United States of America the eighty-seventh.

By the President: ABRAHAM LINCOLN
  WILLIAM H. SEWARD,   Secretary of State

Less than a year later, Lincoln donated his original draft manuscript of the Emancipation Proclamation—most of it in his own handwriting—to a delegation of midwestern women who were raising funds for the care of wounded Union veterans. The women asked Lincoln specifically for the proclamation, as "the most acceptable donation you could possibly make." Lincoln sent the document reluctantly—"I had some desire to retain the paper," he told them—but he agreed that " if it shall contribute to the relief or comfort of the soldiers that will be better." In 1871, the original disappeared in the Great Chicago Fire; fortunately, Lincoln had directed John Hay to make photographic facsimiles of the proclamation.

Reflection

"Many of my strongest supporters urged emancipation before I thought it indispensable, and, I may say, before I thought the country was ready for it," Lincoln later told a group of New Yorkers visiting the White House. "It is my conviction that, had the Proclamation been issued even six months earlier than it was, public sentiment would not have sustained it. . . . I can now solemnly assert, that I have a clear conscience in regard to my action on this momentous question. I have done what no man could have helped doing, standing in my place."

All the motives that led Lincoln to issue the proclamation—depriving the Confederacy of vital human resources, righting a centuries-old crime against Negroes, outflanking the Radicals in Congress, providing northerners with a moral cause, forestalling British intervention, and destroying the institution that was tearing the Union apart—were summed up in his reply to a lawyer in Washington who congratulated him on emancipating the slaves. "It was not only the Negro that I freed," Lincoln replied, "but the white man no less."

Jubilee

After the *Washington Evening Star* published a copy of the Emancipation Proclamation on the afternoon of January 1, a parade of whites and blacks marched past the White House, cheering Lincoln. At one point the president appeared at an upstairs window, but he refused to meet his admirers.

Elsewhere in the city, a group of Negroes assembled in front of the office of the Reverend D. B. Nichols, superintendent of the city's "contraband department" on Twelfth and O Streets. They sang spirituals, including "Go Down Moses" and "I'm a Free Man Now, Jesus Christ Made Me Free." A preacher who called himself "John de Baptis" reminded the audience of "how it was in Dixie, when you worked all day without giving satisfaction. I have worked by the month for six months since I left Dixie, and the money is all my own; and I'll soon eddicate my children. But brethren," he went on, "don't be too free. The lazy man can't go to Heaven. . . . You must depend upon yourself and be honest."

That evening, Nichols addressed another gathering of Negroes at a nearby schoolhouse. Nichols assured them that they were free to work for themselves, but he advised them to start with low wages "and work up like white men." "Thanks be to God!" shouted a contraband from northern Virginia. "Bless that man they call Mr. Lincoln for such a glorious proclamation."

Residents of northern cities marked the occasion with ringing church bells, 100-gun salutes, and resolutions praising the president, although New York remained largely silent. In Boston, many of New England's foremost literary personalities—including Oliver Wendell Holmes, Harriet Beecher Stowe, John Greenleaf Whittier, Francis Parkman, Henry Wadsworth Longfellow, and Edward Everett Hale—gathered at the Music Hall on New Year's afternoon. Following a performance of Beethoven's Fifth Symphony and Mendelssohn's "Hymn of Praise," Ralph Waldo Emerson read a poem he had composed for the occasion: "I break your bonds and masterships,/ And I unchain the slave: / Free be his heart and hand henceforth/ As wind and wandering wave."

In Union-occupied Norfolk, 4,000 Negroes paraded through the city carrying Union flags and cheering the death of slavery, unaware that the proclamation did not apply to them. On the Sea Islands, more than 5,000 former slaves—mostly women—in their holiday best gathered with white teachers and military officers to celebrate the proclamation. At one point the freedmen suddenly broke into song: "My country, 'tis of thee." "I never saw anything to electric," noted Colonel Thomas Higginson, commander of the all-Negro First South Carolina Volunteers. "It made all other words cheap; it seemed the choked voice of a race at last unloosed."

Frederick Douglass praised January 1 as "the most memorable day in American Annals," but warned that slavery had stamped its character on the nation "too deeply and indelibly, to be blotted out in a day or a year, or even in a generation." "The slave will yet remain in some sense a slave, long after the chains are taken from his limbs," predicted Douglass, "and the master will retain much of the pride, the arrogance, imperiousness and conscious superiority and love of power."

Doubts

Most northern metropolitan dailies printed the Emancipation Proclamation on Friday, January 2—often on an inside page, subordinated to the latest news of military events. Moderate Republicans praised the proclamation as a blow for liberty and a much-needed boost to the Union war effort. "The nation may be sick unto speedy death and past help from this and other remedy," wrote George Templeton Strong in his diary, "but if it is, its last great act is one of repentance and restitution."

The *New York Times* deemed the proclamation "a revolution," the start of a new era in the United States. "It changes entirely the relations of the National Government to the institution of Slavery," noted the *Times*. "Hitherto Slavery has been under the protection of the Government; henceforth it is under its ban." Few northern moderates, however, expected or desired the president to further assist Negroes.

Although they praised the proclamation, abolitionists expressed disappointment that Lincoln justified emancipation primarily as a military measure rather than an act of justice. Besides, the proclamation left slavery undisturbed in the border states.

Abolitionists and congressional Radicals doubted that Lincoln would use the proclamation to inaugurate a more aggressive war. They shared Congressman Charles Sedgwick's fear that Lincoln "will stop with the proclamation and take no active and vigorous measures to insure its efficacy."

Residents of the border states gave the Emancipation Proclamation a hostile reception. Even though the proclamation did not apply to them, they understood that it sounded the death knell of slavery in America, and it heightened the feeling of distance between them and the rest of the Union. In Kentucky, the proclamation enraged every segment of the political spectrum. State legislators repeatedly denounced the Lincoln administration, and—even though Kentucky was exempt from the proclamation—approved legislation nullifying it within the state's borders. Union soldiers from the border states echoed civilians' outrage. "I dont want the negro free," decided a private from Missouri. "I dont think I will do much fighting to free the nasty thing. . . . I say the Democrats ougt to go in with the south and kill all the Abolitionists of the north and that will end this war." "[We] volunteered to fight to restore the Old Constitution and not to free the Negroes," a soldier from Kentucky declared, "and we are not a-going to do it."

Across the southern counties of Ohio, Illinois, and Indiana, the proclamation was greeted with scorn by whites fearful that southern freedmen would flee northward. "Ohio will be overrun with negroes," warned one opposition broadsheet. "They will compete with you and bring down your wages, *you* will have to work with them, eat with them, your *wives* and *children* must associate with theirs and you and your families will be degraded to their level." In Illinois, the Democratic majority in the state legislature introduced resolutions demanding an immediate end to the war unless Lincoln withdrew the Emancipation Proclamation.

Opposition in the Midwest stemmed not only from the proclamation itself but also from the widespread perception that Lincoln had abused his executive powers over the past several months by suspending the writ of habeas corpus. The notion of restricting whites' freedom to release Negroes from slavery fueled the mounting discontent. Secret antiwar societies such as the Knights of the Golden Circle and the Society for the Diffusion of Political Knowledge attracted thousands of converts in Illinois and Indiana.

From Bloomington, Illinois, one anxious Republican reported that "this State is on the verge of revolution. . . . South of Springfield deserters of the army can not be arrested. . . . The Democratic press and speakers openly denounce Lincoln as a tyrant and despot; charge him with violating the Constitution and being a worse traitor than Jeff Davis."

Resistance

As many of Lincoln's critics predicted, the Emancipation Proclamation initially strengthened Confederate resistance. Southerners feared that the measure might provoke slave uprisings and, ultimately, a race war within the South.

President Jefferson Davis denounced the proclamation as one of "the most execrable measures in the history of guilty man." In a message to the Confederate congress, Davis predicted that Lincoln's edict could only have "one of three possible consequences—the extermination of the slaves, the exile of the whole white population of the Confederacy, or absolute and total separation of these states from the Unites States."

Lincoln scoffed at such fears. "As to any dread of my having a 'purpose to enslave, or exterminate, the whites of the South,' I can scarcely believe that such dread exists," he told a friend in January. "It is too absurd."

Nevertheless, all efforts to negotiate a compromise peace were now dead. The Emancipation Proclamation "shuts the door of retreat and repentance on the weak and timid," exulted the *Richmond Examiner*," which denounced Lincoln's edict as the "most startling political crime, the most stupid political blunder, yet known in American history."

Yet an element of anxiety began to creep into southerners' pronouncements. As slaves learned of the proclamation through overheard conversations, stray copies of newspapers, and the grapevine telegraph, whites in the Confederacy grew increasingly fearful that their Negroes would accept Lincoln's invitation to freedom.

There were no slave insurrections; southern slaves long ago learned the futility of armed resistance. Instead, the proclamation encouraged more subtle forms of resistance, leading to rising complaints from whites that Negroes were becoming "unfaithful" or "demoralized." And it gave new encouragement to slaves—particularly those along the fringes of the Confederacy—to run away and seek asylum with the Union armies. As a result, increasing numbers of slaveowners in the upper South either sold their slaves to plantations in the interior of Georgia, Alabama, and Mississippi (far away from the temptation of Union forces) or moved to the Deep South.

A Divided Army

Army officials distributed 15,000 copies of the president's emancipation message to Union troops. Many high-ranking officers, conservatives who had never favored emancipation, greeted the proclamation with disdain. General Joseph Hooker, who spent January scheming to replace Burnside as commander of the Army of the Potomac, reported that "perhaps a majority of the officers, especially those high in rank, were hostile to the policy of the government. . . . And a large element of the army had taken sides antagonistic to it, declaring that they would never have embarked in the war had they anticipated this action of the government."

"I did not come out to fight for the nigger or abolition of Slavery," complained a Democratic lieutenant colonel from New York, who suggested that Lincoln "ought to be lashed up to 4 big fat niggers & left to wander about with them the [balance] of his life." "There is an astonishing amount of dissatisfaction among officers & men in this army," claimed a Union captain in Baton Rouge. "The emancipation act is alarming unpopular. . . . There has been a great many resignations." A captain in the Army of the Potomac noted that his troops "say it has turned into a 'nigger war' and all are anxious to return to their homes for it was to preserve the Union that they volunteered."

Nevertheless, a majority of midlevel officers—who tended to be the best-educated segment of the northern army—supported the proclamation, as did Union generals who lacked a political agenda. Combining idealism and pragmatism, they promised to carry out "any policy ordered . . . to be terrible on the enemy."

"Thank God the contest is now between Slavery & freedom, & every honest man knows what he is fighting for," observed one soldier from western New York. A colonel of a regiment from Indiana reported that his troops possessed a "desire to destroy everything that gives the rebels strength. . . . This army," he predicted, "will sustain the emancipation proclamation and enforce it with the bayonet." "I am no Nigger worshipper," added a soldier from Pennsylvania, who supported the proclamation anyway because it was "striking at the root of the Evil   nothing will end this war sooner."

For the Ages

Lincoln was not surprised that the proclamation aroused scorn in certain quarters. In a discussion with Wendell Phillips and other antislavery leaders at the White House on January 25, Lincoln admitted that the proclamation might have done more harm than good. "All I can say now," the president told his guests, "is that I believe the Proclamation has knocked the bottom out of slavery, though at no time have I expected any sudden results from it."

Although the preservation of the Union remained Lincoln's primary goal, he never seriously considered withdrawing the proclamation. "To use a course, but an expressive figure, broken eggs can not be mended," Lincoln wrote to a Unionist Democrat from Illinois. "I have issued the emancipation proclamation, and I can not retract it."

"I struggled nearly a year and a half to get along without touching the 'institution,'" Lincoln reminded his critics, "and when finally I conditionally determined to touch it, I gave a hundred days fair notice of my purpose, to all the States and people, within which time they could have turned it wholly aside, by simply again becoming good citizens of the United States. They chose to disregard it, and I made the peremptory proclamation on what appeared to me to be a military necessity. And being made, it must stand."

If any Confederate states returned to the Union immediately, the president was still willing to allow them to implement gradual emancipation, accompanied by "systems of apprenticeship for the colored people." "With the aid they can have from the general government," Lincoln noted, "they may be nearly as well off, in this respect, as if the present trouble had not occurred."

Nor did Lincoln abandon his campaign for compensated emancipation in the border states. Learning that the proclamation had encouraged slaves in Missouri to flee their masters, the president called several senators into his office and suggested that Congress appropriate $25 million to pay the state's slaveowners to head off potential trouble.

When Joshua Speed came to Washington, Lincoln reminded his old friend of a conversation twenty years earlier, during Lincoln's early years as a lawyer in Illinois. At the time, Lincoln noted that "he had done nothing to make any human being remember that he had lived"; what he wanted more than anything else was to do something "to connect his name with the events transpiring in his day and generation and so impress himself upon them." After issuing the Emancipation Proclamation, Lincoln told Speed, "I believe that in this measure my fondest hopes will be realized."

Hooker's Boys

"I have no idea that a winter campaign is possible in Virginia," reported Charles Francis Adams, Jr., from his camp just south of Washington. Adams believed that the Army of the Potomac, still recovering from the disaster of Fredericksburg, "wants to go to sleep until the spring. . . . Winter hardships are severe enough in the most comfortable camps. Winter campaigns may be possible in Europe, . . . but in this region of mud, desolation and immense distances, it is another matter."

General Ambrose Burnside disagreed. Although his demoralized army was plagued by a steadily mounting sick list and 200 desertions a day, Burnside proposed to lead his troops across the Rappahannock River to a point several miles west of Fredericksburg. By flanking Lee's forces, he hoped to force the Confederates to forsake their defensive positions and fight in the open.

All of Burnside's division commanders opposed the movement. Fearing another disaster, several of them hurried to Washington to ask Lincoln to countermand Burnside's orders. Lincoln asked General Halleck to go down to Burnside's headquarters and examine the ground for himself. "Your military skill is useless to me," the president wrote, "if you will not do this."

Halleck replied that it was not his job to second-guess generals who were commanding armies in the field. Lincoln accepted the rebuke, but he never again asked Halleck for a recommendation on strategic questions.

Blessed by a spell of unusually dry weather, Burnside began his advance on January 19. Within twenty-four hours a torrential rain turned the dirt roads of Virginia into impassable quagmires. Ammunition wagons, artillery, mules, and soldiers slipped and sank into the foot-deep mud. Observing the struggles of the Union troops, rebel pickets on the other side of the Rappahannock held up derisive signs that read, "This Way to Richmond."

After two days, Burnside ordered his wretched soldiers back into camp. They were so short of provisions that some men died of scurvy, while wounded soldiers in hospital tents froze to death for lack of blankets. The army seemed on the verge of mutiny. "I have heard generals, subordinate officers, and men say that they expect to be whipped anyhow, that 'all these fatigues and hardships are for nothing,' and that they might as well go home," reported Carl Schurz from Burnside's headquarters. "The whole army," agreed a private from Rhode Island, "is sick of this miserably managed war."

On January 24, Burnside told Lincoln that he wanted to relinquish his command, "of which he had long been very sick." "I think you are right," Lincoln said. After conferring with Stanton, Lincoln accepted Burnside's resignation and named General Hooker as his replacement.

Hooker's promotion caught many observers by surprise. Known as "Fighting Joe" for his willingness to engage the enemy, Hooker was popular with his men. The northern public praised him for his heroism at Antietam, Malvern Hill, and Williamsburg. Radical Republicans in Congress loved him for his eagerness to crush the South.

But Hooker was a vain, ambitious man who schemed to undermine his superiors. He had openly intrigued against McClellan and Burnside, and he savaged anyone who crossed him. He could not restrain himself from telling a reporter for the *New York Times* in early January that the Lincoln administration was "imbecile and 'played out.'" "Nothing would go right," Hooker argued, "until we had a dictator, and the sooner the better." A handsome man of dubious personal morality, Hooker drank excessively, and his headquarters were a notorious combination of brothel and barroom.

"Hooker does talk badly," Lincoln admitted, "but . . . he is stronger with the country today than any other man." When he informed Hooker by letter of his promotion, Lincoln reminded the general of his recent statement that the nation needed a dictator. "What I now ask of you is military success," Lincoln wrote, "and I will risk that dictatorship."

"He talks to me like a father," Hooker told a friend. "I shall not answer this letter until I have won him a great victory."

British Storms

Violent storms in the North Atlantic in early January delayed the arrival of news from the United States in Great Britain, but by the end of the month the text of the Emancipation Proclamation had appeared in every major British newspaper.

Palmerston's government was not impressed. Foreign Minister Lord Russell feared that Lincoln's message would lead to "acts of plunder, of incendiarism, of revenge" by black slaves. "There seems to be no declaration of a principle adverse to slavery in this proclamation," complained Russell. "It is a measure of war of a very questionable kind."

Among the working and middle classes, however, the Proclamation evoked enthusiasm. In Manchester, where the loss of the cotton trade was producing widespread hardship, a massive gathering of workers sent an encouraging message to Lincoln: "Since we have discerned . . . that the victory of the free north, in the war which has so sorely distressed us as well as afflicted you, will strike off the fetters of the slave, you have attracted our warm and earnest sympathy." A gathering of workingmen in London adopted a similar resolution, celebrating "the steady advance of your policy along the path of emancipation."

"The Emancipation Proclamation has done more for us here than all our former victories and all our diplomacy," observed Henry Adams in London. "It is creating an almost convulsive reaction in our favor all over this country."

The British government was not in the habit of consulting the working classes on political issues, but the widespread agitation in favor of liberty alarmed Palmerston's government and quashed any plans to mediate an end to the American conflict. To maintain the pro-Union momentum, Lincoln urged the workers in Manchester never to forget that the central question of the rebellion was "the attempt to overthrow this government, which was built upon the foundation of human rights, and to substitute for it one which should rest exclusively on the basis of human slavery."

A Presidential OK

In the early weeks of 1863, Radical Republicans and abolitionists pressured Lincoln to fulfill the promise of the Emancipation Proclamation and use Negro troops in combat. The president remained cautious. He told Vice President Hamlin that he was "feeling the public pulse," fearing that the northern public still was not up to it. But when Hamlin and a delegation of ten army officers came to the Executive Mansion to lobby for Negro combat units, Lincoln acknowledged that the time had come to derive some benefit from the Emancipation Proclamation. Lincoln handed Hamlin an order instructing Secretary of War Stanton to form several Negro regiments, although the president insisted that they have white officers.

On January 15, Stanton authorized Governor John Andrew of Massachusetts to raise two regiments of free Negroes. Prominent New England whites and Negro leaders offered to serve as recruiting agents. Meanwhile, the governor pressured wealthy young white men to serve as officers.

Recruiters found northern Negroes less enthusiastic about fighting than at the start of the war. Confederate threats to hang captured Negro soldiers, combined with the federal government's degrading refusal to commission Negro officers, diminished the allure of combat. As the thriving northern wartime economy continued to provide employment opportunities, observers reported that "the blacks here are too comfortable to do anything more than talk about freedom."

Further south, Colonel Thomas Higginson began using his First South Carolina Volunteers to raid the coast of southern Georgia and northern Florida. "Nobody knows anything about these men who has not seen them in battle," reported Higginson. "There is a fiery energy about them beyond anything of which I have ever read." He claimed that their knowledge of local conditions, plus the incentive of freedom for themselves and their families, made them superior to white troops. "No officer in this regiment," Higginson concluded, " now doubts that the key to the successful prosecution of this war lies in the unlimited employment of black troops."

Others remained skeptical. When General Nathaniel Banks replaced

General Butler in New Orleans, he forced all the Negro officers of the colored regiments under his command to resign. Convinced that Negroes were "a race unaccustomed to military service," he then disbanded the Negro regiments and used the troops to guard prisoners of war and sugar plantations.

Negro troops in Louisiana suffered constant abuse from civilians and bigoted white Union soldiers. The subservient behavior and ragged appearance of former field hands exacerbated the racism of Union soldiers in the South. "The average plantation negro was a hard-looking specimen," observed an officer, "with about as little of the soldier to be seen in him as there was of the angel in Michael Angelo's block of marble before he had applied his chisel." A lifetime of slavery produced "plantation manners": "the awkward bowing and scraping . . . a rolling, dragging, moping gait and a cringing manner, with a downcast thievish glance that dared not look you in the eye."

But freedom and military training soon transformed runaway slaves into soldiers. "Yesterday a filthy, repulsive 'nigger,' to-day a neatly-attired man," remarked one Union colonel. "Yesterday a slave, to-day a freeman; yesterday a civilian, to-day a soldier."

Freedmen who joined the Union ranks knew they risked death if captured. Confederate troops did not hesitate to murder Negro prisoners. After capturing several Negroes in uniform, a North Carolina soldier recalled that they were "either bayoneted or burnt. The men were perfectly exasperated at the idea of negroes opposed to them & rushed at them like so many devils."

Nevertheless, Lincoln displayed an increasing willingness to use Negro troops. He spoke of recapturing Fort Sumter and manning it with Negroes, and he urged General John Dix to use Negroes to garrison Fortress Monroe and Yorktown. When congressional Radicals pressed him to give General Frémont another command, Lincoln told them he was considering nominating Frémont to lead a Negro army.

At the end of January, the president drafted a recommendation that General Butler return to the Department of the Gulf to lead Louisiana's Negro regiments in clearing Confederate forces from the lower Mississippi Valley. And in a conference with Senator Sumner and other antislavery leaders at the Executive Mansion, Lincoln spoke of arming 200,000 southern Negroes by the beginning of July.

Sterner Stuff

"It is a common thing to hear Republicans abuse the President and the Cabinet," wrote Noah Brooks on February 4, "and to see Republicans . . . squelch out a message from the White House, or treat it with undisguised contempt."

Despite widespread support among congressional Republicans for Lincoln's policies on the great questions of the war—emancipation, confiscation, and the suspension of habeas corpus—an undercurrent of dissatisfaction was poisoning relations between the lame-duck Congress and the president. Lincoln blamed the growing restlessness on the Union's repeated military losses, but its causes ran deeper than that.

Nearly two years after Lincoln's inauguration, senior Republicans in Congress still resented the president's refusal to follow their lead. Worse, he was expanding presidential power at their expense; by the spring of 1863, Lincoln wielded greater powers than any previous American president.

Republican leaders resented Lincoln's willingness to express his opinion on legislation, especially since his messages to Congress often resembled lectures. Senators blamed Lincoln for assembling an ill-matched Cabinet whose members continued to snipe at one another, and they chafed at Lincoln's persistent attempts to conciliate the border states. Representatives of the border states, meanwhile, misinterpreted the president's solicitude as weakness, and they dispatched delegations to the White House seeking additional concessions.

Abolitionist author Richard Henry Dana visited Washington and decided that "the most striking thing" to him was "the absence of personal loyalty to the President. It does not exist." Incessant political infighting took a toll on Lincoln. Visitors to the Executive Mansion in early February noticed that the president lacked his usual good humor. "I observe that the President never tells a joke now," observed Admiral John Dahlgren. Stress made Lincoln's hands shake; another guest reported that the president looked haggard and worn—"so broken, so dispirited, and so ghostlike." Lincoln claimed to harbor no thoughts of serving a second term. "I have ceased to have any person feeling or expectation in that matter," the president told Wendell Phillips, "so abused and borne upon as I have been."

Fire in the Midwest

In the late winter of 1863, the pro-war political coalition in the North was disintegrating. Radical Republicans spent January and February trying to purge the Union Army of Democratic generals, before the new Congress—with substantially increased Democratic representation—convened in March.

But the Radicals were no longer Lincoln's primary concern. In the Midwest, a rising storm of opposition to the Emancipation Proclamation threatened to overwhelm Unionist sentiment. In the first year of the war, residents of Ohio, Illinois, and Indiana had enlisted enthusiastically to save the Union. After suffering a disproportionate share of northern casualties, however, they felt betrayed to learn that they were also fighting to end Negro slavery in the Confederacy.

Their disillusionment was fed by an agricultural depression caused by the Confederate blockade of the Mississippi River at Vicksburg, preventing midwestern farm products from reaching foreign markets. When the administration called for 500,000 new volunteers in February—followed by congressional approval of the Union's first conscription act on March 3—discontent boiled over. "All who wish to be butchered will please step forward," suggested one newspaper editorial. "All others will please stay at home and defy Old Abe."

"The President tells me he now fears 'the fire in the rear'—meaning the Democracy—especially the Northwest—more than our military chances," Senator Sumner informed a friend in late January. Governor Yates of Illinois warned Lincoln that he was "sitting on a powder keg." Mass meetings in the Midwest protesting emancipation and the war degenerated into violence. Race riots erupted in Detroit when whites attacked Negroes, killing several and burning dozens of homes. Elsewhere, numerous draft officials and Union soldiers home on leave were beaten or murdered.

Feeling that antiwar legislators might seize control of state militias, Yates and Governor Oliver Morton of Indiana prorogued their state legislatures. Lincoln dispatched four army regiments to Illinois to discourage Democratic politicians from obstructing the war effort. Army officers shut down newspapers that protested the administration's policies too strongly.

General McClellan, meanwhile, embarked on a tour of New England, accepting invitations to speak in every major eastern city. Sensing that Lincoln would be vulnerable if he ran for reelection in 1864, Democratic politicians urged McClellan to explore a bid for the presidency.

Respite

By the end of March, General Hooker had transformed the demoralized Army of the Potomac into a force that he called "the finest army on the planet." To check desertions, Hooker used a judicious combination of furloughs and harsh punishments. Soldiers spent more time in drill and field exercise to sharpen their skills and maintain discipline; officers implemented sanitation rules that significantly reduced sickness; quartermasters improved the quality and variety of provisions, including beef, vegetables, potatoes, onions, and fresh bread. Overdue pay finally arrived. Enormous freight trains and fleets of government steamers carried supplies to the army, including 1 million pounds of forage daily to feed its 60,000 horses.

Every corps received its own unique badge, which soldiers wore on their shoulders or caps. Borrowing a page from General Lee's book, Hooker organized his 17,000-man cavalry into a separate corps under General George Stoneman, who made better use of its mobility in skirmishes and expeditions.

Even men who distrusted Hooker admitted that the 130,000 troops under his command were ready for battle. "I have never known men to change from a condition of the lowest depression to that of a healthy fighting state in so short a time," observed one officer.

At the suggestion of Mrs. Lincoln, who knew how much her husband needed a respite from the pressures of Washington, the president sailed down the Potomac in the first week of April to review the army. He arrived at Hooker's headquarters in an early spring snowstorm on the afternoon of April 5.

Lincoln originally intended to spend only a day or two inspecting the troops, but he enjoyed the contrast with Washington so much that he stayed nearly a week. Despite the cold, blustery weather, the president rode bareheaded through the camps as a sign of respect to the enlisted men. Lincoln insisted on visiting all of the hospital tents of General George Meade's Fifth Corps, shaking hands with the wounded men, asking them questions, and leaving them with encouraging words.

As usual, the soldiers gave "Father Abraham" an enthusiastic reception. Although they joked at his ungainly figure, they sensed Lincoln's genuine concern for their welfare. In their eyes, he was "our revered president," "the brother of every soldier." They also noticed the president's weary sadness. "Did you ever see such a look on any man's face?" one soldier asked. "It is an awful load," noted another. "It is killing him."

The tour revived Lincoln physically and mentally, although he told Noah Brooks that "nothing could touch the tired spot within, which was all tired." Impressed by the army's energy, Lincoln was less sanguine about Hooker's judgment. During their conversations, the president began to say, "If you get to Richmond—" but Hooker interrupted him. "Excuse me, Mr. President, but there is no 'if' in the case. I am going straight to Richmond, if I live!"

"That is the most depressing thing about Hooker," Lincoln murmured to a companion with a sigh. "It seems to me that he is over-confident."

Chancellorsville

Before he left, Lincoln told Hooker pointedly that his objective should be the destruction of Lee's army on the other side of the Rappahannock, rather than the capture of Richmond, especially since Hooker's forces outnumbered the rebels nearly two to one. To take full advantage of his numerical superiority, however, Hooker needed to force Lee into the open.

Dividing his army, Hooker sent three corps and Stoneman's cavalry north, crossing the Rappahannock on April 28 several miles beyond the Confederate lines. Meanwhile, the other four corps feigned an attack against Fredericksburg. Forty-eight hours later, the northernmost three corps—70,000 infantrymen—had advanced to a clearing at a crossroads known as Chancellorsville, named after a brick mansion about 10 miles west of Fredericksburg. Hooker ordered them to wait there. "I have Lee's army in one hand and Richmond in the other," he jubilantly announced to his aides.

Gambling that the Union force at Chancellorsville represented the main threat, Lee turned most of his army to face it. On May 1, advance rebel units clashed with Union troops several miles east of Chancellorsville. Hooker froze. Instead of pressing ahead, he ordered his infantry to pull back to the area called the Wilderness, where dense thickets and tangled underbrush negated the Union's superior numbers.

Lee seized the initiative. Again defying convention, he divided his outnumbered troops and ordered General Jackson to launch an offensive against the poorly protected Union right on the afternoon of May 2. Jackson's surprise attack routed the northern troops, until darkness ended the day's fighting.

Hooker might have recovered his losses by counterattacking the following day, especially since the Confederate Army remained divided. But the shaken general withdrew from a superior defensive position to shorten his lines. When the battle resumed he cautiously insisted upon holding in reserve nearly a third of his forces—37,000 men, more than either wing of the Confederate forces.

During the ensuing battle, a cannonball struck Hooker's headquarters. A falling column hit Hooker and rendered him unconscious for over an hour. Although his corps commanders were eager to reclaim the offensive, none of them felt justified in assuming command while Hooker lived. (Lincoln later remarked that "if Hooker had been killed by the shot which knocked over the pillar that stunned him, we should have been successful.")

On the evening of May 4, Hooker—having regained his senses but not his nerve—decided to retreat across the Rappahannock. He had won nothing at a cost of 17,000 casualties, compared with the Confederacy's losses of 13,000.

Lincoln received news of Hooker's retreat on the afternoon of May 6. As he walked into a room where several guests sat waiting, he seemed close to collapse. "I shall never forget that picture of despair," wrote Noah Brooks.

> He held a telegram in his hand, and as he closed the door and came toward us I mechanically noted that his face, usually sallow, was ashen in hue. . . .
>
> Never, as long as I knew him, did he seem to be so broken, so dispirited, and so ghostlike. Clasping his hands behind his back, he walked up and down the room, saying, "My God! my God! What will the country say! What will the country say!"

Facts and Prejudice

"Uncle Abe has at last sensibly concluded to arm the darkey and let him fight," wrote a Union lieutenant to his wife in Ohio. "They are not to be placed by the side of the white soldiers but is to be organized into companies, regiments and brigades by themselves with white officers. This is considered the master stroke of policy. . . . I think the slavery question which has puzzled our fathers for fifty years is now being solved."

In the spring of 1863, Lincoln abandoned his reservations about using Negro soldiers in combat. On March 26, the president encouraged Senator Andrew Johnson—serving as military governor of Tennessee—to raise a Negro army. "The colored population is the great *available* and yet *unavailed* of, force for restoring the Union," Lincoln argued. "The bare sight of fifty thousand armed, and drilled black soldiers on the banks of the Mississippi, would end the rebellion at once."

While Lincoln wrote to Johnson, Colonel Thomas Higginson was leading the First South Carolina Infantry (African Descent) on a raid into northern Florida. Reports from northern white civilians on the Sea Islands, where Higginson trained his troops, praised the martial qualities of the Negro soldiers. "Once they are in they fight like fiends," observed one labor superintendent. "My faith is firm that the best thing that can be done for these men is to put them in the Army. They will learn there sooner than anywhere else that they are men. The improvement & bearing of those who are now in the Army is so marked that every one notices it."

Lincoln kept a close watch on the progress of Higginson's regiment. "I see the enemy are driving at them fiercely, as is to be expected," the president remarked on April 1. "It is important to the enemy that such a force shall *not* take shape, and grow, and thrive, in the South; and in precisely the same proportion, it is important to us that it *shall*."

Although the First South Carolina helped capture Jacksonville, they obtained only about fifty new recruits, because local slaveowners had already taken their human property farther inland. Nevertheless, the Negro soldiers' bravery under fire impressed their commander. Their success helped persuade Lincoln and Stanton to send General Lorenzo Thomas to the Mississippi Valley to raise as many regiments of former slaves as possible. Starting in Kentucky in the first week of April, Thomas recruited 20,000 Negroes in six weeks, mostly former field hands from large plantations. To coordinate the sudden increase in Negro troops, Secretary Stanton established the Bureau of Colored Troops in the War Department on May 22, under the command of Major Charles W. Foster.

Shortly after Thomas left Washington, Lincoln sent General Daniel Ullman to Louisiana to raise a Negro infantry brigade. Ullman encountered opposition from General Banks, who had ordered most Negroes in the New Orleans area to continue to work on cotton plantations. The freedmen could choose to labor on any plantation and received a nominal wage. If they refused to work, military authorities assigned them to public works projects.

Banks's policies perpetuated the despair of slavery under a different guise. "No one can travel from plantation to plantation, from country to country, as I have done, without being strangely impressed with the universal gloom of the negro character," wrote the minister George Hepworth from Louisiana. "They are a sombre race,—a race who show that every effort has been made to crush them,—a race whose hearts have a chain and ball on them. . . . It is very seldom that you hear a good round laugh from a black man. He is timid and fearful, and seems like one walking in a dangerous place in the dark."

Pressured by War Department officials, Banks finally consented to raise a corps of Negro troops known as the "Corps d'Afrique." But Banks staffed the corps with white officers, and limited each regiment to half the usual number of men.

Others were less skeptical. "I am happy to be able to announce to you my complete and eminent satisfaction with the results of the organization of negro regiments in this department," declared General David Hunter in a note to Secretary of War Stanton. "They are imbued with a burning faith that now is the time appointed by God . . . for the deliverance of their race."

"Facts are beginning to dispel prejudices," agreed an editorial in the *New York Tribune*. "Enemies of the negro race, who have persistently denied the capacity and doubted the courage of the Blacks, are unanswerably confuted by the good conduct and gallant deeds of the men whom they persecute and slander."

Grant Disappears

Across the border from northeastern Louisiana, the Confederate garrison at Vicksburg remained entrenched in the last major rebel stronghold on the Mississippi River. Located on a plateau 200 feet above the river, the heavily fortified town stubbornly withstood every Union attack from land or sea. "It was an ugly place," noted Charles Dana, "with its line of bluffs commanding the channel for fully seven miles, and battery piled above battery all the way."

As Grant discovered during the winter of 1862–1863, the only viable approach was landward, from the east. In late April, Union transports began ferrying 23,000 soldiers from their camps on the western side of the Mississippi across the river, 60 miles south of Vicksburg. Then, instead of attacking Vicksburg directly, Grant decided to strike into the interior and threaten Jackson, the state capital, hoping to lure Vicksburg's defenders into the open.

Grant knew he could not rely on an extended supply line in hostile territory, but information provided by Union agents convinced him that there was sufficient beef, cattle, and corn in the surrounding countryside to allow his troops to live off the land. Assured by Stanton that he had "the full confidence of the Government . . . and will be firmly and heartily supported," Grant cut his communications, broke loose from his supply base, and plunged into western Mississippi. For nearly two weeks, no one in Washington knew precisely where Grant's army was.

First Fruits of Emancipation

In heavily Democratic districts throughout the North, opposition to conscription and emancipation mounted. Democratic speakers urged their audiences to strike a blow for liberty by resisting the draft. "When the President called upon them to go and carry on a war for the nigger," declared the editor of an influential Catholic journal in New York, "he would be damned if he believed they would go." "We will not render support to the present Administration in its wicked Abolition crusade," promised a meeting of midwestern Democrats. "We will resist to the death all attempts to draft any of our citizens into the army."

Among Union soldiers, however, civilians' antiwar protests created a backlash of support for the president. At the same time, Lincoln's emancipation policy grew more popular within the army as troops witnessed the damage it inflicted upon the enemy.

"I have always untill lately been opposed to abraham linkins proclamation," observed a private from Pennsylvania, "but i have lately been convinced that it was just the thing that was needed to weaken the strength of the rebls." "The 'inexorable logic of events' is rapidly making practical abolitionists of every soldier," agreed a lieutenant from Kentucky. "I am afraid that I am getting to be an Abolitionist. All right! better that than a Secessionist."

Every month, thousands of slaves, emboldened by the Emancipation Proclamation, fled their masters. In Memphis, newspapers overflowed with advertisements for fugitive slaves. So many runaways sought temporary refuge in Kentucky that the state legislature passed a measure in March 1863 banning from the state all blacks "claiming or pretending to be free" by virtue of the Emancipation Proclamation.

Alarmed by rumors of slave uprisings, captured Confederate officers admitted that the proclamation "had played hell with them." The wife of a planter in Georgia complained that her slaves were in a condition "of perfect anarchy and rebellion. They have placed themselves in perfect antagonism to their owners and to all government and control. We dare not predict the end of all this."

Food production throughout the Confederacy declined, even though many planters converted their fields from cotton to corn, rice, or wheat. Drought and military requisitions exacerbated the shortages. In the spring of 1863, food prices in southern cities reached prohibitive levels, provoking protests and riots by mobs of armed women unable to feed their families. In Richmond, more than 1,000 demonstrators raided warehouses and shops demanding "bread or blood"; only the appearance of President Jefferson Davis at the head of a militia company persuaded the rioters to disperse.

"The Yankees have now made up their minds that this is to be a long war, and they are determined to fight it out to the end," conceded one newspaper editor in Richmond. "They threaten us at every point—Virginia, Eastern Tennessee, Vicksburg, Louisiana, North Carolina, Hilton Head. . . . Our frontier is too extended to be everywhere adequately defended. Gunboats and cavalry-raids will penetrate the heart of the country, stealing niggers and destroying generally. In short, we are fighting at fearful disadvantage with terrible loss."

Siege

"Have you heard anything from Grant?" Lincoln telegraphed to General John Dix, commander of Fortress Monroe. "Do the Richmond papers have anything about . . . Vicksburg?"

On May 18, General Grant's army reappeared outside of Vicksburg. During the previous fortnight, Grant had defeated a Confederate relief force and beaten back an attack by the rebel garrison at Vicksburg, led by General John Pemberton. Now he settled down to starve Vicksburg into submission. Union soldiers commandeered every morsel of food from the surrounding countryside, including bucketfuls of blackberries, mulberries, and red and yellow wild plums.

Surveying the land around Vicksburg, Charles Dana—who was secretly sending dispatches to Stanton about Grant's physical and mental
condition—noticed a "total absence of men capable of bearing arms. Only
old men and children remained. The young men were all in the army or
had perished in it. The South was drained of its youth."

Courage under Fire

Inspired by Grant's aggressiveness, General Nathaniel Banks prepared to
launch an assault against the Confederate citadel of Port Hudson, 240
miles south of Vicksburg. Banks's force of 30,000 troops included two of
the Negro regiments raised in New Orleans—one consisting of free Negroes, the other of former slaves. Their task at Port Hudson was to charge
across an open plain, then up a steep hill into the strongest Confederate
position. Apparently unaware that the Negro regiments would face heavy
fire from rebel sharpshooters, artillery, and shore batteries, their commander regarded the assault as an experiment to determine whether Negroes
would fight. "I shall compromise nothing in making this attack," he insisted. "The negro will have the fate of his race on his conduct."

At ten o'clock on the hot, dusty morning of May 27, 1,000 Negro soldiers began a calm, steady advance toward Port Hudson. Despite blister-
ing enemy fire, they advanced to within 200 yards of the Confederate
entrenchments before rebel cannon devastated their lines. Repeatedly
they regrouped and struggled forward, only to suffer appalling losses.

By sundown, the Union attack had failed all along the line. But eye-
witnesses testified to the courage of the Negro troops. One soldier from
Wisconsin claimed that the Negroes "fought like devils, they made five
charges on a battery that there was not the slightest chance of their taking, just . . . to show our boys that they *could* and *would* fight."

"You have no idea how my prejudices with regard to negro troops have
been dispelled by the battle," wrote a white officer. "They are far superior
in discipline to the white troops, and just as brave." In an editorial, the
New York Times confirmed that the battle of Port Hudson "settles the

question that the negro race can fight with great prowess. . . . It is no longer possible to doubt the bravery and steadiness of the colored race when rightly led."

Meanwhile, a Confederate relief force seeking to disrupt the Union siege at Vicksburg struck Grant's supply base at Milliken's Bend, just south of the town. The base was being used as a training facility for recently recruited Negro troops, most of whom were former slaves who had never fired a gun.

Most of the fighting at Milliken's Bend took place at close quarters. As enraged Confederate soldiers shouted, "No quarter," Negro soldiers gave ground grudgingly toward the river in fierce hand-to-hand combat. The arrival of two Union gunboats forced the rebels to abandon the attack. A northern observer who toured the battlefield shortly afterward testified to the ferocity of the fighting. "Many men were found dead with bayonet stabs," he wrote, "and others with their skulls broken open by butts of muskets." Rebel military authorities reportedly hanged several captured Negro soldiers. Other Negro prisoners were sold back into slavery.

"I never more wish to hear the expression, 'the niggers won't fight,'" wrote a white officer to his family in Illinois. After listening to the comments of other white soldiers, Charles Dana concluded that "the bravery of the blacks in the battle at Milliken's Bend completely revolutionized the sentiment of the army with regard to the employment of negro troops. I heard prominent officers who formerly in private had sneered at the idea of the negroes fighting express themselves after that as heartily in favor of it."

From New Orleans, Samuel Denison reported to Secretary of the Treasury Chase that "the whole army, from colonels down, is thoroughly abolitionized. They have seen the negroes drill and fight, and they want to give them a chance and put down slavery. I have not seen a soldier who has not this feeling."

Meade Assumes Command

"Lee and Hooker both seem moving," mused George Templeton Strong in his diary. "Lee seems to contemplate either an attack on Washington or an invasion of Pennsylvania. . . . I fear Joe Hooker, drunk or sober, is no match for Lee."

At a strategy conference in Richmond in mid-May, General Lee convinced President Jefferson Davis that the best hope for the survival of the Confederacy lay in a second invasion of the North. By leading his seemingly invincible army through the Shenandoah Valley and into Maryland and Pennsylvania, Lee hoped to "turn back the tide of war, that is now pressing the South" and obtain urgently needed supplies for his troops. If he could inflict another crushing defeat on the Army of the Potomac, or perhaps capture Baltimore, the northerners' resolve might crumble, forcing the Lincoln administration to concede the Confederates' independence.

After scraping together 75,000 soldiers from Virginia and the Carolinas, Lee sent the first part of his army across the Potomac into Maryland on June 15. Convinced that Lee's force outnumbered his own, Hooker asked Halleck to transfer to his command the 10,000 Union troops at Harpers Ferry. Halleck refused. Angered, Hooker offered his resignation. When Secretary of War Stanton delivered Hooker's telegram to Lincoln on the evening of June 27, he asked the president for guidance. Without hesitating, Lincoln answered, "Accept his resignation."

Virtually no one except a few Radical Republicans in Congress mourned the loss of Hooker. Later, Lincoln told a reporter that he regarded Hooker "very much as a father might regard a son who was lame, or who had some other incurable physical infirmity." His love for such a son, Lincoln said, "would be even intensified by the reflection that the lad could never be a strong and successful man."

Halleck recommended General George Meade, a corps commander in the Army of the Potomac, as Hooker's replacement. That evening, an army officer in civilian clothes took a train to Frederick, Maryland, and notified Meade at 3 A.M. that he now commanded the Army of the Potomac. Meade accepted the appointment reluctantly; he knew it had ruined the career of each of his predecessors.

Tall, slim, and nearsighted, with a luxuriant gray beard and a reticent manner, Meade in his slouch hat and plain blue uniform resembled a country lawyer or "a good sort of family doctor" more than the leader of the largest army on the continent. An excellent defensive strategist, Meade had fought in every major eastern battle in the past year. His men respected him for his willingness to endure hardships, even if his outbursts of violent temper ("the old snapping turtle," they called him) and his aloof manner—reporters typically saw Meade standing alone, even in the midst of a crowd—kept them at a distance.

Lincoln did not send Meade any telegrams of advice. As 85,000 soldiers of the Army of the Potomac followed the Confederate forces into Pennsylvania, the president was still showing signs of stress and fatigue. A guest at the White House noticed Lincoln's "drooping eyelids, looking almost swollen; the dark bags beneath the eyes; the deep marks about the large and expressive mouth."

Habitually cautious, Meade remained on the defensive, keeping his army between Lee and Washington. Three days after he assumed command, advance units of the Union and rebel armies stumbled into one another about a mile west of the town of Gettysburg.

Victory: East

No one expected to fight a decisive battle at this time or place. Gettysburg was a quiet town of 2,400 inhabitants, located at the junction of ten country roads. To the east rose the hills known as Cemetery Ridge; on the western edge of town stood the heights of Seminary Ridge.

Although General Lee had hoped to tempt the Union Army into taking the offensive, his line of communications was growing dangerously extended, and he needed to force a battle. When Lee heard of the initial skirmish at Gettysburg, he quickly concentrated his forces north of the town in an attempt to strike the dispersed Union Army before General Meade could prepare a defense.

On the first day of the battle, July 1, Confederate forces pushed back the outnumbered Union divisions in hard fighting. During the night, Meade arrived at Gettysburg and reinforced the Union line along Cemetery Ridge. Lee knew he faced a daunting task, attacking an enemy in a strong defensive position with shorter lines of communication, but he believed his troops were invincible.

The battle resumed on the hot, clear afternoon of July 2. Lee sent General James Longstreet to smash the Union left and capture the Round Tops, a pair of hills from which rebel artillery could sweep the Union positions. Simultaneously, he directed General Richard Ewell to attack the Union right. At sundown, it looked as if the combined Confederate assaults might break the northern lines, but a Union counterattack managed to regain nearly all the lost ground. Although Lee declared the day a success, the Army of the Potomac retained control of Cemetery Ridge, and particularly the critical Little Round Top.

In Washington, Lincoln followed the progress of the battle in the War Department's telegraph room. He read the latest dispatches as he paced back and forth, stopping occasionally to trace the position of the armies on a map that hung on the wall.

Lee's decision to launch an all-out attack against the center of the Union line on July 3 sealed the fate of the Confederacy. At three o'clock in the afternoon, 15,000 rebel infantrymen under the command of General George Pickett marched out of the woods and across a wheat field toward Cemetery Ridge, over half a mile away.

Only a handful of Pickett's men reached the Union defenders. Shredded by artillery and rifle fire, more than half were killed or wounded. As the survivors staggered back to the rebel lines, Lee met them and declared, "It was all my fault; get together, and let us do the best we can toward saving that which is left us." The following day, Lee reluctantly decided to retreat into Virginia. Meade chose not to pursue until his own exhausted troops recovered.

Union casualties at Gettysburg totaled nearly 17,000 men, slightly more than the 15,600 Confederate dead and wounded. But the North could replace its losses. The South could not.

At sundown on Sunday, July 4, Lincoln drove in a carriage across the Long Bridge to the line of Union defenses at Arlington. A brigade of troops was forming for an evening review, and the commanding general invited the president to observe the parade. His face drawn and haggard from anxiety, Lincoln asked the regimental bands to play "Lead, Kindly Light." As the president repeated in a barely audible voice the lines of the song—

"Lead, kindly light, amid the encircling gloom . . . Keep thou my feet; I do not ask to see"—the general saw tears coursing down Lincoln's cheeks.

Victory: West

At Vicksburg, Union artillery pounded the rebel garrison incessantly. Union troops edged closer every day, digging tunnels and planting mines, tightening the noose around the city. Within Vicksburg, residents were reduced to eating rats, mules, and boiled sugarcane sprouts. "Our rations have been cut down to one biscuit and a small bit of bacon per day," wrote a delegation of Confederate soldiers to General Pemberton, "not enough scarcely to keep soul and body together, much less to stand the hardships we are called upon to stand."

On the afternoon of July 3, Pemberton met General Grant on a hill outside the city to negotiate terms of surrender. Grant allowed the 29,500 rebel troops in Vicksburg to leave "on parole"—agreeing not to rejoin the Confederate Army. Each Confederate officer was permitted to keep his sidearms and one horse. The rebels "had behaved so well," Grant later explained, "that I did not want to humiliate them. I believed that consideration for their feelings would make them less dangerous during the continuance of hostilities, and better citizens after the war was over."

Union possession of Vicksburg rendered the Confederate position at Port Hudson untenable. Five days later, the 6,400 defenders of Port Hudson surrendered.

The Confederacy was cut in two. Supplies from the southern states west of the Mississippi could no longer reach the increasingly desperate armies of the east. With no rebel force behind them, Grant and Sherman were free to sweep through the interior of Mississippi, Alabama, Tennessee, and Georgia.

9

CREATING FREEDOM

Despite repeated telegrams from Lincoln urging him to pursue and crush the Army of Virginia as it waited to cross the flood-swollen Potomac, General Meade refused to risk an attack. "We have done well enough," Meade insisted. "I did not believe the enemy could be whipped." On July 14, General Lee and his troops retreated unmolested into Virginia.

When he heard that Lee had crossed the Potomac, Lincoln wept. "We had them within our grasp," the president told John Hay. "We had only to stretch forth our hands & they were ours. And nothing I could say or do could make the Army move." Lincoln briefly considered going to the front and assuming command of the Union forces in person. "If I had gone up there," he grumbled, "I could have whipped them myself."

News of the Union victories at Gettysburg and Vicksburg raised northerners' hopes that the end of the rebellion was at hand. Fearful that the Confederacy might surrender before it was thoroughly whipped, Radical congressmen worried that Lincoln might renege on the Emancipation Proclamation to lure dispirited southerners into returning to the Union. Already northern conservatives and southern Unionists were pressuring Lincoln to retract or modify the proclamation to encourage moderates in the South to overthrow the Confederate government.

But Lincoln no longer entertained any hope that Confederate officials would voluntarily rejoin the Union. Besides, the notion of returning freedmen to slavery filled the president with repugnance. "I think I shall not, in any event, retract the emancipation proclamation," Lincoln declared in July 1863, "nor, as executive, ever return to slavery any person who is free by the terms of the proclamation, or by any of the acts of Congress."

Riot

On the morning of July 11, a blindfolded official of the provost marshal's office in New York City began drawing slips of paper from a large hollow wheel outside the Ninth District police headquarters on Third Avenue, on the northern edge of the city. The papers bore the names of male New Yorkers between the ages of twenty and forty-five—those eligible for the nation's first federal military draft.

Violent resistance to conscription had previously erupted in scattered areas in the north, particularly in the border states and the lower Midwest. Local authorities expected some opposition to the draft among the heavily Democratic Irish sections of New York, but the ferocity of the reaction caught them by surprise.

In the summer of 1863, New York City was primed for an explosion. Over the previous fifteen years, the city's population had increased at an extraordinary rate, primarily as a result of immigration from Ireland and Germany. Nearly half of New York's 800,000 residents were foreign-born. Many of those were crammed into squalid tenements in the lower part of Manhattan Island, making the city's Fourth Ward nearly twice as crowded as the notorious slums of London's East End.

Municipal services failed to keep pace with the rise in population. Nearly two-thirds of New York City lacked sewers; many of the sewer lines that existed were so poorly constructed that they frequently were clogged with filth. Epidemics regularly swept through the tenements, giving New York the highest death rate of any city in the civilized world. Merchants sold milk from diseased cattle and coffee tainted with street sweepings and sawdust.

Native-born Americans despised the uneducated and largely Catholic Irish, relegating them to the lowest-paying jobs, where they competed for work with Negroes. Barely able to survive in the best of times, New York's working poor were hit hard by the inflation of wartime; during the first two years of the war, prices rose nearly 40 percent, while wages increased only 12 percent.

In an era when religion and cultural politics determined party affiliation, nearly all Irish immigrants voted Democratic. Suspicious of federal authority, Irish-Americans especially resented the conscription act of March 1863, which convinced them that the government was trampling on the liberties of white Americans, "having the poor man dragged from his family and sent to the war to fight for the negro and not to restore the Union." Workers could afford neither to leave their jobs nor hire a substitute to take their place in the army. Once the draft went into effect, racism and economic distress combined to spark the worst outbreak of rioting in the nation's history.

On the stifling hot, muggy morning of July 13, a band of Irish toughs attacked the Ninth District draft office, smashing furniture and setting the building ablaze as they shouted, "To hell with old Abe." The movement quickly spread throughout the city's working-class sections in the Upper East Side, where violence was such a commonplace means of expressing political grievances that the paving stones of streets, which protesters often tore up and hurled at police or soldiers, were known as Irish confetti.

Rioters cut down telegraph poles to sever police communications, tore up railroad tracks, attacked the police and the provost marshal's guard on the streets, and then began smashing windows and looting shops—especially jewelry stores and saloons. They attacked the homes of abolitionists and assaulted every Negro in sight, invading Negroes' houses and pulling them off steamboats and streetcars to savagely beat them or hang them from lampposts. An English visitor witnessed whites chasing a Negro down an avenue, shouting, "Kill the black son of a bitch!" and "Kill all niggers!" Employers were warned "not to put any niggers to work."

Late in the afternoon, a mob set fire to the Colored Orphan Asylum at Fifth Avenue and Forty-Third Street. Fortunately, most of the children had escaped moments earlier. When firemen attempted to put out the blaze, the rioters destroyed the hydrants. The evening ended with an assault on the City Armory. Throughout the night, bystanders heard laborers threatening to "burn the whole city before they were through," starting with Wall Street and the mansions of the wealthy.

"The town," wrote Herman Melville in disgust, "is taken by its rats." City police could not quell the disorder. Mayor George Opdyke asked local military authorities for help, but there were only about 800 federal troops in the New York metropolitan area. As the city awaited reinforcements, citizens formed vigilante committees and joined volunteer militia regiments to protect their property from the mob. National Guard units set up howitzers at strategic intersections, and naval authorities stationed a gunship off the Battery at the foot of Wall Street, with its cannon protecting the financial district.

Not until the Seventh New York Regiment arrived, early on Thursday morning, did the violence subside. Before the day was over, three more regiments brought the total number of troops in the city to 4,000. After a bloody confrontation between soldiers and rioters near Gramercy Park on the evening of July 16, the uprising collapsed.

Over 120 people lay dead, and nearly $2 million worth of property had been destroyed. New York's Negro population suffered most grievously. "The three days of misrule in New York will be the blackest in its history," mourned Thurlow Weed, who sent a donation of $500 to assist Negro survivors. "That the rioters should have deliberately marked for rapine and murder a class at once the least offending and the most defenseless is a fact in crime at which civilization and humanity revolt and shudder."

Racial prejudice grew stronger in the riot's aftermath. Fearful of renewed trouble, employers refused to hire Negroes; New Yorkers who befriended Negroes found themselves threatened by white laborers. Eventually one-third of the city's black population left to seek better opportunities elsewhere. "How this infernal slavery system has corrupted our blood, North as well as South," lamented George Templeton Strong.

Glory

As white rioters terrorized New York City, the 54th Massachusetts Infantry (Colored) prepared to lead an assault on Fort Wagner, the battery that guarded the entrance to Charleston, South Carolina. Shortly after sundown on July 18, three Union brigades—including the 54th Massachusetts—advanced across a narrow neck of land toward the fort. A ten-hour barrage by Union land artillery and gunboats was supposed to soften the rebel defenses, but the shells did only minimal damage. Most of the march was carried out in silence, except for the exhortations of white officers to their soldiers.

When the Union troops were nearly upon the fort, Confederate gunners opened fire. Hundreds of men fell in the first volley. Within minutes the Union ranks were in complete disarray. Some soldiers continued forward and surged over the parapets, only to be cut down by rebel bayonets. For several minutes a Negro sergeant held an American flag atop one wall of the fort, waiting for reinforcements. But the second wave of attackers hesitated, and the remnants of the 54th were forced to retreat.

More than 250 soldiers of the 54th Massachusetts were dead, wounded, or missing. A witness to their courage under fire declared that "no word of scorn or contempt for negro soldiers will ever be heard from any who beheld that spectacle." "I have changed my opinion of the negroes as soldiers," observed a white Union officer, "and I honor any man who will take command of a body of them against all prejudice."

Northern abolitionists rejoiced at the Negroes' sacrifice. "I have no tears to shed over their graves," insisted Angeline Grimke Weld, "because I see that their heroism is working a great change in public opinion, forcing all men to see the sin & shame of enslaving such men."

By August, there were nearly 50,000 Negro soldiers in the Union Army. White northerners increasingly welcomed their presence in combat, partly because of their bravery, and partly because the use of Negro troops reduced white casualties. The sudden availability of this substantial untapped supply of military manpower also strengthened the will of white northerners to continue the war until military victory was achieved.

In the South, civilian manpower continued to erode, as slaves fled their masters and enlisted in the Union armies. "I have given the subject of arming the negro my hearty support," wrote General Grant in a private letter to Lincoln on August 23. "This, with the emancipation of the negro, is the heavyest [*sic*] blow yet given the Confederacy. . . . I am therefore most decidedly in favor of pushing this policy to the enlistment of a force sufficient to hold all the South falling into our hands and to aid in capturing more."

Military service worked as a vehicle of emancipation in the Union border states as well. Slaves who enlisted in the army automatically earned their freedom; the federal government paid their owners compensation up to $300 per slave. If the government drafted the slave of a loyal master, the slave became free, and his former master received $100 bounty.

Reports of Negro soldiers' courage in combat dispelled any lingering doubts Lincoln had about emancipation as an effective weapon of war. Writing to an old friend in Illinois, Lincoln contrasted the bravery of the 54th Massachusetts with the lawlessness of draft rioters in New York. "Peace does not appear so distant as it did. I hope it will come soon, and come to stay," the president wrote. "And then, there will be some black men who can remember that, with silent tongue and clenched teeth, and steady eye, and well-poised bayonet, they have helped mankind on to this great consummation; while, I fear, there will be some white ones, unable to forget that, with malignant heart, and deceitful speech, they have strove to hinder it."

During a visit to the President's House in August, Frederick Douglass received Lincoln's pledge that he would continue using Negro troops. Nevertheless, Lincoln denied Douglass's request that Negro soldiers receive equal pay with white troops. "We had to make some concession to prejudice," Lincoln explained, but he assured Douglas that "in the end they shall have the same pay as white soldiers."

Having previously described Lincoln as "preeminently the white man's President, entirely devoted to the welfare of white men," Douglass admitted that the president was "the first great man that I talked with in the United States freely, who in no single instance reminded me of the difference between himself and myself, of the difference of color."

A Summer Respite

Washingtonians enjoyed a quiet summer in 1863. The eastern armies, still exhausted from their encounter at Gettysburg, remained on opposite sides of the Rappahannock. No draft riots disturbed Washington's peace. Only 1,000 men from the District were actually drafted, a third of whom were Negroes—including Lincoln's barber and the headwaiter at Willard's Hotel.

Southern sympathizers who had fled Washington for Richmond in the early days of the war drifted back as food shortages in the Confederate capital grew more acute. They found the District transformed by the wartime construction boom, with new houses, shops, and munitions factories driving up the price of real estate. Pigs and cows still wandered along the sidewalks, but the initiation of a municipal garbage service in the summer of 1863 significantly reduced the piles of manure in the streets. City authorities offered farmers and gardeners the opportunity to cart off any remaining dung, free of charge.

On Capitol Hill, still littered with discarded bricks and chunks of mortar, workmen continued their extensive renovation of both houses of Congress. Lincoln insisted that the construction continue despite the wartime emergency. "If people see the Capitol going on," the president explained, "it is a sign we intend the Union shall go on."

Prostitution continued to thrive in Washington. Fashionably decorated mansions on Lafayette Square and the south side of Pennsylvania Avenue served as "fancy houses" catering to army officers. For enlisted men, working-class whites, and Negroes, squalid brothels in Tincup Alley or on Nigger Hill provided overpriced, poisonous liquor and the promise of a late-night brawl.

Crowds gathered on weekends to watch Washington's top amateur baseball team play on the Potomac grounds. In August, John Ford opened his new theater, complete with a double presidential box decorated with dark red wallpaper, lace curtains, American flags, and an upholstered rocking chair for the president.

There were lavish parties in the city with plentiful supplies of turkeys, quail, oysters, and venison. Mary Lincoln, though, seldom appeared at social affairs. She suffered an accident in July when the bolts of the driver's seat in her carriage came loose; apparently someone had unscrewed them in an attempt to injure the president. When the horses panicked, Mary fell out of the carriage and struck her head on a rock. The wound became infected, and she began to complain of headaches. Her outbursts of temper—especially fits of jealousy against young women in her husband's company—grew more violent and unpredictable. She went on extraordinary spending sprees, running up debts of tens of thousands of dollars for jewelry, gowns, and furs. And visions of her dead sons, Willie and Eddie, standing at the foot of her bed, haunted her dreams.

Changing Tide

During the late-summer lull in the war, Lincoln spent much of his time studying local political campaigns in several key northern states. The president was especially anxious because Democrats in Ohio and Pennsylvania had nominated peace candidates for governor. If they won, political pressure to end the war with a compromise settlement would increase substantially.

Democratic speakers revived their customary race-baiting tactics, assuming that the northern public remained ambivalent about emancipation. "Let every vote count in favor of the *white* man, and against the Abolition hordes, who would place negro children in your schools, negro jurors in your jury boxes, and negro votes in your ballot boxes," warned a prominent Democrat in Ohio.

This time the strategy failed. As Secretary of State Seward explained, "Slavery is dead; the only trouble is that the fools who support it from the outside do not recognize this, and will not till the thing is over. . . . So now, though slavery is dead, the Democratic party insists on devoting itself to guarding the corpse."

Events on the battlefield led northern voters to embrace the connection between emancipation and the survival of the Union. The clearest evidence of a shift in sentiment occurred in Baltimore, where supporters of the Unconditional Union Emancipation ticket held a massive rally in Monument Square on October 28. Secretary of the Treasury Chase spoke openly in favor of immediate emancipation in Maryland, and demonstrators carried banners proclaiming UNION, EMANCIPATION AND FREE WHITE LABOR, and SLAVERY IS DEAD — ITS TREASON KILLED IT. Those who remembered how Lincoln had sneaked through the city in disguise two and a half years earlier were stunned by the change. "As the eye took in the vast multitude which surged through the square," wrote one reporter, "one could not help but feel . . . that a great and momentous revolution had occurred."

Republican candidates scored impressive victories in every state. Pennsylvania's Republican governor, Andrew Curtin, won reelection; and Clement Vallandigham, the Democratic antiwar nominee for governor of Ohio, lost in a landslide. A Union candidate won the gubernatorial race in Kentucky; Republicans captured two-thirds of the legislative districts in New York; and Iowa reported a nearly complete Republican sweep.

"The change of opinion on this slavery question since 1860 is a great historical fact, comparable with the early progress of Christianity," declared a Republican in New York. If northern voters had been polled on the Emancipation Proclamation a year earlier, claimed the editor of the *Illinois State Journal,* "there is little doubt that the voice of a majority would have been against it. And yet not a year has passed before it is approved by an overwhelming majority."

A Fine Shot

For a brief time, Lincoln could enjoy the presidency. Congress was out of session, and the Cabinet seldom met to discuss anything other than routine matters. Observers noted that the president wielded power with increasing confidence. "The Tycoon is in fine whack," reported John Hay. "I have rarely seen him more serene and busy. He is managing this war, the draft, foreign relations, and planning a reconstruction of the Union, all at once."

Public criticism of Lincoln diminished. An editorial in the *New York Times* named the president "the most popular man in the Republic." Even longtime critics such as Joseph Medill, editor of the *Chicago Tribune,* admitted that "were an election for President to be held tomorrow, Old Abe would . . . walk over the course."

Between friendly discussions of politics, Lincoln relaxed by participating in marksmanship contests on the White House south lawn. One day a squad of Union soldiers assigned to guard the area heard the sound of rifle fire and hastened to investigate. Not recognizing the stooping president from the back, they gruffly ordered him to stop. Lincoln—who was an excellent shot—was too busy drawing a bead on his target to pay any attention until they came close behind him. When he finally stood up and turned around, the startled soldiers gaped for a moment, and then ran away. "Well," Lincoln declared, "they might have stayed and seen the shooting."

At the end of a day Lincoln preferred to sit in his office alone with his thoughts. "He would sometimes sit for an hour in complete silence," recalled John Nicolay, "his eyes almost shut, the inner man apparently as far from him as if the form in the chair were a petrified image."

In the evenings, the president often attended the theater—sometimes three or four times a week. He especially enjoyed Shakespeare, considering himself an expert on the history plays in which Falstaff appears. Lincoln visited the new Ford's Theater for the first time in October; several weeks later, he went again to see *The Marble Heart,* featuring John Wilkes Booth. Hay dismissed it as a "rather tame" performance.

Shortly after noon on November 18, Lincoln boarded a special train to Gettysburg to attend a ceremony dedicating the new National Soldiers' Cemetery. Although he had been planning his speech for several weeks, the president had written only half of it by the time he left Washington. He completed the address that evening in an upstairs room at the home of his host, Judge David Willis.

All night long, trains brought visitors from all parts of the North into the small Pennsylvania town until every hotel and most private homes were filled with guests. After dinner, a military band stopped by the Willis house to serenade Lincoln, and well-wishers called for "Old Abe, the next President" to say a few words. Lincoln refused. He was tired and had nothing to say, he explained, and went back inside. Seward was less reticent. He announced that he had hoped to see slavery die by peaceful means, but it seemed "he was destined to see it die by the fates of war."

At ten o'clock the following morning, the official procession began winding its way slowly through heavy fog and drizzling rain to the site of the cemetery, about three-fourths of a mile south of Gettysburg. Clad in a new black suit and a black stovepipe hat (still circled with a black band of mourning for his son Willie), Lincoln took his seat on a wooden platform atop Cemetery Ridge, the highest point of the battlefield. The president was not feeling well; he was suffering from a slight fever. Around him the land still bore scars of the three days' fighting in July: trees shattered by bullets and artillery shells, the remains of army horses and mules, and thousands of freshly dug graves, where soldiers from both sides had recently been reinterred.

Witnesses estimated the audience at about 15,000 people, including an unusually high number of women. Not everyone paid strict attention to the proceedings. Nearly half of the crowd spent at least part of the afternoon wandering over the battlefield—some reverentially, others searching for souvenirs.

During the lengthy opening prayer ("a prayer which thought it was an oration," complained John Hay), the clouds parted and the sun broke through. The featured speaker was the former United States senator and governor of Massachusetts, Edward Everett, who delivered a two-hour address from memory. By the time Marshal Ward Lamon rose to introduce the president, it was midafternoon.

With flags and banners draped on the platform behind him, Lincoln praised the dead for sacrificing their lives so the nation could endure and experience "a new birth of freedom." Occasionally he improvised changes to the text of his 256-word message. Five times the audience interrupted the president with scattered applause. A photographer struggled to get a clear shot of Lincoln, but the president ended his speech and sat down before he could set up his equipment.

Most of the crowd was surprised at the brevity of Lincoln's address. Although Hay believed that Lincoln spoke "with more grace than is his wont," one of Lincoln's friends reported that the president "did not appear to think very highly of his own speech." On the return trip to Washington, Lincoln sat alone, with a wet towel cooling his forehead.

Emancipation Assured

In his third annual message, delivered to Congress on December 8, Lincoln reported that the nation had suffered no ill effects from the Emancipation Proclamation. "The crisis which threatened to divide the friends of the Union is past," Lincoln concluded.

According to the president, nearly 100,000 Negro soldiers—half of them combat troops—had enlisted in the Union armies. "In my judgment," Lincoln wrote, "they have aided, and will further aid, the [Union] cause" by depriving the Confederacy of slave labor, and "supplying the places which otherwise must be filled with so many white men. . . . To now abandon them would be not only to relinquish a lever of power, but would also be a cruel and an astounding breach of faith."

Believing that the Confederacy was crumbling, Lincoln proposed generous terms for southern states that wished to return to the Union. The president insisted, however, that any rebels seeking pardon must take an oath to obey all presidential proclamations and acts of Congress abolishing slavery.

He sent the same message to the citizens of Union-occupied Tennessee and Louisiana. Any state applying for readmission to the Union needed to draft a new constitution "recognizing the emancipation proclamation, and adopting emancipation in those parts of the State to which the proclamation does not apply." Besides guaranteeing freedom for Negroes after the war ended, Lincoln sought to bind poor white farmers to the new southern state governments by ending the political dominance of wealthy slaveholders.

Yet the president continued to harbor a preference for a gradual transition between slavery and independence. "It would not be objectionable," Lincoln assured General Nathaniel Banks in Louisiana, if federal officials adopted "some practical system by which the two races could gradually live themselves out of their old relation to each other, and both come out better prepared for the new."

Lincoln's flexibility on racial issues alarmed abolitionists and Radical congressmen. The president "is willing that the negro should be free but seeks nothing else for him," charged Wendell Phillips. To guarantee economic independence for southern Negroes, Radicals called on the Lincoln administration to seize Confederate plantations and distribute the land to freedmen, poor whites, and Union veterans.

Neither Lincoln nor a majority of congressional Republicans supported such confiscatory proposals, but by the end of 1863 the Republican Party was uniting behind a constitutional amendment to abolish slavery forever throughout the nation. Such a measure would eliminate the pockets of slavery left by the Emancipation Proclamation and place emancipation on a more stable legal footing. Lincoln favored the amendment but refused to pressure Congress into passing it. "I can see that time coming," he assured Leonard Swett. "Whoever can wait for it will see it; whoever stands in its way will be run over by it."

Although only six northern states allowed Negroes to vote, congressional support for Negro suffrage in the South also was growing. Following a meeting at the Executive Mansion with Negroes from Louisiana who presented him with a petition, Lincoln privately expressed his support for voting rights for Negroes. He preferred to restrict it, however, to "the very intelligent" and Union army veterans.

A Presidential Sketch

Mary Lincoln marked the dawn of 1864 by putting aside her mourning clothes, appearing at the New Year's Day reception wearing a rich purple velvet gown with white satin fluting around the bottom. The president stood beside her, dressed entirely in black save for white kid gloves (which he hated), shaking hands and saying "How-do" to a line of visitors that included four Negroes "of genteel exterior, and with the manners of gentlemen."

A journalist at the reception wrote that Lincoln's "complexion is clearer, his eyes less lack-luster and he has a hue of health to which he has long been a stranger." (Secretary of State Seward, on the other hand, "looked very much like a molting barnyard fowl among peacocks.") But another epidemic of smallpox was creating panic in the capital. Authorities tried to isolate smallpox cases at Kalorama Hospital on the northern edge of the city while doctors provided free vaccinations to the poor.

Most days the president rose before sunrise, devoting two hours before breakfast to reading, writing, or studying military or political issues. After nearly three years in office, Lincoln still routinely spent five or six hours a day greeting visitors: foreign diplomats, inventors, soldiers seeking promotions, women desiring passes to Richmond, mothers begging pardons for their sons, delegations bearing petitions, politicians looking for favors, admirers asking for his autograph. Even so, the president met only about a tenth of those who sought an audience.

Lincoln usually dined around six o'clock with only a close friend or two, since he and Mrs. Lincoln shared an aversion to state dinners. The First Lady held several levees a week, however, which the president attended whenever his schedule permitted, even though he still felt uncomfortable in a crowd. The only dress code for these affairs was "that people shall appear in decent and clean clothes." Souvenir-hunting guests frequently departed from the Executive Mansion with purloined bits of the furnishings, such as samples of curtains, carpets, and window hangings in the East Room.

Casual acquaintances still struggled to understand Lincoln's personality. "I cannot describe the President; it is impossible," admitted Richard Henry Dana. "He has sobered in his talk, told no extreme stories, and said some good things and some helplessly natural and naive things. You can't help feeling an interest in him, a sympathy and a kind of pity; feeling, too, that his weak points may wreck him or wreck something. His life seems a series of wise, sound conclusions, slowly reached, oddly worked out, on great questions, with constant failures in administration of details and dealings with individuals."

In the early weeks of the year, an aspiring artist, Francis B. Carpenter, arrived in Washington to paint a picture of Lincoln reading the preliminary Emancipation Proclamation to his Cabinet. Carpenter arrived at the White House during a Saturday afternoon reception and saw the president standing, "it seemed to me, solitary and alone, though surrounded by the crowd." When a secretary introduced the artist, Lincoln drew himself up to his full height and asked, "Do you think, Mr. Carpenter, that you can make a handsome picture of *me?*"

For the next six months, Carpenter enjoyed virtually free access to the White House, studying Lincoln at every opportunity. "Absorbed in his papers," Carpenter wrote, "he would become unconscious of my presence, while I intently studied every line and shade of expression in that furrowed face. In repose, it was the saddest face I ever knew. There were days when I could scarcely look into it without crying."

Slaughter

Early in 1864 the President decided to bring General Grant to Washington to replace Halleck as general in chief of the Union armies. Congress honored Grant by reviving the rank of lieutenant general in the army, a grade previously conferred only upon George Washington, shortly before his death.

Grant arrived in the capital just before sundown on March 8. Wearing his rumpled traveling uniform, the general finished half his dinner unnoticed at Willard's Hotel until someone recognized the slightly built, stoop-shouldered figure. One bystander noted that Grant wore an expression "as if he had determined to drive his head through a brick wall, and was about to do it." Later that evening, Lincoln met Grant for the first time. Lincoln led him into a reception in the East Room, where the general was immediately surrounded by admirers chanting, "Grant! Grant! Grant!"

Lincoln appreciated Grant because the general never questioned Lincoln's emancipation policy and refused to get involved in political affairs. Grant "doesn't worry and bother me," the president told a friend. "He isn't shrieking for reinforcements all the time. He takes what troops we can safely give him . . . and does the best he can with what he has got."

At the outset, the president made it clear that Grant's primary objective was the destruction of the rebel army, which Lincoln believed was the only force holding the Confederacy together. Lincoln left decisions about strategy and tactics to Grant.

There were only two rebel armies remaining: General Lee's Army of Northern Virginia and General Joseph E. Johnston's Army of Tennessee. Grant appointed General William Tecumseh Sherman to command the

Union forces in the West and instructed him "to move against Johnston's army, to break it up, and to get into the interior of the enemy's country as far as you can, inflicting all the damage you can against their war resources."

Grant made his own headquarters with the Army of the Potomac, although General Mead retained nominal command of the army. "Lee's army will be your objective point," Grant instructed Meade. "Wherever Lee goes, there will you go also."

On the clear, warm morning of May 4, Meade led his 120,000 troops across the Rapidan River. He planned to move southeast toward Richmond—the seventh campaign by a Union army against the Confederate capital. "Whatever happens," Grant told Lincoln, "there will be no turning back." The following day, the Union general Benjamin Butler landed another 30,000 soldiers on the south side of the James River, between Richmond and Petersburg.

Outnumbered by nearly two to one, Lee decided to strike the Army of the Potomac on May 5 as it marched through the Wilderness, where the forest of tangled underbrush and scrub pines reduced the impact of Grant's superior numbers. After three days of fighting, Union casualties numbered 17,500 men, and the Confederates had lost over 9,000 dead and wounded. Unlike previous Union commanders in Virginia, however, Grant refused to retreat in the face of massive casualties. He ordered Meade to go around Lee and proceed southward, toward Richmond.

Between May 9 and 12 the two armies engaged in the bloodiest fighting of the war at Spotsylvania. "I propose to fight it out on this line if it takes all summer," Grant wired to Lincoln, but when the Union casualty figures reached the North—32,000 men lost in a single week—northern newspaper editors who had previously idolized Grant turned against him. "He is a butcher," agreed Mary Lincoln, "and is not fit to be at the head of an army."

At the dusty town of Cold Harbor, to the southeast, the armies confronted each other again. Grant ordered an attack on the morning of June 3, but rebel sharpshooters entrenched behind multiple rows of earthworks easily drove back the Union assault. After losing 7,000 men in less than twelve hours, Grant ended the slaughter. "I regret this assault more than any one I have ever ordered," he admitted. Quietly, before Lee realized what was happening, Grant withdrew his forces and once more headed southward to begin a siege of Petersburg.

Under Fire

"There are many very bad now in hospital," wrote Walt Whitman from Washington, "so many of our soldiers are getting broke down after two years, or two and a half, exposure and bad diet, pork, hard biscuit, bad water or none at all, etc., etc., so we have them brought up here. Oh, it is terrible, and getting worse, worse, worse. I thought it was bad; to see these I sometimes think is more pitiful still."

Northern criticism of the casualties from Grant's Virginia campaign failed to crack Lincoln's determination to gain a military victory. Privately, however, Lincoln was horrified by the Union losses, and his responsibility for thousands of deaths. He confessed to a friend that he found it very odd "that I, who couldn't cut the head off a chicken, and who was sick at the sight of blood, should be cast into the middle of a great war, with blood flowing all about me." He bore the suffering only by convincing himself that it was part of a divine plan. "The purposes of the Almighty are perfect, and must prevail," the president explained to a Quaker from Pennsylvania. "Surely He intends some great good to follow this mighty convulsion, which no mortal could make, and no mortal could stay."

Lincoln's qualms did not deter him from seeking a second term. By the first week of June, all of Lincoln's challengers for the Republican presidential nomination had faded away, as one state convention after another endorsed Lincoln by an overwhelming majority. Secretary of the Treasury Chase and General Frémont never gained significant support outside of Radical circles, and Grant quashed a movement by the president's opponents to nominate him as an alternative.

To attract Democrats who supported the war Republican officials adopted the label "National Union Party" for the presidential election. Delegates to the National Union convention at the Front Street Theater in Baltimore on June 7 and 8 nominated Lincoln on the first ballot. Disenchanted with Vice President Hamlin's radical views on slavery, Lincoln refused to give the convention any indication of his preference for a running mate. After considerable bickering and confusion in the hot, humid convention hall, the delegates chose a southern War Democrat, Andrew Johnson of Tennessee, to balance the ticket.

There were no surprises in the National Union platform, which elicited little discussion and less debate. The moderate antislavery plank endorsed the federal government's policies, including the Emancipation Proclamation and both congressional Confiscation Acts, and supported a constitutional amendment prohibiting slavery in the United States. Earlier in the year, the Republican-dominated Senate had passed such an amendment; it fell thirteen votes short of the required two-thirds majority in the House, however, when all but four Democratic representatives voted against it.

Radical and moderate Republican congressmen countered by passing the Wade-Davis bill, which imposed strict conditions—including the abolition of slavery—on the readmission of any southern state into the Union. As Congress prepared to adjourn on the morning of July 4, Republican leaders confronted Lincoln in his office at the Capitol and pressed him to sign the measure. The president refused. Congress, he insisted, did not possess the authority to abolish slavery in the reconstructed states.

Later that hot, dusty day, Lincoln rode back to the Executive Mansion, passing a group of Negroes enjoying an Independence Day picnic on the lawn between the mansion and the War Department. It was an irreproachably respectable affair, to raise funds for a school building for local Negro children. Barbers and waiters strolled across the grounds with polished ivory-handled canes; cooks and house servants twirled pastel parasols; light-skinned children swung on swings suspended from the shade trees. "The blacks are right," noted one white Washingtonian. "They and they alone, freed by accident, have lost nothing and gained everything."

There were few able-bodied veteran Union troops in Washington on the Fourth of July in 1864. Lincoln and Secretary of War Stanton had given Grant nearly every available soldier in the area, leaving the capital vulnerable to a rebel raid.

On July 5, the Confederate general Jubal Early and the Second Corps of the Army of Northern Virginia crossed the Potomac River into Maryland. Early hoped to frighten Lincoln into withdrawing enough troops from the Army of the Potomac—encamped outside Petersburg—to relieve the pressure on that beleaguered city.

Lincoln and Stanton reacted slowly to Early's threat. On July 9, Early led 15,000 rebel soldiers in a victorious skirmish against a smaller Union force at the Monocacy River. He camped for the night at Rockville, about 10 miles north of Washington. The following day, Lincoln wired Grant, imploring him to return with a sizable portion of the Union Army "to destroy the enemie's force in this vicinity."

By Monday, July 11, Early's troops could see the Capitol dome in the distance. When rebel soldiers attacked the Union garrison at Fort Stevens, the northernmost point of Washington's defenses, city residents could hear artillery fire in the distance. Eager for a view of the action, Lincoln rode out to the fort and stood calmly on a parapet, looking through a field glass at the advancing Confederate line. Twice he ignored warnings to take shelter as bullets flew past him. When a soldier standing nearby was shot, a Union officer shouted at the president, "Get down, you fool!"

Lincoln and his wife returned to Fort Stevens the following afternoon to witness another Confederate assault. Again the president stood in plain view of the rebel sharpshooters. After a surgeon was killed within three feet of the commander in chief, the fort's commander ordered Lincoln to sit down or be forcibly removed.

Veteran reinforcements from the Army of the Potomac reached Washington that evening. Early's troops retreated into the countryside, but they continued to raid towns in Maryland and Pennsylvania for several weeks. Despite Lincoln's urging, no Union force ventured out to challenge them.

Ill Omens

Lincoln's political destiny rose and fell with the Union's military fortunes. The appalling losses at the Wilderness, Spotsylvania, and Cold Harbor—with Grant no nearer to capturing Richmond—fed northerners' weariness with the war; the most popular song of the summer was "When This Cruel War Is Over."

Problems on the home front exacerbated this discontent. Taxes continued to rise, the federal government's credit was exhausted, and administration officials warned that another draft might be necessary in the fall. What the nation needed, declared Senator Summer, was "a president with brains; one who can make a plan and carry it out."

Lincoln irritated Radical Republicans by killing the Wade-Davis bill with a pocket veto, and by forcing Salmon Chase's resignation from the Cabinet at the end of June. Chase's efforts to ingratiate himself with Lincoln's political enemies had finally exhausted the president's patience; once Lincoln won the presidential nomination, he cut Chase adrift.

Conservative Republicans and War Democrats, on the other hand, grumbled about Lincoln's insistence that the rebels accept emancipation as an essential condition of peace talks. Emancipation as a means of winning the war had become widely popular in the North; it was less tolerable when it threatened to delay the end of the bloodshed. One loyal newspaperman warned Lincoln that northern voters were fearful "that we are not, to have peace *in any event* under this Administration until Slavery is abandoned."

Lincoln nearly backed down. In a draft of a letter to a War Democrat in Wisconsin, the president declared that "if Jefferson Davis wishes . . . to know what I would do if he were to offer peace and re-union, saying nothing about slavery, let him try me."

But Lincoln never sent the letter. Instead, he reaffirmed his intention to maintain the freedom of the nearly 200,000 former slaves who were now serving in the Union armies. Without their help, Lincoln acknowledged, the North's war effort would collapse in less than a month.

"There have been men who proposed to me to return to slavery the black warriors of Port Hudson . . . to conciliate the South," the president told a delegation of midwesterners. "I should be damned in time and eternity for so doing. . . . My enemies pretend I am now carrying on this war for the sole purpose of Abolition. So long as I am President, it shall be carried on for the sole purpose of restoring the Union. But no human power can subdue this rebellion without the use of the emancipation policy, and every other policy calculated to weaken the moral and physical forces of the rebellion."

By mid-August, political experts concluded that Lincoln could never win reelection. "Mr. Lincoln is already beaten. He cannot be elected," decided Horace Greeley. "Everything," mourned the president's secretary John Nicolay, "is darkness and doubt and discouragement."

Lincoln agreed. "You think I don't know I am going to be beaten," the president told General Schuyler Hamilton, "but I do, and unless some great change takes place, *badly beaten.*"

On August 23, Lincoln asked his Cabinet to sign the following memorandum: "This morning, as for some days past, it seems exceedingly probable that this Administration will not be reelected. Then it will be my duty to so cooperate with the President-elect as to save the Union between the election and the inauguration; as he will have secured the election on such grounds that he cannot possibly save it afterward."

The Dilemma of Janus

The Democrats' prospects were not as bright as they appeared. The party was torn between the advocates of peace at any price, and those who insisted that the Union be fully restored. "They must nominate a Peace Democrat on a war platform, or a War Democrat on a peace platform," observed Lincoln, "and I personally can't say that I care much which they do."

Democrats who favored a negotiated peace, such as Clement Vallandigham, persuaded the delegates to the party's national convention to adopt a platform demanding an immediate end of hostilities, "to the end that at the earliest practicable moment peace may be restored on the basis of the Federal Union of the States." The Democratic platform made no mention of slavery.

McClellan was nominated on the first ballot, but the delegates saddled him with a Peace Democrat from Ohio as a running mate. In his acceptance speech, McClellan attempted to distance himself from his party's platform, insisting that there could be no peace without restoration of the Union. Yet McClellan could not run as a Democratic candidate while disavowing the party's position on the war. A popular Currier and Ives cartoon portrayed a two-faced McClellan standing atop a flimsy platform supported by Satan, Jefferson Davis, and Clement Vallandigham. "I accept the nomination and of course stand on the platform," the general said to one side; and to the other, "If you don't like the platform, I refer you to my letter of acceptance."

Union soldiers who had formerly idolized McClellan now abandoned him. A soldier in General Sherman's army reported that his comrades feared McClellan would arrange a compromise peace that would allow the Confederates to keep their slaves. "Then we can fight them again in ten years," he complained. "But let Old Abe settle it, and it is always settled."

Presidential Revival

On August 30, General John B. Hood's Confederate troops evacuated Atlanta, setting fire to the city's factories and warehouses to deny military supplies to the Union armies. Three days later, Sherman's soldiers marched unopposed into the Confederacy's second largest city. "Atlanta is ours, and fairly won," Sherman wired to Stanton.

Reports from other fronts were equally encouraging to Lincoln. To the south, Admiral David Farragut captured Mobile Bay and closed the final gap in the Union navy's blockade of the Gulf Coast. In western Virginia, General Phil Sheridan launched a campaign of destruction that turned the Shenandoah Valley into a smoldering wasteland.

With 5,000 to 10,000 new enlistments every day, Secretary of State Seward was able to reassure voters in the North that there would be no new draft. In late September, Lincoln moved to heal the rift with Republican Radicals by forcing their bête noire, Postmaster General Montgomery Blair, to resign. When the death of Chief Justice Roger Taney on October 12 opened a prized appointment, the president hinted that he might nominate Salmon Chase to replace Taney; Chase promptly endorsed Lincoln's reelection.

Threats

Every week Lincoln received anonymous letters threatening his life. Most he filed away in an envelope marked "Assassination" that he kept in a pigeonhole of his desk; once he pulled out eighty threatening notes to show to a friend from Pennsylvania. "It is no uncommon thing to receive them now," the president explained to the artist Francis Carpenter. "But they have ceased to give me any apprehension."

As the frequency of threats increased, so did the security measures surrounding the president. Lincoln preferred not to be guarded, but Ward Lamon insisted on stationing four plainclothes officers of the city police at the Executive Mansion at all times. One company of mounted troops from Ohio and another company of infantry from Pennsylvania were assigned to guard the entrances.

One August evening, someone shot at Lincoln as he was riding to the Soldiers' Home. The bullet passed cleanly through the crown of his tall black hat. Lamon and Stanton beefed up their precautions, ordering a military escort and special detectives to accompany the president everywhere he went. Still, Lincoln depreciated the danger. "I long ago made up my mind that if anybody wants to kill me, he will do it," he told Noah Brooks. "If I wore a shirt of mail, and kept myself surrounded by a bodyguard, it would be all the same. There are a thousand ways of getting at a man if it is desired that he should be killed."

A Muddy Campaign

It was not a particularly edifying presidential election campaign. Democratic propagandists played the race card, denouncing "Abraham Africanus I" and producing a list of "Lincoln's Ten Commandments" that began with "Thou shalt have no other God but the negro." Republicans countered by branding Democrats as traitors. A typical Republican pamphlet accused Democrats of worshiping "the great and the mighty, the terribly feared, and the wonderfully adored Jefferson Davis, . . . who hatest the poor white man, and whose mission it is to establish the only slave government the world ever saw."

Faced with a choice between Lincoln and McClellan, Radical Republicans swallowed hard and supported Lincoln. "Lincoln's election would be a disaster," Senator Sumner confessed to a close friend, "but McClellan's a damnation."

Northern Negro leaders—including Frederick Douglass—also fell into line behind the president, forgiving his reluctance to issue the Emancipation Proclamation and to use Negro troops. "There are but two parties in the country today," declared a Negro attorney at the national Convention of Colored Men in October. "The one headed by Lincoln is for Freedom and the Republic; and the other, by McClellan, is for Despotism and Slavery."

Lincoln remained anxious until the end. "There was not much doubt about the result of the Baltimore Convention," he told his Cabinet, "but about this thing I am far from certain." When all the votes were counted, Lincoln captured 55 percent of the popular vote, carrying every state in the Union except Kentucky, New Jersey, and Delaware. With a margin of 212 to 21 in the electoral vote, Lincoln became the first president in thirty-two years to win a second term.

Inauguration Day: March 4, 1865

Early on the dark, drizzling morning of Saturday, March 4, President Lincoln rode alone in his carriage down Pennsylvania Avenue to Capitol Hill. Along the way, he passed tourists wading ankle-deep in muddy streets, the result of steady rains over the past week. Fortunate visitors found a place to sleep in the city's crowded hotels; to handle the overflow, Willard's owners sold space on mattresses and cots in its hallways and parlors. Other tourists spent the night in Baltimore, taking the day's first trains on the Baltimore and Ohio tracks to the newly renovated Union Station.

Lincoln entered the Capitol through a side door and spent the rest of the morning signing bills passed in the waning hours of the Thirty-eighth Congress. Outside, under threatening skies, a crowd began to gather in front of the Capitol. Observers noted that there seemed to be fewer spectators than in 1861.

Shortly after eleven o'clock, marshals on horseback stopped the city's streetcars and cleared Pennsylvania Avenue for the inaugural procession. Metropolitan police lined both sides of the street; cavalry patrols stood guard at every intersection. Members of the local Typographical Society, armed with a portable printing press, distributed broadsheets bearing the day's schedule of events.

A light shower began. Struggling through the mud and the windswept rain, the parade, too, seemed smaller than in 1861. The marshal in chief led the way, followed by rows of Union infantry, a squadron of cavalry, and a battery of artillery. Next came the floats, including a model of the iron-clad ship, the *Monitor*, firing blank salutes from the cannon in its revolving turret. There were delegations of visiting dignitaries, veteran reserve regiments, firefighters and fire engines from Washington and Philadelphia, and four companies of Negro troops.

Just before noon, the vice president-elect, Andrew Johnson, entered the Senate chamber arm in arm with Hannibal Hamlin. Before taking the oath of office, Johnson delivered a rambling twenty-minute speech that appeared to be a product of too much whiskey. When the vice president finally sat down, Lincoln bent down to whisper to the parade marshal, "Do not let Johnson speak outside."

When the presidential procession emerged onto the platform at the east portico of the Capitol, the crowd broke into prolonged applause. Spectators waving American flags struggled to get a better view of the president. John Wilkes Booth was part of the crowd on the platform; Booth later boasted that he had been close enough to Lincoln to shoot him that afternoon, had he wished to.

As the Senate sergeant at arms rose and bowed, doffing his shiny back hat, the audience grew silent. Lincoln stepped forward holding his speech, printed in two columns on a half sheet of foolscap. The president had been losing weight for weeks; his cheeks were sunken, and friends thought he looked far older than his fifty-six years. He frequently complained that his hands and feet were cold. Mrs. Lincoln confided to a family member that her husband looked "so broken-hearted, so completely worn out" that "I fear he will not get through the next four years."

Everyone in Washington knew the war was nearly over. Union victories in November at Nashville and Franklin, Tennessee, had crushed the Confederacy's western army. After marching virtually unopposed from Atlanta to Savannah, leaving a path of total devastation in their wake, General Sherman and his 60,000 troops turned north to smash their way through South Carolina, where the war had begun. "The truth is, the whole army is burning with an insatiable desire to wreak vengeance upon South Carolina," Sherman wired to General Halleck. "I almost tremble at her fate, but feel that she deserves all that seems to be in store for her." By March 4, Sherman was slashing his way through the Carolinas to the coast, where he planned to turn northward to reinforce General Grant outside of Petersburg.

Desperate for manpower, the Confederate congress passed a measure in mid-February permitting slaves to enroll in the rebel army. Appalled, Senator Howell Cobb of Georgia claimed that the decision made a mockery of the Confederate rebellion. "The day you make soldiers of them is the beginning of the end of the revolution," Cobb insisted. "If slaves will make good soldiers our whole theory of slavery is wrong."

That was a lesson Lincoln had learned. A month before the inauguration, the House of Representatives had approved the Thirteenth Amendment, prohibiting slavery everywhere in the United States. Lincoln had lobbied strenuously for the measure, promising that "it will bring the war, I have no doubt, rapidly to a close." Even though the president's signature was not necessary, Lincoln signed the amendment, calling it "a King's cure for all the evils. It winds the whole thing up."

Looking out over the crowd on the Capitol steps on Inauguration Day, Lincoln suggested that the war represented God's punishment on North and South for tolerating the sin of slavery for too long. "Fondly do we hope—fervently do we pray—that this mighty scourge of war may speedily pass away," the president continued. "Yet, if God wills that it continue, until all the wealth piled by the bond-man's two hundred and fifty years of unrequited toil shall be sunk, and until every drop of blood drawn with the lash, shall be paid by another drawn with the sword . . . so still it must be said that 'the judgments of the Lord, are true and righteous altogether.'"

Lincoln closed with a wish "to bind up the nation's wounds . . . to do all which may achieve and cherish a just, and a lasting peace, among ourselves, and with all nations." As the spectators gave their loudest cheers of the afternoon, Chief Justice Chase administered the oath of office, and cannons boomed.

Deliverance

On April 4, Union troops entered Richmond, and Lincoln walked un-harmed through the city streets. Black laborers who recognized the presi-dent dropped to their knees and praised him as "the great Messiah." "Bless the Lord," they shouted, "Father Abraham's come."

"Don't kneel to me," a startled Lincoln told them. "That is not right. You must kneel to God only, and thank him for the liberty you will here-after enjoy."

Five days later, General Lee and General Grant met in a private home at the crossroads of Appomattox Court House to negotiate the surrender of the Army of Northern Virginia. Lincoln received the news from Appo-mattox on the evening of April 9. Nowhere in his speeches during the last week of his life did the president provide any glimpse into the role he thought Negro freedmen would play in a reconstructed Union.

Shortly after ten o'clock on the evening of April 14, John Wilkes Booth broke into the presidential box at Ford's Theater and fired his pistol at Lin-coln's head. The president died nine hours later.

As Secretary of the Navy Welles arrived at the White House that morning, he saw several hundred Negroes weeping in a cold rain on Penn-sylvania Avenue. "They seemed not to know what was to be their fate since their great benefactor was dead," Welles noted, "and their hopeless grief affected me more than almost anything else, though strong and brave men wept when I met them."

In South Carolina, freed slaves waited to learn whether Lincoln's death would force them back into slavery. "Uncle Sam is dead, isn't he," they asked. "The Government is dead, isn't it? . . . We going to be slaves again?" One Negro who had fled slavery decided that "I might as well stayed where I was. It 'pears we can't be free, nohow. The rebs won't let us alone. If they can't kill us, they'll kill all our frien's, sure."

10

AFTERMATH

Measured against Lincoln's wartime expectations, the Emancipation Proclamation proved a resounding success. It encouraged slaves in the Confederate states to flee their masters, or at least slow their work and grow insubordinate. The heightened possibility of slave insurrection distracted Confederate officials and lowered morale in the rebel armies.

Once Lincoln publicly defined the war as a conflict between freedom and slavery, any chance of European aid to the Confederacy vanished. In the northern states, emancipation boosted morale by providing a humanitarian ideal to complement the preservation of the Union. And in Washington, the proclamation assured Lincoln of the continued support of Radical Republicans in Congress.

Most important, Lincoln's decision to link emancipation with the use of Negro troops in combat gave the North an abundant source of manpower when white enlistment was faltering. There were 179,000 Negroes in the Union armies at the end of the war, most of whom were former slaves. Lincoln steadfastly maintained that the Union could not have won the war without these troops. Their record in combat lifted northerners' spirits, gave slaves in the Confederacy further incentive to escape, and helped crush southerners' will to resist in the final days of the war.

As Lincoln foresaw, though, there were also negative consequences. The Emancipation Proclamation shattered the northern pro-war coalition; while conservative Republicans eventually returned to support the Lincoln administration, many War Democrats did not. Kentuckians despised the expansion of Union war aims to include abolition, as did Irish-Americans in northern cities.

Since the proclamation freed only slaves in select geographical areas, emancipation arrived piecemeal. Thousands of Negroes remained slaves at the moment of Lincoln's death. Armed resistance in the western Confederacy continued sporadically for two months after Appomattox; in Texas, slaves would later celebrate June 19 as their emancipation day.

Except where slaves freed themselves by escaping from their masters, emancipation depended upon the progress of the Union armies. In areas of the Confederacy undisturbed by northern troops, some planters kept their Negroes enslaved until a Union officer or an agent of the Freedmen's Bureau—bearing a copy of the Emancipation Proclamation—arrived to declare the slaves free in the spring or summer of 1865. Often federal officials disappointed freedmen by recommending that they remain where they were and—in Lincoln's words—"labor faithfully for reasonable wages" whenever possible.

Emancipation occurred last in the northern border states of Delaware and Kentucky. Slaveowners in Kentucky proved especially intractable. Since the Emancipation Proclamation had no legal force there, they continued to hold more than 65,000 Negroes in slavery. White Kentuckians who felt betrayed by the Lincoln administration's racial policies released their frustrations through violence against freedmen, particularly Negro veterans of the Union Army. In August 1865 the state legislature rejected the Thirteenth Amendment, and state officials continued to enforce Kentucky's slave code until the amendment was finally ratified in December.

By emancipating the Confederacy's slaves as a war measure—and not as an act of justice toward the Negro—Lincoln subordinated the ideal of freedom to the preservation of the Union. Emancipation became the means to an end, a by-product of the war. The proclamation consisted of legalistic language designed to stifle any challenges to the abolition of slavery, the sort of language one expected from a generation that devoted enormous time and energy to debates over the constitutional and legal rights of slaveowners. Lincoln left no noble words about liberty for Negroes, no eloquent phrases that could inspire subsequent generations to work toward equality.

Lincoln understood that freedmen would be hard-pressed to overcome the racial prejudices of whites in American society. As he explained to the delegation of Negro leaders who visited him in August 1862, "even when you cease to be slaves you are yet far removed from being placed on an equality with the white race. . . . Go where you are treated the best, and the ban is still upon you." Yet the Emancipation Proclamation contains no hint of any plan to help the former slaves protect their liberty. Nor is there evidence that Lincoln thought deeply about this problem in the months before his death.

There would be no transition from slavery to freedom; no way to learn the meaning of emancipation except through experience in a white-dominated society. Beyond emancipation, the national government made no commitments to southern Negroes. Both whites and blacks would improvise new relationships in communities whose traditions had been uprooted by war.

Those outdated traditions included the eighteenth-century notion that government was based on popular consent. The triumph of Lincoln's principle that the southern states had no right to secede represented a victory for conservative nationalism, the right of a nation to protect its existence. To defeat the Confederate rebellion, Lincoln and Congress substantially extended the power and role of the federal government in the lives of both northern and southern citizens, elevating the nation—as the collective embodiment of freedom—above state and individual liberties.

Lincoln's assumption of expanded executive powers did not survive the war, however. Andrew Johnson's collision with Radical Republicans over the terms of southern reconstruction ended in a complete victory for Congress. For the rest of the century, no American president exercised his authority as aggressively as Lincoln.

This Land Is Ours

Former slaves celebrated their freedom in a variety of ways, most commonly by traveling. Half a million refugee Negroes who had followed the Union armies out of slavery already were far from home, waiting for white authorities to decide their future. Hundreds of thousands more walked away from their former masters and kept walking, simply because they could. Since slaveowners had deliberately broken up Negro families, many freedmen spent months traveling from one southern state to another, searching for long-lost relatives. Others headed for southern or border cities looking for employment other than field work. Some who equated slavery with work refused to labor at all in the first heady months of freedom. Only a small percentage of freedmen migrated to the North.

More than anything else, former slaves desired land of their own. They understood clearly that freedom required economic self-sufficiency, a notion held by white Americans since colonial days. "The way we can best take care of ourselves is to have land, and turn in and till it by our labor," a delegation of Negroes from Georgia told Secretary of War Stanton. "We wants land," insisted a former slave in South Carolina. "dis bery land dat is rich wid de sweat ob we face and de blood ob we back."

Yet the only region where southern Negroes owned substantial amounts of land at the end of the war was South Carolina's Sea Islands, where former slaves managed to purchase sections of the plantations abandoned by rebel landowners. They expected to gain more after General Sherman issued his Special Field Order Number 15 in January 1865, promising tracts of 40 acres of abandoned coastal property to the refugee Negroes who followed him on his march out of Georgia.

By the summer of 1865, 40,000 former slaves were farming their own land successfully on the Sea Islands. Then white planters drifted back to reclaim their property. Despite protests from representatives of the Freedmen's Bureau, President Andrew Johnson decided that the planters retained legal title to the land. (In his third annual message to Congress, Lincoln had similarly proposed that the government restore rebels' property, with the exception of slaves.) Once the freedmen harvested the crops they had planted, they had to either leave or lease plots from the former slaveowners. Those who refused these options were forced off the land by federal troops. At the end of December 1866, fewer than 2,000 Negro landowners remained on the Sea Islands.

A deep-seated respect for property rights led Congress to reject all Radical Republican measures for widespread confiscation and redistribution of Confederate lands. The government opened public acreage in the South for sale to former slaves, but most of this was marginal land. Southern whites steadfastly refused to sell land to Negroes under any but the most desperate circumstances. Although some ex-slaves agreed to work as wage laborers for white landowners (most of whom insisted on planting cotton), this option proved unpopular because it resembled a return to slavery; besides, Negroes were suspicious of labor contracts written by former slaveowners. Instead, a majority of freedmen chose to become sharecroppers or tenant farmers.

The freedmen's second priority was to obtain a basic education for themselves and their children. Again the federal government failed to provide the necessary resources. Congress authorized the Freedmen's Bureau to spend $5,000 to rent and repair schools, but private charities in the North had to supply the teachers. Organizations such as the American Freedmen's Union Commission discovered that the wartime enthusiasm to help the freed slaves quickly waned. Within two years after Appomattox, contributions from the northern public to southern educational missions declined sharply, forcing hundreds of Negro schools across the South to close.

Southern white leaders applauded the failure of northern charity. "If our civilization is to continue," argued Robert Dabney, a clergyman in Virginia, "there must be at the bottom of the social fabric a class who must work and not read." If education elevated Negroes from the lowest rung of southern society, poor whites would have to fill the void.

Empty Liberty

White southerners reacted cautiously to the presence of nearly 4 million free Negroes. Initially, whites feared physical retribution by their former slaves, particularly those who had served in the Union Army. But when the summer and autumn of 1865 passed with few outbreaks of racial violence, southern white leaders regained their confidence and began to devise legal stratagems to return freedmen as far as possible to the condition of slaves.

Taking as their models the "black codes" developed before the war to control free southern Negroes, local governments adopted ordinances that put Negroes under strict police control, stripping them of the right of free movement, preventing them from buying or selling property, and prohibiting them from carrying weapons, testifying in court, or congregating in large groups. "The whites esteem the blacks their property by natural right," reported an official of the Freedmen's Bureau in Georgia. "They still have an ingrained feeling that the blacks at large belong to the whites at large, and whenever opportunity serves, they treat the colored people just as their profit, caprice or passion may dictate."

When Chief Justice Salmon Chase toured the South in the summer of 1865, delegations of Negroes told him "tales of atrocities . . . whippings and cutting off of ears and the like, for crimes of going where they pleased and assuming to act as freemen." Southern whites defended the black codes by arguing that the freedmen were "naturally lazy, criminal, lustful, and seditious," and would refuse to work without a master.

Many northerners who worked with former slaves during and immediately after the war were only slightly less critical of the freedmen's behavior. After several years in Port Royal, one northern missionary complained of Negroes' "skill in lying, . . . their habit of shielding one another," and "their invariable habit of taking a rod when you, after much persuasion, have been induced to grant an inch." A teacher who attempted to manage a Sea Island plantation decided that the freedmen, "in spite of all the nonsense which has been written about them, are a very low and degraded class of beings."

Perceptive observers attributed whites' disillusionment to the fact that former slaves were actually exercising their freedom, instead of following the instructions of their northern mentors. Reporters who traveled through the South noted that freedmen who farmed their own land worked more conscientiously and acted more responsibly than those who labored for someone else. In circumstances where they expected punishment, or distrusted the promises of whites, southern Negroes resorted to the same behavior that had helped them survive slavery.

Fearful that the North was losing the fruits of victory, a coalition of Radical and moderate Republicans in Congress invalidated the black codes and placed the former Confederate states under federal military rule. In March 1866 Congress passed a civil rights bill—over President Johnson's veto—that bestowed citizenship on all persons born in the United States and gave the federal government the power to protect individuals' civil rights. To prevent any legal challenges to Negroes' rights, Congress wrote similar provisions into the Fourteenth Amendment. Former Confederate states had to ratify the amendment to rejoin the Union.

Congressional Republicans displayed less unity on the issue of Negro suffrage. The most radical faction, led by Sumner and Stevens, insisted that freedmen could never secure their rights unless they could defend themselves with the ballot. Yet there remained substantial opposition among northern whites who doubted that Negroes could make intelligent political decisions. "We are familiar with the notion of a nigger servant, bootblack, barber, or field hand, and not familiar with that of a Negro legislator," admitted George Templeton Strong. "To the Northern man of plain, ordinary, common understanding, a colored person helping to regulate our national finances and our foreign relations seems out of place and anomalous."

In 1865, only six northern states allowed Negroes to vote. That autumn, voters in Minnesota, Connecticut, and Wisconsin rejected negro suffrage amendments to their state constitutions; two years later, Ohio and Kansas voted down similar measures. Among Lincoln's former Cabinet members, Seward and Welles openly opposed negro suffrage. "Is it politic, and wise, or right even," Welles asked, ". . . to elevate the ignorant negro, who has been enslaved mentally as well as physically, to the discharge of the highest duties of citizenship?"

When Congress finally approved the Fifteenth Amendment in February 1869, the deciding factor was the desire of Republican leaders to strengthen their party in the South. Since few southern whites joined the

Republican Party, the only alternative was to enfranchise freedmen. More than a few northern states refused to ratify the amendment, however, and it became part of the Constitution in March 1870 only after several former Confederate states ratified it as the price of returning to the Union.

Even then Congress refused to carry out a thorough reorganization of southern society. By leaving whites in control of the vast majority of agricultural land, federal officials permitted southern landowners to control the freedmen by more subtle means—renting them land, extending credit, and keeping them in debt as a form of economic slavery.

By the end of 1870 the wartime impetus to aid the Negro was nearly spent. Abolitionists had achieved their primary goal: the destruction of slavery and the liberation of all male Americans. But that goal looked backward, erasing the legacy of the past. There was no consensus on the next step, or even whether another step was necessary.

Preoccupied by material concerns in postwar America, northerners abandoned freedmen to their own inadequate resources. "The North has nothing to do with the Negroes," maintained Secretary of State Seward. "I have no more concern for them than I have for the Hottentots. . . . They are not of our race. They will find their place. . . . The North must get over the notion of interference with the affairs of the South."

To emancipate slaves in the Confederacy, Lincoln had expanded the power of the federal government during a wartime crisis. "War had removed constitutional obligations and restrictions," he once observed, "and it was our duty to avail ourselves of every necessary measure to maintain the Union." No similar emergency arose in the postwar years, nor did Lincoln's successors share his political skill in balancing competing factions, or his willingness to employ presidential authority to achieve social reform.

The position of southern Negroes steadily deteriorated. By the end of the nineteenth century, segregation was becoming entrenched in local and state laws, reinforced by the threat of lynching. White officials used poll taxes, literacy tests, and grandfather clauses to disenfranchise Negroes. And as the price of cotton declined in the postwar years, Negro sharecroppers and tenant farmers sank deeper into debt.

Looking back, Frederick Douglass concluded that emancipation left the former slave "at the mercy of the men who had robbed him all his life and his people for centuries." Without land of his own—by 1900, nonwhites owned only 600,000 acres of land in the South—the southern Negro was left "on his knees. . . . supplicating the old master class to give him leave to toil."

In August 1908, a white mob sparked a race riot in Lincoln's home town, Springfield, Illinois. Intent on lynching a Negro accused of assaulting a white woman, rioters attacked every Negro they could find, burning and looting Negroes' homes and stores, and shouting "Lincoln freed you, we'll show you where you belong." By the time the National Guard restored order, six people were dead and nearly sixty wounded. "A large part of the white population of Lincoln's home," concluded one reporter, "have initiated a permanent warfare with the negro race."

Emancipation in Memory

Disappointment over the consequences of emancipation did not diminish Lincoln's reputation among American Negroes as their savior. It was not a title Lincoln had sought. He consistently played down his role in destroying slavery, attributing its demise to the "frictions and collisions" of the war. In late October 1864, Sojourner Truth visited Lincoln and told him that he was the only president who had ever done anything for her people. Lincoln replied that he was also "the only one who ever had such opportunity. Had our friends in the South behaved themselves, I could have done nothing whatever."

Nevertheless, Negroes regarded Lincoln as a modern Moses who delivered them from bondage. They ignored the limitations of the Emancipation Proclamation and celebrated January 1—or sometimes September 22—as their independence day. Commemorations usually were held in churches, where a leading member of the community read the proclamation aloud.

After Lincoln died, proposals for negro schools and memorials to celebrate Lincoln's memory generated widespread enthusiasm among American Negroes, especially among Union veterans. Negro soldiers stationed in Missouri donated $5,000 to found the Lincoln Institute in Jefferson City. Another group of nearly 700 enlisted men raised $3,000 for a monument built solely with contributions from Negroes. If it were built "proportionate to the veneration with which the black people hold his memory," one colonel said, "then its summit will be among the clouds."

The culmination was a twelve-foot-high bronze statue of Lincoln standing over a slave. Lincoln's right hand held the Emancipation Proclamation, while his left extended over a slave rising from a kneeling position. A hint of a smile played on Lincoln's face; the former slave wore a grim, determined look. Known as the Freedman's Monument, the statue was dedicated in 1876 in Washington's Lincoln Park, a mile east of the Capitol. In his speech at the ceremony, Frederick Douglass praised Lincoln as the Negroes' liberator, yet he reminded his audience that the Great Emancipator remained the white man's president. "You are the children of Abraham Lincoln," he told them, but "we are at best his step-children; children by adoption, children by force of circumstances and necessity."

Booker T. Washington, the most visible Negro leader at the turn of the century, chose to ignore the contradictions in Lincoln's racial policies. For Washington, Lincoln's importance for American Negroes resided less in the Emancipation Proclamation than the inspirational model Lincoln provided of virtue, hard work, and self-denial. These were the qualities that earned Lincoln a place in a popular reader for Negro schoolchildren as the only white person worthy of emulation. "The more I learn of Lincoln's life," confessed Washington, "the more I am disposed to look at him . . . as a great moral leader, in whose patience, tolerance, and broad human sympathy there is salvation for my race, and for all those who are down, but struggling to rise."

Other Negro leaders were less patient. In 1909, on the hundredth anniversary of Lincoln's birth, a coalition of white and Negro leaders announced that they would convene in New York the following year to seek solutions to the disturbing trends toward anti-Negro violence and heightened discrimination. The conference led to the founding of the National Association for the Advancement of Colored People, which dedicated itself to "the completion of the work . . . the Great Emancipator began."

White Americans' memories of Lincoln centered far less on emancipation than on his leadership of a stronger, reinvigorated nation. The earliest works by white poets about the Civil War ignored Negroes and the Emancipation Proclamation altogether. The former abolitionist James Russell Lowell's "Commemoration Ode," delivered at the Harvard University commencement in July 1865, made no reference to emancipation, celebrating instead the transformation of white America into "a new imperial race." Similarly, Herman Melville's "Battle Pieces" praised the victory of power and authority over the southerners' dream of individual freedom.

With few exceptions, the flood of reminiscences about Lincoln that appeared in the postwar decades focused primarily on his personal life and character. A biography by the former congressman Isaac Arnold, *Abraham Lincoln and the Overthrow of Slavery,* published in 1866, was the only full-length study of Lincoln's role in emancipation. Publication of the late president's speeches and letters, edited by his private secretaries Hay and Nicolay, reinforced whites' perception that Lincoln thought and cared more deeply about the Union than Negroes' rights.

Whites who recognized Lincoln as the Great Emancipator preferred to apply his legacy to groups other than Negroes. Labor organizers in the late nineteenth century quoted selected passages from Lincoln's speeches defending the right of workers to enjoy the fruits of their own labor. Progressive reformers seeking to outlaw child labor pictured a forlorn working-class boy standing at the foot of the Freedmen's Monument, asking plaintively, "What about me?" Anti-imperialists who opposed the United States' annexation of the Philippines in 1896 cited Lincoln's antislavery argument that "no man is good enough to govern another without his consent." But when the fiftieth anniversary of the Emancipation Proclamation arrived in 1913, Congress refused to pass legislation commemorating the occasion.

No quotations from the Emancipation Proclamation grace the Lincoln

Memorial, dedicated in Washington in 1922, although one wall does bear a painting entitled *Emancipation* by Jules Guerin. The text of the Gettysburg Address is written on a tablet on another wall; at the opposite end of the hall, visitors can read Lincoln's Second Inaugural Address. Behind the statue of a seated Lincoln is an inscription that reads,

IN THIS TEMPLE

As in the Hearts Of The People
For Whom He Saved The Union
The Memory of Abraham Lincoln
Is Enshrined Forever.

Nevertheless, Lincoln retained his hold on the affections of most American Negroes. The selection of February as the date of Negro History Week, and later Negro History Month, honored the birthdays of both Lincoln and Frederick Douglass. Perhaps the most powerful image of the civil rights movement during the New Deal was a concert by Marian Anderson at the Lincoln Memorial on Easter Sunday, 1939, after she had been barred from singing at Constitution Hall.

More than two decades later, the Reverend Martin Luther King, Jr., invoked Lincoln's image as the Great Emancipator when he challenged President John F. Kennedy to sign "a second Emancipation Proclamation" outlawing segregation. "The time has come," King insisted, "to let those dawn-light rays of freedom, first glimpsed in 1863, fill the heavens with the noonday sunlight of complete human dignity."

When Kennedy demurred, King organized a massive civil rights rally that culminated in a gathering of 200,000 marchers at the Lincoln Memorial on August 28, 1963. Standing in front of Lincoln's statue, King described the Emancipation Proclamation as "a great beacon of hope to millions of Negro slaves who had been scarred in the flame of withering injustice, . . . a joyous daybreak to end the long night of their captivity."

King closed his speech with an eloquent challenge to white America.

"I have a dream," he said, "that one day this nation will rise up and live out the true meaning of its creed: We hold these truths to be self-evident that all men are created equal."

The moment marked a turning point in King's career, in the modern civil rights movement, and in the image of Abraham Lincoln among African-Americans. Freedom would be won by the descendants of slaves, not bestowed upon them by whites. "Exactly one hundred years after Abraham Lincoln wrote the Emancipation Proclamation *for them*," noted King, "Negroes wrote their own document of freedom in their *own way*."

NOTES

In the following notes, works are cited by the author's name and a brief title upon the first citation; for a full listing, consult the bibliography. If the note cites an author with more than one work in the bibliography, a brief title for the work is always given in the note.

Page

6   "seeking concealment . . .": P. Foner, *Douglass*, p. 71.
6   "nothing but a . . .": Oates, *With Malice*, p. 213.
7   "to free the negroes and . . .": J. McPherson, *Battle Cry*, p. 243.
7   "If you are tame enough . . .": ibid.
7   "The evil days, so dreaded . . .": Mitgang, *Lincoln*, p. 119.
8   "the disease of the . . .": Fehrenbacher, *Recollected Words*, p. 119.
8   "the people of the North . . .": ibid., p. 422.
8   "a great crying" and "an enormous national . . .": Burlingame, *Inner World*, p. 29.
8   "If all earthly power . . .": Cuomo, *Lincoln*, p. 68.
10 "not knowing when, or whether . . .": Oates, *With Malice*, p. 208.
10 "He keeps all . . .": Stampp, *And the War*, p. 182.
10 "gotten up . . . by designing . . .": Donald, *Lincoln*, pp. 275–76.
10 "Why all this excitement . . .": ibid.
10 "While some of us may differ . . .": ibid., p. 275.
11 "There will be no . . .": Basler, *CW* IV, p. 341.

13   "it may much more . . .": Burlingame, *Oral History,* p. 146.

13   "all suburb and . . .": F. Pratt, *Russell Diary,* p. 195.

13   "of a distillery . . .": Kaplan, *Whitman,* p. 274.

14   "least attractive . . .": ibid.

14   "rude colony" and "unfinished . . .": ibid.

14   "the country is wild . . .": Leech, *Reveille,* p. 10.

14   "It was an overgrown . . .": Sherman, *Recollections,* p. 318.

16   "an able, a specious . . .": C. F. Adams, *Autobiography,* p. 89.

16   "must and will . . .": Taylor, *Seward,* p. 107.

16   "dirty abolition sneak . . .": Leech, p. 41.

17   "Why, I myself . . .": F. Pratt, p. 20.

18   "Take him all . . .": Fehrenbacher, *Recollected,* p. 375.

18   "Violence is not . . ." Oates, *With Malice,* p. 215.

20   "Any man is a . . .": P. Smith, *Trial,* p. 23.

21   "The whole commerce . . .": Jefferson, *Notes,* p. 162.

21   "We have the wolf . . .": Brodie, *Jefferson,* p. 442.

21   "an exhausted soil . . .": Kolchin, *American Slavery,* pp. 174–75.

23   "recoiled from active . . .": Schurz, *Autobiography,* p. 169.

23   "Old James Buchanan . . .": Nevins, *Strong,* p. 103.

24   "You have got things . . .": Lewis, *Sherman,* p. 150.

24   "We are a weak . . .": Nevins, *Strong,* p. 109.

25   "Surrounded and guarded . . .": Stampp, *And the War,* p. 197.

25   "Evil was in the air . . .": C. F. Adams, *Autobiography,* pp. 76, 82.

26   "united to produce . . .": Sherman, p. 232.

26   "was so withered . . .": Rice, *Reminiscences,* p. 49.

26   "the outgoing President . . .": C. F. Adams, *Autobiography,* p.

27   "otherwise, the . . .": Fehrenbacher, *Recollected Words,* p. 460.

27   "certainly did not present . . .": Schurz, *Autobiography,* p. 162.

27   "his perfect composure . . .": Kaplan, p. 260.

28   "A galvanized corpse . . .": Foote, *Civil War,* p. 40.

29   "burlesque upon . . .": Cuomo, p. 94.

30   "There has never . . .": Basler, IV, pp. 262–71.

33   "Well, I hardly . . .": *Washington Post,* March 6, 1863.

33   "I cannot say what . . .": ibid.

34   "I do not suppose . . .": C. F. Adams, *Autobiography,* pp. 97–98.

34   "Thank God, we now . . .": Oates, *With Malice,* p. 219.

35   "tempted to say . . .": Nevins, *Strong,* p. 107.

36   "Mr. Lincoln's Inaugural . . .": *New York Times,* March 6, 1861.

36   "the secession conspirators . . .": Stampp, *And the War,* p. 201.

37   "ready to stand . . .": C. F. Adams, *Autobiography,* p. 948.

37   "His speech was just what was . . .": P. Smith, p. 30.

37	"coercive policy of . . .": Mitgang, *Lincoln*, pp. 240–42.
37	"There is no . . .": quoted in *Baltimore Sun*, March 7, 1861.
37	"There is some . . .": Donald, *Lincoln*, p. 284.
37	"a double-tongued document . . .": Foner, p. 72.
38	"entirely ignorant . . .": Donald, *Lincoln*, p. 285.
39	"What seemed . . .": Fehrenbacher, *Recollected Words*, p. 351.
39	"Nothing could possibly . . .": Anderson, *A Public Man*, p. 226.
39	"We didn't know what . . .": C. F. Adams, *Autobiography*, p. 72.
39	"to hold all . . .": Fehrenbacher, *Recollected Words*, p. 328.
40	"Why not? . . .": Fehrenbacher, *Recollected Words*, p. 390.
40	"I now see no . . .": Oates, *With Malice*, p. 220.
40	"I have seen him . . .": Burlingame, *Oral History*, pp. 38–39.
41	"Of all the trials . . .": Fehrenbacher, *Recollected Words*, p. 344.
41	"that he thought . . .": ibid., p. 504.
41	"The clamor for offices . . .": Anderson, p. 241.
41	"the buffaloes on the . . .": Donald, *Sumner*, p. 386.
42	"I had not noticed it . . .": Anderson, p. 241.
42	"In that one . . .": Fehrenbacher, *Recollected Words*, p. 194.
42	"like a man . . .": Oates, *With Malice*, p. 222.
42	"We have scarcely . . .": Donald, *Lincoln*, p. 285.
42	"Those who visited . . .": Schurz, p. 175.
43	"a particularly good . . .": Rice, p. 54.
43	"He is a lank and . . .": Nevins, *Strong*, p. 188.
43	"His evident integrity . . .": ibid., p. 204.
43	"with a shambling . . .": F. Pratt, pp. 22–24.
44	"You should not . . .": Donald, *Lincoln*, p. 285.
44	"Mr. Lincoln is evidently . . .": *New York Times*, April 4, 1861.
44	"no fixed policy . . .": Donald, *Lincoln*, p. 290.
44	"the darkest one . . .": Sherman, p. 242.
44	"unqualified recognition . . .": Oates, *With Malice*, p. 223.
45	"A cold shock . . .": Fehrenbacher, *Recollected Words*, p. 328.
45	"We are at the end . . .": Basler, IV, p. 317, fn.
46	"I must do it.": ibid., p. 317.
46	"The first case . . .": Fehrenbacher, *Recollected Words*, pp. 455–56.
46	"I've known Mr. Lincoln . . .": Johansen, *Douglas*, p. 860.
47	"the honor, the integrity . . .": Basler, IV, p. 332.
47	"he intended to . . .": Fehrenbacher, *Recollected Words*, p. 133.
47	"The whole population . . .": J. McPherson, *Battle Cry*, p. 274.
49	"If you had not . . .": Fehrenbacher, *Recollected Words*, p. 269.
49	"The scene was very novel . . .": Burlingame, *Hay Diary*, p. 22.
49	"A general tempest . . .": ibid., p. 2.

50   "I think to lose Kentucky . . .": Basler, IV, p. 533.

51   "an egotistical . . .": C. F. Adams, *Autobiography*, p. 81.

52   "I . . . told [Lincoln] . . .": Donald, *Sumner*, p. 269.

52   "Some of our northerners . . .": Burlingame, *Hay Diary*, p. 19.

52   "going to free . . .": ibid., p. 22.

52   "are declaring that now . . .": ibid.

52   "the exterminated . . .": ibid., p. 19.

52   "The central idea . . .": ibid., p. 20.

53   "I must take into . . .": Fehrenbacher, *Recollected Words*, p. 432.

53   "We are all born . . .": ibid.

53   "The colored man throughout . . .": ibid., p. 144.

53   "cooked by Niggers . . .": Oates, *With Malice*, pp. 252–53.

53   "false, foolish, wicked . . .": Kaplan, p. 133.

54   "Until I can be satisfied . . .": Niven, *Welles*, p. 222.

54   "Nature has set . . .": Kaplan, p. 122.

54   "A race, degraded for . . .": Donald, *Sumner*, p. 235.

54   "The weak to grow . . .": Cuomo, *Lincoln*, p. 63.

55   "the law means . . .": Fehrenbacher, *Recollected Words*, p. 303.

55   "Can blacks be expected . . .": P. Smith, p. 52.

55   "The enormity of . . .": ibid., p. 51.

56   "go down to . . .": Fehrenbacher, *Recollected Words*, p. 204.

56   "with all the . . .": ibid., p. 195.

56   "What are we to do . . .": Leech, p. 57.

56   "Twenty-four hundred . . .": J. McPherson, *Battle Cry*, p. 322.

57   "everything goes . . .": Burlingame, *Hay Diary*, p. 6.

57   "The difficulty with . . .": Donald, *Lincoln*, p. 285.

57   "I have to say . . .": Trudeau, *Like Men*, p. 8.

57   "We want you damned . . .": ibid.

58   "if I had known . . .": Burlingame, *Hay Diary*, p. 12.

59   "We will, on the contrary . . .": T. Harry Williams, *Radicals*, p. 25.

59   "should occasion offer . . .": ibid.

59   "It is my earnest . . .": Fehrenbacher, *Recollected Words*, p. 9.

60   "You say you have . . .": Butler, *Butler's Books*, p. 257.

60   "Are these men, women . . .": J. McPherson, *Battle Cry*, p. 355.

60   "Until long after Sumter . . .": Donald, *Chase*, p. 20.

60   "the government neither should . . .": Donald, *Lincoln*, p. 343.

61   "striding like a crane . . .": F. Pratt, p. 212.

61   "Washington, now, indeed . . .": ibid., pp. 188–89.

62   "Scott will not . . .": Fehrenbacher, *Recollected Words*, p. 337.

62   "Certainly, bring him . . .": Schurz, p. 178.

62   "As we left . . .": ibid.

64   "We have saved this Union . . .": Brodie, p. 141.

64   "a disgraceful surrender . . .": T. Harry Williams, *Radicals*, p. 22.

64   "Stepped & steamed . . .": Randall, *Lincoln*, p. 210.

64   "It is no part . . .": T. Harry Williams, *Radicals*, p. 26.

65   "They think . . .": Leech, p. 89.

66   "This is not . . .": ibid., p. 106.

66   "a few scarecrow-men . . .": F. Pratt, p. 199.

66   "You are green . . .": Oates, *With Malice*, p. 251.

67   "Are you really . . .": F. Pratt, p. 223.

67   "The fat is in . . .": J. McPherson, *Battle Cry*, p. 348.

67   "Believe me . . .": F. Pratt, p. 211–12.

68   "a most woe-begone rabble . . .": Leech, pp. 103–4.

68   "I'm going home . . .": F. Pratt, p. 233.

68   "I 'spects, massa . . .": ibid.

69   "I have not lost" and "I don't see why . . .": ibid., p. 247.

69   "There is an indefinable . . .": J. McPherson, *Battle Cry*, p. 359.

69   "He has brains . . .": Donald, *Lincoln*, p. 317.

69   "By some strange operation . . .": ibid.

70   "I do not want to carry . . .": Jellison, *Fessenden*, p. 135.

70   "We will be held . . .": J. McPherson, *Battle Cry*, p. 309.

71   "He was slow to move . . .": Hunt, p. 159.

71   "Browning, . . .": Fehrenbacher, *Recollected Words*, p. 62.

72   "The very stomach . . .": P. Foner, p. 115.

72   "If their whole . . .": Trefousse, *Thaddeus Stevens*, p. 112.

73   "is most . . .": Chase, *Diary and Correspondence*, p. 502.

74   "foolish proclamation . . .": Donald, *Lincoln*, p. 316.

74   "Frankly, I say . . .": Niven, *Salmon P. Chase*, p. 281.

74   "will alarm our . . .": Basler, IV, p. 506.

74   "taxed me so . . .": Fehrenbacher, *Recollected Words*, p. 220.

74   "for a great national . . .": Donald *Lincoln*, p. 315.

75   "You have no idea . . .": Jellison, p. 138.

75   "No word describes . . .": Chase, p. 504.

75   "the only real noble . . .": T. Harry Williams, *Radicals*, p. 41.

75   "poor white trash . . .": ibid.

75   "could only come of . . .": Oates, *With Malice*, p. 261.

75   "Fremont's proclamation was . . .": Donald, *Lincoln*, p. 316.

75   "This thunderbolt . . .": Sandburg, *War Years*, I, p. 357.

75   "I think Sumner . . .": Brodie, p. 155.

76   "he can seize them . . .": Basler, IV, pp. 531–33.

76   "How many times . . .": Brodie, p. 155.

76   "It is said we . . .": J. McPherson, *Battle Cry*, p. 356.

77   "The city has a more . . .": Leech, p. 108.

77   "I intend to be careful . . .": Burlingame, *Hay Diary*, p. 25.

78   "armed with plans . . .": F. Pratt, pp. 256–57.

78   "a dotard or . . .": J. McPherson, *Battle Cry*, p. 360.

78   "I can do it all.": Burlingame, *Hay Diary*, p. 30.

78   "an idiot . . .": ibid., p. 289.

79   "Some of the . . .": Sears, *McClellan Papers*, pp. 106–7, 114, 135.

79   "We want our army . . .": Jellison, p. 141.

79   "I begin to despair . . .": Burlingame, *Hay Diary*, p. 286.

80   "Help me to dodge . . .": J. McPherson, *Battle Cry*, p. 364.

80   "You must not fight . . .": Burlingame, *Hay Diary*, p. 29.

80   "The President has lost . . .": Jellison, p. 139.

80   "Lincoln means well . . .": Burlingame, *Hay Diary*, p. 287.

80   "Personally, you . . .": Burlingame, *Oral History*. pp. 54–55.

81   "The idea of conquering . . .": Hunt, p. 159.

81   "I find everybody . . .": ibid.

81   "do not want . . .": Simon, *Grant Papers*, III, p. 4.

81   "if it is necessary . . .": Simon, IV, p. 227.

81   "In all this . . .": Simon, III, p. 4.

81   "Lincoln is soon . . .": Eaton, *History of Confederacy*, p. 236.

82   "Like black birds . . .": Woodward, *Chesnut*, p. 199.

82   "the loose and . . .": Niven, *Chase*, p. 282.

83   "as you deem . . .": E. McPherson, *Political History*, p. 247.

83   "Every means . . .": Burlingame, *Nicolay's Interviews*, p. 145 fn.

83   "as clearly a right . . .": E. McPherson, *Political History*, p. 249.

83   "This will never do . . .": Carpenter, *Six Months*, p. 136.

83   "head & shoulders . . .": Randall, *Lincoln*, pp. 56–57.

84   "all slaves who leave . . .": Trefousse, p. 116.

84   "the slave question . . .": *New York Times*, Dec. 3, 1861.

84   "the integrity of the Union . . .": Basler, V, pp. 35–53.

86   "the President will approve . . .": *New York Times*, Dec. 3, 1861.

87   "Never should any question . . .": Donald, *Lincoln*, p. 345.

87   "the only . . .": Fehrenbacher, *Recollected Words*, p. 433.

87   "no greater disaster . . .": *New York Times*, Dec. 3, 1861.

88   "an opposition party . . .": Nevins, *Strong*, p. 194.

88   "Notify the slaveholders . . .": Mitgang, *Lincoln as They*, p. 279.

88   "The long and short . . .": P. Foner, p. 15.

88   "God won't let . . .": J. McPherson, *Negro's Civil War*, p. 43.

89   "If our soldiers . . .": *New York Times*, Jan. 2, 1862.

90   "the sound of drums . . .": Jacob, *Capital Elites*, p. 47.

90   "Politicians of every . . .": ibid., p. 47.

91   "Rebels have no right . . .": *New York Times*, Jan. 6, 1862.

91   "and carefully read it over . . .": Rice, p. 60.

92   "Peculiar circumstances . . .": J. McPherson, *Battle Cry*, p. 495.

92   "Our nation is . . .": Donald, *Lincoln*, p. 342.

92   "I believe that slavery . . .": J. McPherson, *For Cause*, p. 118.

92   "I thought I hated . . .": ibid., p. 119.

92   "he would have lost . . .": ibid.

92   "we must first conquer . . .": J. McPherson, *Battle Cry*, p. 497.

92   "I don't care a damn . . .": J. McPherson, *For Cause*, p. 119.

93   "For my part . . .": Trudeau, *Like Men of War*, p. 18.

93   "Why have our rulers . . .": Hunt, p. 162.

93   "if the President . . .": Donald, *Lincoln*, p. 331.

93   "The Prest. is an . . .": ibid., p. 328.

93   ""Mr. President, you are . . .": ibid., p. 332.

94   "great negligence . . .": Niven, *Salmon P. Chase*, p. 275.

94   "General, what shall . . .": Oates, *With Malice*, p. 284.

95   "If I tell him . . .": Donald, *Lincoln*, p. 330.

95   "what he intended . . .": Niven, *Salmon P. Chase*, p. 279.

96   "that damned long armed . . .": Donald, *Lincoln*, p. 186.

96   "a low, cunning . . .": Anderson, *Public Man*, p. 210.

96   "painful imbecility . . .": Thomas and Hyman, p. 124.

97   "He would lean . . .": Leech, p. 160.

97   "You gentlemen . . .": Andrews, *The North Reports*, p. 55.

98   "as firm a Democrat . . .": Thomas and Hyman, p. 139.

98   "is just the man . . .": Williams, *Radicals*, p. 90.

98   "who have conversed with . . .": ibid., p. 90.

98   "As soon as I can get . . .": Foote, I, p. 245.

98   "This army has got to . . .": Leech, p. 143.

98   "we have had no war . . .": Thomas and Hyman, p. 146.

99   "Mud, mud . . .": Rhodes, *All for the Union*, p. 46.

100   "Massa done gone . . .": Foote, p. 217.

100   "After this, it certainly . . .": ibid., p. 214.

100   "to be more anxious . . .": T. Harry Williams, *Radicals*, p. 161.

100   "infernal, unmitigated . . .": Leech, p. 126.

101   "Why in_____ain't they . . .": Burlingame, *Hay Diary*, p. 292.

101   "so really angry . . .": ibid.

101   "I am no engineer . . .": ibid., p. 293.

102   "whenever such action . . .": *New York Times*, Dec. 3, 1861.

102   "A stronger and . . .": Schurz, *Autobiography*, p. 190.

102   "Would not the cry . . .": Schurz, *Reminiscences, II*, p. 310.

102   "Wa-al, that reminds me . . .": Nevins, *Strong*, p. 204.

103   "better to keep . . .": Coulter, *Kentucky,* p. 156.

103   "I have no faith in . . .": ibid., p. 157.

104   "good and responsible . . .": Rose, *Rehearsal,* p. 22.

104   "he ought not . . .": Fehrenbacher, *Recollected Words,* p. 358.

104   "Good-bye, General . . .": Rice, p. 142.

105   "I pray that the President . . .": Schurz, *Autobiography,* p. 188.

105   "I want to know . . .": Donald, *Lincoln,* p. 346.

105   "the disease of . . .": Fehrenbacher, *Recollected Words,* p. 119.

105   "In my judgment . . .": Basler, V, p. 145.

106   "just the right thing . . .": Donald, *Lincoln,* p. 347.

106   "a masterpiece of . . .": Oates, *With Malice,* p. 298.

106   "the most diluted . . .": Brodie, p. 156.

106   "rather an excuse for . . .": T. Harry Williams, *Radicals,* p. 158.

106   "Every concession . . .": Donald, *Lincoln,* p. 348.

107   "Immense . . .": Fehrenbacher, *Recollected Words,* pp. 121–22.

108   "I reject it now . . .": Brodie, p. 156.

108   "an awful responsibility . . .": Schurz, *Autobiography,* p. 188.

108   "very much as I . . .": F. Pratt, p. 264.

108   "conceived with the : . .": Donald, *Lincoln,* p. 340.

109   "Going down the Bay . . .": Basler, V, p. 185.

109   "Old Abe is mad . . .": Rice, p. 53.

110   "great ignorance . . .": Donald, *Lincoln,* p. 341.

110   "a very great kindness . . .": Burlingame, *Hay Diary,* p. 36.

110   "I shall work . . .": Donald, *Lincoln,* p. 341.

110   "The less I see . . .": Sears, *Young Napoleon,* p. 164.

111   "The Army is in . . .": Sears, *McClellan Papers,* p. 213.

111   "very much against . . .": Oates, *With Malice,* p. 296.

111   "The recommendation . . .": *Messages and Documents,* p. 324.

111   "It is my profound . . .": Schurz, *Reminiscences,* II, p. 286.

112   "They who in quarrels . . .": J. McPherson, *Battle Cry,* p. 384.

112   "the *Scoundrelism* . . .": Allen, *Great Britain,* p. 483.

112   "unless we soon . . .": Durden, *James Shepherd Pike,* p. 78.

113   "upon a higher moral . . .": ibid.

113   "Although the war . . .": *Messages and Documents,* p. 37.

113   "the insurrectionary government . . .": ibid., p. 326.

114   "Nowhere has the condition . . .": Ford, ed., *Cycle of Adams Letters,* I, p. 122.

114   "As our swarm . . .": ibid., p. 120.

114   "The outcry opened . . .": Sears, *Young Napoleon,* p. 168.

114   "a dead failure . . .": ibid.

114   "they were certain . . .": Leech, p. 163.

114 "was not . . .": Fehrenbacher, *Recollected Words*, p. 63.

115 "The little Napoleon . . .": Hay, *Letters*, p. 57.

115 "I think it is . . .": Basler V, p. 185.

115 "I was much tempted . . .": Sears, ed., *McClellan Papers*, p. 234.

116 "I can't spare . . .": Fehrenbacher, *Recollected Words*, p. 315.

116 "we shuffle and . . .": T. Harry Williams, *Radicals*, p. 159.

116 "too easy and . . .": Trefousse, p. 120.

116 "Patch up a compromise . . .": Brodie, p. 158.

116 "Our accounts say . . .": Ford, *Cycle*, pp. 140–41.

116 "Stevens, Sumner, and . . .": Brodie, pp. 156–57.

118 "must be suppressed . . .": T. Harry Williams, *Radicals*, p. 160.

118 "an asylum for . . .": Leech, p. 242.

118 "the time and manner . . .": Basler, V, p. 169.

118 "It should have . . .": Fehrenbacher, *Recollected Words*, p. 64.

119 "I am so far behind . . .": ibid., p. 295.

119 "had two family . . .": ibid., p. 64.

119 "Lincoln has signed . . .": Nevins, *Strong*, pp. 216–17.

119 "talking relative to the . . .": P. Smith, p. 257.

119 "like a master . . .": Strauberg, *Eyewitness Reports*, p. 77.

120 "clothing, temporary homes . . .": Green, *Washington*, p. 276.

120 "I trust I am not . . .": P. Smith, p. 257.

120 "can now hold up . . .": J. McPherson, *Negro's Civil War*, p. 45.

120 "so much engaged . . .": Jellison, p. 145.

121 "I feel that the . . .": Sears, *McClellan Papers*, p. 252.

121 "No one but McClellan . . .": J. McPherson, *Battle Cry*, p. 426.

122 "We have reached . . .": ibid., p. 428.

122 "The romance of the thing . . .": ibid., p. 429.

122 "weary, care-worn . . .": Donald, *Lincoln*, p. 358.

122 "Well, I cannot take . . .": Nevins, *Strong* p. 218.

123 "So has ended . . .": Donald, *Chase Diaries*, p. 85.

123 "naturally one of the . . .": Ford, *Cycle*, pp. 126–27.

123 "Slavery is written . . .": Rose, *Rehearsal*, p. 57.

124 "sly . . . docile and submissive . . .": ibid., pp. 58, 128, 140.

124 "are just such . . .": Ford, *Cycle*, p. 118.

124 "My impression from what . . .": ibid., pp. 131–33.

125 "hanger-on at Washington . . .": T. Harry Williams, *Radicals*, p. 136.

125 "It is time slavery . . .": ibid., p. 55.

125 "Please let me have . . .": ibid., p. 136.

126 "this looks in the . . .": Rose, p. 145.

126 "I don't believe . . .": J. McPherson, *Negro's Civil War*, p. 164.

126 "Negros—plantation negroes . . .": ibid.

126 "slavery and martial law . . .": Basler, V, p. 222.

127 "No commanding general . . .": ibid., p. 219.

127 "not so far from . . .": Venet, *Neither Ballots nor Bullets*, p. 42.

128 "protracted by the obstinacy . . .": T. Harry Williams, *Radicals*, p. 138.

128 "Our progress has . . .": Sears, *McClellan Papers*, p. 209.

128 "All accounts . . ." and "That effort . . .": ibid., p. 271.

129 "I am trying to . . .": Fehrenbacher, *Recollected Words*, p. 324.

129 "is the only object . . .": Leech, p. 173. My discussion of Washington in the summer of 1862 relies heavily upon Leech's excellent study.

129 "I think the time is near . . .": Basler, V, p. 236.

129 "It is perfectly . . .": Sears, *McClellan Papers*, p. 275.

129 "The net is quietly . . .": ibid., p. 276.

130 "the sickening sight of the battlefield . . .": ibid., p. 288.

130 "a curious scene . . .": Lowenfels, ed., *Whitman's War*, p. 87.

132 "not one in a hundred . . ." and "a docile people . . .": Green, p. 277.

133 "To my unsophisticated . . .": Burlingame, *Brooks*, p. 57.

133 "Such a decree . . .": Basler, V, pp. 278–79.

133 "A bad habit . . .": Leech, p. 174.

134 "lost his mind . . .": Nevins, *Strong*, p. 233.

135 "a flatterer, a deceiver . . .": Foote, p. 527.

135 "as big a liar . . .": Ford, *Cycle*, p. 181.

135 "A liar might be . . .": Fehrenbacher, *Recollected Words*, p. 474.

136 "Slavery must perish . . .": Donald, *Chase Diaries*, p. 97.

136 "too cautious . . .": Sears, *Young Napoleon*, pp. 244–45.

136 "The Govt has . . .": Sears, *McClellan Papers*, pp. 322–23.

137 "I never leave . . .": Sears, *Young Napoleon*, p. 217.

137 "only be prompted by . . .": Foote, p. 515.

137 "It is considered . . .": Sears, *Young Napoleon*, p. 216.

137 "I did not expect . . .": Rhodes, p. 64.

138 "We cannot make out . . .": Nevins, *Strong*, p. 235.

138 "imbecile, a coward . . .": P. Smith, p. 264.

138 "it is not on our . . .": Poore, *Reminiscences*, p. 109.

138 "wishes to outgeneral . . .": P. Smith, p. 264.

138 "maintain your ground . . .": Basler, V, p. 298.

138 "I expect to maintain . . .": ibid., p. 292.

139 "General, I understand . . .": Nevins, *War*, II, p. 144.

139 "Things had gone on . . .": Carpenter, pp. 20–21.

139 "He would look out . . .": Bates, *Telegraph Office*, p. 36.

140 "I want you to go . . .": Hunt, p. 160.

140 "Hamlin, you have often . . .": ibid.

140 "was much moved . . .": ibid., p. 160.

140   "You need more men . . .": Oates, *With Malice,* p. 307.

140   "too big a lick.": Fehrenbacher, *Recollected Words,* pp. 434.

140   "Wait. . . . Time is . . .": ibid., p. 435.

140   "Your achievements . . .": Sears, ed., *McClellan Papers,* p. 339.

141   "Rest is what we . . .": Rhodes, p. 65.

141   "gathered berries . . .": Foote, p. 519.

141   "either a . . .": J. McPherson, *Negro's Civil War,* pp. 46–47.

141   "The time will come . . .": Hunt, p. 161.

141   "My belief is unshaken . . .": Ford, *Cycle,* pp. 162–63.

142   "seemed to infuse . . .": Rhodes, p. 66.

142   "will never measure . . .": Sears, *Young Napoleon,* p. 227.

142   "become entangled . . .": Foote, p. 530.

142   "but after what he had . . .": Nevins, *War,* II, p. 157.

143   "If I had succeeded . . .": Sears, *McClellan Papers,* p. 350.

143   "upon the highest . . .": ibid., pp. 344–45.

143   "If anyone thinks . . .": J. McPherson, *For Cause,* p. 121.

143   "The tendency of public . . .": Thomas and Hyman, p. 231.

143   "Slavery must be . . .": J. McPherson, *For Cause,* p. 120.

143   "this thing of guarding . . .": J. McPherson, *Battle Cry,* p. 502.

144   "It seemed that . . .": Sears, *McClellan Papers,* p. 348.

145   "I am very anxious . . .": Foote, p. 533.

145   "as honest a man . . .": Brodie, p. 164.

145   "The President is not . . .": T. Williams, *Radicals,* p. 163.

146   "Treason must be made . . .": Brodie, p. 166.

146   "Let me confiscate . . .": ibid.

146   "You can form no . . .": J. McPherson, *Battle Cry,* p. 496.

147   "it would have been . . .": Jellicoe, p. 146.

147   "whole soul was . . .": Nevins, *War,* II, p. 149.

147   "a *decision* at once . . .": Basler, V, pp. 317–19.

148   "I regard the . . .": Trudeau, p. 17.

148   "I was as nearly . . .": Foote, p. 524.

148   "to meddle . . .": Fehrenbacher, *Recollected Words,* pp. 469–70.

149   "Until this time . . .": Beale, *Welles Diary,* p. 71.

149   "He was 'earnest in the conviction . . .' ": ibid.

149   "does not drive . . .": T. Williams, *Radicals,* p. 3.

150   "How I wish the . . .": Fehrenbacher, *Recollected Words,* p. 18.

150   "civilized warfare . . .": Oates, *With Malice,* p. 309.

150   "It is startling . . .": Donald, *Lincoln,* p. 365.

150   "They come now . . .": Fehrenbacher, *Recollected Words,* p. 64.

150   "plantation carts . . .": J. McPherson, *Negro's Civil War,* p. 61.

151   "The President cannot . . .": T. Williams, *Radicals,* p. 164.

151   "Will disappoint, and I fear . . .": Jellison, p. 146.

151   "has shaped . . .": Fehrenbacher, *Recollected Words*, p. 368.

152   "the severest justice . . .": Basler, V, p. 330.

152   "The government seems . . .": Nevins, *Strong*, p. 244.

153   "Everything he does . . .": Kaplan, p. 271.

153   "does not lead . . .": Nevins, *Strong*, p. 245.

153   "Not a spark of genius . . .": Foote, p. 524.

153   "stumbling, halting . . .": P. Smith, p. 244.

153   "The simple truth is . . .": Foote, p. 524.

153   "The great phenomenon . . .": J. McPherson, *Battle Cry*, p. 496.

153   "The time has come . . .": Nevins, *War*, II, p. 147.

154   "If we succeed in . . .": Ford, *Cycle*, p. 165.

154   "Suppose that all the . . .": Burlingame, *Oral History*, p. 49.

155   "to take some . . .": Oates, *With Malice*, p. 310.

155   "I said to the Cabinet . . .": Carpenter, p. 21.

156   "to return to . . .": Basler, V, pp. 336–37.

156   "the measure goes beyond . . .": Niven, *Welles*, p. 419.

156   "dreaded any . . .": Hendrick, *Lincoln's War Cabinet*, p. 418.

157   "and go home . . .": ibid., p. 420.

157   "an arbitrary and despotic . . .": ibid., p. 422.

157   "How much better . . .": Chase, *Diary*, p. 99.

158   "the last measure . . .": Carpenter, p. 22.

159   "those blunders which have . . .": ibid., pp. 174–75.

160   "entertained a notion . . .": Trudeau, p. 18.

160   "Place arms in the hands . . .": Brodie, p. 157.

160   "Certainly we hope . . .": Trudeau, p. 18.

160   "We don't want to . . .": ibid.

160   "the rear-guard of . . .": Donald, *Lincoln*, p. 367.

160   "I would raise . . .": Brodie, p. 160.

161   "we want to save . . .": Hunt, p. 162.

161   "some dead niggers . . .": Brodie, p. 160.

161   "For my part . . .": Trudeau, p. 18.

161   "I have no hobby . . .": J. McPherson, *Battle Cry*, p. 502.

161   "I am using them . . .": Simon, ed., V, p. 311.

161   "These people . . .": Chase, p. 377.

161   "Phelps has gone . . .": Trudeau, p. 25.

162   "These men . . .": Chase, pp. 311–13.

162   "Let England . . .": P. Smith, p. 287.

162   "I am receiving . . .": Trudeau, p. 13. For my discussion of Lane's efforts to recruit black troops, I am heavily indebted to Noah Andre Trudeau's work.

162   "regiments of persons . . .": ibid., pp. 13–14.

162   "Give them a fair chance . . .": ibid., p. 14.

162   "With one exception . . .": ibid.

162   "It would . . .": Fehrenbacher, *Recollected Words*, p. 64.

162   "all colored men offered as . . .": Basler, V, p. 357.

163   "Here, directly in . . .": Sears, ed., *McClellan Papers*, p. 384.

163   "I find the forces . . .": Foote, pp. 595–96.

164   "would be a greater nuisance . . .": Hay, p. 59.

164   "The stomach . . .": Mitgang, *Lincoln*, pp. 298–300.

164   "The more I see of slavery . . .": J. McPherson, *For Cause*, p. 118.

164   "The institution of slavery . . .": ibid.

164   "began to see . . .": Chase, p. 377.

165   "There is but one . . .": Mitgang, *Edward Dicey*, p. 47.

165   "were never more . . .": J. McPherson, *Negro's Civil War*, p. 89.

165   "We may as well . . .": ibid., p. 69.

166   "The crowd continually . . .": Hay, p. 58.

166   "will issue no proclamation . . .": Donald, *Lincoln*, p. 366.

166   "What I *cannot* do . . .": Basler, V, p. 343.

166   "The truth is . . .": ibid., pp. 345–46.

166   "this government cannot . . .": ibid., pp. 350–51.

167   "I do not think . . .": T. Harry Williams, *Radicals*, p. 171.

167   "Lincoln is doing . . .": P. Smith, p. 245.

167   "an Ass . . . for the . . .": ibid., p. 244.

167   "I do not hesitate . . .": P. Foner, ed., *Douglass*, p. 256.

167   "a damn humbug": J. McPherson, *Battle Cry*, p. 509.

168   "You and we . . .": Basler, V, pp. 370–75.

169   "This is our country . . .": J. McPherson, *Battle Cry*, p. 509.

169   "Pray tell us . . .": J. McPherson, *Negroes' Civil War*, p. 93.

169   "an itinerant Colonization . . .": P. Foner, *Douglass*, pp. 266–70

169   "Stand firm on . . .": Foote, p. 608.

169   "faithfully carry out . . .": Sears, ed., *McClellan Papers*, p. 394.

169   "it will take . . .": ibid., p. 395.

169   "Now I am to . . .": Fehrenbacher, *Recollected Words*, p. 129.

170   "Do you remember . . .": J. McPherson, *Battle Cry*, p. 505.

170   "There is not one . . .": Basler, V, p. 389 (fn.)

170   "I would save . . .": Basler, V, pp. 388–89.

171   "You should issue . . .": Rice, p. 88.

171   "The air of this city . . .": Ford, *Cycle*, p. 178.

172   "leave Pope to get . . .": Sears, ed., *McClellan Papers*, p. 416.

172   "so wrathful . . .": Sears, *Young Napoleon*, p. 254.

172   "It really seemed . . .": Burlingame, *Hay Diary*, p. 37.

173 "It's another . . .": Foote, p. 640.

173 "We have had a . . .": ibid., p. 642.

173 "Open sneering at . . .": ibid., p. 643.

173 "Everyone you met . . .": ibid., p. 645.

173 "Well, John . . .": Burlingame, *Hay Diary*, p. 38.

173 "We must hurt this enemy . . .": ibid.

174 "to avoid great disaster.": Foote, p. 645.

174 "Unless something . . .": ibid.

174 "I beg of you to . . .": ibid., p. 648.

174 "the destruction . . .": Thomas and Hyman, p. 220.

174 "conversations amounted . . .": Niven, *Chase*, p. 295.

174 "A terrible and . . .": Sears, ed., *McClellan Papers*, p. 428.

175 "he seemed wrung . . .": Basler, V, p. 404 (fn.)

175 "he felt almost ready . . .": ibid.

175 "I must have . . .": Donald, *Lincoln*, p. 371.

175 "I cannot but feel . . .": Foote, p. 649.

175 "The order is mine . . .": ibid., p. 648.

175 "has acted badly . . .": Burlingame, *Hay Diary*, pp. 38–39.

175 "What is the use . . .": ibid., p. 40.

176 "The will of God prevails . . .": Basler, V, pp. 403–4.

176 "his mind was burdened . . .": ibid., p. 404 (fn.)

176 "I am almost ready . . .": ibid., p. 404.

177 "We cannot afford . . .": Foote, p. 662.

177 "a very complete . . .": J. McPherson, *Battle Cry*, p. 555.

177 "If the Federals . . .": ibid., p. 556.

177 "turn out Lincoln . . .": Nevins, *Strong*, pp. 255–56.

177 "We could end the war . . .": Basler, V, p. 501.

178 "Disgust with our . . .": Nevins, *Strong*, p. 256.

178 "This changing from . . .": Donald, *Lincoln*, p. 373.

178 "Tale-telling and . . .": ibid.

178 "only special gift is . . .": Nevins, *Strong*, p. 256.

178 "if possible to save . . .": Nevins, *War*, II, p. 220.

178 "bullied by those . . .": T. Harry Williams, *Radicals*, p. 179.

178 "sufficient grasp of mind . . .": ibid., p. 180.

178 "The truth is that . . .": Rice, pp. 527, 536.

179 "few very radical . . .": Donald, *Lincoln*, p. 373.

179 "I hope it will not be . . .": Basler, V, pp. 419–21.

179 "As commander-in-chief . . .": ibid.

180 "When the rebel . . .": Donald, *Chase Diaries*, p. 150.

181 "find and hurt this . . .": Nicolay and Hay, *Lincoln*, p. 153.

181 "I am for sending . . .": Basler, V, p. 415.

181   "There never was . . .": Nicolay and Hay, *Lincoln,* p. 155.

182   "a fight between . . .": ibid.

182   "the old women . . .": Nevins, *War,* II, p. 231 (fn.)

182   "It has been a . . .": Sears, ed., *McClellan Papers,* pp. 461–62.

182   "Destroy the rebel . . .": Basler, V, pp. 426.

182   "Time was of no . . .": Nicolay and Hay, *Lincoln,* p. 157.

183   "In a second . . .": J. McPherson, *Battle Cry,* p. 540.

183   "There was nothing . . .": Nicolay and Hay, *Lincoln,* p. 158.

183   "The men are loading . . .": J. McPherson, *Battle Cry,* p. 540.

183   "We are in the midst . . .": Sears, ed., *McClellan Papers,* p. 468.

183   "Lee's army was ruined . . .": J. McPherson, *Battle Cry,* p. 543.

184   "Who can tell . . .": Nevins, *War,* II, p. 225.

184   "send all the troops . . .": Sears, ed., *McClellan Papers,* p. 468.

184   "Where is the splendid . . .": Nevins, *War,* II, p. 226.

184   "This is a woful . . .": Nicolay and Hay, *Lincoln,* p. 160.

184   "our victory was . . .": Sears, ed., *McClellan Papers,* p. 470.

184   "Why did we not . . .": Rhodes, p. 74.

184   "If McClellan had only . . .": Nevins, *War,* II, p. 230.

185   "well educated but . . .": ibid.

185   "they did not mean . . .": Burlingame, *Hay Diary,* p. 41.

185   "if he did not keep . . .": Rice, p. 531.

185   "My idea of this war . . .": Nevins, *War,* II, p. 193.

185   "Gentlemen, Why . . .": Fehrenbacher, *Recollected Words,* p. 417.

186   "I have, as . . .": Chase, pp. 87–88.

187   "I made a solemn vow . . .": Carpenter, pp. 89–90.

187   "I can always . . .": Fehrenbacher, *Recollected Words,* p. 425.

187   "I know very well . . .": Chase, p. 88.

187   "By the President . . .": Text is in Basler, V, pp. 433–36.

189   "It was not my way . . .": Carpenter, pp. 23–24.

190   "all reference to . . .": Chase, p. 89.

190   "The Proclamation does not . . .": ibid.

190   "A club . . . to beat . . .": J. McPherson, *Battle Cry,* p. 557.

191   "The difficulty . . .": Rice, pp. 535–36.

191   "if the President . . .": Carpenter, p. 88.

195   "No mistake . . .": Basler, V, p. 438.

195   "What I did . . .": ibid.

196   "this righteous decree . . .": Oates, *With Malice,* p. 320.

196   "every mistake . . .": Donald, *Lincoln,* p. 378.

196   "The President may be . . .": Nevins, *War,* II, p. 237.

196   "The President, as President . . .": Jellison, pp. 155–56.

196   "a measure of justice . . .": Donald, *Lincoln,* p. 378.

196 "A poor *document* . . .": Nevins, *War*, II, p. 234.

197 "Immediate and absolute . . .": Mitgang, pp. 307–8.

197 "A paper pronunciamento . . .": Laas, p. 187 (fn.).

197 "What is liberty . . .": Van Deusen, p. 333.

197 "If utter desperation . . .": Mitgang, p. 304.

198 "A gigantic usurpation . . .": Mitgang, p. 313.

198 "the atrocity . . .": Donald, *Lincoln*, p. 378.

199 "a proposal for the . . .": J. McPherson, *Battle Cry*, p. 560.

199 "the crowning act . . .": P. Smith, p. 293.

199 "as black of soul . . .": Franklin, p. 68.

199 "I cannot make . . .": Sears, ed., *McClellan Papers*, pp. 481–82.

199 "disgust, discontent . . .": Nevins, *War*, II, p. 238.

199 "submit to the . . .": Sears, ed., *McClellan Papers*, p. 490.

199 "the remedy for . . .": ibid., p. 494.

199 "Abraham 'has gone' . . .": J. McPherson, *For Cause*, p. 121.

199 "The God of battle . . .": ibid., p. 122.

200 "Nothing should stand . . .": J. McPherson, *Battle Cry*, p. 559.

200 "Sick and tired . . .": J. McPherson, *For Cause*, p. 123.

200 "I don't want to fire . . .": ibid., p. 122.

200 "The principle asserted . . .": Franklin, pp. 72–73.

200 "Where he has no power . . .": Mitgang, p. 320.

200 "nothing less than the . . .": *New York Times*, September 28, 1862.

200 "was a most wonderful . . .": Burlingame, *Hay Diary*, p. 41.

200 "all seemed to feel . . .": ibid.

201 "two such races . . .": Merrill, pp. 142, 210.

201 "to prevent the Radicals . . .": Rice, p. 533.

201 "was followed by . . .": Basler, VIII, p. 49.

201 "This, looked soberly . . .": Basler, V, p. 444.

202 "The foundations . . .": Fehrenbacher, *Recollected Words*, p. 23.

202 "From the expiration . . .": ibid.

202 "wished it distinctly . . .": Rice, p. 61.

203 "Early one morning . . .": Werner, p. 39.

203 "gloom and despondency . . .": Nevins, *War*, II, p. 297.

203 "They say they are . . .": ibid., p. 296.

203 "I kept McClellan . . .": Fehrenbacher, *Recollected Words*, p. 43.

203 "was playing false . . .": Burlingame, *Hay Diary*, p. 232.

204 "with his long legs . . .": Foote, p. 748.

204 "Hatch, Hatch . . .": ibid., p. 749, and Donald, *Lincoln*, p. 386.

204 "Are you not . . .": Basler, V, pp. 460–61.

204 "Will you pardon me . . .": ibid., p. 474.

205 "There is no doubt . . .": Allen, p. 480.

205 "We must continue to be . . .": ibid., p. 481.

206 "The Constitution as . . .": J. McPherson, *Battle Cry*, p. 560.

206 "I told you so . . .": Donald, *Lincoln*, p. 382.

206 "the Proclamation has not . . .": King, p. 199.

206 "if it be true . . .": J. McPherson, *Battle Cry*, p. 560.

206 "literally bending . . .": Donald, *Lincoln*, p. 382.

206 "introverted look . . .": ibid.

206 "We are indeed . . .": Basler, V, p. 478.

207 "'Abolition Slaughtered' . . .": J. McPherson, *Battle Cry*, p. 561.

207 "It was not . . .": Donald, *Lincoln*, p. 384.

207 "would be glad to hear . . .": Rice, p. 276.

207 "You need not be . . .": ibid.

207 "felt like the boy . . .": Sandburg, I, p. 611.

208 "tried long . . .": Fehrenbacher, *Recollected Words*, p. 32.

208 "This has been a . . .": Rhodes, p. 80.

208 "Little Mac has gone . . .": Nevins, *War*, p. 332.

208 "How fortunate for us . . .": ibid., p. 333.

209 "they have made . . .": Sears, ed., *McClellan Papers*, p. 520.

209 "In parting from you . . .": ibid., p. 521.

209 "stand by General Burnside . . .": Foote, p. 757.

209 "Recruits come . . .": Chase, p. 319.

210 "they have done well . . .": ibid., p. 330.

210 "it needs but . . .": J. McPherson, *Negro's* Civil War, p. 166.

210 "Just think how infamous . . .": Nevins, *Strong*, p. 283.

211 "She is very beautiful . . .": Green, p. 268.

211 "Washington is just now . . .": Andrews, p. 39.

212 "His hair is grizzled . . .": Burlingame, *Brooks*, pp. 13–14.

213 "weary and care worn . . .": King, p. 200.

213 "Mr. Lincoln's whole soul . . .": Donald, *Lincoln*, p. 397.

213 "Without slavery . . .": Basler, V, pp. 518–37.

215 "by the hallucination . . .": Foote, p. 810.

215 "We have always . . .": Nevins, *War*, p. 339.

216 "I never saw . . .": Werner, p. 33.

216 "There never was . . .": Fehrenbacher, *Recollected Words*, p. 67.

216 "Order the army . . .": Nevins, *Strong*, p. 278.

217 "It's an army of lions . . .": ibid.

217 "Above us . . . within speaking . . .": Werner, p. 35.

217 "It can hardly be . . .": J. McPherson, *Battle Cry*, p. 572.

217 "There has been enough . . .": Nevins, *War*, p. 350.

217 "My first battle . . .": Werner, p. 36.

218 "Oh those men . . .": Nevins, *War*, p. 350.

218   "have borne, silently . . .": J. McPherson, *Battle Cry*, p. 574.

218   "The men cannot be . . .": Hunt, p. 162.

218   "The general indignation . . .": Nevins, *Strong*, p. 281.

218   "a growing dread . . .": King, pp. 206–7.

218   "The Army of the Potomac . . .": T. Harry Williams, *Radicals*, p. 238.

218   "We are now . . .": Donald, *Lincoln*, pp. 402–3.

219   "You know the old lady . . .": King, p. 207.

219   "The President is . . .": Nevins, *War*, p. 351.

219   "folly, stupidity . . .": Jellison, p. 156.

219   "They may do as they please . . .": Donald, *Lincoln*, p. 402.

219   "The feeling is everywhere . . .": Nevins, *War*, p. 355.

219   "is awfully shaken . . .": ibid.

220   "if there was . . .": Fehrenbacher, *Recollected Words*, p. 496.

220   "They wish to . . .": ibid., p. 67.

220   "If one goes . . .": ibid., p. 129.

220   "Now I have the . . .": T. Harry Williams, *Radicals*, p. 211.

221   "I was never in . . .": Green, p. 254.

221   "miasmatic swamp . . .": ibid., p. 255.

222   "At once, the freedmen . . .": J. McPherson, *Battle Cry*, p. 578.

223   "there would be a rebellion . . .": Franklin, p. 90.

223   "would not . . .": Fehrenbacher, *Recollected Words*, p. 129.

223   "a great impulse . . .": Brodie, p. 159.

223   "I have studied . . .": Donovan, p. 117.

223   "The President is occupied . . .": Randall, p. 167.

223   "The President says he would not . . .": ibid.

224   "command and require . . .": Basler, VI, pp. 23–26.

225   "The year has not . . .": Rhodes, p. 85.

225   "I was in hope . . .": Werner, p. 37.

225   "There were no sugar . . .": ibid., p. 51.

225   "Now no more . . .": P. Smith, p. 302.

227   "Anyone who behaves . . .": Burlingame, *Brooks*, p. 15.

227   "With a sincere . . .": ibid.

227   "his heavy eyes brightening . . .": ibid., p. 17.

227   "I never, in . . .": Fehrenbacher, *Recollected Words*, p. 397.

228   "Now, this signature . . .": ibid.

228   "Three hours' hand-shaking . . .": Carpenter, p. 87.

228   "The South had fair warning . . .": ibid.

228   "a fit and necessary . . .": Basler, VI, pp. 28–31.

229   "I wish I could . . .": Bates, p. 145.

232   "I had some desire . . .": Basler, VI, p. 539.

232   "Many of my . . .": Carpenter, p. 77.

233   "It was not only . . .": Fehrenbacher, *Recollected Words*, p. 507.

233   "and work up like white men . . .": Franklin, p. 107.

233   "how it was in Dixie . . .": Different versions of this speech may be found in Franklin, pp. 106–7; J. McPherson, *Negro's Civil War*, p. 62; and P. Smith, p. 302. See also the *New York Times*, January 2, 1863, and the *Washington Post*, January 2, 1863.

234   "I break your bonds . . .": Franklin, pp. 110–11.

234   "I never saw anything . . .": ibid., p. 118.

234   "the most memorable day . . .": P. Foner, *Douglass*, p. 306.

234   "too deeply and indelibly . . .": ibid., pp. 310–12.

235   "The nation may be . . .": Nevins, *Strong*, p. 286.

235   "It changes entirely . . .": *New York Times*, Jan. 3, 1863.

235   "will stop with the . . .": T. Harry Williams, *Radicals*, p. 215.

235   "I don't want . . .": J. McPherson, *For Cause*, p. 122.

235   "[We] volunteered to fight . . .": ibid., pp. 122–23.

235   "Ohio will be . . .": Donald, *Lincoln*, p. 417.

236   "the most execrable measures . . .": Franklin, p. 125.

236   "one of three possible . . .": Donovan, p. 113.

236   "As to any dread . . .": Basler, VI, p. 49.

237   "shuts the door . . .": Franklin, p. 124.

237   "perhaps a majority . . .": T. Harry Williams, *Radicals*, pp. 240–41.

237   "I did not . . .": J. McPherson, *For Cause*, p. 122.

238   "There is an astonishing . . .": ibid., p. 123.

238   "say it has turned . . .": ibid.

238   "any policy ordered . . .": Thomas and Hyman, p. 266.

238   "Thank God the . . .": J. McPherson, *For Cause*, p. 121.

238   "desire to destroy . . .": J. McPherson, *Second Revolution*, p. 35.

238   "I am no . . .": J. McPherson, *For Cause*, p. 122.

238   "All I can say . . .": Fehrenbacher, *Collected Words*, p. 120.

238   "To use a coarse . . .": Basler, VI, p. 48.

239   "I struggled nearly . . .": ibid., pp. 48–49.

239   "he had done . . .": Fehrenbacher, *Recollected Words*, p. 413.

240   "I have no idea . . .": Ford, *Cycle*, p. 203.

240   "Your military skill . . .": Basler, VI, p. 31.

241   "I have heard generals . . .": Nevins, *War*, II, p. 433.

241   "The whole army . . .": T. Harry Williams, *Radicals*, p. 240.

241   "of which he had long . . .": Burlingame, *Brooks*, p. 21.

241   "I think you are right . . .": Donald, *Lincoln*, p. 411.

241   "imbecile and . . .": ibid.

241   "Hooker does . . .": Fehrenbacher, *Recollected Words*, p. 375.

241   "What I now ask . . .": Basler, VI, pp. 78–79.

241   "He talks to me . . .": Nicolay and Hay, p. 174.

242   "acts of plunder . . .": Donald, *Lincoln*, p. 379.

242   "Since we have . . .": Basler, VI, p. 65 (fn).

242   "the steady advance . . .": ibid., p. 89 (fn).

242   "The Emancipation Proclamation has . . .": Ford, I, p. 243.

242   "the attempt to overthrow . . .": Basler, VI, pp. 63–65.

243   "feeling the public pulse . . .": Hunt, p. 163.

243   "the blacks here are . . .": J. McPherson, *Negro's Civil War*, p. 173.

243   "Nobody knows . . .": ibid., pp. 166–67.

244   "a race unaccustomed . . .": Trudeau, p. 34.

244   "The average . . .": J. McPherson, *Negro's Civil War*, p. 171.

244   "Yesterday a . . .": ibid.

244   "either bayoneted . . .": J. McPherson, *Battle Cry*, p. 566.

245   "It is a common thing . . .": Burlingame, *Brooks*, p. 22.

245   "the most striking thing . . .": Donald, *Lincoln*, p. 424.

245   "I observe that the . . .": ibid., p. 426.

246   "I have ceased . . .": Fehrenbacher, *Recollected Words*, p. 120.

246   "All who wish . . .": Nevins, *War*, p. 389.

246   "The President tells me . . .": Nevins, *War*, pp. 367–68.

247   "the finest army . . .": Nicolay and Hay, p. 175.

247   "I have never known . . .": J. McPherson, *Battle Cry*, p. 585.

248   "our revered . . .": Burlingame, *Inner World*, p. 82.

248   "Did you ever see . . .": ibid.

248   "It is an awful load . . .": ibid.

248   "nothing could touch . . .": Burlingame, *Brooks*, p. 43.

248   "That is the most depressing . . .": ibid., p. 240 (fn.).

249   "I have Lee's army . . .": Nevins, *War*, p. 441.

249   "if Hooker had . . .": Fehrenbacher, *Recollected Words*, p. 478.

250   "I shall never forget . . .": Burlingame, *Brooks*, pp. 241–42 (fn.).

250   "Uncle Abe has at last . . .": Trudeau, p. 48.

250   "The colored population . . .": Basler, VI, p. 149.

250   "Once they are in . . .": J. McPherson, *Negro's Civil War*, p. 168.

251   "I see the enemy . . .": Basler, VI, p. 158.

251   "No one can travel . . .": J. McPherson, *Negro's Civil War*, p. 56.

252   "I am happy . . .": J. McPherson, *Negro's Civil War*, p. 167.

252   "Facts are beginning to . . .": ibid., pp. 168–69.

252   "It was an ugly place . . .": Dana, p. 36.

252   "the full confidence . . .": McFeely, p. 130.

253   "When the President called . . .": J. McPherson, *Battle Cry*, p. 609.

253   "We will not render . . .": ibid.

253   "I have always . . .": J. McPherson, *For Cause*, p. 125.

253 "The 'inexorable logic' . . .": ibid., p. 126.
253 "had played hell . . .": J. McPherson, *Negro's Civil War*, p. 65.
254 "of perfect anarchy . . .": P. Smith, p. 383.
254 "The Yankees have now . . .": Nevins, *Strong*, p. 323.
254 "Have you heard . . .": Basler, VI, p. 232.
254 "Do the Richmond . . .": ibid., p. 210.
255 "total absence of . . .": Dana, p. 53.
255 "I shall compromise . . .": Trudeau, p. 39.
255 "fought like devils . . .": ibid., p. 44.
255 "You have no idea . . .": J. McPherson, *Negro's Civil War*, p. 185.
255 "settles the question . . .": *New York Times*, June 11, 1863.
256 "Many men were found . . .": Dana, p. 86.
256 "I never more wish . . .": J. McPherson, *Negro's Civil War*, p. 186.
256 "the bravery of the blacks . . .": Dana, p. 86.
256 "the whole army . . .": Chase, p. 396.
256 "Lee and Hooker . . .": Nevins, *Strong*, p. 324.
257 "turn back the tide . . .": Nevins, *War*, III, p. 83.
257 "Accept his resignation . . .": Thomas and Hyman, p. 273.
257 "very much as a father . . .": Burlingame, *Brooks*, p. 242 (fn.).
257 "a good sort . . .": Donald, p. 445.
258 "drooping eyelids . . .": ibid.
259 "It was all my fault . . .": Wheeler, p. 323.
260 "Our rations have been . . .": Nevins, *War*. p. 71.
260 "had behaved so well . . .": ibid., p. 72.
261 "We have done . . .": J. McPherson, *Battle Cry*, p. 663.
261 "We had them . . .": Burlingame, *Hay Diary*, p. 67.
261 "If I had gone . . .": ibid.
262 "I think I shall not . . .": Basler, VI, p. 365.
263 "having the poor man . . .": Cook, p. 61.
263 "Kill all niggers . . .": ibid., p. 77.
264 "The town is taken . . .": ibid., p. 156.
264 "The three days . . .": Weed, *Memoirs*, vol. II, p. 436.
264 "How this infernal . . .": Nevins, *Strong*, p. 342.
265 "no word of scorn . . .": Trudeau, p. 87.
265 "I have changed . . .": ibid.
265 "I have no tears . . .": J. McPherson, *Negro's Civil War*, p. 191.
266 "I have given the subject . . .": ibid.
266 "Peace does not appear . . .": Basler, VI, p. 410.
266 "We had to make . . .": Oates, *With Malice*, p. 356.
266 "preeminently the white man's . . .": ibid.
266 "the first great man . . .": ibid., p. 357.

267 "If people see . . .": Leech, p. 279.
268 "Let every vote count . . .": J. McPherson, *Battle Cry*, pp. 685–86.
268 "Slavery is dead . . .": Burlingame, *Hay Diary*, p. 73.
269 "As the eye took in . . .": Burlingame, *Brooks*, p. 77.
269 "The change of opinion . . .": Nevins, *Strong*, p. 408.
269 "there is little doubt . . .": J. McPherson, *Battle Cry*, p. 688.
269 "The Tycoon is in . . .": Donald, *Lincoln*, p. 449.
269 "were an election . . .": ibid., p. 458.
270 "Well, they might . . .": Burlingame, *Hay Diary*, p. 311 (fn.).
270 "He would sometimes sit . . .": Nevin, *War*, p. 451.
271 "(a prayer which thought . . .": Burlingame, *Hay Diary*, p. 113.
271 "with more grace . . .": ibid.
271 "did not appear . . .": Burlingame, *Brooks*, p. 89.
272 "The crisis which . . .": Message is in Basler, VII, pp. 36–56.
272 "recognizing the emancipation . . .": Basler, VI, p. 365.
272 "It would not be . . .": ibid.
272 "is willing that the . . .": J. McPherson, *Battle Cry*, p. 701.
273 "I can see . . .": Fehrenbacher, *Recollected Words*, p. 440.
273 "The very intelligent . . .": Basler, VII, p. 243.
273 "of genteel exterior . . .": Donald, *Lincoln*, p. 475.
274 "complexion is clearer . . .": Burlingame, *Brooks*, p. 100.
274 "looked very much . . .": ibid., p. 99.
274 "I cannot describe . . .": P. Smith, p. 499.
274 "it seemed to me . . .": Carpenter, p. 19.
275 "Absorbed in his papers . . .": ibid., p. 30.
275 "as if he had . . .": J. McPherson, *Battle Cry*. p. 721.
275 "doesn't worry and . . .": Donald, *Lincoln*, p. 497.
276 "to move against . . .": J. McPherson, *Battle Cry*, p. 722.
276 "Lee's army will be . . .": ibid.
276 "Whatever happens . . .": ibid., p. 726.
276 "I propose to fight . . .": ibid., p. 731.
276 "He is a butcher . . .": Donald, *Lincoln*, 515.
276 "I regret this assault . . .": Nevins, *War*, IV, p. 43.
277 "There are many very . . .": ibid., p. 64.
277 "that I, who . . .": Donald, *Lincoln*, p. 514.
277 "The purposes of the . . .": Basler, VII, p. 535.
278 "The blacks are right . . .": Leech, pp. 329–30.
279 "to destroy the enemie's . . .": Basler, VII, p. 437.
279 "Get down . . .": Leech, p. 343.
280 "a president with brains . . .": Donald, *Lincoln*, p. 524.
280 "that we are out . . .": ibid., p. 529.

280 "if Jefferson Davis . . .": Basler, VII, p. 501.

280 "There have been men . . .": ibid., pp. 506–7.

281 "Mr. Lincoln is . . .": Nevins, *War,* p. 529.

281 "Everything is darkness . . .": Sears, *Young Napoleon,* p. 367.

281 "You think I . . .": Fehrenbacher, *Recollected Words,* p. 196.

281 "This morning . . .": Basler, VII, p. 514.

281 "They must nominate . . .": Donald, *Lincoln,* p. 530.

281 "to the end that . . .": E. McPherson, *Political History,* p. 419.

282 "I accept the . . .": Sears, *Young Napoleon,* pp. 378–79.

282 "Then we can fight . . .": ibid., p. 379.

282 "Atlanta is ours . . .": J. McPherson, *Battle Cry,* p. 774.

283 "It is no . . .": Fehrenbacher, *Recollected Words,* p. 83.

283 "I long ago . . .": Oates, *With Malice,* p. 416.

283 "the great and the mighty . . .": Nevins, *War,* IV, pp. 114–15.

283 "Lincoln's election would be . . .": Brodie, p. 197.

284 "There are but two . . .": Donald, *Lincoln,* p. 541.

284 "There was not much . . .": Nevins, *War,* IV, p. 139.

285 "Do not let Johnson . . .": Donald, *Lincoln,* p. 565.

285 "So broken-hearted . . .": ibid., p. 568.

286 "The truth is . . .": J. McPherson, *Battle Cry,* p. 826.

286 "The day you make . . .": ibid., p. 835.

286 "it will bring . . .": Fehrenbacher, *Recollected Words,* p. 384.

286 "A King's cure . . .": Basler, VIII, p. 254.

286 "Fondly do we . . .": ibid., pp. 332–33.

287 "Don't kneel to me . . .": Donald, *Lincoln,* 576.

287 "They seemed not to know . . .": P. Smith, p. 570.

287 "Uncle Sam . . .": Rose, *Rehearsal,* p. 346.

287 "I might as well have . . .": J. McPherson, *Negro's Civil War,* p. 307.

290 "even when you cease . . .": Basler, V, p. 372.

291 "The way we can best . . .": J. McPherson, *Negro's Civil War,* p. 299.

291 "We wants land . . .": ibid., p. 298.

292 "If our . . .": Ginzberg and Eichner, p. 216.

293 "The whites esteem . . .": ibid., p. 145.

293 "tales of atrocities . . .": P. Smith, p. 638.

293 "naturally lazy . . .": Berlin, *Slaves Without,* p. 384.

293 "skill in lying . . .": Rose, *Rehearsal,* p. 363.

293 "in spite of . . .": ibid., p. 364.

294 "We are familiar with . . .": P. Smith, p. 728.

294 "Is it politic . . .": ibid., p. 668.

295 "The North has . . .": ibid., p. 667.

295 "War had . . .": Fehrenbacher, *Recollected Words,* p. 470.

296   "At the mercy of . . .": J. McPherson, *Negro's Civil War,* p. 300.

296   "Lincoln freed you . . .": Petersen, p. 167.

296   "A large part of . . .": ibid.

296   "the only one . . .": Fehrenbacher, *Recollected Words,* p. 116.

297   "proportionate to . . .": Petersen, p. 56.

297   "You are the children . . .": ibid., p. 168.

297   "The more I learn of . . .": ibid., p. 173.

298   "What about me?": ibid., p. 159.

299   "The time has come . . .": ibid., p. 354.

299   "a great beacon of hope . . .": *New York Times,* August 29, 1963.

300   "Exactly one hundred years after . . .": Petersen, p. 357.

SELECT BIBLIOGRAPHY

There is more published material on the Civil War than on any other period in U.S. history, and there are more biographies of Abraham Lincoln than of any other American. These souces are of uneven quality, however, and a great deal of myth has become mixed with fact over the past century and a half. Readers who wish to return to original souces should begin by consulting the multi-volume *Collected Works of Abraham Lincoln*. The *Reminiscences of Abraham Lincoln,* collected and edited by Allen T. Rice, contains interesting and entertaining recollections by "distinguished men" of Lincoln's time, but students must keep in mind that the volume was published more than twenty years after Lincoln's death. In an attempt to verify the accuracy of statements attributed to Lincoln, Don and Virginia Fehrenbacher have compiled an excellent and valuable volume, *Recollected Words of Abraham Lincoln,* which attempts to gauge the reliability of several hundred contemporary witnesses who claim to have recorded Lincoln's words.

Diaries, letters, and memoirs of the era abound. Among the most helpful for this study were John Hay's letters and diary, the diaries of Salmon Chase and Gideon Welles, the autobiography of Charles Francis Adams, Jr., the observations of journalists Noah Brooks and William Howard Russell, the letters of George McClellan, and historian James McPherson's *For Cause and Comrades,* a collection of letters written by soldiers on both sides of the conflict.

Contemporary newspaper reports of military events were frequently unreliable, partly due to military censorship. Nevertheless, I found journalists' eyewitness accounts of civilian affairs valuable for the details they provided, particularly in the *New York Times, Washington Post,* and *Baltimore Sun.* Diplomatic correspondence from the preemancipation period may be found in *Message and Documents, 1862–63, Part I,* published by the Government Printing Office.

Among the multitude of secondary sources on Lincoln and the Civil War, several stand out for the insights they provide. I am deeply indebted to David Donald's excellent biography, *Lincoln,* for its analysis of Lincoln's political style as president. James McPherson's *Battle Cry of Freedom* is the single most comprehensive, gracefully written volume that blends military and political history. Two multivolume narratives—Shelby Foote's *The Civil War* and *The War for the Union* by Allan Nevins—delve into military affairs in more detail.

Abbott, Richard H. *The Republican Party and the South, 1855–1877.* Chapel Hill: University of North Carolina Press, 1986.

Adams, Charles Francis. *An Autobiography.* Boston: Houghton Mifflin Company, 1916.

Adams, George Worthington. *Mary Logan: Reminiscences of the Civil War and Reconstruction.* Carbondale, IL: Southern Illinois University Press, 1970.

Allen, H.C. *Great Britain and the United States: A History of Anglo-American Relations.* New York: St. Martin's Press, 1955.

Anderson, Frank Maloy. *The Mystery of "A Public Man."* Minneapolis: University of Minnesota Press, 1948.

Andrews, J. Cutler. *The North Reports the Civil War.* Pittsburgh: University of Pittsburgh Press, 1955.

Barnes, Thurlow Weed. *Life of Thurlow Weed: Vol. II: Memoir of Thurlow Weed.* New York: Da Capo Press, 1970.

Basler, Roy P., ed. *Collected Works of Abraham Lincoln.* 8 volumes. New Brunswick, NJ: Rutgers University Press, 1953.

Bates, David Homer. *Lincoln in the Telegraph Office.* New York: The Century Company, 1907.

Beale, Howard K., ed. *Diary of Gideon Welles.* New York: W. W. Norton, 1960.

Belz, Herman. *A New Birth of Freedom: The Republican Party and Freedmen's Rights, 1861 to 1866.* Westport, CT: Greenwood Press, 1976.

Berlin, Ira, et al. *Free at Last: A Documentary History of Slavery, Freedom, and the Civil War.* New York: New Press, 1992.

———, et al., eds. *Freedom: A Documentary History of Emancipation, 1861–1867.* Cambridge, Eng.: Cambridge University Press, 1985.

———. *Slaves Without Masters: The Free Negro in the Antebellum South.* Oxford, Eng.: Oxford University Press, 1974.

Blaine, James G. *Twenty Years of Congress: From Lincoln to Garfield.* Norwich, CT: Henry Bill Publishing Company, 1884.

Bogue, Allan G. *The Earnest Men: Republicans of the Civil War Senate.* Ithaca, NY: Cornell University Press, 1981.

Boritt, Gabor S., ed. *Lincoln, the War President.* New York: Oxford University Press, 1992.

———, ed. *Lincoln's Generals.* New York: Oxford University Press, 1994.

Bradley, Erwin S. *Simon Cameron: Lincoln's Secretary of War.* Philadelphia: University of Pennsylvania Press, 1966.

Brodie, Fawn M. *Thaddeus Stevens: Scourge of the South.* New York: W. W. Norton, 1959.

———. *Thomas Jefferson: An Intimate History.* New York: W. W. Norton, 1974.

Browne, Francis Fisher. *The Everyday Life of Abraham Lincoln.* Chicago: Browne & Howell, 1913.

Burlingame, Michael. *The Inner World of Abraham Lincoln.* Urbana, IL: University of Illinois Press, 1994.

———, and John R. Turner Ettlinger, eds. *Inside Lincoln's White House: The Complete Civil War Diary of John Hay.* Carbondale, IL: Southern Illinois University Press, 1997.

———, ed. *Lincoln Observed: Civil War Dispatches of Noah Brooks.* Baltimore: Johns Hopkins University Press, 1998.

———, ed. *An Oral History of Abraham Lincoln: John G. Nicolay's Interviews and Essays.* Carbondale, IL: Southern Illinois University Press, 1996.

Butler, Benjamin F. *Butler's Book.* Boston: A. M. Thayer & Co., 1892.

Cain, Marvin R. *Lincoln's Attorney General: Edward Bates of Missouri.* Columbia, MO: University of Missouri Press, 1965.

Carpenter, Francis B. *Six Months at the White House with Abraham Lincoln.* New York: Hurd and Houghton, 1866.

Catton, Bruce. *Never Call Retreat.* Garden City, NY: Doubleday & Company, 1965.

Chancellor, Sir Christopher, ed. *An Englishman in the American Civil War.* New York: New York University Press, 1971.

Chase, Salmon P. *Diary and Correspondence of Salmon P. Chase.* New York: Da Capo Press, 1971.

Cohen, Rosetta Marantz, and Samuel Scheer, eds. *The Work of Teachers in America.* Mahwah, NJ: Lawrence Erlbaum Associates, 1997.

Cook, Adrian. *The Armies of the Streets.* Lexington, KY: University Press of Kentucky, 1974.

Coulter, E. Merton. *The Civil War and Readjustment in Kentucky.* Gloucester, MA: Peter Smith, 1966.

Cox, LaWanda. *Lincoln and Black Freedom*. Columbia, SC: University of South Carolina Press, 1981.

Crawford, Martin, ed. *William Howard Russell's Civil War: Private Diary and Letters, 1861–1862*. Athens, GA: University of Georgia Press, 1992.

Cuomo, Mario, and Harold Holzer, eds. *Lincoln on Democracy*. New York: HarperCollins, 1990.

Current, Richard N. *Lincoln and the First Shot*. Philadelphia: J. B. Lippincott Co., 1963.

Dana, Charles A. *Recollections of the Civil War*. New York: D. Appleton and Company, 1898.

Davis, David Brion. *Slavery and Human Progress*. New York: Oxford University Press, 1984.

———. *The Problem of Slavery in Western Culture*. Ithaca, NY: Cornell University Press, 1966.

Dennett, Tyler, ed. *Lincoln and the Civil War in the Diaries and Letters of John Hay*. New York: Dodd, Mead & Company, 1939.

Donald, David Herbert. *Charles Sumner and the Coming of the Civil War*. New York: Alfred A. Knopf, 1961.

———. *Inside Lincoln's Cabinet: The Civil War Diaries of Salmon P. Chase*. New York: Longmans, Green and Co., 1954.

———. *Lincoln*. New York: Simon & Schuster, 1995.

Donovan, Frank Robert. *Mr. Lincoln's Proclamation: The Story of the Emancipation Proclamation*. New York: Dodd, Mead, 1964.

Duberman, Martin B. *Charles Francis Adams*. Boston: Houghton Mifflin Company, 1961.

———, ed. *The Anti-Slavery Vanguard: New Essays on the Abolitionists*. Princeton, NJ: Princeton University Press, 1965.

Durden, Robert Franklin. *James Shepherd Pike: Republicanism and the American Negro, 1850–1882*. Durham, NC: Duke University Press, 1957.

Eaton, Clement. *A History of the Southern Confederacy*. New York: The Free Press, 1965.

Egan, Ferol. *Frémont: Explorer for a Restless Nation*. Garden City, NY: Doubleday & Company, 1977.

Fehrenbacher, Don. *Lincoln in Text and Context*. Stanford, CA: Stanford University Press, 1987.

———. *Prelude to Greatness: Lincoln in the 1850's*. Stanford, CA: Stanford University Press, 1962.

———, and Virginia Fehrenbacher, eds. *Recollected Words of Abraham Lincoln*. Stanford, CA: Stanford University Press, 1996.

Fermer, Douglas. *James Gordon Bennett and the New York Herald*. Woodbridge, U.K.: Boydell Press, 1986.

Fields, Anne. *Life and Letters of Harriet Beecher Stowe*. Boston: Houghton Mifflin, 1897.

Flower, Frank. *Edwin McMasters Stanton*. Akron, OH: Saalfield Publishing Company, 1905.

Fogel, Robert William. *Without Consent or Contract: The Rise and Fall of American Slavery*. New York: W. W. Norton, 1989.

Foner, Eric. *Free Soil, Free Labor, Free Men: The Ideology of the Republican Party Before the Civil War*. London: Oxford University Press, 1970.

Foner, Philip S. *The Life and Writings of Frederick Douglass: Vol. III: The Civil War*. New York: International Publishers, 1952.

Foote, Shelby. *The Civil War: A Narrative*. New York: Random House, 1958.

Ford, Worthington Chauncey, ed. *A Cycle of Adams Letters, 1861–1865*. Boston: Houghton Mifflin, 1920.

———, ed. *Letters of Henry Adams (1858–1891)*. Boston: Houghton Mifflin, 1930.

Franklin, John Hope. *The Emancipation Proclamation*. Garden City, NY: Doubleday & Company, 1963.

Frederickson, George M. *The Inner Civil War: Northern Intellectuals and the Crisis of the Union*. New York: Harper & Row, 1968.

Garner, Stanton. *The Civil War World of Herman Melville*. Lawrence, KS: University Press of Kansas, 1993.

Gienapp, William E. *The Origins of the Republican Party, 1852–1856*. New York: Oxford University Press, 1987.

Ginzberg, Eli, and Alfred S. Eichner. *Troublesome Presence: Democracy and Black Americans*. New Brunswick, NJ: Transaction Publishers, 1993.

Graebner, Norman A., ed. *Freedom in America: A 200-Year Perspective*. University Park, PA: Pennsylvania State University Press.

———, ed. *Politics and the Crisis of 1860*. Urbana, IL: University of Illinois Press, 1961.

Grant, Ulysses S. *Memoirs and Selected Letters*. New York: The Library of America, 1990.

Green, Constance McLaughlin. *Washington: Village and Capital, 1800–1878*. Princeton, NJ: Princeton University Press, 1962.

Gunderson, Robert Gray. *Old Gentlemen's Convention: The Washington Peace Conference of 1861*. Madison, WI: University of Wisconsin Press, 1961.

Hassler, Warren W., Jr. *General George B. McClellan: Shield of the Union*. Baton Rouge, LA: Louisiana State University Press, 1957.

Hay, John. *Letters of John Hay and Extracts from Diary*. New York: Gordian Press, 1969.

Hendrick, Burton J. *Lincoln's War Cabinet*. Gloucester, MA: Peter Smith, 1946.

Higginson, Thomas Wentworth. *Contemporaries*. Boston: Houghton Mifflin, 1899.

Hochfield, George E., ed. *Henry Adams: The Great Secession Winter of 1860–61 and Other Essays*. New York: A. S. Barnes and Co., 1958.

Holzer, Harold, ed. *Dear Mr. Lincoln: Letters to the President*. Reading: Addison-Wesley Publishing Company, 1993.

Howard, Victor B. *Black Liberation in Kentucky: Emancipation and Freedom, 1862–1884*. Lexington, KY: University Press of Kentucky, 1983.

Hunt, H. Draper. *Hannibal Hamlin of Maine: Lincoln's First Vice-President*. Syracuse, NY: Syracuse University Press, 1969.

Isely, Jeter Allen. *Horace Greeley and the Republican Party*. New York: Octagon Books, 1965.

Jacob, Kathryn A. *Capital Elites*. Washington, D.C.: Smithsonian Institution Press, 1995.

Jellison, Charles A. *Fessenden of Maine: Civil War Senator*. Syracuse, NY: Syracuse University Press, 1962.

Johannsen, Robert W., ed. *Letters of Stephen A. Douglas*. Urbana, IL: University of Illinois Press, 1961.

————. *Lincoln, the South, and Slavery*. Baton Rouge, LA: Louisiana State University Press, 1991.

————. *Stephen A. Douglas*. New York: Oxford University Press, 1973.

Johnson, Berman E. *The Dream Deferred: A Survey of Black America, 1840–1896*. Dubuque, IA: Kendall/Hunt Publishing Company, 1993.

Kaplan, Justin. *Walt Whitman: A Life*. New York: Simon & Schuster, 1980.

King, Willard L. *Lincoln's Manager: David Davis*. Cambridge, MA: Harvard University Press, 1960.

Klein, Philip Shriver. *President James Buchanan: A Biography*. University Park, PA: Pennsylvania State University Press, 1962.

Klement, Frank. *The Copperheads in the Middle West*. Chicago: University of Chicago Press, 1960.

Laas, Virginia Jeans, ed. *Wartime Washington: The Civil War Letters of Elizabeth Blair Lee*. Urbana, IL: University of Illinois Press, 1991.

Larsen, Arthur J. *Crusader and Feminist: Letters of Jane Grey Swisshelm, 1858–1865*. Westport, CT: Hyperion Press, 1976.

Leech, Margaret. *Reveille in Washington, 1860–1865*. New York: Grosset & Dunlap, 1941.

Levine, Bruce. *Half Slave and Half Free: The Roots of Civil War*. New York: Hill and Wang, 1992.

Lewis, Lloyd. *Sherman: Fighting Prophet*. New York: Harcourt, Brace and Company, 1958.

Litwack, Leon F. *North of Slavery: The Negro in the Free States, 1790–1860*. Chicago: University of Chicago Press, 1961.

Livermore, Mary A. *My Story of the War*. Hartford, CT: A. D. Worthington and Company, 1896.

Lowenfels, Walter. *Walt Whitman's Civil War*. New York: Da Capo Press, 1961.

McDonough, James Lee. *War in Kentucky: From Shiloh to Perryville*. Knoxville, TN: University of Tennessee Press, 1994.

McFeely, William S. *Grant: A Biography*. New York: W. W. Norton, 1981.

McPherson, Edward. *The Political History of the United States of America During the Great Rebellion, 1860–1865*. New York: Da Capo Press, 1972.

McPherson, James M. *Abraham Lincoln and the Second American Revolution*. New York: Oxford University Press, 1990.

———. *Battle Cry of Freedom: The Civil War Era*. New York: Oxford University Press, 1988.

———. *For Cause and Comrades: Why Men Fought in the Civil War*. New York: Oxford University Press, 1997.

———. *The Negro's Civil War*. New York: Pantheon House, 1965.

McReynolds, Edwin C. *Missouri: A History of the Crossroads State*. Norman, OK: University of Oklahoma Press, 1962.

Manakee, Harold R. *Maryland in the Civil War*. Baltimore: Maryland Historical Society, 1961.

Martin, Isabella D., and Myrta Lockett Avary, eds. *Mary Boykin Chesnut: A Diary from Dixie*. Gloucester, MA: Peter Smith, 1961.

Merrill, James M. *William Tecumseh Sherman*. Chicago: Rand McNally, 1971.

Metzler, Milton, ed. *Thoreau: People, Principles, and Politics*. New York: Hill and Wang, 1963.

Mitgang, Herbert, ed. *Lincoln as They Saw Him*. New York: Rinehart and Company, 1956.

———. *Edward Dicey: Spectator of America*. Chicago: Quadrangle Books, 1971.

Monaghan, Jay. *Abraham Lincoln Deals with Foreign Affairs*. Lincoln, NB: University of Nebraska Press, 1945.

Nash, Howard P., Jr. *Stormy Petrel: The Life and Times of General Benjamin F. Butler*. Rutherford, NJ: Fairleigh Dickinson University Press, 1969.

Neely, Mark E., Jr. *The Last Best Hope of Earth: Abraham Lincoln and the Promise of America*. Cambridge, MA: Harvard University Press, 1993.

Nevins, Allan, ed. *A Diary of Battle: The Personal Journals of Colonel Charles S. Wainwright, 1861–1865*. New York: Harcourt, Brace, 1962.

———. *Diary of the Civil War, 1860–1865: George Templeton Strong*. New York: Macmillan, 1962.

————. *Frémont: Pathmarker of the West.* New York: Longmans, Green & Co., 1955.

————. *The War for the Union.* 4 volumes. New York: Charles Scribner's Sons, 1971.

Nicolay, John G., and John Hay. *Abraham Lincoln: A History.* Chicago: University of Chicago Press, 1966.

Niven, John. *Gideon Welles: Lincoln's Secretary of the Navy.* New York: Oxford University Press, 1973.

————. *Salmon P. Chase.* New York: Oxford University Press, 1995.

Oates, Stephen B. *Abraham Lincoln: The Man Behind the Myths.* New York: Harper & Row, 1984.

————. *With Malice Toward None: The Life of Abraham Lincoln.* New York: Harper & Row, 1977.

Paludan, Phillip Shaw. *The Presidency of Abraham Lincoln.* Lawrence, KS: University Press of Kansas, 1994.

Petersen, Merrill D. *Lincoln in American Memory.* New York: Oxford University Press, 1994.

Pisani, Camille Ferri. *Prince Napoleon in America, 1861.* Bloomington, IN: Indiana University Press, 1959.

Poore, Benjamin Perley. *Perley's Reminiscences of Sixty Years in the National Metropolis.* Philadelphia: Hubbard Brothers, 1886.

Potter, David M. *The Impending Crisis: 1848–1861.* New York: Harper & Row, 1976.

Pratt, Fletcher, ed. *William Howard Russell: My Diary North and South.* New York: Harper & Brothers, 1954.

Pratt, Julius. *A History of United States Foreign Policy.* Englewood Cliffs, NJ: Prentice-Hall, 1961.

Randall, J. G. *Lincoln the President: Springfield to Gettysburg, Vol. 2.* New York: Dodd, Mead & Company, 1945.

Ransom, Roger L. *Conflict and Compromise: The Political Economy of Slavery, Emancipation, and the American Civil War.* Cambridge, Eng.: Cambridge University Press, 1989.

Reynolds, David S. *Walt Whitman's America: A Cultural Biography.* New York: Alfred A. Knopf, 1995.

Rhodes, Robert H., ed. *All for the Union: The Civil War Diary and Letters of Elisha Hunt Rhodes.* New York: Vintage Books, 1992.

Rice, Allen T. *Reminiscences of Abraham Lincoln by Distinguished Men of His Time.* New York: North American Publishing Co., 1886.

Rolle, Andrew. *John Charles Frémont: Character as Destiny.* Norman, OK: University of Oklahoma Press, 1991.

Rose, Willie Lee. *Rehearsal for Reconstruction: The Port Royal Experiment.* New York: Vintage Books, 1967.

————. *Slavery and Freedom*. New York: Oxford University Press, 1982.

Rumyantseva, Nelly, ed. *Marx and Engels on the United States*. Moscow: Progress Publishers, 1979.

Russel, Robert R. *Critical Studies in Antebellum Sectionalism*. Westport, CT: Greenwood Publishing Company, 1978.

Sandburg, Carl. *Abraham Lincoln: The War Years*. New York: Harcourt, Brace & World, 1939.

Schneller, Robert J., Jr. *A Quest for Glory: A Biography of Rear Admiral John A. Dahlgren*. Annapolis, MD: Naval Institute Press, 1996.

Schurz, Carl. *The Autobiography of Carl Schurtz*. New York: Charles Scribner's Sons, 1961.

————. *The Reminiscences of Carl Schurz*. New York: The McClure Company, 1907.

Scrugham, Mary. *The Peaceable Americans of 1860–1861*. New York: Octagon Books, 1976.

Sears, Stephen W., ed. *The Civil War Papers of George B. McClellan: Selected Correspondence, 1860–1865*. New York: Ticknor and Fields, 1989.

————. *George B. McClellan: The Young Napoleon*. New York: Ticknor & Fields, 1988.

Sherman, John. *Recollections of Forty Years in the House, Senate, and Cabinet*. New York: Greenwood Press, 1968.

Simon, John Y., ed. *The Papers of Ulysses S. Grant*. Carbondale, IL: Southern Illinois University Press, 1970.

Smalley, Donald, and Bradford Allen Booth, eds. *North America, by Anthony Trollope*. New York: Alfred A. Knopf, 1951.

Smith, Elbert B. *The Presidency of James Buchanan*. Lawrence, KS: University Press of Kansas, 1975.

Smith, George Winston, and Charles Judah. *Life in the North During the Civil War: A Source History*. Albuquerque, NM: University of New Mexico Press, 1966.

Smith, Page. *Trial by Fire: A People's History of the Civil War and Reconstruction*. New York: McGraw-Hill Book Company, 1982.

Stampp, Kenneth. *America in 1857: A Nation on the Brink*. New York: Oxford University Press, 1990.

————. *And the War Came*. Baton Rouge, LA: Louisiana State University Press, 1967.

————. *The Peculiar Institution: Slavery in the Ante-Bellum South*. New York: Random House, 1956.

Stewart, James Brewer. *Holy Warriors: The Abolitionists and American Slavery*. New York: Hill and Wang, 1976.

Straubing, Harold Elk. *Civil War Eyewitness Reports*. Hamden, CT: Archon Books, 1985.

Taylor, John M. *William Henry Seward: Lincoln's Right Hand.* New York: HarperCollins, 1991.

Thomas, Benjamin P. *Abraham Lincoln: A Biography.* New York: Alfred A. Knopf, 1952.

————, and Harold M. Hyman. *Stanton: The Life and Times of Lincoln's Secretary of War.* New York: Alfred A. Knopf, 1962.

Thorndyke, Rachel Sherman, ed. *The Sherman Letters: Correspondence Between General Sherman and Senator Sherman from 1837 to 1891.* New York: Da Capo Press, 1969.

Trefousse, Hans. *Thaddeus Stevens: Nineteenth-Century Egalitarian.* Chapel Hill, NC: University of North Carolina Press, 1997.

Trudeau, Noah Andre. *Like Men of War: Black Troops in the Civil War, 1862–1865.* Boston: Little, Brown, 1998.

Van Deusen, Glyndon. *William Henry Seward.* New York: Oxford University Press, 1967.

Venet, Wendy Hamand. *Neither Ballots nor Bullets: Women Abolitionists and the Civil War.* Charlottesville, VA: University Press of Virginia, 1991.

Villard, Henry. *Memoirs of Henry Villard.* Boston: Houghton, Mifflin, and Company, 1904.

Vinovskis, Maris A., ed. *Toward a Social History of the American Civil War.* Cambridge, Eng.: Cambridge University Press, 1990.

Watterson, Henry. *The Compromises of Life.* Freeport: Books for Libraries Press, 1906.

————. *"Marse Henry": An Autobiography.* New York: George H. Doran, 1919.

Welles, Gideon. *Lincoln and Seward.* Freeport, NY: Books for Libraries Press, 1969.

Wells, Damon. *Stephen Douglas: The Last Years, 1857–1861.* Austin, TX: University of Texas Press, 1971.

Werner, Emmy E. *Reluctant Witnesses: Children's Voices from the Civil War.* Boulder, CO: Westview Press, 1998.

Wheeler, Richard. *Voices of the Civil War.* New York: Thomas Y. Crowell, 1976.

Williams, Kenneth P. *Lincoln Finds a General.* New York: Macmillan, 1964.

Williams, T. Harry. *Beauregard: Napoleon in Gray.* Baton Rouge, LA.: Louisiana State University Press, 1955.

————. *Lincoln and His Generals.* New York: Alfred A. Knopf, 1963.

————. *Lincoln and the Radicals.* Madison, WI: University of Wisconsin Press, 1965.

————. *McClellan, Sherman and Grant.* New Brunswick, NJ: Rutgers University Press, 1962.

Wills, Garry. *Lincoln at Gettysburg: The Words That Remade America.* New York: Simon & Schuster, 1992.

Wilson, Forrest. *Crusader in Crinoline: The Life of Harriet Beecher Stowe.* Philadelphia: J. B. Lippincott Company, 1941.

Woodson, Thomas, et al., eds. *Nathaniel Hawthorne: The Letters, 1857–1864.* Columbus, OH: Ohio State University Press, 1987.

Woodward, C. Vann, and Elisabeth Muhlenfeld, eds. *The Private Mary Chesnut: The Unpublished Civil War Diaries.* New York: Oxford University Press, 1984.

INDEX